Internet Literacy

Fred T. Hofstetter

University of Delaware

with World Wide Web site by

Pat Sine

University of Delaware

Irwin McGraw-Hill

Boston   Burr Ridge, IL   Dubuque, IA   Madison, WI   New York   San Francisco   St. Louis
Bangkok   Bogotá   Caracas   Lisbon   London   Madrid
Mexico City   Milan   New Delhi   Seoul   Singapore   Sydney   Taipei   Toronto

Irwin/McGraw-Hill

A Division of The **McGraw-Hill** Companies

Internet Literacy

domestic   2 3 4 5 6 7 8 9 0   VNH VNH   3 2 1 0 9
international   1 2 3 4 5 6 7 8 9 0   VNH VNH   3 2 1 0 9 8

ISBN 0-07-029387-2

VP/Editorial director: Michael Junior
Sponsoring editor: Rhonda Sands
Developmental editor: Kyle Thomes
Project manager: Terri Edwards
Production supervisor: Rich DeVitto
Cover and interior designer: Gary Palmatier, Ideas to Images
Cover photographer: Tom Brakefield
Cartoonist: Gary Palmatier, Ideas to Images
Editorial assistant: Stephen Fahringer
Compositor: Ideas to Images
Typefaces: Utopia and Gill Sans
Printer: Von Hoffmann Press, Inc.

The credits on page xvi are an extension of this copyright page.

Library of Congress Cataloging-in-Publication Data
Hofstetter, Fred T. (Fred Thomas), 1949–
    Internet literacy / by Fred T. Hofstetter ; with a World Wide Web
site by Pat Sine.
       p.   cm.
    Includes bibliographical references and index.
    ISBN 0-07-029387-2 (acid-free paper)
    1. Internet (Computer network). 2. Computer literacy. I. Sine,
Pat. II. Title.
TK5105.875.I57H65 1998
004.67'8—dc21   97-43031
                                                                              CIP

International Edition
Copyright © 1998. Exclusive right by The McGraw-Hill Companies, Inc., for manufacture and export. This book cannot be re-exported from the country to which it is consigned by The McGraw-Hill Companies, Inc. The International Edition is not available in North America.

When ordering this title, use ISBN 0-07-115730-1

http://www.mhhe.com

Dedication

This book is dedicated to the memory of the four people who made my childhood special: Aunt Irene, Uncle Guy, and Grandma and Grandpa Jones. Never was a child shown more love, caring, and devotion. I wish every child could be so fortunate as to have such super relatives.

In Memoriam Amantem

Irene Trenor Landerman, 1899–1969

Guy N. Landerman, 1896–1965

Benjamin F. Jones, 1896–1971

Margaret E. Trenor Jones, 1904–1996

Contents

Introduction

INTERNET is the buzzword of the century. Never before has a technology spread so rapidly. Never has an invention enabled so many people to do so many things—things that are strategically important to life in the information society. So strategic that being able to use the Internet has become a basic skill. So important that understanding the Internet and knowing how to communicate over it has become a literacy.

Internet literacy is what this book's about. The goal is to provide a course of study that will enable students to acquire the conceptual background and the online skills needed to become Internet literate. An important feature of this book is the way it avoids unnecessary jargon and computer terms. By focusing on the tasks that an Internet literate person should be able to accomplish, and by using software that makes those tasks easy to accomplish, this book provides a course of instruction that any college student or motivated high school student can successfully complete.

Another key feature is the way this book teaches the student how to create Web pages and publish them on the World Wide Web. After learning how to use Internet search engines to conduct research, students complete a Web page creation tutorial that steps through the process of online writing and documenting Internet resources with proper bibliographic style. Thus, the student becomes a creator and a contributor, not just a consumer, of the Internet. Along the way, the student creates a home page and a Web page résumé. Several students have reported that putting their résumés on the Web helped them find jobs.

The course is organized into seven parts. Part One defines the Internet and explains how it is changing the world. After defining the basic Internet services of electronic mail, listserv, newsgroups, chat, telnet, FTP, and the World Wide Web, the book explains how they are being used across a broad range of industries to provide people with important new capabilities, including telecommuting, home shopping, government services, and interactive television. Especially relevant to college students are the sections on teaching, learning, and interconnected scholarship.

Part Two covers the logistics of getting connected to the Internet. Students learn about Internet service providers and how to connect via telephone modems, Ethernet, ISDN, or cable modems. Then the students go online and learn how to surf the Net using a World Wide Web browser. This initial online experience is designed in such a way as to provide students with the maximum amount of Internet benefit through a minimum knowledge of technical terms and computing concepts. More knowledge of the inner workings of the Net comes in later parts of the book. Here, the focus is on ease of use and learning how to get to places and find things without getting too technical.

In Part Three, students learn how to communicate over the Internet, first through electronic mail, and then via listserv and newsgroups. Step-by-step tutorial exercises allow students to practice key concepts and develop online skills. A chapter on Internet etiquette covers rules, courtesies, and ethics that all users should observe when communicating online.

Part Four is a tutorial on how to use Internet search engines to find things online via subject-oriented searches, key word searching, concept searches, and metasearching. Students learn how to search scholarly databases of refereed articles as well as more general sources. In addition to searching for text, students learn how to conduct multimedia searches for pictures, animations, audio, and video. In support of online writing, students learn the proper bibliographic style for citing Internet resources. MLA, APA, and CMS styles are covered.

In Part Five, students learn how to establish a presence on the Internet by creating Web pages and mounting them on the World Wide Web. A chapter on Web page creation strategies helps students choose the proper tool for the task at hand. A chapter on Web page design teaches screen design principles and shows how to lay out Web page elements effectively. Then, students learn how to create a home page and a Web page résumé and publish documents on the Web. By linking their home page to their résumé and to other online resources, students experience how hyperlinks can create a world of interconnected scholarship.

Part Six brings the students' Web pages to life by showing how to use multimedia on the Internet. After making a waveform audio recording, students learn how sounds, movies, and animations can be linked to Web pages and made to play via helper applications, plug-ins, and Java applets. A multimedia tour of the Web provides access to the large number of multimedia creation tools for making active Web pages.

Even though the Internet has already become an essential part of life in the information society, the Net still is in many ways an emerging technology that is inspiring debates about how it should evolve and become regulated. Accordingly, Part Seven gets the students involved in planning for the future of the Internet by discussing and debating the societal issues of equity, privacy, security, protectionism, censorship, decency, copyright, and fair use. Then students learn about the emerging technologies of the multimedia backbone, Internet talk radio, the real-time streaming protocol, artificial intelligence, voice recognition, text-to-speech conversion, image recognition, intelligent agents, videoconferencing, Internet phone services, Webcasting, virtual reality, wireless communications, and Internet PCs.

The book concludes by showing students how to use the Internet for continued learning about the exciting new products that will be invented during the coming decades. The best listservs, newsgroups, and Web sites for keeping up with this fast-paced field are identified, and students learn how to subscribe for free.

WORLD WIDE WEB SITE

Accompanying this book is an Internet Literacy Web site by Pat Sine. It's called the "Interlit" Web site—Interlit stands for Internet Literacy. The address of the site is http://www.udel.edu/interlit. It provides quick and easy access to all of the Internet resources and examples referred to in this textbook. In addition to making it easy to find things, the Interlit Web site can help save you money, because almost all of the resources it uses are available free of charge.

Icons coordinate what you read in this book with what you will find at the Interlit Web site. When you see an icon in the margin of this text, you will know that you can go to the Interlit Web site for quick and easy access to that item. For example, in the Web page creation tutorial, where the book provides a layout analysis of exemplary Web pages, the Interlit Web site provides hot links that enable you to visit the exemplars and try them out. By providing access to exemplary Web pages across the curriculum, the Interlit Web site enables students to study models of good online writing in every discipline.

END-OF-CHAPTER EXERCISES

Throughout the course, end-of-chapter exercises provide practical, hands-on assignments for students to complete outside of class. The instructor can adjust the depth and rigor of the course by deciding which assignments to require. Highly motivated students can go ahead and complete all of the exercises, to harness the full potential of the Internet.

BASIC WINDOWS AND MACINTOSH TUTORIALS

At six strategic locations in this book, Windows and Macintosh tutorials have been provided for technologically challenged students who may need help completing basic computing tasks. The tutorials are presented at the point where students will first need them. For students or instructors who want to locate the basic Windows and Macintosh tutorials at other times, Appendix A shows where to find them.

WHAT YOU WILL NEED TO USE THIS BOOK

Internet Literacy works with both Netscape Communicator and Microsoft Internet Explorer on both Windows and Macintosh computers. In order to complete the exercises and tutorials in this book, the student will need to have access to a Windows PC or a Macintosh running either Netscape Communicator or Microsoft Internet Explorer. The student will also need an Internet account that provides the basic Internet services of e-mail, listserv, newsgroup, FTP, telnet, and the Web. This account must include at least four megabytes of Web space in which students will create their Web pages. Students who do not already have Internet access should refer to Part Two of this book, which provides a detailed explanation and comparison of the options for getting connected to the Internet. While high-speed connections work best, all of the exercises in this book can be completed via modem over an ordinary telephone line.

INTERNET TOOLKIT

By working through the tutorial exercises in this book, the student will acquire a toolkit full of utilities for authoring Web pages, manipulating images, recording and editing sound, creating animations, and maintaining a Web site. Appendix B lists the utilities used in this book. Any of these utilities that the student does not already have can be downloaded from the Interlit Web site. Utilities are provided for both Windows and Macintosh computers.

ACKNOWLEDGMENTS

I have many people to thank for making this project possible, but most of all, I want to acknowledge all of my students, who inspired this book through their enthusiastic participation in the experimental courses that were the precursors to what we now know as *Internet Literacy*. I learn more from my students than from anyone else, and I look forward to every class, not so much to teach, as to learn.

University of Delaware Research Professor L. Leon Campbell provided valuable service as the author's "intelligent agent" on the Internet. Almost daily, Leon sent the author information about issues, trends, and new developments gleaned from his extensive surfing of the network. Leon is a valued friend and colleague.

Susan Brynteson, Director of Libraries at the University of Delaware, read and commented on the section on Copyright and Fair Use, as did Lisa Livingston, Director of CUNY's Instructional Media Division and chair of the CCUMC Fair Use Working Committee. I am grateful for the guidance they provided. All educators owe a debt of gratitude to Lisa for her dedication to creating the *Fair Use Guidelines for Educational Multimedia*.

Pat Sine, Manager of the Instructional Technology Center at the University of Delaware, created the Interlit Web site that supports this book. Pat served as an invaluable resource throughout this project, and I am grateful for her expertise, dedication, and numerous contributions.

Dr. Primo Toccafondi, coordinator of the University of Delaware's degree programs in Southern Delaware, helped the author teach Internet Literacy in a distance learning format. I will always be grateful to Toc for his many suggestions and helpful comments on drafts of the text, as well as for his camaraderie. Making new friends is one of the lifelong rewards of working on projects like this one.

As the result of a videoconference organized by my friends Jack Chambers and Kathy Clower at Florida Community College in Jacksonville, I met Will Philipp, who directs the distance learning programs at PBS. Will teamed with me and Rich Fischer, Associate Provost for Continuing and Distance Education at the University of Delaware, to create the PBS *Internet Literacy* TeleWEBcourse, which uses this book as its text. I'm grateful to Jack, Kathy, Will, and Rich, and to their wonderful staffs.

Rhonda Sands of McGraw-Hill served as this book's editor. I thank Rhonda for her many contributions, both editorial and otherwise. I am especially grateful for the thorough manner in which McGraw-Hill conducted external reviews of this text prior to its publication. I want to thank the following reviewers for their many insights and suggestions:

Ron Berry, *Northeast Louisiana University*

Roger Lee, *Houston Community College*

Tim Eichers, *Northern Virginia Community College*

Bret Ellis, *Brigham Young University, Hawaii Campus*

Daris Howard, *Ricks College*

Robert Hubbard, *Albertus Magnus College*

Tim Kennedy, *Bellevue Community College*

Pratap P. Reddy, *Raritan Valley Community College*

Robert Youngblood, *Arizona State University*

Credits

Many of the screen representations, logos, and icons appearing here are registered trademarks of their respective owners and are used by permission.

We would like to thank the following organizations and individuals for allowing us to include their graphics in the book:

Adobe Systems, Inc.
Aladdin Systems, Inc.
Alberto Ricci
Alchemy Mindworks, Inc.
Allegiant Technologies, Inc.
Amazon.com, Inc.
America Online, Inc.
American Journalism Review and NewsLink Associates
Andy Carvin
Andy's Netscape HTTP Cookies Notes
answers.com
Apple Computer, Inc.
AT&T Corp.
BigFoot Partners L.P.
Cable News Network, Inc.
Casio Computer Co., Ltd.
CAUSE
Center for Democracy & Technology
Charles Schwab & Co., Inc.
Cicada Web Development
CIO Communications, Inc.
Claris Corporation
CMP Media, Inc.
CNET, Inc.
CommerceNet Consortium
Compuserve, Inc.
Connectix Corporation
Cookie Central
Corel Corporation
Creative Labs, Inc.
Crypto.Com
Cornell Research Foundation (CU-SeeMe)
Dartmouth University
Deja News, Inc.
Democratic National Committee
Digital Equipment Corporation
DIRECTV, Inc.
Discreet Data Research
Dragon Systems, Inc.
Eastman Kodak Company
Educational Testing Service
Educom

EFnet #irchelp channel operators
Electronic Desktop Project, California State University
Electronic Frontier Foundation
Electronic Privacy Information Center
Elysium Ltd.
Encyclopedia Britannica, Inc.
Engineering Information Inc.
ERIC
Erol's
Excite, Inc.
FBI
FCC
Filez
FlyCast Communications Corporation
Four11 Corp.
General Magic, Inc.
Generic Top Level Domain Memorandum of Under- standing (gTLD-MoU)
Georgia Institute of Technology
GifBuilder
Global Schoolnet
go2net, Inc.
Gordon Publications
HyperMedia Communications Inc.
InfiNet
Information Access Company
Infoseek Corporation
Internet Privacy Coalition
Internet Shopping Network
InterNIC
Ipswitch, Inc.
Ircle
Jasc, Inc.
Joe Koeniger
JPayne
Kairos
Kevin Savetz Publishing
Kidlink Society
La Maison Européenne de la Photographie
LC&D Internet Publishing
LiveUpdate

Luckman Software Corporation
Lycos, Inc.
Macromedia, Inc.
Mecklermedia Corporation
Microsoft Corporation
Microsoft Network
MIDIWorld
Musée du Louvre
NASA
National Geographic Society
National Science Foundation
NCSA
NetDay
Netscape Communications Corporation
Northwest Computer Services
NYSE Inc.
Open Market, Inc.
Ovid Technologies, Inc.
Pacific Coast Feather Company
Paul Burchard
PhotoDisc, Inc.
Picture Network International, Ltd., and its content suppliers
Pietro Di Micli
Pitsco, Inc
PKWARE, Inc.
PointCast, Inc.
Prodigy Services Corporation
Progressive Networks, Inc. and/or its licensors
pulver.com, Inc.
Quarterdeck Corporation
Republican National Committee
Robert Bradley
Robert H Zakon
Scholastic Inc.
Seiko Epson Corporation
Smithsonian Institution
SoftQuad, Inc.
SoundEffects
Starwave Corp. and ESPN Inc.
State of Delaware
Sun Microsystems, Inc.
Switchboard Inc. & Database America Inc.

Syllabus Press Inc.
Technology & Learning
TERC
THE Journal
The Internet Mall, Inc.
The List
The McKinley Group, Inc.
The Miami Herald
The Nasdaq Stock Market, Inc.
The Palace, Inc.
The Princeton Plasma Physics Laboratory (PPPL)
The Recreational Software Advisory Council (RSAC)
The Rotherwick Firewall Resource
The Stalker's Home Page
The Weather Channel
Thorsten Lemke
Time Inc. New Media
Time Warner Inc.
Tjerk Vonck & mIRC Co. Ltd.
Tom Christiansen
TravelGram
Tristan Savatier
TrustE
U.S. Copyright Office, Library of Congress
University of Delaware
University of Houston College of Education
University of Mississippi
University of Waterloo
Unusual Solutions, Inc.
US House of Representatives
VDOnet Corporation
Vinay Kumar
Virage Inc.
VocalTec Inc.
Web Cast SIG
White House
WhoWhere? Inc.
Wired Ventures Inc.
World Wide Web Consortium
Xing Technology Corporation
Yahoo, Inc.

Part One

Understanding the Internet

Many people have a cloudy understanding of the Internet. Some books even represent the Internet as a cloud in diagrams that illustrate how people communicate over the Net.

This part of the book will remove the clouds by defining what the Internet is, describing what you can do with it, and demonstrating how it is changing the world.

1 Definitions

After completing this chapter, you will be able to:

- **Define the Internet, describe how large it is, and find out how fast it is growing.**

- **Know when you are really "on" the Internet.**

- **List and define the eight basic Internet services of e-mail, listserv, newsgroups, chat, FTP, telnet, Gopher, and the World Wide Web.**

- **Explain what is meant by client-server computing.**

- **Understand the Internet naming system of domains and subdomains.**

- **Provide a brief history of the Internet, explaining how it grew from its humble origins into the worldwide network that we enjoy today.**

TECHNICAL terms can scare people. Especially when computers are involved, technical terms can make things so hard to understand that people may shy away from learning how to do things that really are quite simple. This book purposefully avoids unnecessary jargon. The goal is to enable you to take advantage of the wonderful resources on the Internet without having to learn a lot of technical terms. There are certain terms, however, that an Internet literate person must know. This chapter defines those terms.

WHAT IS THE INTERNET?

The Internet is a worldwide connection of more than 10 million computers and 45,000 networks that follow the Internet Protocol (IP). The Internet Protocol was invented for the U.S. Department of Defense Advanced Research Projects Agency (ARPA). The goal was to create a network that would continue to function if a bomb destroyed one or more of the network's nodes; information would get rerouted automatically so it could still reach its address. As a result of this bomb-proof design, any user on the Internet can communicate with any other user, regardless of their location.

Figure 1-1 illustrates the web that is formed by the interconnections of computers on the Internet in the United States. More than 190 countries and territories around the world are similarly connected to the Internet, forming a worldwide telecommunications network.

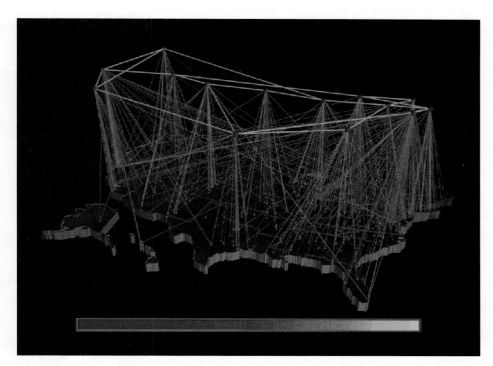

Figure 1-1 "NSFNET T1 Backbone and Regional Networks." Rendered by Donna Cox and Robert Patterson, National Center for Supercomputing Applications/University of Illinois. This image is a visualization study of inbound traffic measured in billions of bytes on the NSFNET T1 backbone for September 1991. The traffic volume range is depicted from purple (zero bytes) to white (100 billion bytes). The data was collected by Merit Network, Inc. The NSFNET is one of the most important parts of the Internet in the United States.

WHEN ARE YOU "ON" THE INTERNET?

New users are sometimes confused about when they are "on" the Internet. Just because you are connected to another computer does not necessarily mean you are "on" the Internet. For example, a lot of computer companies run bulletin-board services (BBSs) to which you can connect by running a so-called terminal program. A **terminal program** is a computer software utility that allows you to dial up to a remote computer using a telephone modem. Dialing up to a BBS with a terminal program does not put you on the Internet for two reasons: (1) the BBS does not use the Internet Protocol (IP); (2) the BBS is not part of the Internet. Therefore, you are not connected to the Internet when you dial up to a BBS.

It is also possible to use a terminal program to dial up to a computer that is connected to the Internet. While connected to that remote computer, you can access Internet services, such as electronic mail. However, you are not really "on" the Internet, because your terminal program is not using the Internet Protocol. The computer to which you are connected is on the Internet, but you are not.

In order to be really "on" the Internet, your computer needs to be using the Internet Protocol. Then you can use programs like Netscape Navigator and the Microsoft Internet Explorer to access the World Wide Web and other Internet services. Chapter 3 explains how you can get your computer connected to the Internet via the Internet Protocol over ordinary telephone lines, higher-speed digital telephone lines, and superfast broadband coaxial cable. Then you will really be "on" the Internet.

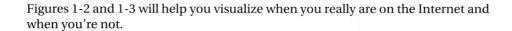

Figures 1-2 and 1-3 will help you visualize when you really are on the Internet and when you're not.

Figure 1-2 You are really "on" the Internet when your computer is using the Internet Protocol to access Internet resources directly.

Figure 1-3 You are not really "on" the Internet when your computer is dialed up as a terminal to a computer that accesses the Internet for you.

WHO IS USING THE INTERNET?

People from all walks of life are using the Internet. Business professionals, stockbrokers, government workers, politicians, doctors, teachers, researchers, students, monks, kids, the elderly, soldiers, parents, entertainers, police, social workers, pilots, waiters, disk jockeys, and movie stars—virtually everyone who wants to succeed in the information society is using the Internet.

According to the *Electronic Information Report,* 21 million people subscribed to online services in 1996, up 45% from 1995 (*Investor's Business Daily* 26 Mar 97). Extensive surveys, profiles, and statistics on who uses the Internet can be found by following the Interlit Web site links to the Georgia Tech Web Surveys.

HOW FAST IS THE INTERNET GROWING?

Figure 1-4 shows how fast the Internet is growing. Currently, the Internet is doubling in size about every four months. A recent study of Internet use patterns conducted by Nielsen Media Research and CommerceNet indicates that recent Internet growth is coming from newcomers who are older, less affluent, and inclined to spend less time online than previous long-term Internet users. The study also found that business users increasingly are buying products and services through the World Wide Web. For more information, follow the Interlit Web site links to the CommerceNet report.

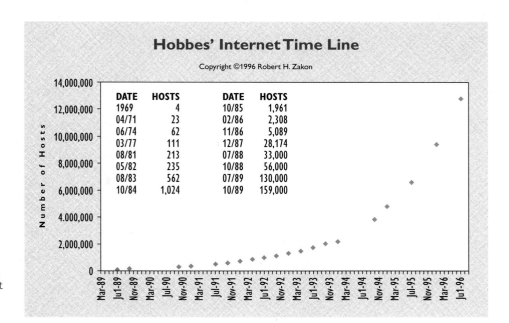

Figure 1-4 How fast the Internet is growing. For more information, follow the Interlit Web site links to Hobbes' Internet Time Line.

WHAT ARE THE INTERNET SERVICES?

What people do on the Internet is organized according to services defined by protocols that specify how information moves across the Net. The most popular protocols include electronic mail (e-mail), listserv, newsgroups, chat, File Transfer Protocol (FTP), telnet, Gopher, and the World Wide Web.

Figure 1-5 Electronic mail queues up in your in box.

Electronic Mail

The most often used protocol is electronic mail, which is also known as e-mail. Every registered user on the Internet has an e-mail address. E-mail is a great way to communicate, because it avoids the delays caused by playing telephone tag. As depicted in Figure 1-5, mail queues up in your "in box," and you read and respond to it at your convenience. Many users read their electronic mail several times a day. You will learn how to use electronic mail in Chapter 6.

Listserv

Listserv stands for "list server" and is built on top of the e-mail protocol. Listservs work like electronic mailing lists, sending e-mail messages to people whose names are on the list. You join a listserv by e-mailing a message to it, saying you want to subscribe. Then, whenever someone sends e-mail to the listserv, you will receive a copy in your e-mail. Likewise, when you send e-mail to the listserv, everyone on the listserv will get a copy of your message, as depicted in Figure 1-6. Thus, listserv is a simple way for groups of people to communicate with one another through e-mail.

There are thousands of listservs on the Internet. You will learn how to find out about listservs and join them in Chapter 7.

USENET Newsgroups

A more highly organized way for groups of people to communicate is through USENET newsgroups. USENET is an electronic bulletin-board service consisting of newsgroups, newsfeeds, and newsreaders. Once you subscribe to a newsgroup, you use a newsreader to access the group's newsfeed. Figure 1-7 shows how information in the newsfeed is organized according to topics. In addition to reading information on existing topics, you can add your own comments and create new topics, thereby participating in a virtual conference on the Internet.

Don't be confused by the use of the word *news* in the term *newsgroup.* While some newsgroups are devoted to what is traditionally known as news, a newsgroup can contain discussions on any topic. In Chapter 8, you will learn how to find out what newsgroups exist and how to join them.

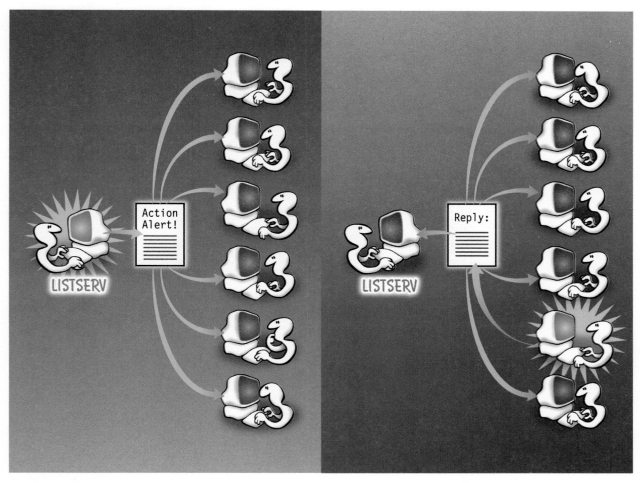

Figure 1-6 Listservs distribute messages to people whose names are on an electronic mailing list.

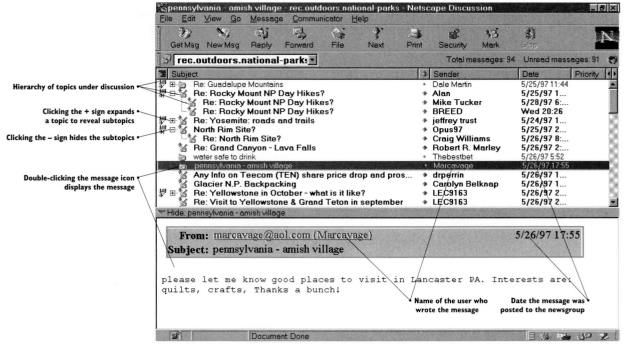

Figure 1-7 USENET Newsgroups organize information according to topics.

Chat

A very popular form of real-time communications on the Internet is Internet Relay Chat (IRC), which enables people to converse with one another over the Internet. As you type a message on your computer keyboard, the people you're chatting with see what you type almost immediately, and you can simultaneously see what they type in reply. Figure 1-8 shows a conversation in progress.

The conversations are organized according to channels; each channel is a different conversation that's going on. There are thousands of existing chat channels that you can join, or you can create your own channel. In Chapter 9, you'll learn about free Windows and Macintosh software you can get for doing chat.

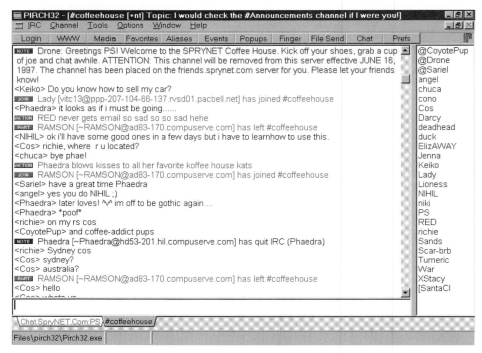

Figure 1-8 An Internet Relay Chat in progress on the Internet.

FTP

FTP stands for File Transfer Protocol. It is the standard method for transferring files over the Internet from one computer to another. FTP can be used as a verb as well as a noun. For example, if you want someone to send you a file, you can ask them to FTP it to you.

Figure 1-9 is an artist's impression of how FTP can transfer files across the Internet. You will learn how to use FTP in Chapter 22.

Telnet

Once you log on to your local network, telnet lets you log in remotely to other networks on the Internet, as depicted in Figure 1-10. If you do not have a logon on the remote computer, you can often gain access by logging on as "anonymous."

Like the names of many Internet services, telnet can be used as a verb. For example, you can tell someone to telnet to your computer to retrieve a file you left there for them. You will learn how to use telnet in Chapter 10.

Figure 1-9 FTP transfers files over the Internet from one computer to another.

Figure 1-10 Telnet lets you log in remotely to other networks on the Internet.

Gopher

Gopher is a play on words. It was invented in 1991 at the University of Minnesota, home of the Golden Gophers. Its function on the Internet is to help you "go fer" things. As depicted in Figure 1-11, you navigate through a hierarchy of menus to locate and download texts, pictures, audio clips, and videos. Thus, Gopher is a protocol for organizing information hierarchically on the Internet.

As the first information-harvesting tool that made the Internet easy enough for the average person to navigate, the Gopher spread quickly all over the world. In just a few short years, however, the Gopher had been eclipsed by the more popular World Wide Web.

Figure 1-11 Gopher enables you to find information by navigating through a menu of menus to locate what you want.

World Wide Web

The World Wide Web (WWW) is a networked hypertext system that allows documents to be shared over the Internet. Developed at the European Particle Physics Center (CERN) in Geneva, Switzerland, the Web's original purpose was to let researchers all over the world collaborate on the same documents without needing to travel anywhere physically.

Hypertext is a word coined by Ted Nelson (1965). It refers to text that has been linked. When you view a hypertext and click a word that has been linked, your computer launches the object of that link. The links give the text an added dimension, which is why it is called hyper.

When it was released in 1991, the Web was purely text-based. In 1993, the National Center for Supercomputer Applications (NCSA) released Mosaic, a graphical user

Figure 1-12 The World Wide Web is the most popular service on the Internet.

interface that made the Web extremely easy to use. In addition to text, Mosaic allowed Web pages to contain pictures, with links to audio and video as well. This led to the Web's becoming the most popular service on the Internet. As depicted in Figure 1-12, the Web enables you to follow links to documents and resources all over the world.

In 1994, Netscape Communications Corporation was started by some of Mosaic's developers, and over the next few years, a program called Netscape Navigator become the most popular Web browser. Microsoft also created a Web browser called the Microsoft Internet Explorer, which now ships as part of Windows. The popularity of Netscape Navigator and the Microsoft Internet Explorer diminished the need for continued work on Mosaic, and in 1997, the NCSA quietly discontinued work on it, opting instead to work on other advanced Internet technologies.

You will learn how to browse the World Wide Web in Chapter 4, use it for research in Chapter 11, and create your own Web pages in Part Five. You can learn more about the history of the Web by following the Interlit Web site links to the W3C World Wide Web Consortium. By following the links to Tim Berners-Lee, you can read a fascinating interview in *Technology Review Online* with the person credited with inventing the Web.

WHAT IS CLIENT-SERVER COMPUTING?

Client-server computing is an important concept on the Internet. Think about what the Internet is: a worldwide connection of millions of computers. Think about what these computers do: they send and receive information. That's what client-server computing is all about. When a computer sends information, the computer is a server. When a computer receives information, the computer is a client. The term client-server computing refers to the manner in which computers exchange information by sending it (as servers) and receiving it (as clients).

Any computer on the Internet can be a client or a server. For example, when you surf the World Wide Web with a browser such as Netscape Navigator or the Microsoft Internet Explorer, your computer is a client, because you are receiving information from other computers on the World Wide Web. The computers that send the information are the servers; computers devoted to serving Web pages are called Web servers.

Sometimes a server needs to obtain additional information in order to answer a request from a client. At the moment when the server requests information from another computer, the server becomes a client. When the server obtains the information it needs, it routes the information back to you, fulfilling its role as your server.

You will encounter the terms *client* and *server* a lot. If you are a little confused at first, don't fret. Just remember that client means "receive" and server means "send." If you play tennis, this will be easy to remember, because when you serve a tennis ball, you send it, hopefully very fast, to your opponent! Another aid to remembering correct usage is the fact that both server and send begin with an *s.*

WHAT ARE DOMAINS AND SUBDOMAINS?

Every computer on the Internet has a unique Internet Protocol (IP) address. An IP address consists of four numbers separated by periods. The numbers range from 0 to 255. The smallest address is 0.0.0.0 and the largest is 255.255.255.255. The number of IP addresses this scheme allows is 256^4, which is 4,294,967,296. This provides room for adding more computers as the network grows.

IP addresses can be hard to remember. For example, the Web server at the Library of Congress has the IP address 140.147.248.7. The White House is at 198.137.241.30. The Smithsonian is 160.111.7.240. If you had to remember numbers like these, the Internet would not be very user-friendly.

To make IP addresses easier for human beings to remember, a Domain Name System (DNS) was invented to permit the use of alphabetic characters instead of numbers. For example, instead of having to remember that the Library of Congress is at 140.147.248.7 you can use its domain name www.loc.gov. The White House is www.whitehouse.gov, and the Smithsonian is www.si.edu.

Domain names have the format:

`hostname.subdomain.top-level-domain`

In the United States, top-level domains normally consist of one of the following:

`.edu`	educational
`.com`	commercial
`.gov`	government
`.mil`	military
`.net`	network support centers
`.org`	other organizations

In the rest of the world, top-level domains are usually country codes, such as *FR* for France. The subdomain refers to the network to which a computer is connected, and the host name refers to the computer itself. For example, in the domain name www.louvre.fr, which is the World Wide Web server at the famous Louvre museum in Paris, the top-level domain *fr* indicates that the server is located in France, the subdomain *louvre* tells you that the server is on the Louvre's network, and the host name *www* identifies this computer as the Louvre's World Wide Web server.

On February 4, 1997, the Internet International Ad Hoc Committee (IAHC) announced seven new top-level-domain names. When this book went to press, the new names were not yet implemented; you can check the status of the new domain names by following the Interlit Web site links to the Generic Top Level Domain Memorandum of Understanding. The seven new names are:

`.firm`	for businesses, or firms
`.store`	for businesses offering goods to purchase
`.web`	for entities emphasizing activities related to the WWW
`.arts`	for entities emphasizing cultural and entertainment activities
`.rec`	for entities emphasizing recreation/entertainment activities
`.info`	for entities providing information services
`.nom`	for those wishing individual or personal nomenclature

BRIEF HISTORY OF THE INTERNET

The Internet originated when the Advanced Research Projects Agency (ARPA) of the United States Department of Defense began a network called ARPANET in 1969. Its goal was to support military research about how to build a network that could continue to function in the midst of partial outages that could be caused by bomb attacks. Instead of giving the network the responsibility for routing the information, the computers on the network shared equally in the responsibility for ensuring that the communication was accomplished. The messages were divided into packets that wound their way through the network on an individual basis. Each packet contained some information and the address of the destination to which it was to be delivered. If one of the computers along the way stopped functioning, such as in a bomb attack, the packets would automatically find an alternate route to their destinations. Thus, every computer on the network was treated as a peer. That's why, to this day, no computer on the Internet is more important than any other, and no one computer is in charge.

During the 1970s, universities began using the Internet Protocol to connect their local networks to the ARPANET. Access to the Pentagon's computers on the

ARPANET was tightly controlled, but the university computers were permitted to communicate freely with one another. Because the IP software was public-domain, and the basic technology made joining the network relatively simple, the Internet became more diverse. It didn't cost much to join the Internet, because each local network simply paid for its connection to the nearest node. As the network grew, it became more valuable as it embraced larger user populations, social groups, and resources. Diversity posed security risks, however, and in 1983 the military segment broke off and became MILNET.

In 1986, the National Science Foundation (NSF) began the NSFNET, a backbone that connected the nation's five supercomputer centers at high speed. NSF upgraded the network repeatedly, setting a blistering pace for technical advancement. In 1991, NSF lifted the restriction that prohibited commercial entities from using the backbone. By 1994, the NSFNET was carrying 10 trillion bytes of Internet traffic per month. In 1995, NSFNET reverted to a research network, and the U.S. Internet backbone traffic is now routed through interconnected network providers.

Attempts to continue expanding and speeding up the Internet continue. A consortium of research universities is creating an even faster network named "Internet II." President Clinton has pledged financial support to help build it. For a complete chronology of the Internet, follow the Interlit Web site links to the Hobbes' Internet Time Line.

E X E R C I S E S

1. Find out the domain name of the computer network at your school or place of work. If you have an e-mail address on that network, the domain name will be the part of your e-mail address after the @ sign. For example, if your e-mail address is SantaClaus@toymakers.northpole.com, the domain name is toymakers.northpole.com.

2. How well-connected are the people in your life? How many of your friends and relatives have access to the Internet? What about your school or workplace: Do you have convenient access to the Internet there? How about your home—do you have Internet access at home? Do you believe that having access to the Internet should be a high priority for anyone planning to succeed in the twenty-first century?

3. Match the Internet services on the left with the description of what they enable you to do.

___E___ e-mail	A. Participate in an online conference about a particular topic.
___D___ listserv	B. Transfer a file from one computer to another.
___A___ USENET newsgroups	C. A global hypertext system.
___F___ chat	D. Send a message to a list full of people.
___B___ FTP	E. Send a message to an individual.
___G___ telnet	F. Converse with one or more people in real time over the Internet.
___H___ Gopher	G. Log on remotely to another computer on the Internet.
___C___ World Wide Web	H. A hierarchically organized menuing system.

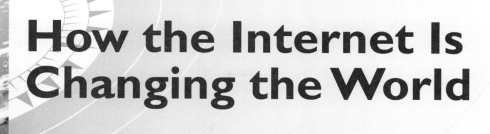

2 How the Internet Is Changing the World

After completing this chapter, you will be able to:

▪ **Describe how the Internet is changing the world by means of a process called convergence.**

▪ **Tell what percentage of the population is telecommuting already.**

▪ **Know where the hottest shopping sites are on the Net.**

▪ **Guage the extent to which commercial advertising is paying for services available "for free" on the Internet.**

▪ **Understand how government officials and politicians are using the Internet.**

▪ **Realize how the Internet is revolutionizing the publishing industry.**

▪ **Share the vision of how the Web is capable of hosting an interconnected world of research and scholarship.**

▪ **Understand how the Net provides educators with a powerful medium for more actively involving students in the teaching and learning process.**

F YOU had to summarize in one word how the Internet is changing the world, that word would be *convergence;* on the Internet you can see how all of our traditional ways of communicating are converging into a networked supermedium, as depicted in Figure 2-1.

No matter how you want to encode your message—whether through text, image, video, audio, print, or speech—you can communicate it digitally over the Internet. Digitization is changing the kind of world we live in. It's an instantaneously connected world. It's highly productive. It knows no bounds, and it gives everyone an equal chance.

Because the Net cannot see racial differences, age, sex, or physical handicaps, it doesn't discriminate. Except, perhaps, it does discriminate against the unconnected, because in an information society, to be cut off from the network is to be disenfranchised.

Figure 2-1 The forces of digitalization are converging traditional forms of communication into a networked supermedium.

MERGERS AND ALLIANCES

Bane, Bradley, and Collis (1995:2) compare the forces of digitalization to the gravity of a wormhole in *Star Trek*, pulling recognizable industries through it and transforming them into something unrecognizable on the other side. Indeed, these forces have caused an unprecedented number of mergers and alliances as corporations jockey for position in the converged world. There were 1,563 high-tech mergers in 1995, up from 879 in 1994. The total value of the transactions was $82.8 billion, up from $69.2 billion a year earlier. According to a Broadview Associations LLP survey, 64% of companies are considering more mergers and partnerships (*Information Week* 29 Jan 96: 28).

For example, Microsoft and the satellite TV broadcast company DirecTV are forming an alliance to offer digital information and entertainment services that can be displayed on a TV set or a computer screen (*New York Times* 12 Mar 96: C2). Microsoft partnered with NBC to create the MSNBC network at http://www.msnbc.com, which uses the brand power of a TV network to transition people to become online users, and makes the online service become a regular part of the way people use television (*Broadcasting & Cable* 6 May 96: 43). Compaq Computer and Thomson Consumer Electronics have teamed up to produce devices that combine the functions of PCs and televisions. Compaq is the biggest PC seller, and Thomson is the largest U.S. maker of TV sets (*Investor's Business Daily* 23 May 96: A3).

High-tech mergers are not limited to the United States. America Online, in partnership with the Japanese trading company Mitsui and the business publishing company Nihon Keizai Shimbun (Nikkei), is establishing an online service in Japan offering a broad range of Japanese-language material (*Financial Times* 9 May 96: 17). Nintendo, Microsoft, and Japan's Nomure Research Institute are collaborating to deliver a high-speed online service that will beam content such as sports news, online shopping, and entertainment via a TV broadcasting satellite system (*Financial Times* 27 Jun 96: 15). Deutsche Telekom, France Telecom, and Sprint have formed an alliance called Global One to provide worldwide voice, data, and video services for corporate clients. Global One will be competing against Uniworld, formed by AT&T and four European telecom operators, and Concert, formed by British Telecommunications and MCI (*Financial Times* 1 Feb 96: 16). Electronic Arts, the largest producer of video game software, has purchased Johannesburg-based software distributor Vision Software, which is building import operations in Kenya and four central African countries (*New York Times* 9 Apr 96: C5).

TELECOMMUTING

For a large percentage of the population, the Internet is becoming the workplace. According to a Deloitte & Touche report, telecommuting (working from home, using computers, modems, and fax machines) accounted for 45% of all new jobs from 1987 to 1992 (*Atlanta Constitution* 2 Jan 94: E2). A survey by Work/Family Directions found that 20 to 40% of employees would like to telecommute (*Wall Street Journal* 14 Dec 93: B1). More than half of U.S. businesses permitted telecommuting in 1996, with 1.5 million companies having telecommuting policies in place (*USA TODAY* 18 Jun 96: E7). The California earthquakes made many new converts to telecommuting, given the significant long-term damage to traffic routes around Los Angeles (*Investor's Business Daily* 27 Jan 94: 4). In addition to reducing traffic congestion, telecommuting can cut pollution, as an Arthur D. Little study points out. For example, a 10 to 20% reduction in trips would save 3.5 billion gallons of gas yearly (*Atlanta Constitution* 2 Dec 93: A19). Telecommuting has also had an impact on the clothing industry, causing suit sales to plummet as more people work from home (*St. Petersburg Times* 3 Jan 94: 19).

In 1996, the Internet created 1.1 million new jobs (*Internet Index* 16 Apr 97). As the Internet grows and creates even more online jobs, the number of telecommuters will continue to increase.

BUSINESS, ADVERTISING, AND ONLINE SHOPPING

The Net is changing how the world shops. Instead of wearing yourself out trekking from store to store trying to find the size and style you like and then having to wait in line to pay for it, teleshopping services let you shop from home. A Yankelovich Partners survey found that 60% of respondents have tried either online or television shopping. Most cited convenient hours and a secure environment as the reasons they liked the service. Electronic home shopping sales have surged to more than $3 billion annually and are forecast to rise to anywhere from $30 billion to $250 billion in the next 10 years (*Miami Herald* 18 Jan 94: C1). The 1997 Price Waterhouse Technology Forecast predicts that electronic commerce on the Web will reach at least $44 billion annually by 2000, and possibly as much as $200 billion (*Toronto Globe & Mail* 26 Feb 97).

In 1996, corporations spent $266.9 million advertising products on the Web. While the amount of sales conducted over the Net is not yet very large, it is expected that online shopping will eventually surpass the traditional storefront marketplace in sales volume. Wal-Mart, the nation's largest retail company, is doubling the number of items that will be available to persons who shop on the Internet, making it possible for shoppers to purchase 80,000 different products online (*Financial Times* 27 Mar 97). Chrysler Corporation expects that 25% of its sales in 2001 will be conducted online; only 1.5% are online today (*Internet Index* 16 Apr 97).

CORPORATE OVERVIEW
INTERNET INDEX

Table 2-1 lists the Web addresses of some Internet shopping services and describes what they do. You can follow the links to all of these online shops at the Interlit Web site. For more-detailed statistics on commercial use of the Net, follow the Interlit Web site links to the Internet Index.

Table 2-1   World Wide Web Online Shopping Locations

World Wide Web Address	What You'll Find There
http://www.internetmall.com The Internet **MALL**	27,000 companies organized according to floors. First Floor, Books & Media; Second Floor, Travel & Fun; Third Floor, Technology Center; Fourth Floor, Fashion; Fifth Floor, Gifts; Sixth Floor, Household; plus six more floors.
http://tips.internet.com T.I.P.S.	Wide range of information technology products, including network connections, Internet providers, World Wide Web products, digital cameras, video products, and more
http://www.amazon.com **A**	Online bookstore that stocks millions of different titles
http://www.isn.com ISN	Internet Shopping Network (ISN) for computer products, software, and multimedia accessories
http://www.expedia.com **Expedia**	Microsoft Expedia travel shop where step-by-step wizards help you research your travel plans and book flights, hotels, and rental cars
http://www.yahoo.com/Business_and_Economy/Companies/Shopping_Centers/Online_Malls **YAHOO!**	Extensive list of Internet shopping sites on the Web

The Internet is changing the face of business. Online shopping and banking are creating a cashless society by eliminating the need for printed money. Brokerage firm Charles Schwab says 20% of its business already comes from electronic stock and mutual fund orders. Schwab is expanding that to include electronic payment capability, and it predicts that online orders will represent 30 to 40% of order entry in the next four to five years (*St. Petersburg Times* 23 May 96: E6). To visit Schwab on the Web, follow the Interlit Web site links to Charles Schwab.

Advertising pays the cost of providing some of the Web's best services, much like advertising covers the cost of television broadcasts so you can watch TV "for free." For example, Figure 2-2 shows how commercial ads pay for the popular search engine Yahoo at http://www.yahoo.com. FlyCast Communications estimates that most Web sites fill only about 50% of their allotted advertising space, often using the remainder for in-house ads or giving it away free to steady customers. FlyCast wants to become the Web's advertising liquidator, selling unused ad space through an electronic auction system (*Wall Street Journal* 24 Feb 97). FlyCast's AdAgent

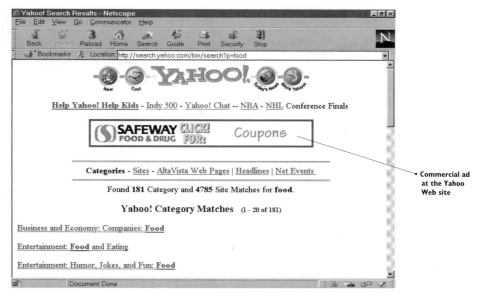

Figure 2-2 Commercial advertising pays for the Yahoo search engine, making it "free" to users on the Internet.

provides media buyers with complete, real-time control over Web ad campaign planning, market testing, execution, and performance monitoring. Leading agencies and Web advertising buyers use FlyCast's unique real-time buying capability to make traditional ad buys and to make real-time buys over an open exchange, a concept similar to financial market trading. You can learn more about this effort by following the Interlit Web site links to FlyCast.

 Advertising also pays for the Internet's amazing PointCast Network, shown in Figure 2-3. The PointCast Network is a free news and information service available via the Internet that allows you to personalize the service according to your interests. PointCast's Smart Screen™ technology automatically begins running headline news when your computer is idle. Figure 2-4 shows the wide variety of news content to which you can subscribe, including local news, weather, sports, and lifestyles. In addition to the custom news content you choose, PointCast also

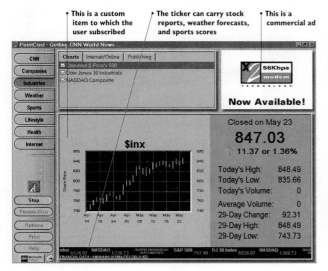

Figure 2-3 Sample screen from the PointCast Network.

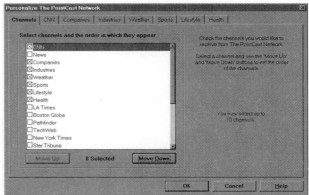

Figure 2-4 PointCast lets you customize the newsfeeds according to your lifestyle, geographical location, and interests.

displays commercial advertising that pays for the service and makes it "free" to end users like yourself. Thus, PointCast uses the same financial model that made commercial television a success. You can download the PointCast Network by following the Interlit Web site links to PointCast's Web site.

GOVERNMENT SERVICES, POLITICS, AND NATIONAL DEFENSE

Government officials have turned increasingly to the Internet for solutions to problems inherent in governance. The Net makes services more widely available and enables municipalities to respond more quickly to emergencies and disasters. You can access a wealth of information by following the Interlit Web site links to the U.S. Government Consumer Information Center in Pueblo, Colorado. At the Internal Revenue Service Web site pictured in Figure 2-5, you can learn about the tax code, download tax forms, and file your income tax return over the telephone. By following the links to North Communications, you can find out about touch-screen kiosks that state and local governments are deploying to increase access to government services.

Videoconferencing and the Internet provide ways for politicians to reach, canvass, and broaden their constituencies. The Internet has become so important in getting elected to public office that almost every political candidate has a Web site. For example, Figures 2-6 and 2-7 show the Democratic and Republican Web sites, respectively. For an index of political candidate Web sites, follow the Interlit Web site links to "Political Candidates."

Countries that want to be competitive in the new global economy are quickening the pace of the development of their national information superhighways. When this book went to press, more than 70 countries were already connected.

Figure 2-5 You can download tax forms at the Internal Revenue Service Web site. To visit this site, follow the Interlit Web site links to the IRS.

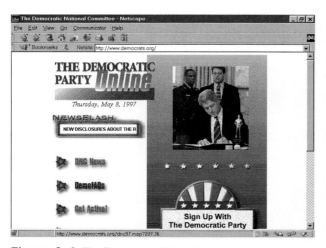

Figure 2-6 The Democrats' Web site.

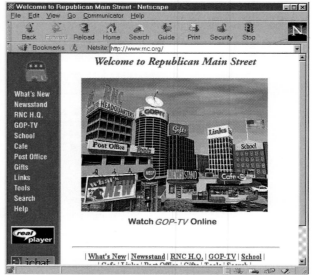

Figure 2-7 The Republicans' Web site.

The United States relies so much on the Internet that perhaps even more devastating than a nuclear attack would be an electronic invasion of the computer networks without which this country would grind to a halt. Such a form of electronic attack is known as **information warfare**. According to Central Intelligence Agency Director John Deutch, the trend toward increased corporate reliance on telecommunications and networks is making the United States more vulnerable to information warfare tactics. "The electron, in my judgment, is the ultimate precision-guided munition. Virtually any single 'bad actor' can acquire the hardware and software needed to attack some of our critical information-based infrastructures.... We have evidence that a number of countries around the world are developing the doctrine, strategies and tools to conduct information attacks" (*Wall Street Journal* 26 Jun 96: B6). Deputy U.S. Attorney General Jamie Gorelick warns that "an electronic Pearl Harbor" is a very real danger. About 250,000 intrusions into Defense Department computer systems are attempted each year, with about a 65% success rate (*BNA Daily Report for Executives* 17 Jul 96: A22).

As President of the United States, George Bush criticized the CIA for being so slow to issue reports that the White House learned more about world developments by watching commercial TV. The government now uses the Internet to provide officials with live online newsfeeds from news organizations such as CNN, which is on the Web at http://www.cnn.com. For more information about the use of information technologies in defense applications, follow the Interlit Web site links to the Defense Advanced Research Projects Agency (DARPA).

ELECTRONIC PUBLISHING

The Internet is changing how we read newspapers by eliminating the need for the paper and offering customization with search engines that can find not only text but graphics, audio, and video as well. According to The Kelsey Group, more than 2,700 newspapers are experimenting with electronic ventures, compared to only 42 in 1989; contributing to the need for these experiments is the fact that half of young people aged 18 to 24 do not read newspapers at all (*U.S.News & World Report* 16 May 94: 60). Table 2-2 lists a few of the newspapers you can read on the Web.

Table 2-2 A Few of the Newspapers on the World Wide Web

Newspaper	Web Address
New York Times	http://www.nytimes.com
Raleigh [NC] News & Observer	http://www.nando.net
San Francisco Chronicle	http://sfgate.com/chronicle/index.shtml
San Jose [CA] Mercury News	http://www.sjmercury.com
USA Today	http://www.usatoday.com
Virginian-Pilot	http://www.pilotonline.com
4,000 other links to newspapers, magazines, broadcasters, and news services	http://www.newslink.org

Dow Jones publishes an electronic version of its flagship *Wall Street Journal* and also offers an online service called *Personal Journal* that delivers selected stories based on customer demand (*Miami Herald* 12 Sep 93: C3). Imagine what a time-saver this is. Suppose you are an educator and you want the latest news in education, but you have little interest in sports. Instead of having a newspaper delivered that is 2% education and 40% sports, you get a newsfeed of all the educational articles from all of the "papers." Executives at Mercury Center, the electronic extension of the *San Jose Mercury News,* predict that reader loyalty will increase because electronic publishing gives a newspaper the tools to focus on small parts of the market, offering topics that may not interest a general audience (*New York Times* 7 Feb 94: C1).

TELEVISION AND ENTERTAINMENT

The Internet is competing with television for people's free time. A survey conducted by the Emerging Technologies Research Group shows Internet users spending an average of 6.6 hours a week on the Net, time previously spent watching TV, listening to the radio, or making long-distance phone calls. The average session was 68 minutes (*Tampa Tribune* 12 Jan 96: B&F1). A Nielsen study reported similar results, concluding that Internet users spend more time online than TV viewers spend with their VCRs. Twenty-four million people in the United States and Canada are already on the Internet. The Nielsen study also found that women comprise about one-third of all Internet users, far more than previously thought (*Dow Jones News* 30 Oct 95).

TEACHING AND LEARNING

The benefits of computer-based learning are well-documented by Professor James Kulik (1985, 1986, 1991, and 1994) and his associates at the University of Michigan. During the past 20 years, Kulik has analyzed hundreds of controlled experiments on the effectiveness of computer-based learning. Overall, the findings indicate that average learning time has been reduced significantly (sometimes by as much as 80%), and achievement levels are more than a standard deviation higher (a full letter grade in school) than when computers are not used.

The Internet is enabling educators to make use of computer-based learning strategies online. By linking universities, colleges, schools, and homes into a worldwide network, the Internet is helping to break down the distinctions between grade levels. The Internet is enabling students of all ages to collaborate on worldwide projects, share discoveries, and develop strategies for acquiring knowledge in a social context.

It is difficult for a teacher to provide this kind of environment for each student in a traditional classroom. Since there is only one teacher for many students, it is physically impossible for a teacher to support each student's individual needs. The World Wide Web helps by providing students with an interconnected world of knowledge to explore. Screen capture and downloading enable students to collect what they discover and construct a framework for organizing and understanding. Since the learner is portrayed as an active processor who explores, discovers, reflects, and constructs knowledge, the trend to teach from this perspective is known as the constructivist movement in education.

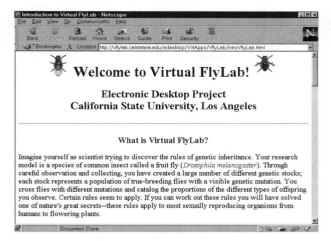

Figure 2-8 The Virtual FlyLab lets you breed fruitflies and explore the laws of genetic inheritance.

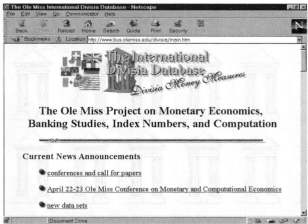

Figure 2-9 The Divisia Database lets you download monetary aggregates for countries around the world.

Suppose you're a biology student learning the laws of genetic inheritance. As illustrated in Figure 2-8, the Virtual FlyLab lets you breed fruit flies, formulate hypotheses, and run statistical procedures, creating a framework for discovering and validating genetic laws. You can breed your own fruit flies by following the Interlit Web site links to the Virtual FlyLab.

Imagine an economics student investigating monetary aggregates for countries around the world. Instead of using the simple-sum aggregates supplied officially by the central banks, the student can download the raw data to conduct experiments uncontaminated by inconsistent methods of index construction. By following the Interlit Web site links to the Divisia Database shown in Figure 2-9, you can scroll down and ask to see the monetary aggregates of any country in the world. Then you can copy and paste the data from the Web page into a spreadsheet, where you can manipulate it as you wish.

Figure 2-10 Java rotations of a model of a benzene molecule. Rotating the chemical model leads the user to discover that the centers of the six carbon atoms and six hydrogen atoms in benzene are coplanar.

One of the most difficult problems in teaching chemistry is to help students visualize the structure of chemical models. In a textbook, students are limited to a static photo showing only one position. On the Web, using active technologies such as Sun's Java, students can rotate chemical models by clicking and dragging with a mouse. For example, Figure 2-10 shows different stages in the rotation of a model of a benzene molecule on a Java Web page. To try this and other chemical models on the Web, follow the Interlit Web site links to the Java Molecule Viewer.

Science teachers are using the Internet to provide students with collaborative learning experiences, access to scientific databases, and virtual visits to science laboratories. Reporting on the New Jersey Networking Infastructure in Education project, Friedman, Baron, and Addison (1996) cite several compelling examples of science study via the Internet. Students gather samples from local pond water, measure chemical characteristics, examine organisms, and share observations with peers over the Internet. An ocean weather database that tracks ships at sea enables students to calculate the speed and direction of oceangoing vessels and predict arrival times. Students visit the Plasma Physics Laboratory at Princeton University to access data from fusion experiments as quickly as Princeton scientists. As pictured in Figure 2-11, you can even run a tokamak nuclear fusion reactor.

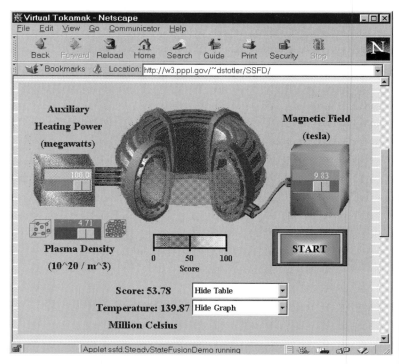

Figure 2-11 By manipulating the sliders that control the plasma density, heating power, and magnetic field, you can learn how these parameters interact, and you'll develop an intuitive feel for the process that scientists go through in designing tokamak reactors.

Table 2-3 lists the Web sites you can visit to learn more about these projects. All of these projects are linked to the Interlit Web site. For the latest information, follow the Interlit Web site links to the New Jersey Networking Infastructure in Education.

Table 2-3   Web Sites for Science Study on the Internet

Type	Topic	URL
Collaboration	Pond water	http://njnie.dl.stevens-tech.edu/curriculum/water.html
Collaboration	Temperature	http://njnie.dl.stevens-tech.edu/curriculum/temp/intro.html
Databases	Ships at sea	http://njnie.dl.stevens-tech.edu/curriculum/oceans/stowaway.html
Databases	Sunspots	http://www.users.interport.net/~jbaron/solar.html
Science labs	Fusion	http://ippex.pppl.gov/ippex/
Science labs	DNA research	http://morgan.rutgers.edu

NATIONAL GEOGRAPHIC SOCIETY

The National Geographic Kids network (Kids Net) combines online computer activity with real-life interactions and experimentation. Electronic mail engages children in cooperative learning across the Internet. For example, consider the Acid Rain Project shown in Figure 2-12. Students designed acid-rain collectors and inspected tombstones for acid-rain damage. After compiling and analyzing the data, students shared results through e-mail. The result provided a comparison of acid-rain damage throughout the United States and Canada. For more information, follow the Interlit Web site links to the Acid Rain Project.

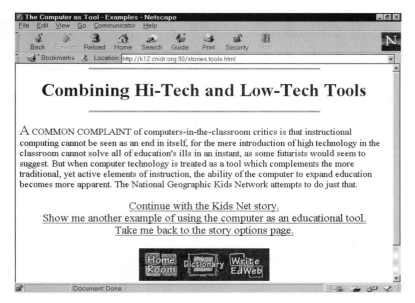

Figure 2-12 The Acid Rain Project at the National Geographic Kids Network.

Another online collaborative network is organized by the KIDLINK Society. Since 1990, KIDLINK has united 60,000 children aged 10 to 15 from 85 countries. Online discussions use Internet chat rooms. Kids can connect at any time to join conversations on a wide range of subjects. For more information, follow the Interlit Web site links to the KIDLINK Society.

INTERCONNECTED SCHOLARSHIP

The Internet affords researchers an unprecedented opportunity to create an interconnected world of scholarship. Imagine having every scholarly paper mounted on the World Wide Web, with hypertext links that put you just a mouse click away from calling up the source materials referenced in the article. Such was the dream of Tim Berners-Lee when he began making plans to create the Web back in the early 1980s. At that time, the tools for creating Web pages were primitive, however, and mounting documents on the Web required technical skills that exceeded what the average scholar had the time to learn and use. Happily, there now are Web page creation utilities for the world's most popular word processors—Microsoft Word and WordPerfect. After just a few mouse clicks, scholars can create Web pages out of any research paper.

The author believes that when the word processors used to author scholarly papers become capable of creating Web pages, all scholars should assume the responsibility of putting their research papers on the Web. Then the Web crawlers will find the papers and index them into the Internet's search engines. Automatically, a world of interconnected scholarship arises.

Unfortunately, most scholars do not yet know how to create Web pages, and since most journals still don't publish the full text of their articles on the Web, the publishers are not making this happen either. The author believes it's time to change that. By helping everyone who reads this book learn how to create Web pages and mount them on the Web, it is hoped that the Web page creation tutorial in Part Five will contribute to making the world of interconnected scholarship happen sooner rather than later.

E X E R C I S E S

1. Give examples of how the Internet has affected (*a*) the nation as a whole, (*b*) your local community, and (*c*) your personal life.

2. In your chosen career or profession, would telecommuting be appropriate? How would it help or hinder your work?

3. This chapter described how the Internet is changing the world through mergers and alliances, telecommuting, home shopping, electronic publishing, and computer-based learning. How else do you see the Internet changing the world?

4. Kinko's operates a nationwide videoconferencing network. Anyone can go into a Kinko's and buy videoconferencing time. Visit your local Kinko's and ask to see their videoconferencing facilities. Do you think videoconferencing will become a viable business at Kinko's? For whom and for what purpose? Would you use it in your line of work or for personal matters? Why or why not?

5. Compare the advantages and disadvantages of home shopping as you see them. What impact will home shopping have on traditional stores and shopping malls?

6. Visit a local realtor and find out whether they use the Internet to sell homes. If so, ask what the benefit is; if not, find out why the realtor does not use the Net.

7. How is your state and local government using the Internet? Do your local politicians have Web sites? Does your state have kiosks in public places to provide better access to government services? If so, what services are available through kiosks in your state?

8. Is your doctor connected to the Internet? Ask about this during your next appointment. Find out how your doctor uses the network to stay current and learn about new procedures, such as by reading the Online Journal of Clinical Trials.

9. Think of an example showing how a computer helped you learn something. What was the subject matter? What role did the computer play? Did you learn better because of the computer? Why or why not?

10. What percentage of your teachers used the Internet to enhance your educational experience when you were in elementary school? What percentage of teachers do you believe will be using the Internet as a teaching and learning tool by the year 2010?

11. How do you believe the Internet will affect the future of schooling? For example, do you believe that if the Information Superhighway could serve all the nation's educational software to children at home, there would be no further need for schools as we know them? Are there any aspects of schooling that technology cannot replace?

12. Of all the different kinds of occupations you can think of, which ones need the Internet the most? The least? What is your chosen occupation? Why will you need to know about the Internet to do well in your line of work?

13. In what occupations, if any, should the ability to create Web pages be a prerequisite for employment?

Part Two

Getting On the Internet

Almost everyone reading this book has already been on the Internet. You have probably already surfed the Web, for example, and you may consider yourself pretty good at surfing. But do you know the most cost-effective way to connect to the Internet from your locale? Do you understand the theory of surfing well enough to truly glide across the Net and find things quickly?

This part of the book will enable you to get more out of the Internet by helping you understand how best to connect and surf the Net.

3

Getting Connected

After completing this chapter, you will be able to:

- ▪ **Understand the purpose and function of an Internet service provider (ISP).**

- ▪ **Find out who the ISPs are in your locale.**

- ▪ **Compare the advantages and disadvantages of the different transport mediums, including plain old telephone lines, high-speed broadband cables, digital telephone lines, and television cables.**

- ▪ **Understand the difference between connecting to the Internet via terminal programs and TCP/IP connections.**

- ▪ **Decide the best way to connect, given your particular circumstances.**

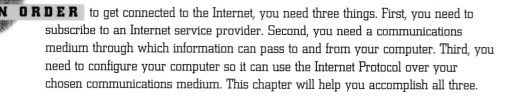 **N ORDER** to get connected to the Internet, you need three things. First, you need to subscribe to an Internet service provider. Second, you need a communications medium through which information can pass to and from your computer. Third, you need to configure your computer so it can use the Internet Protocol over your chosen communications medium. This chapter will help you accomplish all three.

INTERNET SERVICE PROVIDERS

A three-letter acronym that an Internet-literate person should know is ISP, which stands for Internet service provider. The ISP provides you with Internet services, including access to the World Wide Web, e-mail, listserv, and newsgroups. Unless you belong to an institution such as a school, college, or university that provides Internet services to its faculty, staff, and student body for free, you will probably need to pay your ISP an ongoing fee.

In the past, some Internet service providers charged an hourly fee. If you use the Internet a lot, paying by the hour can be very expensive. Listed below are some ISPs that provide unlimited usage for a flat fee of about $20 per month.

America Online

America Online, also known as AOL, is one of the most popular Internet service providers. The number of AOL subscribers has skyrocketed to 8 million (Mercury Center Morning Page 16 Apr 97), causing some overloading of the network. As this book goes to press, AOL is working to upgrade its network to reduce the number of busy signals that users have reported when trying to connect. By the time you read this, the problems hopefully will be solved. To find out more about AOL, go to http://www.aol.com.

AT&T WorldNet

AT&T WorldNet is a nationwide Internet Service Provider. New members get five hours of Internet access per month for $4.95. If you use AT&T WorldNet Service beyond five hours, you get charged $2.50 for each additional hour. Or you can pay a flat fee of $19.95 per month for unlimited usage. You can find AT&T WorldNet on the Web at http://www.att.com.

CompuServe Interactive

CompuServe Interactive (CSi) is a nationwide online service that has 5.3 million subscribers (Mercury Center Morning Page 16 Apr 97). In its 6 May 1997 issue, *PC Magazine* rated CSi as the best online service. To find out more about CompuServe, go to http://www.compuserve.com.

Microsoft Network

The Microsoft Network (MSN) was launched at the same time as Windows 95, which came bundled with the software needed to connect and subscribe to MSN. As this book goes to press, MSN has 2.2 million subscribers (Mercury Center Morning Page 16 Apr 97). To find out more about the Microsoft Network, go to http://www.msn.com.

Prodigy Internet

Prodigy is a nationwide online service that got started through a partnership of Sears and IBM. Prodigy Internet offers up to 10 hours per month of Internet access for $9.95 per month. Additional time is $2.50 per hour. Unlimited access costs $19.95 per month. For more information, go to http://www.prodigy.com.

Regional and Local Networks

By looking up "Internet Services" in the yellow pages of your telephone directory, you will probably find some regional and local ISPs listed in addition to the nationwide service providers discussed so far. For example, in the mid-Atlantic states from Virginia to Massachusetts, a regional ISP called Erol's provides Internet services with the promise that users will not encounter the busy signals or long delays that are alleged to occur at other ISPs. To contact Erol's, call 1-800-376-5772, or go to http://www.erols.com.

An excellent source for finding out about other ISPs in your area is on the Web at http://thelist.internet.com. See the Interlit Web site for this and other links to ISP directories.

School and College Networks

It is common for schools and colleges to operate computer networks that provide Internet services "for free" to their faculty, staff, and students. If you are lucky enough to belong to such a user community, your local school or college serves as your ISP. Since these services are free, however, the resources are sometimes inadequate to meet the demand, and it is not uncommon for members of school and college networks to also subscribe to one of the commercial ISPs. Some campuses have even negotiated deals with commercial ISPs to get a lower price for individuals to subscribe to the commercial service.

TRANSPORT MEDIUM

The transport medium is the physical connection over which information travels between your PC and your Internet service provider. Most often the transport medium is a wire or a cable that you can see and touch. It is also possible to use wireless connections such as cell phones and satellites that communicate via radio signals. Depending upon the medium you wish to use, you will need to have specific hardware installed in your computer to handle the communication.

Telephone Modems

The most common means of connecting to the Internet from home is via plain old telephone service, also known as POTS. In order to communicate with the Internet over an ordinary telephone line, your computer must have a modem. The term **modem** is a combination of the terms *mo*dulate and *dem*odulate, which describe how your computer sends and receives digital information over analog phone lines. Modems are so popular that most computers being sold today come with modems built in. Older models require the addition of external modems that connect to your computer's serial port, or modem cards that plug into one of your computer's expansion slots. Figure 3-1 contains a block diagram that describes how modems work.

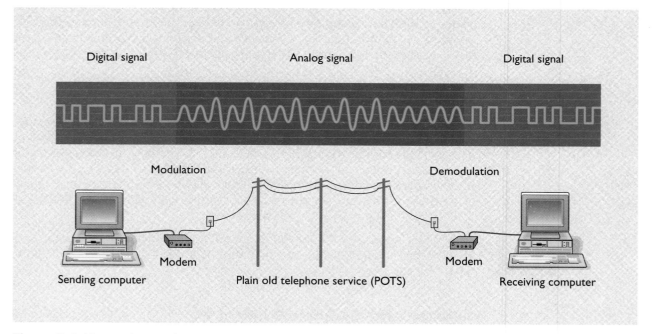

Figure 3-1 How modems work.

Modems have gotten steadily faster as computer technology has advanced. Modem speed is important because it determines how long you have to wait for information to arrive. Modem speed is often expressed in units known as bps, which stands for bits per second, or Kbps, which stands for kilobits [a thousand bits] per second. Common speeds are 14,400 bps (14.4 Kbps), 28,800 bps (28.8 Kbps), 33,600 bps (33.6 Kbps), and 56,000 bps (56 Kbps). For example, information traveling at 14,400 bps takes twice as long to arrive as it would at 28,800 bps.

Just because you have a superfast modem, such as 56 Kbps, does not necessarily mean information will actually travel that fast to and from your computer. The telephone lines and the equipment (routers and switches) that the lines pass through on their way to your ISP may preclude your superfast modem from using its highest speed. Before you invest in the high cost of a superfast modem, you should check with your ISP to make sure that you will actually be able to achieve the highest speed on your particular network. Many modems have built-in compression and decompression features that enable them to pack information more tightly in the communication packets, thereby achieving an actual transmission rate higher than what they're rated at. This feature only works, however, for data that have not already been compressed.

As datacommunications technology continues to advance, modems will continue to increase in speed. Someday, the so-called high speeds discussed in this book will seem slow. For example, Paradyne is already marketing a system called HotWire that uses a rate-adaptive digital subscriber line (RADSL) modem that can send data at speeds of up to 2 million bits per second, making it possible to send video over ordinary telephone lines (*Tampa Tribune* 21 Sep 96: B&F1). If you're tempted to purchase such a modem, however, first make sure that your ISP can support it.

Ethernet

The invention of Ethernet (pronounced *ee-thur-net*) in Bob Metcalfe's Harvard Ph.D. thesis in 1973 was a datacommunications breakthrough that fueled the explosion of local area networks (LANs) throughout academia and industry. Ethernet networks transmit data at high speed, up to 10 megabits per second (Mbps). (*Mega* means "a million," so 10 megabits means 10 million bits.) At Ethernet speeds, a file that takes 10 minutes to transmit over a 14.4 Kbps modem arrives in just 1 second. Actual downloading times may vary, depending on the number of users sharing the Ethernet, network traffic, and compression schemes.

If you're working at a school or company that has its PCs connected to the Internet at high speeds, chances are the communications medium is an Ethernet. At first, Ethernet required the use of coaxial cable, which is the kind of wire used in cable TV. Now there is a so-called 10BaseT Ethernet that can use ordinary twisted-pair telephone wiring. There's also a new 10/100BaseT Ethernet that can move data at rates up to 100 megabits per second.

Token Ring

Token Ring is another type of high-speed network. Like Ethernet, it began using coaxial cable as its physical transport medium. But there's an important difference in the design. Ethernet works on the principle of collision detection. The more users are attached to an Ethernet, the more their data collide. The Ethernet resolves the collisions and delivers the data just fine, but the transmission speed slows down. Token Ring networks avoid collisions by passing data in tokens that move around the network in a ring; hence the name Token Ring. Because the data never collide, Token Ring networks are less prone to slow down as the number of users increases. Token Ring networks typically run at 4 or 16 Mbps, although it's possible to run them even faster. The faster the connection, the higher the cost. Just like Ethernet requires you to have an Ethernet card installed in your computer, so also does Token Ring require you to have a special card installed in your computer, to which the network cable attaches.

ISDN

ISDN stands for Integrated Services Digital Network. It's the digital telephone system that is being installed by regional Bell companies in most of the United States; when this book went to press, about 60% of the country could get ISDN.

ISDN signals are carried over two or more 64 Kbps (64,000 bits per second) circuit-switched channels to carry voice and data, and a lower-speed packet-switched channel that carries control signals. The Basic Rate Interface (BRI) service of ISDN is 144 Kbps, made up of two 64 Kbps data channels and one 16 Kbps control channel. The Primary Rate Interface (PRI) service uses 23 data channels and a 64 Kbps control channel to boost the data rate to 1,544 Kbps (1.544 Mbps), which is capable of real-time videoconferencing in addition to more traditional data services.

In order to use ISDN to connect to the Internet, you will need to contact both your local telephone company and your Internet service provider, to find out whether ISDN is available in your area and to make sure your ISP supports it. ISDN lines cost more than ordinary phone lines, so be prepared to pay more for the higher data rate.

Cable Modems

The term *cable modem* is an oxymoron. Unfortunately, cable modem has already become an established industry term, so it's too late to correct the misuse of the phrase. You'll probably notice the problem as you continue reading this description of what cable modems do. Think about the cable that brings television services into your neighborhood (or imagine such a cable if your neighborhood doesn't have cable TV). It's a coaxial cable. From the reading you did earlier in this chapter, you know that Ethernet works over coaxial cable. When cable TV companies get into the ISP business and begin providing Internet services over TV cables, they use Ethernet. So what's the problem with the term *cable modem?* Ethernet doesn't need a modem, because the signal is already digital! Nevertheless, the industry refers to the network cards used to connect PCs to TV cables as cable modems, and we're stuck with the term, like it or not.

Although cable modems are not very common today, some communities already use them. For example, the high-speed @Home cable Internet access service is available in Fremont, California, for $34.95 per month. The package includes unlimited Internet access, use of a cable modem, e-mail and chat functions, and a customized Web browser. TCI, the cable provider in the Fremont area, will gradually expand the service to cable subscribers in Arlington, Illinois, and Hartford, Connecticut. Meanwhile, Comcast plans to offer @Home in Baltimore and Philadelphia, and Cox Cable will introduce it in San Diego and Orange County, California (*Broadcasting & Cable* 9 Sep 96: 55).

The research firm Dataquest expects high-speed cable modem sales to increase more than tenfold, to 900,000 annually by the year 2000 (*USA Today* 29 May 96: 1B).

WAYS TO CONNECT

There are two basic ways you can connect to an Internet service provider, namely, via terminal programs and through the Internet's TCP/IP protocol.

Terminal Programs

Most PCs come with a terminal program that lets you connect as a "terminal" to access bulletin boards and other dial-up services. If you check with your Internet service provider, you can find out whether dial-up terminal access is available and what services are supported. This does not really put you "on" the Internet, however, because terminal programs do not use the Internet Protocol (IP). In order to really be on the Internet, you need a TCP/IP connection.

TCP/IP Connections

The complete, formal name for the protocol that connects computers to the Internet is TCP/IP. You already know what IP stands for: Internet Protocol. TCP stands for Transmission Control Protocol.

True to its name, TCP governs how information gets transmitted in packets over the Internet. If the information is too large to fit in a single packet, multiple packets get sent. TCP takes care of dividing the information into packets, routing the packets to their destination, and assembling the information when it arrives. If the packets arrive out of sequence, TCP puts them back together in the right order. TCP can even detect when errors occurred on the transmission line to alter the information, in which case TCP asks for the errant packets to be retransmitted.

Depending on what kind of transport medium connects your PC to the Internet, you must have either PPP, broadband, or ISDN-compatible TCP/IP software installed on your computer.

PPP

PPP stands for Point-to-Point Protocol, which you use if you are connecting to the Internet via ordinary telephone lines and a modem. PPP comes built into Windows 95. Windows 3.1 users can get PPP from a variety of sources. For example, PPP comes bundled with *Netscape Navigator Personal Edition,* which you can buy at computer stores.

When your computer connects to the Internet via PPP, your modem dials up to a PPP port at your local Internet service provider (ISP) network. You must be a registered user of this network before you can connect to it via PPP. There is a list of ISPs by area code on the Web at http://thelist.com.

BROADBAND

On a high-speed local area network such as an Ethernet or a Token Ring, each PC contains a network card to which the broadband cable attaches. The vendor of the network card provides the TCP/IP software needed to connect that brand of card to the network. Such software normally ships along with the network card and an instruction manual telling how to install it.

ISDN

Your local telephone company will either supply or specify the kind of network card you will need in order to connect an ISDN line to your computer. The card will arrive along with the TCP/IP software needed to connect that brand of card to the network. Follow the instructions in the card's manual to install it.

COMPARING THE WAYS TO CONNECT

To summarize the many alternatives presented in this chapter, Table 3-1 compares the different ways to connect to the Internet. By studying this comparison, you should be able to select an option that suits your needs and budget.

Table 3-1   Internet Connection Comparison Matrix

Transport Medium	Time to Transmit 100 KB Picture	Time to Transmit 900 KB Audio	Time to Transmit 10 MB 30-Second Movie	Estimated Monthly Communications Cost
14.4 Kbps Modem	55 seconds	500 seconds	93 minutes	$12
28.8 Kbps Modem	28 seconds	250 seconds	46 minutes	$12
33.6 Kbps Modem	24 seconds	214 seconds	40 minutes	$12
56 Kbps Modem	14 seconds	128 seconds	24 minutes	$12
128 Kbps ISDN	6 seconds	56 seconds	10 minutes	$35
3 Mbps Cable Modem	0.27 seconds	2.4 seconds	27 seconds	$35-50

Note: Cable modem speeds vary, depending on the number of simultaneous users of the local cable network.

E X E R C I S E S

1. Check the yellow pages of your phone book and find out how many Internet service providers are listed there. Call at least three ISPs and find out how much unlimited Internet service costs, and at what transmission speeds. What is the most cost-effective ISP in your area?

2. Go to http://www.thelist.com and find out how many ISPs are listed under your area code. Are there more or fewer ISPs listed on the Web than you can find listed under "Internet Services" in the yellow pages of your telephone book?

3. If your local school, company, or library has a local area network, find out what network topology it is (Ethernet or Token Ring) and what speed it has. Also find out whether the network is connected to the Internet, and if it is, what percentage of the PCs connected to the network can access the Internet.

4. Contact your local telephone company and find out whether ISDN services are available to homes in your neighborhood. Find out how much it costs to get an ISDN connection. Make sure you ask about ongoing as well as one-time costs. What services are available via ISDN in your neighborhood? Can you get video conferencing? Does it cost more than lower-bandwidth services?

5. Ask around and find out what percentage of your friends' homes have ISDN installed. Do you think this percentage will increase? Why or why not?

6. Contact your local cable TV company to find out if cable modems are available. If not, register a complaint that your cable company is behind the times. If both cable modems and ISDN are available to you, compare their speeds, costs, and range of services.

4

Surfing the Net

After completing this chapter, you will be able to:

- Know what it means to "surf" the Net.

- Select a Web browser and use it to go surfing.

- Understand the elements of a Uniform resource locator (URL).

- Know how to go to any URL on the World Wide Web.

- Visit some of the most exciting sites on the World Wide Web.

- Understand the concepts of linking and browsing.

- Understand the concepts of a Web page, a home page, and a default page.

- Manipulate a window by sizing, scrolling, hiding, maximizing, and switching among multiple windows.

- Navigate using the browser's buttons and shortcut keys.

- Poke around a Web site by manipulating its URL.

- Avoid distractions and stay focused on the purpose for which you visited a Web site.

- Bookmark your favorite Web sites for quick recall whenever you want to visit them again.

- Know how to create more screen space to display the maximum amount of a Web page inside your browser window.

OST of the people reading this book have probably already had their first surfing experience. Many may consider themselves adept at surfing, and some could even be addicted to it.

Whether or not you have surfed the Net, studying the concepts in this chapter will enable you to become a better surfer than if you "just do it." Especially if you have become addicted, the techniques you learn here will enable you to gain control over the Net, instead of allowing it to control you.

WHAT IS SURFING?

In telecommunications, the term **surfing** means to browse by going from place to place in search of something that interests you. On TV, you surf by changing channels continually until you find a program you want to watch; this is known as channel surfing. On the Net, surfing means to use a program called a browser to go from site to site in search of information that interests you.

The most popular form of browsing occurs on the World Wide Web. As you learned in Chapter 1, the Web is a worldwide hypertext system that interconnects millions of documents. The connections are made through links, which can be textual or graphical. A **link** is a hot spot which, when selected, triggers the object of the link. You select the link by clicking on the word or picture that triggers it. Progressively clicking through the Web by triggering the links that interest you is known as **browsing**, a term synonymous with surfing the Net.

SELECTING A WEB BROWSER

Netscape and Microsoft make the most popular Web browsers. Almost everyone on the Web uses either Netscape Navigator or Microsoft Internet Explorer. You can use either one to complete the tutorial exercises in this chapter.

If you do not already have a browser, you can purchase one at any computer store. Before you spend money buying a browser, however, you should know that both Netscape and Microsoft make their browsers available freely for educational purposes. If you are a teacher or a student, you qualify for a free copy. The person in charge of computing at your school can tell you how to get one.

USING A WEB BROWSER

Before you can start using a Web browser, you must accomplish two tasks:

- You must have a computer that has a "real" Internet connection following the Transmission Control Protocol/Internet Protocol (TCP/IP). Chapter 3 describes how to get such a connection through an ordinary phone line, a digital ISDN phone line, or a high-speed broadband network.

- If the browser is not installed on your computer, you must install it. Follow the installation instructions that came with your browser.

With your computer connected to the Internet, you can start your Web browser and get ready to surf. Typically you start your Web browser by double-clicking on one of these icons:

Netscape   Internet
Navigator 4.0   Explorer

UNDERSTANDING URLS

Every place you can go on the Web has an address known as a **URL**, which stands for *U*niform *r*esource *l*ocator. Most often the resources are hypertext documents, but they can also be pictures, sounds, movies, animations, or application software. URLs can also bring up newsgroups, chat rooms, search engines, and real-time audio and video streams.

Elements of a URL

A URL can have several parts, which always appear in this order:

- protocol
- server name
- port number (optional)
- filename (optional)
- anchor (optional)

Here is what the different parts of a URL mean:

protocol	Protocols include http, gopher, ftp, mailto, and news; the most popular protocol is http, which stands for *h*yper*t*ext *t*ransfer *p*rotocol. Every Web page's URL begins with *http*.
server name	The server name is the Internet address of the computer or file server on which the resource resides.
port number	Port numbers rarely appear in URLs because almost every file server is on the Web's default port, which is port 80.
filename	The filename is the name the file has on the server. If the file is in a folder or subfolder on the server, the filename includes the path to the file as well as the name of the file. If a URL that begins with *http* does not contain a filename, the default filename (usually *index.html*) gets served.
anchor	The anchor is a named bookmark within an HTML file. Anchors are optional. If a URL does not contain an anchor, the browser begins display at the start of the file.

The following analysis shows how the various parts of a URL get combined into a specific address on the World Wide Web. This example is the URL for the professional experience section of the author's résumé.

```
http://www.udel.edu/fth/resume.html#professional
```

protocol	http
server name	www.udel.edu
filename	fth/resume.html
anchor	professional

In most cases, a URL simply consists of a protocol, a server name, and a filename, such as http://www.udel.edu/fth/resume.html.

Web Sites

Every hypertext document on the World Wide Web resides on one of the computers connected to the network. The place where the hypertext document is stored on that computer is known as its **Web site**. Every Web site has a URL.

For example, Sony's Web site is http://www.sony.com. CNN's Web site is http://www.cnn.com. Netscape is at http://www.netscape.com. Microsoft is http://www.microsoft.com. Do you notice the similarity in these corporate Web site addresses? Almost every company in the world has a Web site address in the form of http://www.*company_name*.com.

Web Pages

Like books, each document on the Web consists of one or more pages. Each page in a Web document is known as a **Web page**. Unlike the pages in books, however, Web pages can contain more information than you can see at once. Scroll bars let you move the page up and down inside your browser window, which displays the text and graphics on the Web page.

Every Web page has a URL. For example, the URL of the author's résumé is http://www.udel.edu/fth/resume.html. By analyzing this URL, you can see how this Web page is stored in the *fth* folder (*fth* is the author's initials) at the University of Delaware's Web site. The filename of the Web page is *resume.html*. The filename extension *html* is the standard format used for documents on the Web. HTML stands for *h*yper*t*ext *m*arkup *l*anguage. You will learn more about HTML in Part Five. For now, read on, to get ready to begin surfing or to become a better surfer.

SURFING CONCEPTS AND TECHNIQUES

Surfing the Net is a lot more involved than channel surfing a television. Instead of just flipping through the relatively limited number of channels available on a TV, surfing the Net enables you to navigate a world full of interconnected information, discover new sites you didn't know existed, keep track of where you've been so you can easily get there again, and download things that interest you. By practicing the surfing concepts and techniques presented here, you can master the art of navigating the Net so you can get where you want quickly and accomplish your purpose for going there.

Entering URLs

Oftentimes you will have been given a specific URL that you want to go to. For example, you may have seen an ad for a Sony product that told you to go to the Web site http://www.sony.com for more information. To go there (or to any other site for which you know the URL), you simply type the URL into your Web browser's URL field, and press the Enter key. If your browser's URL field is not visible, follow the steps in Table 4-1 to get it on your screen.

Table 4-1 How to Go to a URL

Netscape Navigator	Microsoft Internet Explorer
▶ Netscape Navigator calls the URL field the Location field.	▶ Microsoft Internet Explorer calls the URL field the Address field.
▶ If the URL field is not visible, pull down the View menu and click Show Location Toolbar.	▶ If the URL field is not visible, pull down the View menu, select Toolbars, and if the Address Bar is not checked, select the Address Bar to display it. If the URL field still is not visible, click your right mouse button on the Toolbar and select Address Bar.
▶ Click once inside the URL field to position your cursor in it.	▶ Click once inside the URL field to position your cursor in it.
▶ Type the URL you want to go to.	▶ Type the URL you want to go to.
▶ Press Enter.	▶ Press Enter.

To activate the URL field so you can type a URL into it, click once inside the URL field to position your cursor there. Erase any URL that might be there currently by dragging your mouse over the URL to select it, then press the Delete key to delete it. Or you can just position your cursor at the end of the URL and backspace over the URL to delete it. Now type **http://www.sony.com** and press Enter. Your browser takes you to the Sony site.

Home Pages

Home is a relative concept. For example, a person from London considers England as home. To fly to Hawaii, that person takes off from London's Heathrow airport. When someone from Los Angeles flies to Hawaii, the plane takes off from the Los Angeles airport. So it is on the Web, where your **home page** is your taking-off point. Many people create their own home page, to which they link the documents and resources they want people who visit their home page to be able to access. Almost every company has a home page, as do government offices, schools, and colleges. Home pages organize and help you access the information at that site. For example, if you were considering going to graduate school at Princeton University, you could find out a lot about it by going to their home page at http://www.princeton.edu.

There's a huge mass of information out there on the Net. Other people's home pages help you make sense out of their stuff. Eventually, after you complete the Web page creation tutorial in Part Five, your home page will organize and help other people make sense out of your stuff.

Default Pages

If you go to a Web site without specifying what document to view, you will get that site's default page. For example, when you went to http://www.sony.com, you were taken to the default page of the Sony site. The default page is often the home page of the company or person who owns the site. In Part Five, you will learn how to create a default page for your Web site.

Scrolling Pages

Unlike books, Web pages can contain more information than you can see all at once. When a Web page contains more information than can fit on the screen, a scroll bar will appear. A **scroll bar** is a control that lets you move the contents of a window up or down to reveal more information.

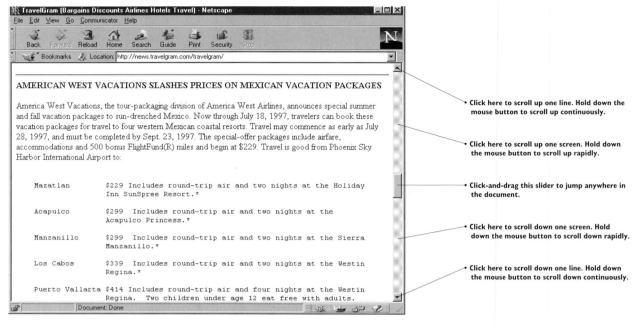

Figure 4-1 Using a scroll bar to reveal different parts of a Web page.

Figure 4-1 shows where to click on a scroll bar in order to move the window's contents line by line, screen by screen, or skip to any part of the page. A good Web page on which to practice scrolling is the TravelGram International Travel Newsletter at http://news.travelgram.com. Go there now; remember that instead of needing to type the entire URL, you can get there by simply typing news.travelgram.com into your browser's URL field and pressing ⌈Enter⌋. Now practice the scroll bar techniques in Table 4-2 using the scroll bar you will find at the right edge of your browser's window.

Table 4-2   How to Use a Vertical Scroll Bar

▶ You'll find the scroll bar at the right edge of the window. The scroll bar consists of a down arrow, an up arrow, and a slider.

▶ Click the down arrow at the bottom of the scroll bar a few times. Notice how each click moves the document down one line. Now hold down the mouse button on the down arrow to scroll down continuously.

▶ Click the up arrow at the top of the scroll bar a few times. Notice how each click moves the document up one line. Now hold down the mouse button on the up arrow to scroll up continuously. Keep the mouse button pressed until you get back up to the top of the document.

▶ Click on the area of the scroll bar above the down arrow. Each time you click this part of the scroll bar, the document moves down one screen. Notice how the slider moves to indicate how far down the document you've gone.

▶ Click on the area of the scroll bar below the up arrow. Each time you click this part of the scroll bar, the document moves up one screen, and the slider moves to indicate how far up the document you've gone.

▶ Finally, practice dragging the slider to jump to different places in the document. To drag the slider, you position your mouse on it, then hold down the mouse button while you move the slider up or down. When you release the mouse button, the document jumps to the new position. Practice dragging the slider to the bottom, middle, and top of the document.

Triggering Links

Links are perhaps the most important surfing concept, because without links, there would be no Web! Links form the pathways that interconnect the documents and resources on the Web. You activate a link by triggering it. There are two kinds of triggers: hypertext and hyperpicture.

HYPERTEXT LINKS

Hypertext triggers consist of one or more words that you click to trigger the events that are linked to the text. Hypertext triggers are also known as hot words, because they make things happen when you click them. So you can tell which words are hot, the hypertext triggers are underlined and printed in a different color than the rest of the text. Links you haven't visited are normally colored blue, and visited links are dark pink.

You can change the default color of the hot words by modifying your browser's preferences. To change the color of the hot words in Netscape Navigator, you pull down the Edit menu, choose Preferences, click Colors, and click the color swatches for Visited Links and Unvisited Links. In Microsoft Internet Explorer, you pull down the View menu, choose Options, click the General tab, and click the color swatches for Visited and Unvisited links. Even though you can change the colors, however, it is recommended that you not modify them unless you have a special reason for doing so.

Sometimes the color selections you make have no effect on the colors you see on a Web page. That's because it's possible for the Web page author to preset the hot words to specific colors that you cannot change. Unless the author has preset the colors on the Web page, the color preferences you choose will take effect.

HYPERPICTURE LINKS

Hyperpicture triggers are pictorial hot spots that you click to trigger events linked to images on the screen. The images can be little icons or larger graphics. It is also possible to have more than one hot spot in a picture; clicking different parts of the picture can trigger different links.

Well-designed Web pages make it obvious where to click to make different things happen. Poorly designed pages can be confusing when it's not clear what will happen when you trigger a link. In Part Five, you will learn how to design Web pages that make it clear what will happen when the user triggers a link.

Figure 4-2 shows a Web page with an interesting combination of hypertext and hyperpicture links. Its URL is http://www.ets.org/body.html. Point your browser there (to "point" your browser means to go to the URL) and try triggering the different hypertext and hyperpicture links.

Navigation Buttons and Keys

At the top of your browser you should see a row of navigation buttons with names like Forward, Back, Home, and Stop. Figure 4-3 shows how the buttons appear in Netscape Navigator, and Figure 4-4 shows the navigation buttons in Microsoft Internet Explorer. If these navigation buttons are not showing on your screen, you can make them visible by following the steps in Table 4-3.

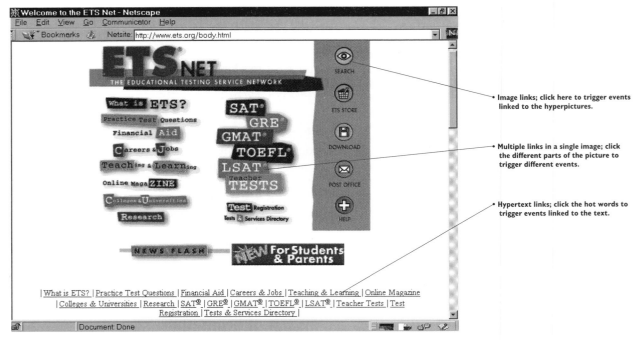

Figure 4-2 Analysis of a Web page with a combination of hypertext and hyperpicture links.

Figure 4-3 Navigation buttons in Netscape Navigator.

Figure 4-4 Navigation buttons in Microsoft Internet Explorer.

Table 4-3 How to Make Your Browser's Navigation Buttons Visible

Netscape Navigator	Microsoft Internet Explorer
▶ Pull down the View menu.	▶ Pull down the View menu and choose Toolbars.
▶ Choose Show Navigation Toolbar.	▶ If Standard Buttons is not checked, choose Standard Buttons.
	▶ If the navigation buttons still do not appear, right-click the toolbar and choose Standard Buttons.

One of the most useful navigation buttons is Back. If you end up someplace you didn't want to go, clicking the Back button will return you to the page from which you triggered the ill-chosen link. Conversely, the Forward button will move you ahead to pages that you visited previously during your current browsing session.

Any time you want to return to your browser's default home page, just click the Home button. If you want to change your browser's default home page, follow the steps in Table 4-4.

Table 4-4 How to Change Your Browser's Default Home Page

Netscape Navigator	Microsoft Internet Explorer
▶ Pull down the Edit menu and choose Preferences.	▶ Pull down the View menu and choose Internet Options.
▶ Select the Navigator category to make the Navigator options appear.	▶ Click the General tab, if it not already selected.
▶ In the Home Page group, enter the URL of the desired home page.	▶ In the Address field, type the URL of your desired home page.
▶ Click OK to close the dialog.	▶ Click OK to close the dialog.

Use the Stop button if you want to interrupt your browser. Sometimes it may appear as though the Internet has gotten stuck after you click on a trigger to go somewhere. If you wait for a while with no response, try clicking the Stop button to cancel the request, and then click the trigger again. This will usually get things moving again. Another use of the Stop button is to cancel a process that is taking too long. For example, you may have clicked a trigger that downloads a movie which could take more than an hour to arrive over a slow Internet connection. Clicking the Stop button interrupts the download so you do not have to wait an hour.

Manipulating URLs

There are some tricks you can play with URLs to help you find information. For example, suppose you've been told to go to the URL http://www.cnet.com/ Content/Features/Howto/IE4tips for a list of tips to help you use the Microsoft Internet Explorer. You find the list helpful, and you're curious what else is available at this site. By progressively stripping off the subfolder names of the path to the original document you were given, you can go to the higher levels of the Web site, and use them as surfing-off points. For example, http://www.cnet.com/Content/ Features/Howto takes you to a menu of tips and tricks for improving your use of other software packages. Stripping off the last part of the URL (i.e., /Howto) and trying http://www.cnet.com/Content/Features brings up a list of feature articles available at the CNET site. Going all the way back to http://www.cnet.com takes you to the CNET home page.

It's easy to manipulate URLs in this manner by using your browser's URL field. Click once in the field, position your cursor at the end of the URL, and backspace to erase the last part of the URL. If your browser's URL field is not visible, follow the steps in Table 4-1 to make it appear. Click once inside the URL field to position your cursor there, erase anything that already appears in the field, type the URL **http://lcweb.loc.gov/exhibits/flw/flw03.html** and press Enter to go there. Then complete the following exercise, which will help you learn how to manipulate a URL:

▶ Position your cursor at the end of the URL field and use the backspace key to erase the last part of the URL, which is /flw03.html. Press Enter. Your Web browser displays the Web page of the manipulated URL.

▶ Once again, position your cursor at the end of the URL field, and use the backspace key to erase the last part of the URL, which is /flw. Press Enter to go to the manipulated URL.

▶ Repeat this process for each part of the URL until all you have in the URL field is http://lcweb.loc.gov—this is the URL of the Library of Congress Web server. LOC stands for Library of Congress.

Partial URLs

Many people are unaware of one of the greatest time-savers in typing URLs. Both Netscape Navigator and Microsoft Internet Explorer allow you to type partial URLs. A **partial URL** is a shortened form of a complete URL, which the browser automatically expands into a complete URL. For example, the complete URL of the Weather Channel is http://www.weather.com, but you don't need to type all of that to get there. Follow these steps to learn how to use partial URLs:

▶ Begin by typing the complete URL http://www.weather.com into your Browser's URL field, and press Enter. Your browser takes you to the Weather Channel. Now click Home to return to your browser's home page.

▶ Repeat the process, but this time, only type www.weather.com and press Enter. Notice how your browser automatically fills in the http:// for you and takes you to the Weather Channel. Almost every Web address begins with http:// and by not having to type that specifically, you can save a lot of time. Click Home to return to your browser's home page.

▶ Now try weather.com to see if your browser still takes you to the Weather Channel.

▶ Finally, try typing the single word weather. Where does your browser take you now?

Coping with "File Not Found" Errors

The Web is a work in progress. People are adding new Web pages and revising things all the time. Sometimes, these changes can cause URLs that worked previously to become invalid. For example, at the Microsoft site www.microsoft.com, Microsoft reorganized the Web pages from which you download software. This caused URLs that worked previously to result in "File Not Found" errors.

If you get a "File Not Found" error, try manipulating the URL by removing the last part of it. Start by removing the filename, and see if the URL takes you somewhere useful. If that doesn't work, try removing the folder names. By progressively stripping off the filename and then the folders, you can usually get the URL to take you to a Web page from which you can browse to what you need.

Sizing and Positioning Your Browser Window

Normally, when you surf the Net, you will want your browser's window to be full screen so you will be able to view the maximum amount of the document you are reading. There are times, however, when you will want the browser to be less than full screen. For example, you might want to have two browser windows open simultaneously so you can do side-by-side comparisons of the information at different Web sites. Table 4-5 shows how to size and position a window.

Table 4-5   How to Size and Position a Window

Desired Window Movement	Windows 3.1	Windows 95	Macintosh
Maximize the window	Double-click the title bar or click the ▲ icon.	Double-click the title bar or click the ☐ icon.	Click the ▦ icon in the upper-right corner of the window.
Unmaximize the window	Double-click the title bar or click the ⬍ icon.	Double-click the title bar or click the ⧉ icon.	Click the ▦ icon in the upper-right corner of the window.
Size the window	Click and drag the corners or the sides of the unmaximized window.	Click and drag the corners or the sides of the unmaximized window.	Click and drag the lower-right corner of the unmaximized window.
Move the window	Click and drag the title bar of the unmaximized window.	Click and drag the title bar of the unmaximized window.	Click and drag the title bar of the unmaximized window.

Get your Web browser running, and practice the steps in Table 4-5. Make your window fill the screen; then make it small. Size the window to make it long and narrow, then short and wide. With practice, you will form your own personal habits for how large or small you prefer your windows to be for different purposes.

Working with Multiple Windows

Windows and the Macintosh are both multitasking operating systems. That means you can have more than one task running at a time. If you are writing a term paper, for example, you can have your word processor running at the same time as your Web browser. When you get an idea from surfing the Web, you can quickly switch to your word processor and make a note of that idea.

To work with multiple windows, you need to know how to make a particular window become visible when you want to view it, and how to hide the window when you want something else on your screen. Table 4-6 shows how to do this.

Table 4-6   How to Hide and Reveal a Window

Desired Window Movement	Windows 3.1	Windows 95	Macintosh
Hide a window	Click the window's ▼ icon.	Click the window's ▬ icon.	Click in a different window.
Show a hidden window	Hold down the Alt key and press Tab until the window's icon appears.	Hold down the Alt key and press Tab until the window's icon appears.	Use the drop-down menu by selecting the icon that appears in the upper-right corner.

Try working with multiple windows now. Get your Web browser running, then hide it. Now get your word processor running, and hide it. Follow the instructions in Table 4-6 to make your Web browser visible again. Now make your word processor become visible. Avoid the temptation to start a new instance of the running program; you want to make the running copy of the program become visible, not start a new instance of the program.

Focusing on a Purpose

You need to be careful out on the Web to remain focused on the reason why you are browsing. The whole world of interconnected information is available to you, and it's loaded with distractions. Novices invariably surf off into unintended directions and may spend hours pursuing things off course. Sometimes this can be fun and adventurous, but if it becomes habitual, you could waste a lot of time.

Be mindful of the purpose for which you are using the Net, and try to remain focused. If you avoid the distractions, you can usually find what you are looking for quickly.

Distractions to Avoid (or to Enjoy)

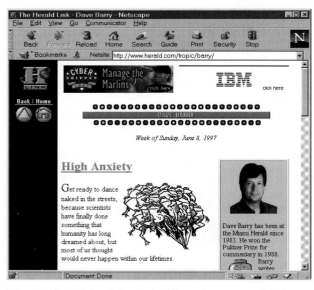

Mass-market retailers have discovered the potential of the Internet to advertise products. Many Web sites sell advertising space. When you visit a site that contains commercial advertising, you will likely encounter a "tickler" in the form of an attractive graphic enticing you to click and launch the ad, as illustrated in Figure 4-5. Since the tickler usually appears on screen first, you may be tempted to click on the ad before your information arrives.

Because commercial Web sites are usually highly developed, they tend to contain some of the more interesting pages on the Web. You may enjoy checking them out from time to time. You need to be careful, however, not to form a habit of meandering. Your time is limited, and you need to use it wisely. It's better to form the habit of not surfing off into unintended directions, and make such an adventure the exception, rather than the rule.

Figure 4-5 Advertising on the Net entices you to click the ad to launch a commercial product presentation.

Bookmarking Your Favorite Sites

Web browsers have built-in support for bookmarks, which make it quick and easy for you to take note of your favorite Web pages and return to them later on. In a Web browser, a bookmark is a pointer to a Web page that enables you to jump directly to that page, without having to navigate the Web to get there.

As you surf the Net and become familiar with the wealth of resources available there, you will begin to favor certain sites over others. To save time getting to your favorite sites, you can bookmark them. To bookmark a site on the Web, follow the steps in Table 4-7.

Table 4-7   How to Bookmark a Web Page

Netscape Navigator	Microsoft Internet Explorer
▶ 🦊 Pull down the Bookmarks menu.	▶ 🗔 Pull down the Favorites menu.
▶ Click Add Bookmark.	▶ Click Add to Favorites.
	▶ Click OK.

To jump to a site that you've bookmarked, simply pull down your browser's bookmark menu, and select the bookmark you want. Your browser will take you to the bookmarked Web page.

Using Bookmark Folders

It's possible to organize your bookmarks in folders. This is recommended if you have a lot of bookmarks, so you can organize them according to topics. To create a bookmark folder, follow the steps in Table 4-8.

Table 4-8 How to Create a Bookmark Folder

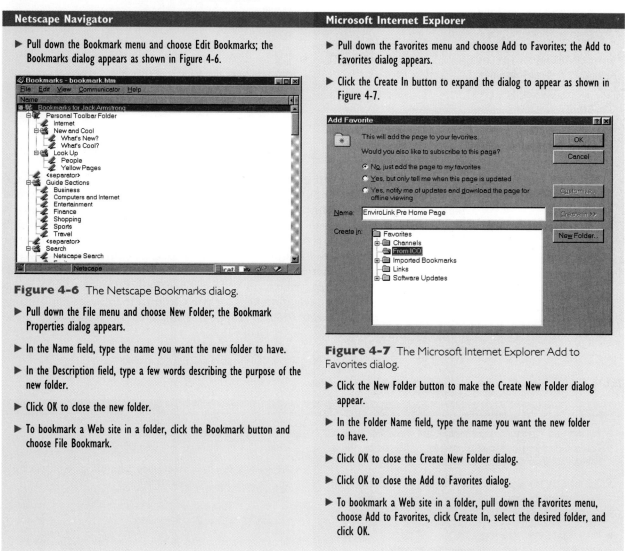

Netscape Navigator	Microsoft Internet Explorer
▶ Pull down the Bookmark menu and choose Edit Bookmarks; the Bookmarks dialog appears as shown in Figure 4-6.	▶ Pull down the Favorites menu and choose Add to Favorites; the Add to Favorites dialog appears.
	▶ Click the Create In button to expand the dialog to appear as shown in Figure 4-7.

Figure 4-6 The Netscape Bookmarks dialog.

▶ Pull down the File menu and choose New Folder; the Bookmark Properties dialog appears.

▶ In the Name field, type the name you want the new folder to have.

▶ In the Description field, type a few words describing the purpose of the new folder.

▶ Click OK to close the new folder.

▶ To bookmark a Web site in a folder, click the Bookmark button and choose File Bookmark.

Figure 4-7 The Microsoft Internet Explorer Add to Favorites dialog.

▶ Click the New Folder button to make the Create New Folder dialog appear.

▶ In the Folder Name field, type the name you want the new folder to have.

▶ Click OK to close the Create New Folder dialog.

▶ Click OK to close the Add to Favorites dialog.

▶ To bookmark a Web site in a folder, pull down the Favorites menu, choose Add to Favorites, click Create In, select the desired folder, and click OK.

Retracing Your Steps

Both Netscape Navigator and Microsoft Internet Explorer remember your most recently visited sites and make it possible for you to jump back to a previous site without having to press the Back button repeatedly to back through the sites one by one. To jump back to a site you previously visited, follow the steps in Table 4-9.

Table 4-9 How to Jump Back to a Site Previously Visited

Netscape Navigator	Microsoft Internet Explorer
▶ Pull down the Go menu; your most recently visited Web sites will be listed there.	▶ Pull down the File menu; your most recently visited Web sites will be listed in the third-last section of the menu.
▶ Select the site you want to jump to, and your browser will take you there.	▶ Select the site you want to jump to, and your browser will take you there.
▶ You can also pull down the Communicator menu and choose History for an index of the sites you visited.	▶ You can also click the History button to reveal a history of the Web sites you've visited. Click a category in the history to expand it, then click a Web site to go there.

Creating More Screen Space

No matter how large your computer screen is, you will sometimes wish it were larger, so more information would fit on it. There are a couple of tricks you can play to increase the viewing area of your Web browser. First, and most obvious, is to maximize the size of your browser window, following the instructions provided in Table 4-5. More subtle is to turn off some of the options that make your browser use extra screen space. For example, turning off the display of the URL field saves a little screen space and increases the viewing area inside the browser. Turning off the navigation buttons frees even more screen space. You can still navigate, using your browser's shortcut navigation keys, or you can turn the navigation buttons back on again when you want them to reappear. Table 4-10 shows how to do these things in your browser.

Table 4-10 How to Increase the Browser's Viewing Area

Netscape Navigator	Microsoft Internet Explorer
▶ Pull down the View menu, choose Toolbars, and choose Hide Location Toolbar to free the screen space taken up by the URL window. (To reverse this, choose Show Location Toolbar.)	▶ Pull down the View menu, choose Toolbars, and click any of the toolbars that are checked to turn them off.
▶ Pull down the View menu, choose Toolbars, and choose Hide Navigation Toolbar to free the screen space used by the navigation buttons. (To reverse this, choose Show Navigation Toolbar.)	▶ Pull down the View menu and see if the Status Bar option is checked; if so, click Status Bar to turn the status bar off.
▶ Pull down the View menu, choose Toolbars, and choose Hide Personal Toolbar to free the screen space used by the personal toolbar. (To reverse this, choose Show Personal Toolbar.)	▶ To turn the toolbars back on, pull down the View menu, select Toolbars, and click the toolbars to turn them back on.
▶ Pull down the View menu and see if the Toolbar option is checked; if so, click Toolbar to turn the toolbar off.	▶ To turn the status bar back on, pull down the View menu and select Status Bar.

VISITING SELECTED WEB SITES

Having studied the browsing principles and techniques presented so far in this chapter, now you're ready to go out on the Net and do some serious surfing. The remainder of this chapter consists of an illustrated list of recommended Web sites.

Following the instructions provided in Table 4-1, How to Go to a URL, you should visit each one of these sites, using the URL printed alongside the name of each site. You'll probably want to bookmark most of these sites, to make them easy for you to visit subsequently. To bookmark a site, follow the instructions provided in Table 4-7, How to Bookmark a Web Page.

CNN

At http://www.cnn.com you will find the Cable News Network (CNN) Web site. Figure 4-8 shows how it presents a menu of local, national, and world news; sports and weather information; and special features including health, style, and travel. Be sure to scroll down to see information that doesn't appear all at once on your screen. This is a large Web page that you need to scroll in order to reveal it all. Click on your interests, and become informed.

Internet Mall

Fulfill your shopping fantasies at http://www.internetmall.com. Here you will find some of the finest shops in the world, as illustrated in Figure 4-9. If you don't find the item you want by browsing through the stores, use the Search Mall feature to find the product you want.

Figure 4-8 The Cable News Network site at http://www.cnn.com.

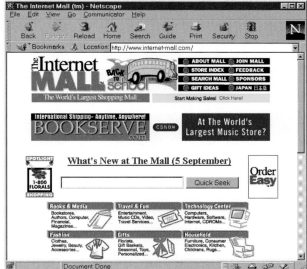

Figure 4-9 You can just browse, or you can actually buy products at http://www.internetmall.com.

Figure 4-10 The ESPN Sportszone site at
http://espn.sportszone.com.

ESPN

At http://espn.sportszone.com you can find all the latest information about your favorite sport. As illustrated in Figure 4-10, you can choose basketball, hockey, baseball, soccer, golf, football, tennis, auto racing, and more. Be sure to scroll down to peruse all of the sports headlines; this is a large Web page that won't appear on your screen all at once.

Global SchoolNet

Pictured in Figure 4-11, the Global SchoolNet Foundation (GSN) links kids around the world with a global Web-based educational network. Formerly called FrEdMail (Free Educational Mail), GSN originated with a group of teachers in San Diego more than a decade ago. With no budget and minimal support, they began a grass-roots movement to create an educational information infrastructure that is now internationally recognized. To learn more and to meet the Global SchoolNet team, go to http://www.gsn.org.

NASA Goddard Space Flight Center

How fortunate we are that NASA conducts an outreach program to the schools. At the Goddard Space Flight Center site pictured in Figure 4-12, you can click the Education button to bring up an index of education links. Programs for K–12 include program descriptions and sample lesson materials correlated to the national standards in mathematics, science, and technology education. Higher-education programs provide support for postdoctoral opportunities and resources. You will find the NASA Goddard Space Flight Center on the Web at http://pao.gsfc.nasa.gov.

Figure 4-11 The Global SchoolNet Foundation site at
http://www.gsn.org.

Figure 4-12 The NASA Goddard Space Flight Center at
http://pao.gsfc.nasa.gov.

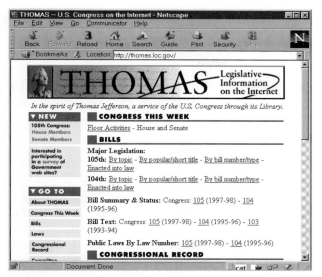

Figure 4-13 Located at http://thomas.loc.gov, THOMAS is operated for the U.S. Congress by the Library of Congress.

Government Online (THOMAS)

Named after Thomas Jefferson, THOMAS is a Web-based information service of the U.S. Congress. As shown in Figure 4-13, you can visit the THOMAS site to find out what is happening on the floor of the House and the Senate, check the status of pending bills and legislation, and read the Congressional Record. Also online are historical documents and an index of U.S. Government Information Services. You can also find out the e-mail address of any senator or congressional representative, and find out how your representatives voted on recent legislation. To check how well you are being represented, visit THOMAS at http://thomas.loc.gov.

Louvre

Figure 4-14 shows how the world-famous *Musée du Louvre,* the largest museum in western Europe, is online at http://mistral.culture.fr/louvre. Here you will find an electronic version of the Louvre magazine, a schedule of cultural activities, a guide to the collections, the history of the buildings, and thousands of images, including the famous Mona Lisa.

Newspapers

The American Journalism Review (AJR) News Link site provides access to the top-10 rated online newspapers, plus more than 4,000 other links to newspapers, magazines, broadcasters, and news services around the world. As you can see from the list of awards along the right margin of Figure 4-15, this is one of the top-rated sites on the Web.

Figure 4-14 The famous *Musée du Louvre* is on the Web at http://mistral.culture.fr/louvre.

Figure 4-15 You can access thousands of online newspapers at the AJR News Link site at http://www.newslink.org.

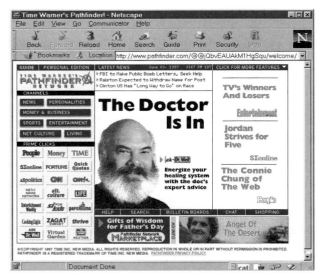

Figure 4-16 Time Inc. New Media's Pathfinder Network is at http://pathfinder.com.

Pathfinder

Another top-rated Web site is Time Inc. New Media's Pathfinder site. Figure 4-16 shows how it provides access to a wide range of news channels and information services. Particularly useful is Quick Quotes, which you can use to find the current value of any stock.

Real Estate Classifieds

If you're looking to buy or sell a house, you should go to Yahoo's Real Estate Classifieds at http://classifieds.yahoo.com/realestate.html. As illustrated in Figure 4-17, you can click the city or state of your choice to find out what's for sale there. For each property listed, not only do you find out the specifications, price, and person's name to click to inquire via e-mail, but you also can click a "Map It" button to bring up a map showing where the property is. You can even zoom in and out on the map to check the size and location of the neighborhood.

Scholastic Network

The Scholastic Network is an online educational subscription service for teachers and students in elementary and middle schools. Figure 4-18 shows how you can find out about award-winning projects, educational games, professional discussions, conversations with special guests, and opportunities to work with well-known children's book authors and scientists. There is a selection of free stuff for teachers and kids, as well as a subscription service for which Scholastic charges a modest fee. You can get a 14-day free trial at the Scholastic Network, which is on the Web at http://www.scholastic.com.

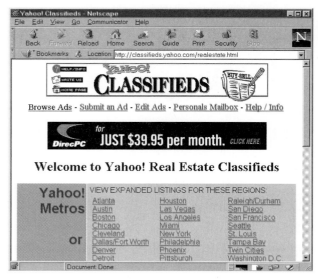

Figure 4-17 Yahoo's Real Estate Classifieds at http://classifieds.yahoo.com/realestate.html.

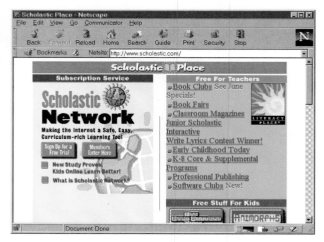

Figure 4-18 The Scholastic Network has a subscription service as well as a collection of free stuff for teachers and kids.

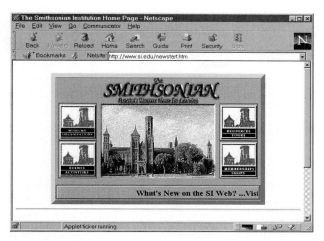

Figure 4-19 The Smithsonian Institution is on the Web at http://www.si.edu.

Smithsonian

The Smithsonian Institution sponsors many Internet services that provide access to materials from its various museums and research arms. For example, the National Air and Space Museum, the National Museum of American Art, and the National Museum of Natural History are all online. You can search the Smithsonian databases, join discussion groups, and explore information on the Smithsonian's many museums, galleries, research centers, and offices. Figure 4-19 shows how you can access all of these resources on the Web at http://www.si.edu.

Stock Exchanges

You can find the New York Stock Exchange (NYSE) on the Web at http://www.nyse.com. Designed as an educational tool for investors, students, and teachers, this Web site presents the NYSE in its role as publisher, generator of news, patron of education, sponsor of scholarly research, and storehouse of statistical data. Figure 4-20 shows how the NYSE Web site enables you to begin a tour of the world's largest ($9.5 trillion global market value) securities market. Also on the Web is the NASDAQ Stock Market, which is at http://www.nasdaq.com. Figure 4-21 shows how the NASDAQ site has surround video and RealAudio to spark your monetary instincts. RealAudio is a real-time streaming protocol that will be discussed in Chapter 9.

TERC

TERC is a nonprofit research and development organization committed to improving mathematics and science teaching and learning. Founded in 1965, TERC is internationally recognized for creating innovative curricula, fostering the professional development of teachers, pioneering creative uses of technology in

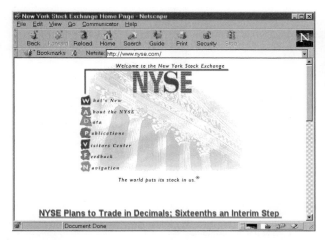

Figure 4-20 The New York Stock Exchange is on the Web at http://www.nyse.com.

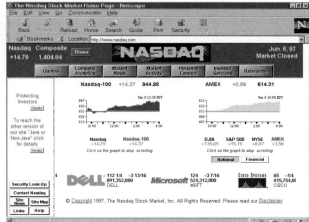

Figure 4-21 The NASDAQ Stock Market's Web site has surround video and RealAudio at http://www.nasdaq.com.

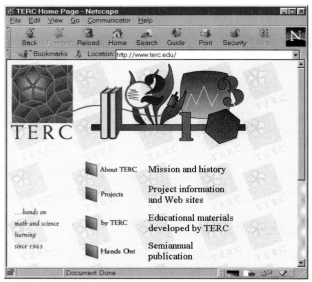

Figure 4-22 The TERC Home Page at http://www.terc.edu.

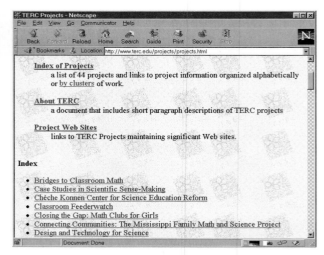

Figure 4-23 Some of the innovative projects you can visit at the TERC Web site.

education, helping educators understand and benefit from the results of educational research, and developing equitable opportunities for underserved learners. You can learn more about TERC and the programs it sponsors by going to http://www.terc.edu. Figure 4-22 shows the TERC home page, and Figure 4-23 lists a few of the TERC projects that come up when you click the Projects button. This is a long list of projects, so make sure you scroll down to peruse them all.

Weather Channel

Weather is one of life's common denominators because everybody seems to care about it. You can find out the current weather conditions and forecast for almost every city in the United States and in many international cities at The Weather Channel Web site. Figure 4-24 shows how you'll find it on the Web at http://

Figure 4-24 Learn the weather forecast for almost any city at http://www.weather.com.

Figure 4-25 Animated graphics make the flags wave at the White House Web site at http://www.whitehouse.gov.

Figure 4-26 Resources available at the White House Web site.

www.weather.com. Clicking the name of a city on the forecasts ticker brings up a detailed weather report for that city, complete with local and regional doppler radar and weather satellite maps.

White House

To kindle your patriotic spirit, visit the White House at http://www.whitehouse.gov. After watching the flags wave (they're animated images) in Figure 4-25, you can scroll down and access the resources in Figure 4-26. In addition to taking a tour and writing e-mail to the President and Vice President, you can get briefings on hot topics and the latest federal statistics. There's also a White House Help Desk and a White House for Kids, which is intended to help young people become more active and informed citizens.

MANAGING YOUR WEB BROWSER'S CACHE

When you surf the Web, your browser keeps copies of the most recently visited Web sites in a place on your hard disk called the cache (pronounced *cash*). As you navigate back and forth around the Web, and you revisit one of the sites in the cache, your browser will check to see if the time stamp on the Web site has changed since your local copy was cached. If the site has not changed, the browser will redisplay the site from the cache, instead of downloading it again. Thus, the cache speeds your use of the Web and reduces traffic on the Net.

How to Manipulate the Cache

It is possible to change the size and location of the browser's cache. You can also purge (i.e., delete) the cache, which you might want to do if you have been reading sensitive information that you would not want someone else using your computer to find. Purging the cache can also fix problems when Web pages don't work properly, especially Web pages with Java. To manipulate your cache, follow the steps in Table 4-11.

Table 4-11   How to Manipulate the Cache

Netscape Navigator	Microsoft Internet Explorer
▶ Pull down the Edit menu and choose Preferences; the Preferences dialog appears.	▶ Pull down the View menu and choose Internet Options; the Internet Options dialog appears.
▶ If the Advanced category has not been expanded, double-click the word *Advanced* to display the options beneath it; one of these options will be *Cache*.	▶ If the General tab isn't already selected, click the General tab.
▶ Click the Cache option; the Cache settings will appear as shown in Figure 4-27.	▶ The Temporary Internet Files group contains your cache controls. Click the Settings button to make the cache settings appear, as shown in Figure 4-28.

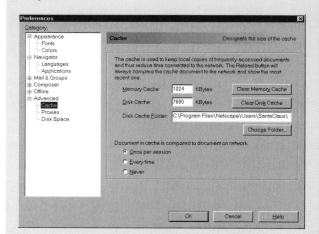

Figure 4-27 The Netscape cache settings.

▶ The Memory Cache setting is the amount of RAM devoted to caching Web resources. You will probably not want to change this. If you want to clear the RAM cache, click the Clear Memory Cache button.

▶ The Disk Cache setting is the amount of space devoted to caching Web resources on your hard disk drive. To clear the hard disk cache, click the Clear Disk Cache button.

▶ The Disk Cache Folder field shows the name of the folder where your cache is located. Do not change this unless you really know what you are doing. Most users never need to change the location of the cache. To view the contents of the cache, use the Windows Explorer or the Macintosh Finder to inspect this folder.

▶ When you are done manipulating the cache, click OK to close the Preferences dialog.

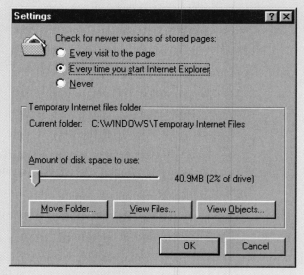

Figure 4-28 The Internet Explorer cache settings.

▶ You can change the percent of your hard disk that is used for the cache by dragging the slider. Do not change this unless you really want to modify this setting; most users never need to change this.

▶ To move the cache to a different folder, click the Move Folder button. Do not do this unless you really know what you are doing. Most users never need to change the location of the cache.

▶ To view the contents of your cache, click the View Files button.

▶ Click OK to close the cache settings dialog.

▶ To purge the cache, click the Delete Files button in the Temporary Internet Files group.

▶ Click OK to close the Internet Options dialog.

E X E R C I S E S

These exercises are intended to be done in order, beginning with number 1, and progressing sequentially down through the rest of them.

1. Get your Web browser running if it isn't already, and go to the URL

    http://place.scholastic.com/EL/software/soft597.htm.

2. Use your mouse to resize the dimensions of the browser window. Notice how the information inside the window flows to fit the shape that you make the window. If you cannot grab the frame of the window and resize it with your mouse, the window might be maximized. Double-click the window's title bar to unmaximize it. If you have trouble, refer to Table 4-5 for help.

3. Make the browser window invisible by minimizing it. Now make the window visible again. If you have trouble doing this, refer to Table 4-6 for help.

4. Practice using the scroll bar to move the document up and down inside your browser window. Fix your eyes on a line of text near the bottom of the screen and practice moving it to the top, and then back down to the bottom of the screen. Practice dragging the scroll button to jump to different parts of the Web page. Drag the button all the way to the bottom to get to the end of the page, then drag it back to the top.

5. Increase your browser's viewing space by turning off the display of the URL field and the navigation buttons. Notice how you can see more of the document when these options are turned off. If you have trouble doing this, refer to Table 4-10 for help.

6. Turn the URL field back on. Explore the higher levels of that URL by stripping off items from the end of it. For example, what do you find at http://place.scholastic.com/EL/software? What's at http://place.scholastic.com/EL? How about http://place.scholastic.com?

7. Bookmark the site you are on now. Then go to the URL http://www.amazon.com. After the new screen appears, see if you can return to the site you just bookmarked by accessing it from your browser's bookmark menu. If you have trouble, refer to Table 4-7 for help.

Part Three

Communicating over the Internet

The most powerful use of the Internet is for communicating with other users. Never before has a communications medium made it so quick and easy and cost-effective to communicate with tens of millions of users all over the world. So great is the benefit that the Internet can truly be called a supermedium for communicating.

In this part of the book, you will learn how to use **electronic mail**, which is a store-and-forward type of communications medium between two people; **listserv**, a way of communicating ideas to a specific group of people; **newsgroups**, which work like online conferences that people can visit on the Net as if they were attending a conference physically; **chat rooms** and other real-time environments for carrying on live conversations; and **telnet**, which you can use to log on remotely to computers on the Internet.

Before you begin communicating on the Information Superhighway, however, you should learn some of the rules of the road. Therefore, we begin with a discussion of Internet etiquette.

5 Internet Etiquette (Netiquette)

After completing this chapter, you will be able to:

- ☐ Define the term *netiquette* and explain its derivation.

- ☐ Understand the difference between commercial and educational use of the Internet.

- ☐ Know what it means to "spam" someone on the Internet, and what to do if someone spams you.

- ☐ Understand the concept of lurking, and know when you should lurk.

- ☐ Know what it means to "flame" someone on the Internet.

- ☐ Understand the concept of SHOUTING on the Internet and become sensitized to not overdoing it.

- ☐ Recognize the more common smileys and other emoticons used on the Internet, and know how to look up the meaning of less common symbols.

- ☐ Understand what the more common three-letter acronyms mean, and know where to go on the Web to look up more esoteric acronyms.

- ☐ Understand some of the more commonly used Internet jargon, and know where to find a more complete listing of Internet terms and definitions.

NETIQUETTE is a term coined by combining the words "Internet etiquette" into a single name. Netiquette is the observance of certain rules and conventions that have evolved in order to keep the Internet from becoming a free-for-all in which tons of unwanted messages and junk mail would clog your in-box and make the Information Superhighway an unfriendly place to be. This chapter presents the rules for commercial versus educational use of the Internet, suggests a way for you to become a good citizen of the Net (network citizens are called **Netizens**), and defines everyday terms and jargon used on the Net.

NETIQUETTE GUIDELINES

In the "Netiquette Guidelines" section of the Interlit Web site, you'll find links to the official rules of etiquette and ethics for responsible use of the Internet. Chief among these is RFC 1855, which was developed by the Responsible Use of the Network (RUN) Working Group of the Internet Engineering Task Force (IETF). This document consists of a bulleted list of specifications that organizations can use to create their own guidelines. For example, Arlene Rinaldi's award-winning Netiquette Home Page, which is entitled "The Net: User Guidelines and Netiquette," contains the Netiquette guidelines used at Florida Atlantic University. The introduction explains how use of the Internet is a privilege, not a right:

> The use of the network is a privilege, not a right, which may temporarily be revoked at any time for abusive conduct. Such conduct would include, the placing of unlawful information on a system, the use of abusive or otherwise objectionable language in either public or private messages, the sending of messages that are likely to result in the loss of recipients' work or systems, the sending of "chain letters" or "broadcast" messages to lists or individuals, and any other types of use which would cause congestion of the networks or otherwise interfere with the work of others.

Developed in conjunction with the American Association for Higher Education and EDUCOM, Frank Connolly's *Bill of Rights and Responsibilities for Electronic Learners* is a succinct and eloquent statement of Netiquette guidelines. To read these guidelines, follow the links to the *Bill of Rights* at the Interlit Web site. Also linked to the Interlit Web site is a related article by Connolly entitled "Intellectual Honesty in the Era of Computing."

Using an Old Testament format to summarize the "Netiquette Guidelines" linked to the Interlit Web site, Figure 5-1 lists the Ten Commandments of Computer Use, which were developed by the Computer Ethics Institute in Washington, DC.

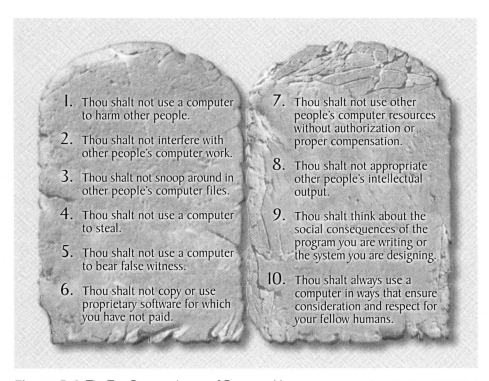

Figure 5-1 The Ten Commandments of Computer Use

Source: http://cpsr.org/dox/cei.html

COMMERCIAL VERSUS EDUCATIONAL USE

A clear and apparent danger is the potential use of the Internet by companies to send advertising via e-mail. It is highly unethical for any company to use e-mail as a means of mass-mailing advertising to users of the Internet. If you receive unwanted advertising in your e-mail, you should write a message back to the sender stating how irritated you are about this, why it threatens the environment of the Internet, and how you plan to get all of your friends to boycott that company's products for breaking the commercial rule of Netiquette, which is: "The mass mailing of commercial advertising is not permitted via electronic mail on the Internet."

To provide a way for users to protest junk mail on the Internet, the Canadian Advertising Foundation is implementing an e-mail system for consumer complaints and plans to publicize the names of advertisers and products that violate the commercial rule of Netiquette (*Toronto Star* 26 Feb 97). Meanwhile, the Nevada State Senate has introduced a bill that would make sending unsolicited advertising to e-mail accounts a misdemeanor. "Most e-mail users pay for their service, so unsolicited e-mail is like receiving direct mail with postage due," says the senate's majority leader. California, Virginia, and Connecticut are considering similar legislation (*St. Petersburg Times* 3 Mar 97).

SPAM

On the Internet, the term **spam** refers to unwanted messages posted to newsgroups or sent to a list of users through e-mail. The term can be used either as a verb or a noun. To spam means to send unwanted messages to a list of users on the Internet. Likewise, unwanted messages that you receive are called spam. Spamming has become so pervasive that it's estimated that unwanted messages account for 5 to 30% of the 15 million messages received by America Online subscribers each day (*Washington Post* 13 Jun 97).

Perhaps the most obvious form of spam is commercial advertising, which is the most unethical use of e-mail on the planet. There are other forms of spam, however. For example, there are a lot of chain letters circulating on the Internet. Chain letters are spam. Don't send or forward them. If you get one, send a polite message to the originator stating that chain letters are an unethical use of the Internet, and that the sender should be ashamed of so littering the Information Superhighway.

There is an example of a chain letter at the Interlit Web site. The title of this letter is "Share the Wealth of the Internet!" Not only did this chain letter use e-mail as its transmission medium, but it blatantly advocated the use of newsgroups to spread the message. Such use of the Internet is improper and highly unethical. Be a good Netizen; never originate or participate in such a spam, and discourage anyone who spams you from ever doing so again.

Some useful suggestions for fighting spam are found at the Interlit Web site. If you follow the links to "Fight Spam on the Internet," you'll find a tutorial entitled "How to Complain to Providers About Spam."

LURKING

To **lurk** means to participate in a conversation on the Internet without responding to any of the messages. You receive and read the messages, but you don't say anything in return. Thus, you're lurking!

It is not unethical to lurk. To the contrary, it is often a good idea to lurk at first. For example, suppose you join a listserv that has been going on for a while. Instead of jumping right in and writing something that may make you seem really out of touch with what's going on, it's smarter to lurk for a while, so you can pick up the gist of the conversation before joining in.

The same guideline applies to newsgroups. Before you begin writing messages in a newsgroup, spend some time looking around at what has been written previously in that newsgroup. When you write something, you want it to seem like you know what's going on. It's inconsiderate to write messages that waste the time of other users on the Net.

FLAMES

On the Internet, a **flame** is a message written in anger. The term flame can be used either as a verb or a noun. To flame someone is to send them an angry message. Angry messages that people send you are known as flames.

You need to be careful, especially if you have a temper. Form the habit of thinking carefully about what you write, and proofread it several times before you send it. Make sure the message really conveys the emotions you want to communicate. If you're real mad and send a hastily written flame, you may regret it later on. When you cool off a few minutes later, you may wish you could tone down the message a little, but it's too late, because the message has already been sent, and unfortunate damage may be done to your relationship with the receiving party.

FIREFIGHTERS

Sometimes flaming can get out of hand, especially when it occurs in a newsgroup or a listserv with a lot of users. People start sending more-heated messages, and things can get ugly. Someone has to step in and write a message intended to restore peace. Since that puts an end to the flames, such peacemakers on the Internet are known as **firefighters**.

SHOUTING

Messages written on the Internet are normally written in lowercase letters, with capital letters appearing only at the start of the first word of each sentence, and on proper nouns, such as the term Internet. WHEN YOU WRITE IN ALL CAPS, ON THE OTHER HAND, YOU'RE SHOUTING! **Shouting** means to add emphasis by writing in all capital letters.

In general, you shouldn't shout on the Internet. You already have the full attention of the person reading your message, and you do not need to shout unless you REALLY want to add emphasis to something. Shouting is almost always regarded in poor taste, however, so do it sparingly, if at all.

If you hit the [Caps Lock] key by mistake, everything you enter will be written in all caps. Don't turn on the [Caps Lock] option unless you really want to shout.

SMILEYS AND EMOTICONS

  One of the problems inherent in text messages is that you cannot see the body language or facial expression of the person sending the message. Not knowing for sure whether something is said in jest can lead people to make false assumptions about the intent of a message. You need to be careful, because miscommunication can cause serious problems.

To give the person reading your message a clue as to what your emotions are, emoticons were invented. **Emoticons** are combinations of a few characters which, when turned sideways, conjure a facial expression. The most common form of emoticon is the **smiley**, which conveys a happy facial expression. Turn your book clockwise, and you will see how the characters :) convey a happy face. The smiley often has a nose :-) and sometimes winks ;-) at you. Left-handed people can use a left-handed smile (: which can also have a nose (-: and can wink (-; at you.

Emoticons are not always happy. For example, :(is a frown, and :-(is a frown with a nose. Someone really sad may be crying :~~(while someone obnoxious may stick out the tongue :-P at you. You can even convey drooling :-P~~ with an emoticon. There are hundreds of these faces. For a more complete list, go to the Interlit Web site and follow the links to smileys and emoticons.

THREE-LETTER ACRONYMS (TLAs)

To shorten the amount of keyboarding required to write a message, some people use three-letter acronyms, which are appropriately known as TLAs. A **three-letter acronym** (TLA) is a way of shortening a three-word phrase such as "in my opinion" by simply typing the first letter of each word, such as imo. The author is not a proponent of three-letter acronyms, because life on the Internet is already filled with enough jargon, abbreviations, and technical terms. TLAs are so common, however, that no book about Internet literacy would be complete without mentioning them. Some of the more common three-letter acronyms are:

brb	=	be right back
bbl	=	be back later
imo	=	in my opinion
lol	=	laughing out loud
j/k	=	just kidding
oic	=	oh, I see
ott	=	over the top (excessive, uncalled for)
thx	=	thanks
wtf	=	what the f**k (not very nice, imo)

There are also two-letter acronyms, such as:

np = no problem

re = hi again, as in "re hi"

wb = welcome back

b4 = before

Some of these are more intuitive than others! There are also acronyms with more than three letters, including:

bbiaf = be back in a flash

hhoj = ha ha, only joking

imho = in my humble opinion

morf = male or female?

nhoh = never heard of him/her

rotfl = rolling on the floor laughing

rtfm = read the f**king manual (not nice at all, imho)

ttfn = ta ta for now

For a more complete list of TLAs, the Interlit Web site has a link you can take to the IRC prelude Web page at http://deckard.mc.duke.edu:8080/irchelp/new2irc.html. IRC stands for Internet Relay Chat, a technology you will learn more about in Chapter 9. TLAs are commonly used in chat rooms, where people save time typing by substituting acronyms for spelled-out phrases.

JARGON ON THE NET

Table 5-1 contains a list of terms you are likely to encounter out on the Net. For a more complete list of Internet jargon, go to the Interlit Web site and follow the links to the Web's official "Jargon File" site. You can also get a printed copy of the Jargon File, which is called *The New Hacker's Dictionary* (MIT Press, ISBN 0-262-68092-0).

Table 5-1 Commonly Used Internet Jargon

Technical Term	What It Means
admin	Administrator; the person in charge on a computer
ASCII	American Standard Code for Information Interchange; the file format of a plain-text (*.txt*) file
avatar	An icon or representation of a user in a shared virtual reality
back door	A hole in the security of a system deliberately left in place by designers or maintainers
bandwidth	The volume of information per unit of time that a computer, person, or transmission medium can handle
banner	Opening screen containing a logo, author credits, or copyright notice
baud	Bits per second, a measure of telecommunication speed
BBS	Electronic bulletin-board system
beta	Mostly working, but still under test
bit	Binary digit; a computational quantity that can take on one of two values, such as true and false, or 0 and 1

Table 5-1   *(Continued)*

Technical Term	What It Means
byte	Eight bits; 1 byte can hold 1 ASCII character (see *ASCII*)
channel	The basic unit of discussion in an IRC; see *IRC*
channel op or chanop	Someone who is endowed with privileges on a particular IRC channel
cookie	A handle, transaction ID, or other token of agreement between cooperating programs; also, a record of the mouse clicks made by a user at a Web site
cracker	Someone who breaks security or intentionally causes operational problems on a computer system
egosurfing	Typing your own name as a key word into an Internet search engine
emoticon	A character combination used in e-mail or news to indicate an emotional state; the most famous is the smiley :)
FAQ	Frequently asked question; also, a list of frequently asked questions and their answers
firefighter	A peacemaker on the Internet who intervenes to stop a flame war
firewall	Provides security by preventing unauthorized data from moving across a network
flame	To send an e-mail message intended to insult or provoke; also used as a noun to refer to the insulting e-mail message
flame war	An acrimonious dispute conducted via e-mail or newsgroups
flamer	A person who flames habitually
giga	A billion; abbreviated G, as in GB, meaning a billion bytes, which is also called a *gigabyte*
hacker	A person who enjoys exploring the details of programmable systems and how to stretch their capabilities; someone who can program quickly. Sometimes the term *hacker* is incorrectly used to refer to a programmer who causes trouble intentionally on a network; the proper term is *cracker*
IRC	Internet Relay Chat, a worldwide "party line" network that allows one to converse with others in real time in chat rooms on the Internet
ISP	Internet service provider, a company that sells Internet access
kilo	A thousand; abbreviated K, as in KB, meaning a thousand bytes, which is also called a *kilobyte*
lurker	One of the silent majority in an electronic forum who posts occasionally or not at all but reads the group's postings regularly
mega	A million; abbreviated M, as in MB, meaning a million bytes, which is also called a *megabyte*
MUD	Multi User Dimension; also Multi-User Dungeon
mudhead	Someone addicted to a MUD
Netiquette	Network etiquette
newbie	Someone new to the network or to a newsgroup
newsgroup	One of Usenet's many discussion groups; see *Usenet*
nick	Short for a nickname; in a chat room, every user must pick a nick
ping	A tiny network message sent by one computer to check for the presence and alertness of another computer
POTS	Plain old telephone service
rave	To persist in discussing a specific topic when other users wish you would drop it
snail mail	Paper mail, as opposed to electronic mail
sneakernet	Term used to refer to transporting data by carrying physical media such as diskettes from one computer to another, instead of transferring the data over the Internet

Table 5-1 *(Continued)*

Technical Term	What It Means
spam	To send unwanted messages to newsgroups or listservs; also used as a noun to refer to the unwanted messages
surf	To browse the Internet in search of interesting stuff, especially on the World Wide Web
sysop	The operator of a bulletin-board system
TCP/IP	Transmission Control Protocol/Internet Protocol; the wide-area networking protocol that makes the Internet work
URL	Uniform resource locator, an address that identifies a document or resource on the World Wide Web
Usenet	A distributed bulletin-board system hosting more than 10,000 newsgroups
virus	A cracker program that searches out other programs and infects them by embedding a copy of itself in them. When these programs are executed, the embedded virus is executed too, thus propagating the infection
wannabee	A would-be hacker; see *hacker*
yo-yo mode	The state in which the system is said to be when it rapidly alternates several times between being up and being down

E X E R C I S E S

1. Use your favorite word processor to compose a message to send people who spam you. Save the message on your hard drive so you will have it ready to copy and paste into your e-mail response to people who send you unwanted messages. If you don't know how to create a text file, follow the instructions in Table 6-10.

2. Use your favorite word processor to write a mock mail message, which you won't actually send anyone—this is just for the purpose of the exercise. Now practice SHOUTING in the message. Make different parts of the message be in uppercase. Read the message, and consider the effect that the shouting has. Decide whether and when you should shout in your messages. Remember that since you already have the attention of the person reading your message, you should SHOUT only when such added emphasis is warranted. Again, shouting is generally discouraged on the Internet.

3. Go to one or more of the smiley sites you'll find in the smiley section of the Interlit Web site, and browse the list of emoticons you will find there. What are your favorite emoticons? Which emoticons do you find too esoteric (that is, too hard to understand) for general use on the Internet?

4. Go to the "Jargon File" site linked to the jargon section of the Interlit Web site, click the link to browse the jargon file as hypertext, scroll down to the Ts, and in the section on talk, browse the list of three-letter acronyms you will find there. Which TLAs do you think an Internet-literate person should know? Which ones are too esoteric for general use on the Internet?

5. Go to the Bill of Rights and Responsibilities site by following the links in the "Netiquette" section of the Interlit Web site. Read carefully the *Bill of Rights and Responsibilities for Electronic Learners* that you will find there. Do you agree with all of the items covered in this Bill of Rights? What do you disagree with? Do you plan to abide by these guidelines? Do you think they leave out anything important? What's not covered that should be?

6

Electronic Mail

After completing this chapter, you will be able to:

- ☐ **Understand what an e-mail account is and know how to get one set up for you.**

- ☐ **Select an e-mail client for use in sending, receiving, and filing e-mail messages.**

- ☐ **Configure your e-mail client so you can begin using e-mail.**

- ☐ **Send, receive, answer, forward, and file e-mail messages.**

- ☐ **Create a signature file that will identify who you are at the end of your e-mail messages.**

- ☐ **Know how to attach files to your e-mail messages.**

- ☐ **Use an address book to keep track of the e-mail addresses of people to whom you send mail.**

- ☐ **Create a mailing list that enables you to send a message to several people at once.**

- ☐ **Search your stored mail messages to find things you've filed for future reference.**

- ☐ **Deal with unwanted mail and detect fake mail IDs.**

- ☐ **Encrypt your mail so only the person receiving it can read it.**

LECTRONIC mail has revolutionized the way people communicate when they can't talk in person. No longer must people wait for traditional postal mail delivery, which has become known as "snail mail" due to its comparative slowness. On the Internet, if both the sender and the receiver log on frequently, it is possible to exchange several messages with someone in a single day.

Electronic mail is highly efficient. It's probably the greatest time-saver in the world. Because you must initiate the reading of your e-mail by running your e-mail software, you read e-mail only when you decide to do so. Thus, e-mail does not interrupt your workday. If you are too busy to read e-mail, or if you are on vacation, your e-mail queues up in your in-box, waiting patiently for the next time you log on. When you travel, you can dial up and read your e-mail using almost any telephone line anywhere in the world. You can even avoid the need for a phone line if your computer is equipped for wireless communications.

GETTING AN ACCOUNT ON A HOST COMPUTER

Before you can begin using e-mail, you must have an **account**. An account enables you to log on to the computer that hosts your e-mail service. The computer that hosts your account is known as your e-mail **host computer**. On the host computer, your account consists of file space where your e-mail queues up waiting for you to read it, and a login procedure that enables you to log on and access your files.

You get the account from your Internet service provider (ISP). Chapter 3 tells you how to select an ISP in your locale. When the ISP sets up your account, you will be told what the name of your account is. Usually this is your own name (such as fred.hofstetter) or your initials (such as fth) or a nickname (such as freddie). If your account name is something impersonal like a number, such as 02737, ask your ISP how to go about changing the number to something more user-friendly. On some computers, for example, you can change your account number into an alphanumeric name by typing **username**, pressing Enter, and following the instructions that will appear on screen. Be careful, because once you choose a name, many computers will not allow you to change it.

In addition to being told the name of your account, you will be given a password that you must enter each time you log on to your account. The password prevents other unauthorized users from logging on under your name and gaining access to your mail. Most host computers permit you to change your password. If your ISP is running Unix, for example, you can change your password by typing **passwd**, pressing Enter, and following the instructions that will appear on screen. Choose a password that you will remember, but don't select one that's easy to guess, because you don't want someone malicious to guess your password and sign on under your name. That person could send offensive mail under your name and cause problems for you. Don't use your first or last name as your password, for example. If you are known to love Corvettes, don't make Corvette your password. Choose something unlikely to be guessed. Include a combination of letters, numbers, and special characters. If you ever suspect that someone has guessed your password, change it immediately. Above all, remember your password. ISPs don't like it when you forget your password and they have to reset it for you.

Your ISP will also tell you the IP address of the computer that hosts your e-mail account. The IP address will be in domain-name format, such as copland.udel.edu. You will need to know all three items—your account name, password, and host computer's IP address—in order to complete the tutorial exercises in this chapter.

SELECTING AN E-MAIL CLIENT

The software program that you use to read your e-mail is known as an **e-mail client**. Both Netscape and Microsoft include e-mail clients in their Web browser software suites. This chapter contains detailed instructions on how to use the Netscape and Microsoft e-mail clients. You are free to choose either one for use in this tutorial.

Netscape Messenger

The e-mail client in Netscape Communicator is called Netscape Messenger. As this book goes to press, Netscape has the largest share of the Web browser market, meaning that most users already have Netscape Messenger.

Microsoft Outlook Express

The e-mail client in Microsoft Internet Explorer is called Outlook Express. Since Microsoft Internet Explorer now ships as part of the Windows operating system, almost everyone who purchases a new Windows-based PC is going to have Outlook Express. It's possible that your copy of Microsoft Internet Explorer may be set to bring up some other e-mail client, such as Microsoft Exchange or Microsoft Outlook. If that happens when you work through the exercises in this chapter, you can change mail packages by following these steps:

▶ Pull down the Microsoft Internet Explorer's View menu and choose Options; the Options dialog appears.

▶ Click the Programs tab.

▶ Pull down the Mail menu and choose Outlook Express mail.

▶ Click OK to close the Options dialog.

CONFIGURING YOUR E-MAIL CLIENT

You must configure your e-mail client before you can begin reading mail. Configuring an e-mail client means telling it the essential information it needs to know, such as the IP address of your ISP's host computer and the name of your e-mail account. You can also set preferences that determine whether the mail will get deleted from the host or stay there after it gets downloaded to your computer. To configure your e-mail client, follow the steps in Table 6-1.

Table 6-1　How to Configure an E-mail Client

Netscape Communicator	Microsoft Internet Explorer
▶ Get Netscape running, if it isn't already. Pull down the Edit menu and choose Preferences.	▶ Get Internet Explorer running, if it isn't already.
▶ Double-click the Mail & Groups category if it's not already expanded, then select Mail Server. The Preferences dialog appears as shown in Figure 6-1.	▶ Select the Mail icon to drop the menu down, and select Read Mail.
	▶ You may get a dialog box asking you to select a folder for your mail; select the Inbox folder, unless you want your mail kept somewhere else.
	▶ Since you have not set up Internet Explorer for mail, the Internet Connection Wizard will launch. The Wizard will ask you several questions.
	▶ First, the Wizard asks for your Internet mail display name, as shown in Figure 6-3. The author typed **Fred T. Hofstetter** here.
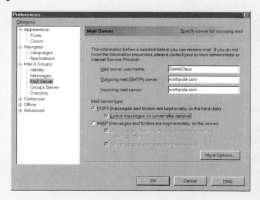	
Figure 6-1 The Netscape Preferences dialog showing the Mail Server options.	
▶ In the Mail Server user-name field, type the name of the account you obtained by following the instructions for getting an e-mail account earlier in this chapter. Do not enter your complete e-mail address into this field; all that goes here is the name of your account.	**Figure 6-3** The Internet Connection Wizard presents a series of five screens that ask you setup questions.

Table 6-1 *(Continued)*

Netscape Communicator	Microsoft Internet Explorer
▶ Set the mail server type to POP3 or IMAP. POP stands for Post Office Protocol and transfers the mail to your computer. IMAP stands for Internet Message Access Protocol and leaves the mail on the server. If you want to learn more about the difference between POP and IMAP, click the POP versus IMAP icon at the Interlit Web site.	▶ Second, the Wizard asks for your e-mail address. Your e-mail address is your account name, followed by an @ sign, followed by the domain name of your ISP's host computer. For example, if your account name is SantaClaus and your host computer is northpole.com, you would type **SantaClaus@northpole.com**
▶ Click the Identify category; the Preferences dialog appears as shown in Figure 6-2. In the Your Name field, type your full name, if it is not there already. In the Email address field, type your e-mail address, if it is not there already. Your e-mail address is your account name, followed by an @ sign, followed by the domain name of your ISP's host computer. For example, if your account name is SantaClaus and your host computer is northpole.com, your e-mail address is: SantaClaus@northpole.com	▶ Third, the Wizard asks whether you want the mail server to be set up as POP3 or IMAP. Choose POP3 if you want your mail to be transferred to your computer, or click IMAP to leave it on the server. Then you enter the name of your incoming mail server and your outgoing mail server, which in the case of Santa Claus would be **mail.northpole.com**. Figure 6-4 shows how Santa would complete this step.

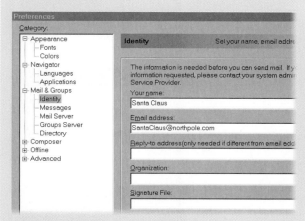

Figure 6-2 The Netscape Preferences dialog showing the Identity options.

▶ Click OK to close the Preferences dialog.

Figure 6-4 The Wizard's Mail Server setup screen.

▶ The Wizard will ask you to enter your e-mail logon name and password.

▶ The Wizard will ask for your Internet mail account name; type the name you want this to be. Santa Claus would type something like "Northpole mail" here, for example.

▶ Next, the Wizard will ask whether you're using a phone line or a network connection; answer accordingly.

▶ If you have multiple connections to the Internet, the Wizard will ask what Internet connection to use. You should choose the same connection you made when you configured your Web browser, unless you have a reason for doing otherwise.

▶ When the Wizard's done, the Microsoft Internet Explorer will fetch your mail.

Having configured the e-mail client, now you're ready to send and receive mail. Read on.

SENDING MAIL

To send someone an e-mail message, follow the steps in Table 6-2. The first time you do this, address the message to yourself, so you will have a message waiting to be read when the next part of this chapter teaches you how to read mail.

Table 6-2   How to Send E-mail

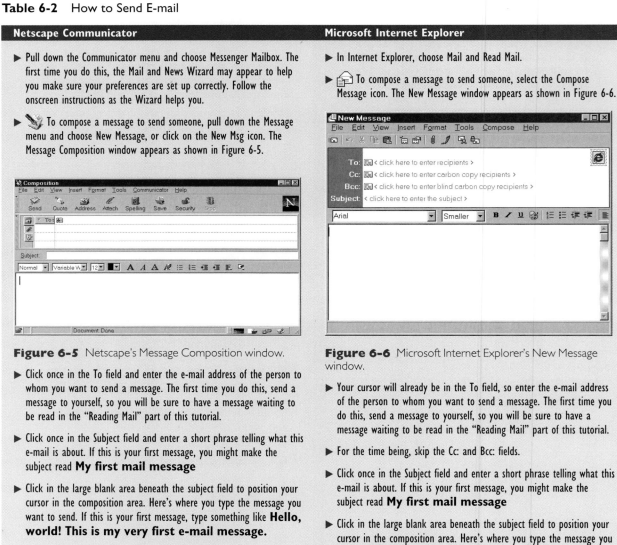

Netscape Communicator	Microsoft Internet Explorer
▶ Pull down the Communicator menu and choose Messenger Mailbox. The first time you do this, the Mail and News Wizard may appear to help you make sure your preferences are set up correctly. Follow the onscreen instructions as the Wizard helps you.	▶ In Internet Explorer, choose Mail and Read Mail.
▶ To compose a message to send someone, pull down the Message menu and choose New Message, or click on the New Msg icon. The Message Composition window appears as shown in Figure 6-5.	▶ To compose a message to send someone, select the Compose Message icon. The New Message window appears as shown in Figure 6-6.

Figure 6-5 Netscape's Message Composition window.

Figure 6-6 Microsoft Internet Explorer's New Message window.

▶ Click once in the To field and enter the e-mail address of the person to whom you want to send a message. The first time you do this, send a message to yourself, so you will be sure to have a message waiting to be read in the "Reading Mail" part of this tutorial.

▶ Click once in the Subject field and enter a short phrase telling what this e-mail is about. If this is your first message, you might make the subject read **My first mail message**

▶ Click in the large blank area beneath the subject field to position your cursor in the composition area. Here's where you type the message you want to send. If this is your first message, type something like **Hello, world! This is my very first e-mail message.**

▶ Click the Send button to send the message.

▶ Your cursor will already be in the To field, so enter the e-mail address of the person to whom you want to send a message. The first time you do this, send a message to yourself, so you will be sure to have a message waiting to be read in the "Reading Mail" part of this tutorial.

▶ For the time being, skip the Cc: and Bcc: fields.

▶ Click once in the Subject field and enter a short phrase telling what this e-mail is about. If this is your first message, you might make the subject read **My first mail message**

▶ Click in the large blank area beneath the subject field to position your cursor in the composition area. Here's where you type the message you want to send. If this is your first message, type something like **Hello, world! This is my very first e-mail message.**

▶ Click the Send button; the message gets put in your queue of messages waiting to be sent.

▶ To really send the message, click the Send and Retrieve button.

READING MAIL

To read your electronic mail, follow the steps in Table 6-3.

Table 6-3   How to Read E-mail

Netscape Communicator	Microsoft Internet Explorer
▶ If the Inbox is not already visible, pull down the Communicator menu and choose Messenger Mailbox to make the Inbox window appear.	▶ If you are not already in Outlook Express, choose Mail from the Internet Explorer menu and choose Read Mail; the Outlook Express window appears.
▶ To find out if you have new mail waiting for you, click the Get Msg button. If the Password dialog appears, type your password and click OK.	▶ In Outlook Express, select your Inbox by clicking it once. If you chose IMAP when you configured your mail in Table 6-1, your inbox is a subfolder of the messages folder on your mail server; if you chose POP3, click the Inbox in your Outlook Express folder.
▶ The Getting New Messages dialog appears, as shown in Figure 6-7, to display the status of the retrieval of your mail.	▶ The Getting Mail dialog appears, as shown in Figure 6-9, to display the status of the retrieval of your mail.

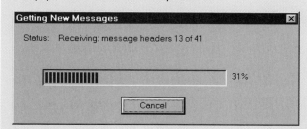

Figure 6-7 The Getting New Messages dialog.

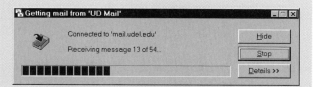

Figure 6-9 The Outlook Express Getting Mail dialog.

▶ If new mail has arrived, the Inbox window will display a menu of your incoming mail messages, as shown in Figure 6-8.

▶ If new mail has arrived, the Inbox window will display a menu of your incoming mail messages, as shown in Figure 6-10.

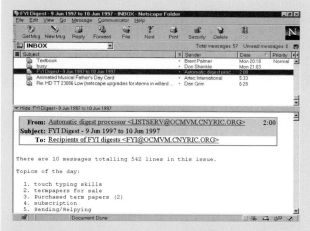

Figure 6-8 The Netscape Inbox displays a menu of incoming mail messages.

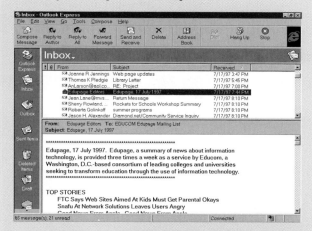

Figure 6-10 The Outlook Express Inbox displays a menu of incoming mail messages.

▶ To preview a message, click its title once, and the message will appear in the window at the bottom of the screen. To read a message, double-click on its title, and the text of the message will appear in a message window. When you are done reading the message, close the message window.

▶ To preview a message, click its title once, and the message will appear in the window at the lower right. To read the message, double-click its title; the message will appear in a Message window. When you are done reading the message, close the message window.

▶ In your Inbox, the mail message will be marked as having been read. It will stay on your computer unless you delete it.

▶ In your Inbox, the mail message will be marked as having been read. The message will stay on your computer unless you delete it.

▶ If you want to delete the message, click on its title once to select it, then click the Delete button.

▶ ✗ If you want to delete the message, click on its title once to select it, then click the Delete button.

ANSWERING MAIL

Once you get started using e-mail regularly, you will find that something you will often want to do is respond to a message someone sent you. Instead of having to go through all of the steps needed to send a totally new message, you can simply reply to the message while it is on your screen. To reply to a message, follow the steps in Table 6-4.

Table 6-4 How to Reply to an E-mail Message

Netscape Communicator	Microsoft Internet Explorer
▶ While viewing the message, click the Reply button, then choose To Sender or To All.	▶ While viewing the message, click the Reply to Author or Reply to All button. A shortcut for replying to the author is to press Ctrl-R; to reply to all, press Shift-Ctrl-R.
▶ A shortcut for replying to the sender is to press Ctrl-R, and to reply to all, press Shift-Ctrl-R.	▶ A new message window will automatically appear, addressed to the author. Enter your reply, then send the message as usual.
▶ A new message window will automatically appear, addressed to the sender. Enter your reply, then send the message as usual.	

FORWARDING MAIL

Sometimes you will receive mail that you want to send a copy of to someone else. Instead of having to go through all of the steps needed to copy and paste the message into a new message window, you can simply forward the message. To forward an e-mail message, follow the steps in Table 6-5.

Table 6-5 How to Forward an E-mail Message

Netscape Communicator	Microsoft Internet Explorer
▶ While viewing the message, click the Forward button; a new Message window will appear.	▶ While viewing the message, click the Forward Message button; a new Message window will appear.
▶ In the To field, enter the e-mail address of the person to whom you want to forward the message.	▶ In the To field, enter the e-mail address of the person to whom you want to forward the message.
▶ In the body of the message, enter anything more that you want to send along with the message, such as a few words indicating why you're forwarding this.	▶ In the body of the message, enter anything more that you want to send along with the message, such as a few words indicating why you're forwarding this.
▶ Send the message as usual.	▶ Send the message as usual.

FILING E-MAIL MESSAGES

Occasionally you will receive an important message that you want to keep so you can refer to it later on. Instead of deleting it, you can file it. To file an e-mail message means to move it into a different folder on your hard drive besides the in-box folder where your incoming mail accumulates. There are three processes to learn related to filing e-mail messages: creating an e-mail folder in which to hold your messages, filing mail into an e-mail folder, and retrieving filed mail whenever you want to read it again.

Creating an E-mail Folder

To file mail, you can create different folders regarding different topics. To create an e-mail file folder, follow the steps in Table 6-6.

Table 6-6 How to Create an E-mail File Folder

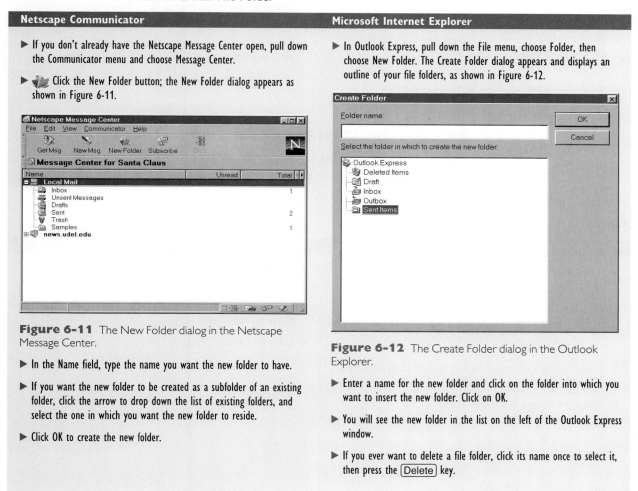

Netscape Communicator	Microsoft Internet Explorer
▶ If you don't already have the Netscape Message Center open, pull down the Communicator menu and choose Message Center.	▶ In Outlook Express, pull down the File menu, choose Folder, then choose New Folder. The Create Folder dialog appears and displays an outline of your file folders, as shown in Figure 6-12.
▶ Click the New Folder button; the New Folder dialog appears as shown in Figure 6-11.	
Figure 6-11 The New Folder dialog in the Netscape Message Center.	**Figure 6-12** The Create Folder dialog in the Outlook Explorer.
▶ In the Name field, type the name you want the new folder to have.	▶ Enter a name for the new folder and click on the folder into which you want to insert the new folder. Click on OK.
▶ If you want the new folder to be created as a subfolder of an existing folder, click the arrow to drop down the list of existing folders, and select the one in which you want the new folder to reside.	▶ You will see the new folder in the list on the left of the Outlook Express window.
▶ Click OK to create the new folder.	▶ If you ever want to delete a file folder, click its name once to select it, then press the [Delete] key.

Filing Mail into an E-mail Folder

You can file mail in any e-mail folder on your computer. Follow the steps in Table 6-7.

Table 6-7   How to File an E-mail Message

Netscape Communicator	Microsoft Internet Explorer
▶ Get your Inbox window on screen. You will see the messages in your Inbox. If there are no messages waiting for you there, click the Get Msg button to see if any mail awaits. If not, you will have to wait until someone sends you mail before you can complete this exercise. One sure way to get mail is to send yourself a message!	▶ Get your Outlook Express window onscreen and select your Inbox. You will see the messages in your Inbox. If there are no messages waiting for you there, click the Send and Receive button to see if any mail awaits. If not, you will have to wait until someone sends you mail before you can complete this exercise. One sure way to get mail is to send yourself a message!
▶ Click once on the title of the message you want to file, to select it.	▶ Right click the message you want to file, to select it, and when the menu pulls down, choose Move To. This will bring up a Move dialog that lets you select the folder you want to file the message in.
▶ Click the File button; a menu drops down showing the names of your file folders.	▶ Another way to file e-mail is to click and drag the title of the message and drop it into the folder you want to file the message in.
▶ Select the name of the folder in which you want to file the mail, and the message will be moved into that folder.	

Retrieving Mail from an E-mail Folder

Filing mail would serve no purpose without a way to retrieve it when you want to refer to it again. To retrieve a filed e-mail message, follow the steps in Table 6-8.

Table 6-8   How to Retrieve a Filed E-mail Message

Netscape Communicator	Microsoft Internet Explorer
▶ Pull down the Communicator menu and choose Message Center; the Message Center window appears.	▶ In Outlook Express, click one of the folders shown on the left of the Outlook Express window.
▶ If your mail folders are not visible, double-click on Mail to reveal them.	▶ An Inbox window will appear, displaying the titles of the mail messages filed in this folder.
▶ Double-click on the name of the folder from which you want to retrieve a filed e-mail message.	▶ To retrieve a message, double-click its title.
▶ An Inbox window will appear, displaying the titles of the mail messages filed in this folder.	
▶ To retrieve a message, double-click its title.	

CREATING A SIGNATURE FILE

When you send someone an e-mail message, it's nice to include information about yourself, so the person receiving the message will know something about you, such as your street address, where you work or go to school, and your telephone number. To keep from having to enter this information each time you send an e-mail message, you can create a **signature file**, which is a block of text that automatically gets appended to the e-mail messages you originate.

To create a signature file, you use any word processor or text editor to create a text file containing the information you want to have appear at the bottom of your e-mail messages. You should not make the lines in a signature file longer than about

72 characters, otherwise they may wrap when people with small screens read your message, and wrapping will throw off the formatting. When you save the file, make sure you save it in plain text format, in the file folder of your choice. Table 6-9 shows how to create a file folder; follow these steps whenever you need to create a new file folder to hold the files you create. Table 6-10 shows how to create a plain text file. To make your e-mail client automatically attach the signature file to the e-mail messages that you send, follow the steps provided in Table 6-11.

Table 6-9 How to Create a File Folder

Windows 3.1	Windows 95	Macintosh
To create a directory with Windows 3.1 and compatibles, you use the Windows File Manager. You will find the File Manager's icon in the Main group on the Windows desktop. If the Main group is not visible, pull down the Communicator menu and select Main to bring it up, then double-click the File Manager icon to launch the File Manager. Figure 6-13 shows how the File Manager provides a visual diagram of how all the files are organized on your computer. You can double-click on any folder to see a list of the files contained in it.	To create a folder with Windows 95, you use the Explorer. To get the Explorer started, use the Windows 95 Start button. If the Start button is not visible on your screen, hold down `Ctrl` and press `Esc`, and the Start button will appear. Click the Start button and choose Programs. You will find the Explorer listed on the Programs menu. Click on the Explorer to get it running. Figure 6-14 shows how the Explorer provides a visual diagram of how all the files are organized on your computer. You can click on any folder to see a list of the files contained in it.	To create a folder on the Macintosh, you use the New Folder command in the File menu of the Finder. If you have no programs running, then you are already in the Finder; if you have other programs running, select the icon in the upper right corner of the screen. Whatever icon appears will vary, depending on what programs you have running. When the menu drops down, select ☐ Finder. Figure 6-15 shows how the Finder provides a visual diagram of how all the files are organized on your computer. You can click on any folder to see a list of the files contained in it.

Figure 6-13 The File Manager uses a filing cabinet metaphor.

To create a new directory for your application, follow these steps:

▶ Click the icon that represents the hard drive in which you will create the directory.

▶ Pull down the File menu and select Create Directory to bring up the Create Directory dialog.

▶ For this tutorial, create a directory called *Interlit*. Assuming your hard drive is C, type **c:\interlit**

▶ Click OK. The directory should now appear in the list of directories displayed by the File Manager. If it does not, scroll to the top of the list on the left side of the File Manager and double-click on the *c:* you will find there.

▶ Close the File Manager by pulling down its File menu and choosing Exit.

Figure 6-14 The Explorer provides a visual overview of all the files and folders on your computer.

To create a new folder, follow these steps:

▶ Click the icon that represents the hard drive on which you will create the folder.

▶ Pull down the File menu, select New, and select Folder. The new folder will appear with the name *New Folder*.

▶ For this tutorial, make the name of the new folder be *Interlit*. Since the name *New Folder* is already selected, you can change the name by simply typing **interlit**

▶ Press `Enter` to complete the creation of the new folder.

▶ Close the Explorer by clicking on the ☒ in the upper right corner of the window.

Figure 6-15 The Macintosh desktop.

To create a new folder, follow these steps:

▶ Select File from the menu bar, then select New Folder. The new folder will appear in whatever window is active or on the desktop, if no windows are active. For this tutorial, select your hard drive so the folder will be opened there.

▶ The folder will be created with the name *untitled folder*. Select the name by clicking it once. Then type the new name. For this tutorial, make the name of the new folder be *Interlit*.

Table 6-10   How to Create a Plain Text File

Windows 3.1	Windows 95	Macintosh
▶ Pull down the Program Manager File menu and choose Run to make the Run dialog appear.	▶ Click the Start button, and choose Run to make the Run dialog appear.	▶ Double-click the icon for SimpleText.
▶ Type **notepad** and press Enter. A Notepad window will appear.	▶ Type **notepad** and press Enter. A Notepad window will appear.	▶ A window with the name *untitled* will appear.
▶ Type the text you want the file to contain. Figure 6-16 contains a model to follow for creating a signature file.	▶ Type the text you want the file to contain. Figure 6-16 contains a model to follow for creating a signature file.	▶ Type the text you want the file to contain. Figure 6-16 contains a model to follow for creating a signature file.
▶ When you are done, pull down the Notepad's File menu and choose Save to make the Save dialog appear. Use the Save dialog to save the file in the directory of your choice.	▶ When you are done, pull down the Notepad's File menu and choose Save to make the Save dialog appear. Use the Save dialog to save the file in the folder of your choice.	▶ When you are done, pull down SimpleText's File menu and choose Save to make the Save dialog appear. Use the Save dialog to save the file in the folder of your choice.

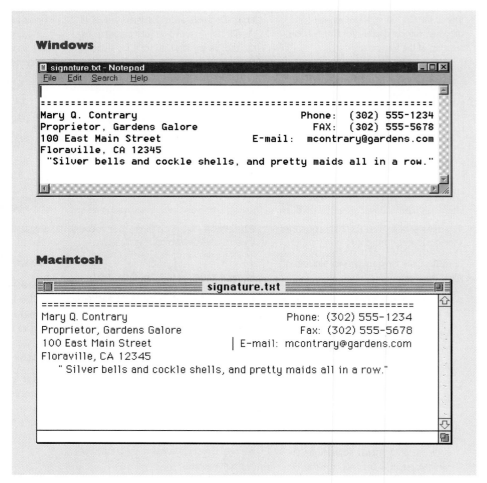

Figure 6-16 A sample signature file showing a person's name, title, address, telephone, fax, e-mail address, and a little saying. When this file gets appended to an e-mail message, the line of equal signs at the top of the file will serve as a divider between the text of the e-mail message and the signature file.

Table 6-11 How to Set Up a Signature File

Netscape Communicator	Microsoft Internet Explorer
▶ Pull down the Edit menu, choose Preferences, and select Mail and Groups Preferences.	▶ In Outlook Express, pull down the Tools menu and choose Stationery.
▶ Double-click the Mail & Groups category, if it's not already expanded, then select Identity; the Preferences dialog appears as shown in Figure 6-17.	▶ When the Stationery dialog appears, click the Signature button; the Signature dialog appears as shown in Figure 6-18.
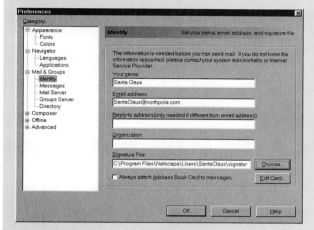	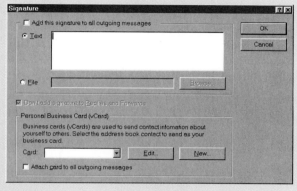
Figure 6-17 The Identity Category of the Netscape Preferences dialog.	**Figure 6-18** The Outlook Express Signature dialog.
▶ Enter the complete path/filename of your signature file into the Signature File field, or click the Choose button, which will bring up a Signature File dialog that will help you locate the file and enter the filename for you.	▶ Click the option for File. Enter the complete path/filename of your signature file into the Signature File field, or click the Browse button, which will bring up a Browse dialog that will help you locate the file and enter the filename for you.
▶ Click OK. If your signature file is longer than four lines, you will get a warning that it exceeds the recommended four lines, but it's OK for it to be a little longer. After all, screen space is free! Be aware, however, that it is not good Netiquette to have excessively long signature files.	▶ You could also click the option for Text and type or paste your signature file into that space.
	▶ You'll also want to click on the choices of when to use your signature file.
	▶ Click OK to close the Signature dialog, then click OK to close the Stationery dialog.

Eventually, you will want to add to your signature file the address of the World Wide Web home page that you will create in Part Five. You can edit your signature file at any time by using your text editor to open your signature file, change it as you like, and save it again.

NOTE If you make a change to your signature file while you have your e-mail software running, the change you make may not take effect right away, because your e-mail client reads the signature file only at the start of the session. To make changes to the signature file take effect, shut down your e-mail client by closing all of your Netscape or Microsoft Internet Explorer windows, then restart it.

MIME ATTACHMENTS

MIME stands for *M*ultipurpose *I*nternet *M*ail *E*xtensions. MIME is a protocol that lets you attach a file to a mail message. When you send the mail message, the attached file goes along with it. When a user receives the message, the attached file gets decoded and stored on the user's computer, where the file can function just like it does on your PC. If the file contains text, you can read it on your PC. If the file is a bitmap, you can see the picture. If it's an audio file, you can hear it. If it's a movie, you can watch it. Any kind of file can be transmitted as a MIME attachment, as long as both the sender and the receiver have a MIME-compliant e-mail client. The e-mail clients in both Netscape Communicator and Microsoft Internet Explorer support MIME. To learn how to send attached files via MIME, follow the steps in Table 6-12.

Table 6-12   How to Attach Files to E-mail Messages

Netscape Communicator	Microsoft Internet Explorer
▶ From your Netscape Inbox, click the New Msg button, and create the mail message to which you want to attach a file.	▶ From Outlook Express, click the Compose Message button and create the mail message to which you want to attach a file.
▶ 🖉 Before you send the message, click the Attach button, and, in the popout menu that will appear, choose File. The File to Attach dialog will appear.	▶ 🗋 Before you send the message, click the Insert File button to make the Insert Attachment dialog appear.
▶ Enter the complete path/filename of the file you want to attach, or use the controls to locate the file and click on its name to enter it into the Filename field.	▶ Enter the complete path/filename of the file you want to attach, or use the controls to locate the file and click on its name to enter it into the Filename field.
▶ Click Open to complete the Attach dialog. The file is now attached to your mail message.	▶ Click Attach to complete the Insert Attachment dialog. The file is now attached to your mail message.
▶ Send the mail message as usual.	▶ Send the mail message as usual.

ADDRESS BOOKS

Before you can send e-mail to someone, you must know the person's e-mail address. To avoid having to look up a person's e-mail address every time, you can record it in an **address book**, which is an index of the e-mail addresses you want to keep track of for future use. To address an e-mail message to someone in your address book, you simply go into your address book, click the person's name, and choose the Send Mail option. This makes an e-mail composer screen appear with the person's e-mail address filled in automatically.

Adding a Name to Your Address Book

To add a name to your address book, follow the steps in Table 6-13.

Table 6-13   How to Add a Name to Your Address Book

Netscape Communicator	Microsoft Internet Explorer

▶ Pull down the Communicator menu and choose Address Book; the Address Book window appears as shown in Figure 6-19.

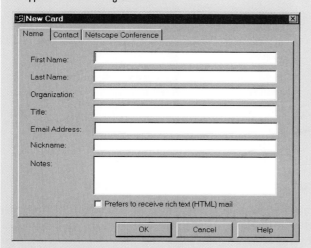

Figure 6-19 The Netscape Address Book window.

▶ To add a name, click the New Card button. The New Card dialog appears as shown in Figure 6-20.

Figure 6-20 The New Card dialog.

▶ In the blanks provided, fill in the person's first name, last name, e-mail address, and a nickname.

▶ If you know the person reads mail with an HTML-enabled e-mail reader, leave the Prefers to Receive HTML option checked; otherwise, uncheck that option.

▶ If you want to include information about the person's street address, phone, and fax numbers, click the Contact tab and fill out that information.

▶ Click OK to close the Add User dialog, and you will see how the person has been added to your Address Book.

▶ If you ever want to change any of this information, just double-click the user's name in your Address Book.

▶ In Outlook Express, click the Address Book icon; the Address Book window appears as shown in Figure 6-21.

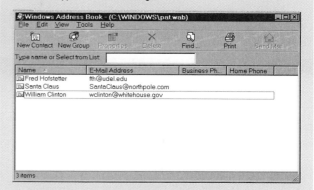

Figure 6-21 The Outlook Express Address Book window.

▶ To add a name, click the New Contact button. The New Contact dialog appears as shown in Figure 6-22.

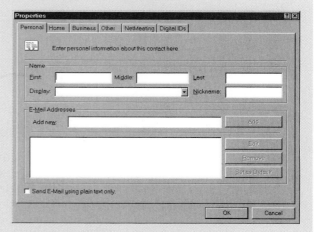

Figure 6-22 The New Contact dialog.

▶ In the blanks provided, fill in the person's first name, last name, e-mail address, and a nickname.

▶ By choosing the other tabs, you can add other information such as a home and business address.

▶ Click OK to close the New Contact dialog, and you will see how the person has been added to your Address Book.

▶ If you ever want to change any of this information, just double-click the user's name in your Address Book.

Addressing E-mail to Someone Listed in an Address Book

To address an e-mail message to someone listed in an address book, follow the steps in Table 6-14.

Table 6-14   How to Address Mail to Someone Listed in an Address Book

Netscape Communicator	Microsoft Internet Explorer
▶ From your Inbox window, press the New Msg button to make the Compose window appear.	▶ From the Outlook Express menu, choose Compose Message to make the New Message window appear.
▶ Click the Address Book button.	▶ In the To, Cc, and Bcc fields you'll notice little address card icons at the left. Click the address card icon in the To field to bring up the Select Recipients dialog.
▶ Click once on the name of the person to whom you want to address the message.	▶ Click once on the name of the person to whom you want to address the message.
▶ Click the To, Cc, or Bcc button, depending on whether you want the person to receive the original message, a carbon copy, or a blind carbon copy.	▶ Click the To, Cc, or Bcc button, depending on whether you want the person to receive the original message, a carbon copy, or a blind carbon copy.
▶ Click OK to close the Address Book; the person's name appears in the address part of your message.	▶ Click OK to close the Select Recipients dialog; the person's name appears in the address part of your message.

Addressing E-mail to Groups of People

As social beings, it's natural for computer users to want to communicate with groups of people. You might be working on a project at work or at school, for example, and you'd like to send a message to all of the people working on that project with you. Instead of having to enter each person's e-mail address each time you want to send the group a message, you can use your Address Book to create mailing lists consisting of as many users as you like. To create a mailing list, follow the steps in Table 6-15.

Table 6-15   How to Create a Mailing List

Netscape Communicator	Microsoft Internet Explorer
▶ Pull down the Communicator menu and choose Address Book to make the Address Book window appear.	▶ From the Outlook Express menu, choose Address Book to make the Address Book window appear.
▶ Click the New List button. The Mailing List dialog appears as shown in Figure 6-23.	▶ Click the New Group button. The Properties dialog for the group appears as shown in Figure 6-24.

Table 6-15 *(Continued)*

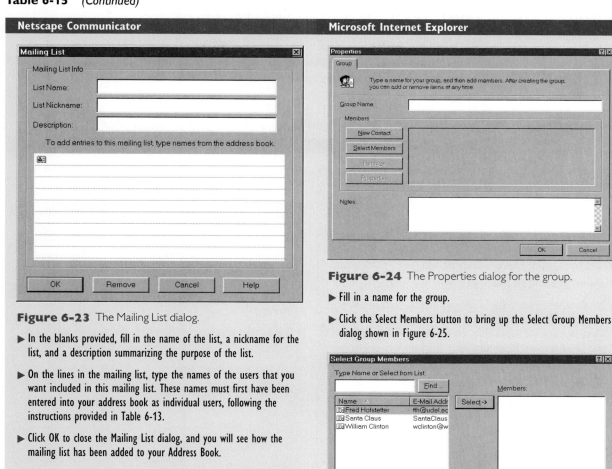

Netscape Communicator

Figure 6-23 The Mailing List dialog.

▶ In the blanks provided, fill in the name of the list, a nickname for the list, and a description summarizing the purpose of the list.

▶ On the lines in the mailing list, type the names of the users that you want included in this mailing list. These names must first have been entered into your address book as individual users, following the instructions provided in Table 6-13.

▶ Click OK to close the Mailing List dialog, and you will see how the mailing list has been added to your Address Book.

▶ If you ever want to change any of this information, just double-click the mailing list's name in your Address Book.

Microsoft Internet Explorer

Figure 6-24 The Properties dialog for the group.

▶ Fill in a name for the group.

▶ Click the Select Members button to bring up the Select Group Members dialog shown in Figure 6-25.

Figure 6-25 The Select Group Members dialog.

▶ Add names from your Address Book to the group by double-clicking on them or by clicking once and then clicking Select. If you want to include someone who is not already in your Address Book, click New Contact and proceed as before.

▶ When you are finished, click OK.

▶ If you ever want to change any of this information, just double-click the group's name in your Address Book.

To send mail to the people in a mailing list, address the mail to the name of the mailing list, following the instructions provided in Table 6-2.

FINDING THINGS CONTAINED IN E-MAIL MESSAGES

When you have a lot of accumulated mail, you will eventually lose track of where everything is. Happily, you can search your mail messages to find things. To search an e-mail message, follow the steps in Table 6-16.

Table 6-16 How to Search for Things in an E-mail Message

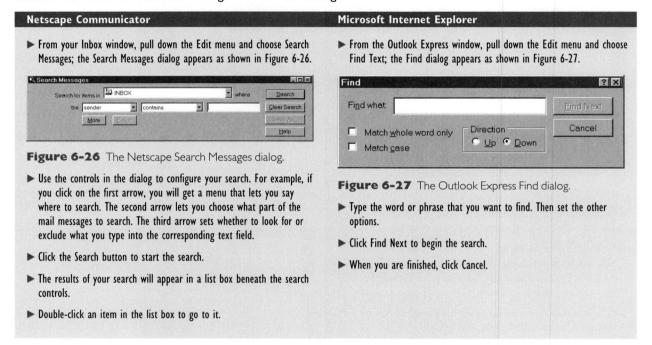

Netscape Communicator

▶ From your Inbox window, pull down the Edit menu and choose Search Messages; the Search Messages dialog appears as shown in Figure 6-26.

Figure 6-26 The Netscape Search Messages dialog.

▶ Use the controls in the dialog to configure your search. For example, if you click on the first arrow, you will get a menu that lets you say where to search. The second arrow lets you choose what part of the mail messages to search. The third arrow sets whether to look for or exclude what you type into the corresponding text field.

▶ Click the Search button to start the search.

▶ The results of your search will appear in a list box beneath the search controls.

▶ Double-click an item in the list box to go to it.

Microsoft Internet Explorer

▶ From the Outlook Express window, pull down the Edit menu and choose Find Text; the Find dialog appears as shown in Figure 6-27.

Figure 6-27 The Outlook Express Find dialog.

▶ Type the word or phrase that you want to find. Then set the other options.

▶ Click Find Next to begin the search.

▶ When you are finished, click Cancel.

DEALING WITH UNWANTED E-MAIL

There are two ways to deal with unwanted e-mail: just delete it, or send a reply indicating your disdain for the unwanted mail. If you believe the unwanted mail is illegal, such as a mail message containing child pornographic material or other criminal activity, you can report the transmission by forwarding it to the appropriate authorities. For example, you can find out how to contact your local FBI office at http://www.fbi.gov/fo/fo.htm. It may help to send mail to the postmaster at your Internet service provider, informing your ISP of the unwanted activity, and asking for it to be stopped. To send mail to your postmaster, assuming your ISP is northpole.com, you would address the mail to postmaster@northpole.com.

USING MAIL FILTERS

You can block mail from unwanted sources by using mail filters. A mail filter blocks mail that comes from e-mail addresses that you forbid. To set a mail filter, follow the steps in Table 6-17.

Table 6-17   How to Block Unwanted Messages with a Mail Filter

Netscape Communicator	Microsoft Internet Explorer
▶ Pull down the Communicator menu and choose Message Center. ▶ Pull down the Message Center's Edit menu, and choose Mail Filters. ▶ In the Mail Filters dialog, click the New button to create a new filter. The Filter Rules dialog appears. ▶ Enter the criteria for the messages you want to block. For example, Figure 6-28 shows how to block junk mail from famous.junk.com.	▶ From the Outlook Express window, pull down the Tools menu and choose Inbox Assistant. *Note:* The Inbox Assistant is only available if you chose POP3 instead of IMAP when you configured your mail server. If you chose IMAP, these instructions do not apply. ▶ In the Inbox Assistant dialog, click Add. ▶ Enter the criteria for the messages you want to block. For example, Figure 6-29 shows how to block junk mail from cyberpromo.com.

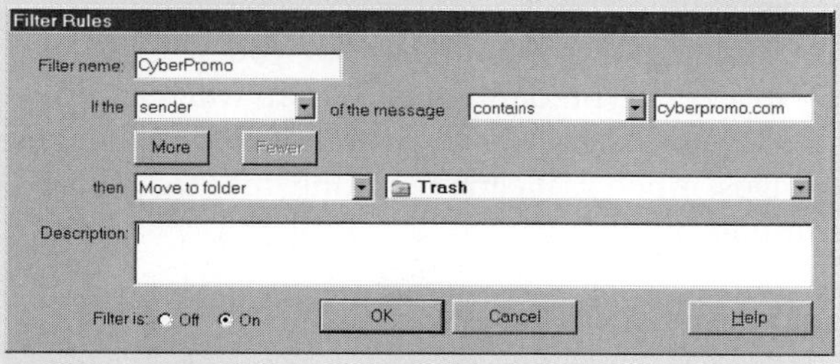

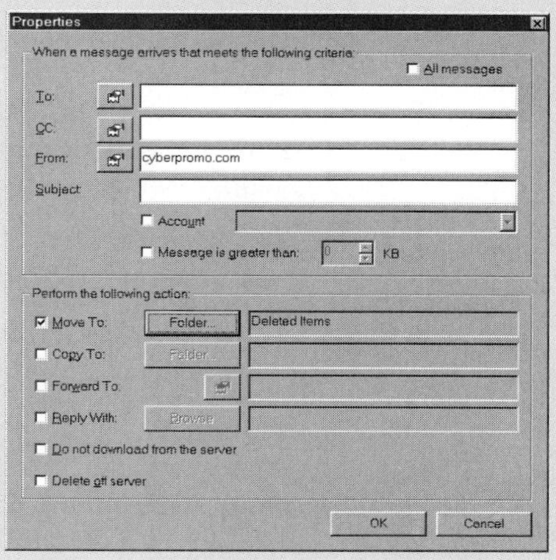

Figure 6-28 The Netscape Filter Rules dialog.

▶ Click OK to close the Filter Rules dialog. Your new rule appears in the Mail Filters dialog.

▶ Click OK to close the Mail Filters dialog.

Figure 6-29 The Outlook Express Filter Rules dialog.

▶ Click OK to close the Filter Rules dialog. Your new rule appears in the Inbox Assistant dialog.

▶ Click OK to close the Inbox Assistant dialog.

DETECTING FAKE MAIL IDs

If you get mail saying it's from someone that you doubt actually wrote the message, such as a message from your boss giving you a million-dollar raise, it's possible that someone used a bogus From field when they sent you the message. You can get more information about where the message came from by revealing the headers of the mail message, as instructed in Table 6-18.

Table 6-18   How to Detect Fake Mail IDs

Netscape Communicator	Microsoft Internet Explorer
▶ With a message selected, pull down the View menu, choose Headers, then choose All. The complete header information appears at the top of the e-mail message. ▶ To return to viewing normal headers, pull down the View menu, choose Headers, then choose Normal.	▶ With a message selected, pull down the File menu, choose Properties, then click the Details tab. ▶ Click OK to exit this dialog.

ENCRYPTING YOUR MAIL

If you are concerned about privacy, you may want to consider **encrypting** your e-mail messages. Encrypting means to run the message through an encoder that uses an encryption key to alter the characters in the message. Unless the person wanting to read the message has the encryption key needed to decode it, the message appears garbled.

Consider a simple example of an encryption key "123" that will shift each successive character in the message by 1, 2, or 3 characters in the alphabet. So encrypted, the message "Hello world" appears as "Igomq zptoe." In practice, encryption keys are much longer, and the encoding process is so complex that you would need a supercomputer to crack the key to an encrypted message. As you will learn in Part Seven, legislation is pending that would allow the government to obtain a court order to decode encrypted messages, much as it can tap phone lines to listen in on conversations of suspected criminals today.

While it is beyond the scope of this book to provide a complete tutorial on encrypting mail, it's easy to get you started.

To learn more about encryption in Netscape, click the Security icon in the toolbar of any message window.

In Microsoft Outlook Express, choose the Tools menu, then click Options. In the Options dialog, click the Security tab and select the check box "Encrypt contents and attachments for all outgoing messages." In the Advanced Settings, you can even set an encryption algorithm.

E-MAIL PRIORITIES

Both Netscape and Microsoft support a priority-setting option that lets you set the priority of an e-mail message. You set this option when you send a message, and when it arrives at its destination, it has a priority flag indicating how important it is. The person receiving the messages can sort them in order of priority, and read the most important ones first. To set the priority for an e-mail message, follow the steps in Table 6-19.

Table 6-19 How to Set the Priority of an E-mail Message

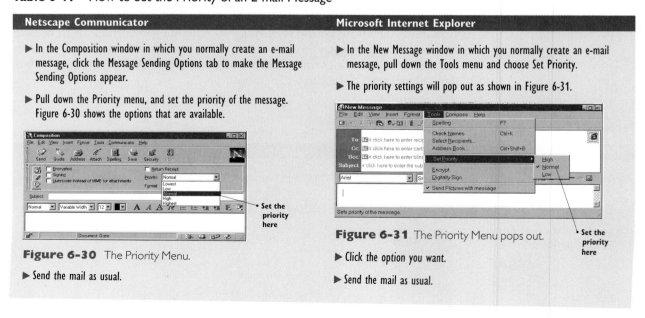

Netscape Communicator	**Microsoft Internet Explorer**
▶ In the Composition window in which you normally create an e-mail message, click the Message Sending Options tab to make the Message Sending Options appear.	▶ In the New Message window in which you normally create an e-mail message, pull down the Tools menu and choose Set Priority.
▶ Pull down the Priority menu, and set the priority of the message. Figure 6-30 shows the options that are available.	▶ The priority settings will pop out as shown in Figure 6-31.

Figure 6-30 The Priority Menu.

Figure 6-31 The Priority Menu pops out.

▶ Send the mail as usual.

▶ Click the option you want.

▶ Send the mail as usual.

SPELL CHECKING

As a final touch, before you send the e-mail message, you may want to spell check it and correct any spelling mistakes.

To spell check an e-mail message with Netscape, click the Spelling icon in the New Message window.

If you're using Microsoft Internet Explorer, and you have Microsoft Office installed on your computer, a spelling option appears on the Tools menu of your Outlook Express New Message window. To spell check a message, pull down the Tools menu and choose Spelling.

E X E R C I S E S

1. Practice sending e-mail messages to yourself. Send yourself one message, then use your e-mail client to get your new mail, and see if you can read the message you sent yourself. Then send several messages to yourself without reading them yet. Tell your e-mail client to get your new mail, and see whether all of the messages arrive. Notice how each message will bear a time stamp telling when it was written.

2. Find a couple of friends who have e-mail addresses, and practice sending and receiving messages with them. Try using the forward feature to forward mail received from one friend to another.

3. Create e-mail file folders named after two of your friends, and practice filing the mail they send you into their respective e-mail folders. Later on, use the Explorer or the File Manager to inspect the mail messages in each file folder. Does this make it easier to find messages than if you kept them all in the same file?

4. To save time addressing messages to your e-mail friends, enter their e-mail addresses into your Address Book. Practice sending your friends messages that you address by selecting their names from the Address Book instead of having to type their e-mail addresses. How much time does this save you per message?

5. Reveal the full headers on an e-mail message that someone sends you. What additional information can you glean from the complete headers as to who sent the message and how it got routed to your computer?

6. Use your Web browser to visit http://lcweb.loc.gov/global/legislative/voting.html and check the voting record of members of Congress to find out whether your congressional representatives are voting the way you want them to. Send e-mail to express your views. Point-and-click e-mail addresses are available for every member of Congress at http://www.yahoo.com/Government/Legislative_Branch/ Congressional_E_Mail_Addresses.

7 Listserv

After completing this chapter, you will be able to:

- **Describe how listserv works through e-mail protocols.**

- **Find out the names of listservs in your discipline or any other subject that interests you.**

- **Subscribe to a listserv.**

- **Know when to lurk on a listserv.**

- **Respond to messages received from a listserv.**

- **Send new messages to a listserv.**

- **File messages received from a listserv.**

- **Unsubscribe from a listserv.**

N OW that you know how to send and receive electronic mail, you are ready to take advantage of the powerful capabilities of **listserv**, which is an Internet resource that uses e-mail protocols to distribute messages to lists of users. The messages get served to everyone whose name is on the list. Hence the name listserv.

There are tens of thousands of listservs that this chapter will enable you to join. Almost every subject imaginable has a listserv already set up for people to receive and exchange information about that topic. When someone sends a message containing new information to the listserv, everyone on the list receives a copy of the message.

Some listservs are **moderated**, meaning that someone screens incoming messages before they get distributed to the list. Most listservs are not moderated, meaning that you can freely send messages to the listserv.

HOW TO SUBSCRIBE TO A LISTSERV

Since it uses e-mail protocols that virtually every user of the Internet already knows, listserv is easy to learn and use. To join a listserv, you send its host computer an e-mail message saying that you want to subscribe. For example, suppose you want to join EDUPAGE, which is a listserv that sends you news about new technology three times each week. To subscribe to EDUPAGE, follow the steps in Table 7-1.

Table 7-1 How to Subscribe to a Listserv

▶ Use your e-mail client to create a new message window.

▶ Address the message to **listproc@educom.unc.edu**

▶ Leave the subject line blank, and as your message, type:
  Subscribe EDUPAGE *Firstname Lastname*

▶ Replace *Firstname* and *Lastname* with your first and last names.

▶ Send the message.

Do not expect to receive an instant reply, because it may take a while for your new subscription to get processed. Within a day or two, however, you will receive an e-mail reply from the server letting you know that you are now subscribed to the EDUPAGE listserv. You will also be given instructions on how to unsubscribe, should you ever decide that you no longer want to belong to the listserv.

Since hundreds of thousands of people are subscribed to EDUPAGE, it is tightly controlled by the people who moderate it. Its purpose is to serve more like an electronic news service that distributes technology news rather than to permit people to discuss things via the listserv. Therefore, if you try to post messages to the EDUPAGE listserv after you join it, you will probably receive a reply from the moderator explaining that EDUPAGE does not enable discussions among the members of the listserv.

FINDING LISTSERVS IN YOUR PROFESSION

You can use the Web to find out about listservs across a broad range of disciplines and professions. Click the listserv icon at the Interlit Web site, or go to one of the listserv search tools listed in Table 7-2.

Table 7-2 Listserv Search Tools

Name of Search Tool	Web Address
TileNet/Lists	http://tile.net/listserv
Liszt Directory of Email Discussion Groups	http://www.liszt.com
Search the List of Lists	http://catalog.com/vivian/interest-group-search.html

RECOMMENDED LISTSERVS

The author would like to recommend a few listservs to you. These deal with technology and focus especially on emerging trends and issues regarding the Internet.

EDUPAGE

Instructions for joining EDUPAGE were provided earlier in this chapter in Table 7-1, "How to Subscribe to a Listserv." If you haven't already joined EDUPAGE, please do so. It's the best single source for keeping up with what's happening, imho.

Netsurfer Digest

Netsurfer Digest is a great way to keep up with the latest hot spots on the Internet. To join the Netsurfer listserv, follow these steps:

▶ Address an e-mail message to **nsdigest-request@netsurf.com**

▶ Leave the subject line blank, and as your message, type: **subscribe nsdigest-text**

▶ Send the message.

Online Insider

Another great source of information about the Internet is Seidman's Online Insider, which you will find on the Web at http://techweb.cmp.com/ng/online_insider/. Past issues (all the way back the premier issue in September 1994) are found there. The Web site is nice because the issues are in HTML with links to all the places Seidman references. To receive the Online Insider in your e-mail, follow these steps:

▶ Address an e-mail message to **listserv@peach.ease.lsoft.com**

▶ Leave the subject line blank, and as your message, type:

    Subscribe ONLINE-L *Firstname Lastname*

▶ Replace *Firstname* and *Lastname* with your first and last names.

▶ Send the message.

HTML-GROUP

All of the listservs described so far are moderated; individual users are not permitted to write messages to the listserv directly. HTML-GROUP is a listserv that does allow users to write messages directly. It is an Internet e-mail discussion list for those beginning to learn HTML. Users discuss Web authoring, tips, secrets, and software tools. Both novices and veteran HTML authors are invited to join, with the more experienced sharing tips with novices.

To help underwrite the expense of the list, members are asked to pay a nominal voluntary annual subscription fee of $6. The fee is voluntary in that, if you can't afford it, you will not be denied access. To subscribe to HTML-GROUP, follow these steps:

▶ Address an e-mail message to **listserv@AirGunHq.com**

▶ Leave the subject line blank, and as your message, type:

   SUB HTML-GROUP *your_e-mail_address*

▶ Replace *your_e-mail_address* with your e-mail address.

▶ Send the message.

RECEIVING LISTSERV MESSAGES: REMEMBER TO LURK!

The easiest part of belonging to a listserv is receiving the messages the listserv will send you. The messages sent by the listserv appear automatically in your e-mail in-box, where you read them like any other e-mail message. As illustrated in Figure 7-1, the From field of your e-mail message will indicate that it came from the listserv.

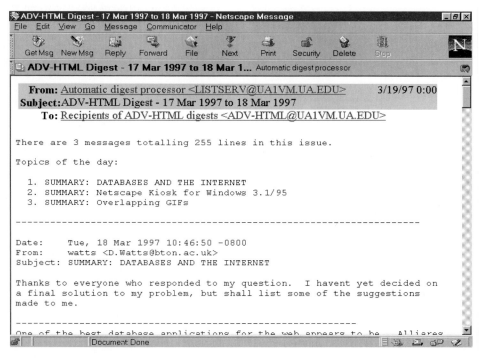

Figure 7-1 The From field indicates that an e-mail message came from a listserv.

If you join a listserv that allows you to send as well as to receive messages, remember the advice that was provided in Chapter 5, on Netiquette. Before you jump in and start originating your own messages, remember to lurk for a while, reading without responding, until you get the gist of the ongoing conversation.

RESPONDING TO A LISTSERV MESSAGE

It's easy to respond to a listserv message, because the address of the listserv will already be in the From field of the listserv message. To respond, simply press your Reply button, and enter your response just like you would send an ordinary e-mail message. Remember that your reply will be sent to lots of people, however, so make sure that what you write pertains to the purpose of the listserv. It is unethical to use listservs for other than their intended purpose.

SENDING A NEW MESSAGE TO A LISTSERV

When you join a listserv, you will be told how to address new messages that you want to send to the listserv. Since listserv addresses can be technical and hard to remember, it's a good idea to enter this address in your e-mail client's Address Book, so you won't forget it. To send a new message to the listserv, you send e-mail to this address, just as if you were sending mail to an individual user. Once again, please remember that your message will be sent to lots of people; make sure it is a proper use of the listserv.

NOTE Each listserv has two addresses that you will want to keep track of. First is the **listserv address**, which is the address to which you sent your subscribe command. At the end of this chapter, you'll learn about other commands that you can send the listserv. Second is the **list address** that the listserv will tell you to use when you want to send messages to everyone on the list. The listserv will tell you the list address in responding to your subscribe command.

FILING MESSAGES RECEIVED FROM LISTSERVS

Occasionally you may receive a message from a listserv that you want to file for later reference. Since messages from listservs arrive as e-mail messages, you can click your File button and file them, just like any other e-mail message.

HOW TO PAUSE A LISTSERV

If you plan to be away from your computer for a while, you may want to send a command to the listserv to make it stop sending messages to you. To pause a listserv, send it the following command:

SET NO MAIL

To resume the listserv, send the following command:

SET MAIL

Because there are several software packages that listserv owners can use to manage their listservs, not all listservs respond to the same set of commands. If a listserv does not respond to the SET NO MAIL command, for example, you may need to unsubscribe to get it to stop sending you messages, then subscribe again when you want to resume.

FINDING OUT WHO BELONGS TO A LISTSERV

It's natural to be curious about who belongs to a listserv. When you send messages to a listserv, everyone on the list gets a copy of your message. To find out who is getting a copy, send the following command to the listserv:

REVIEW *listname*

If that doesn't work, try:

WHO *listname*

Replace *listname* with the name of the list. The listserv will respond by e-mailing you a list of its members. *Note:* The REVIEW and WHO commands must be sent to the listserv address, not the list address. If you send a command to the list address, every member of the list will get it; this can be embarrassing, and it marks you as a neophyte on the Net.

HOW TO UNSUBSCRIBE FROM A LISTSERV

Sometimes you join a listserv only to find that its content doesn't meet your needs, or you get sent so many messages that you just cannot keep up with them. In either case, you will probably want to unsubscribe from the listserv. To unsubscribe, follow the steps in Table 7-3:

Table 7-3 How to Unsubscribe from a Listserv

▶ Address a mail message to the listserv address, which is the address you used when you joined the listserv. For example, if you want to unsubscribe from the HTML-GROUP listserv, address the message to **listserv@AirGunHq.com**

▶ Leave the subject line blank, and as your message type **SIGNOFF** followed by the name of the listserv. For example, to unsubscribe from the HTML-GROUP listserv, you would type **SIGNOFF HTML-GROUP**

▶ Send the message.

The server will respond by sending you a message indicating that your name has been taken off the list.

NOTE Do not send the signoff message to the list address. Doing so will not sign you off the list. Rather, your signoff message will go to every member of the list, marking you as a novice who doesn't fully understand how to use a listserv.

LISTSERV COMMAND SUMMARY

Table 7-4 contains a summary of some of the commands you can send a listserv. For a more complete list, send the listserv the command **LISTSERV REFCARD**.

Table 7-4   Listserv Commands

Listserv Command	What the Command Does
SUBSCRIBE listname *full_name*	Subscribes you to the list, or changes the name under which you were previously subscribed; replace *full_name* with your name.
SUBSCRIBE listname ANONYMOUS	Subscribes you to the list anonymously, if the listserv allows that for this list.
REVIEW listname	Get information about a list, including who owns it and who belongs to it.
SET NOMAIL	Make the listserv stop sending you messages (to resume, send the command **SET MAIL**).
RELEASE	Find out information about the listserv software being used to run this listserv, and who maintains the server.
SIGNOFF listname	Unsubscribes you from the list.
SET listname CONCEAL	Hide yourself from REVIEW.
SET listname NOCONCEAL	Let yourself be listed by REVIEW.
SHOW STATS	Show statistics about the listserv.
SEARCH listname keyword1 <keyword2...>	Search the listserv archives; for more search options, send the **LISTSERV REFCARD** command.
QUERY listname	Queries your set of options on the listserv; use **SET** to change them.
LISTSERV REFCARD	Makes the listserv e-mail you a reference card listing commands users can send the listserv.

EXERCISES

1. Following the instructions provided in this chapter, join the following three listservs: EDUPAGE, Netsurfer Digest, and Seidman's Online Insider. Read all three for a while, until you decide which one you like best. Maybe you will want to remain subscribed to all three! But if you don't, unsubscribe from the one(s) you no longer want to receive.

2. Using one of the listserv search tools listed in Table 7-2, find an unmoderated listserv that interests you, and subscribe to it. Lurk for a while until you get used to the conversation, then try sending your own message to the listserv. Make sure your message fits the stated purpose of the listserv. If it makes sense in the context of the conversation, ask a question in your message, and see whether anyone responds with the information you are seeking.

3. Send a command to the listserv you joined in exercise 2 to find out who belongs to the listserv. If you have trouble doing this, review the listserv commands in Table 7-4.

8

Usenet Newsgroups

After completing this chapter, you will be able to:

■ **Understand how Usenet newsgroups originated as a grassroots effort by students who wanted a better way to organize conversations over the Internet.**

■ **Visualize how the hierarchical structure of a newsgroup mirrors the manner in which physical conferences are organized.**

■ **Use your Web browser to list the newsgroups available through your Internet service provider.**

■ **Subscribe to the newsgroup(s) of your choice.**

■ **Read and respond to topics in a newsgroup, and post new topics that you want to initiate.**

■ **Understand the difference between moderated and unmoderated newsgroups.**

■ **Know when it is too late to cancel a message that you have written in a newsgroup.**

■ **Find out about newsgroups in your field of study or line of work.**

W ONDERFUL as they may be, e-mail and listserv have some shortcomings. While e-mail is a great way for individuals to exchange messages with one another, and listserv makes it easy to send mail to lists of people, it's not easy to maintain your train of thought in a conversation conducted via e-mail. That's because e-mail queues up in your in-box on a variety of topics, requiring your mind to shift gears continually as you read mail on different subjects.

Enter the Usenet newsgroup, a resource invented in the late 1970s by students who wanted a better way to converse over the Internet on specific topics. In this chapter, you will learn how Usenet newsgroups enable users to hold virtual conferences over the Internet. You'll find out what newsgroups exist in your profession, learn how to join and participate in a newsgroup, and know how to go about creating a new newsgroup.

For more background on how Usenet started, follow the links to "Usenet History" at the Interlit Web site.

COMPUTER CONFERENCING

Usenet newsgroups are based on the concept of computer conferencing. Just as physical conferences are held on different topics around the country, so do Usenet newsgroups concentrate on a given subject. Just as physical conferences consist of a series of meetings dealing with different topics within the subject of the conference, so do newsgroups divide into topics that make it easy for you to participate in the discussion that interests you. The main difference between a physical conference and a newsgroup is that the Internet is bounded neither by time nor by space—anyone can participate in any discussion at any time from any place where there is an Internet connection. Another advantage of newsgroups is that you can participate simultaneously in discussions of topics that would otherwise be mutually exclusive at a physical conference, at which simultaneous sessions are held of which you can attend only one at a time.

UNIVERSE OF USENET NEWSGROUPS

There are more than 10,000 Usenet newsgroups on the Internet. Newsgroups have names like rec.bicycles.racing that describe what the group's about. The different parts of a newsgroup name are separated by periods. Common prefixes are *news* for newsgroups that actually deal with news, *comp* for discussions about computers, *sci* for science, *soc* for social issues, *talk* for debates on controversial subjects, *rec* for recreation, and *misc* for miscellaneous topics that don't fit into the other categories.

USENET HIERARCHY

Usenet newsgroups are organized hierarchically. In each newsgroup, there is a list of topics. Under each topic, there is a list of subtopics. Under each subtopic comes a list of messages that users have written in response to that subject. By traversing this hierarchy with a newsgroup reader, you can quickly go to any part of a newsgroup and participate in the topic of your choice.

Messages written in a newsgroup are called **postings** or **articles**. The articles look like e-mail between one user and another, but instead of just being sent between people, the postings can be read by anyone in the world with Usenet access.

NEWSGROUP READERS

A program that enables you to read and participate in a newsgroup is known as a **newsgroup reader**. Both Netscape Communicator and the Microsoft Internet Explorer have newsgroup readers built in. Netscape's newsgroup reader is called Collabra. Both make it easy for you to participate in a newsgroup by clicking on a graphical map that shows the hierarchical outline of topics and subtopics in a newsgroup. Figure 8-1 shows how the hierarchy gets displayed when you read a newsgroup with Netscape Collabra, and Figure 8-2 shows how Microsoft Internet Explorer displays the same newsgroup.

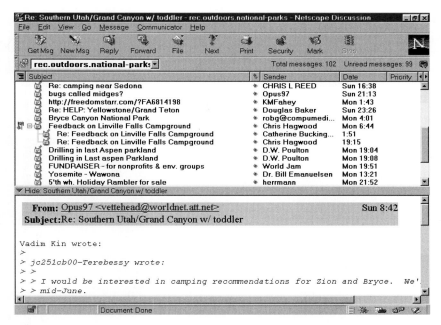

Figure 8-1 How Netscape Collabra displays a newsgroup.

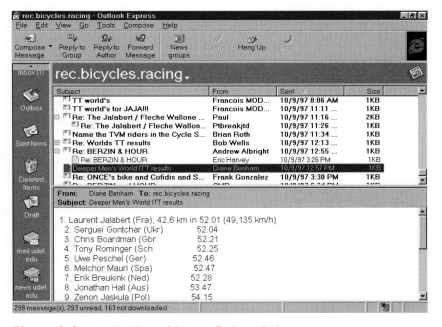

Figure 8-2 How the Microsoft Internet Explorer displays a newsgroup.

CONFIGURING YOUR NEWSGROUP CLIENT

Before you can read news, you need to configure your newsgroup client. In order to do this, you need to know the name of your newsgroup server. It will be a domain name; if you were Santa Claus, for example, the newsgroup server would be named something like news.northpole.com. If you do not know the name of your newsgroup server, ask your Internet service provider. Then follow the steps in Table 8-1 to prepare your browser for reading newsgroups.

Table 8-1   How to Configure Your Newsgroup Client

Netscape Communicator	Microsoft Internet Explorer
▶ Get Netscape Communicator running, pull down the Edit menu, and choose Preferences; the Preferences dialog appears.	▶ Get Microsoft Internet Explorer running, click the Mail button, and choose Read News.
▶ If the Mail & Groups category is not expanded, click the plus sign to expand it.	▶ Since you haven't read news before, the Internet Connection Wizard appears, as shown in Figure 8-4.
▶ Click the Groups Server category; the Preferences dialog appears as shown in Figure 8-3.	

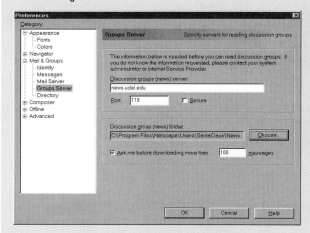

Figure 8-3 The Groups Server category of the Netscape Preferences dialog.

▶ In the Discussion groups (news) server field, type the name of the newsgroup server that you got from your Internet service provider.

▶ Leave the port set to 119, unless you've been instructed otherwise.

▶ Click OK to close the Preferences dialog.

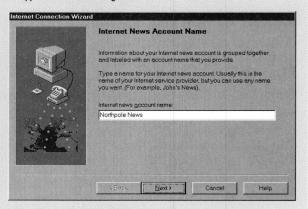

Figure 8-4 The Internet Connection Wizard helps you configure your newsgroup client.

▶ The Wizard will ask you a series of questions. First, the Wizard asks you to type your name as you want it to be displayed when you write a newsgroup message; type your name, then click Next.

▶ Second, the Wizard will ask you to type your e-mail address. Do so, then click Next.

▶ Third, the Wizard asks you to enter your Internet news server name. Type the name of the newsgroup server that you got from your Internet service provider, and click Next.

▶ Fourth, the Wizard asks you to enter a friendly name. Type the name you want this to be. Santa Claus would type something like "North Pole News," for example.

▶ The Wizard will ask whether you're using a phone line or a network connection; answer accordingly.

▶ If you have multiple connections to the Internet, the Wizard will ask what Internet connection to use. You should choose the same connection you made when you configured your Web browser, unless you have a reason for doing otherwise.

▶ When the Wizard is done, it will ask you to click Finish to complete the configuration. Click Finish.

▶ The Wizard will download the list of newsgroups available from your newsgroup server. To learn how to choose a newsgroup from this list, proceed to the next part of this tutorial, "Choosing a Newsgroup."

CHOOSING A NEWSGROUP

Your Internet service provider subscribes to a number of newsgroups from which you can choose one or more that you would like to read. To get a list of the newsgroups from which you can choose, follow the steps in Table 8-2.

Table 8-2   How to Choose a Newsgroup

Netscape Communicator	Microsoft Internet Explorer
▶ Pull down the Communicator menu and choose Collabra Discussion Groups; the Netscape Message Center appears, as shown in Figure 8-5.	▶ In order to select a newsgroup, you need to make Outlook Express list the names of the available newsgroups. If you just ran the Internet Connection Wizard in the previous section of this chapter, the list is already on your screen; proceed to the next step. Otherwise, in Outlook Express, click the 🌐 icon next to the name of your news server in the left-hand column. This will change the menu, as shown in Figure 8-7. Select News Groups.

Figure 8-5 The Netscape Message Center.

▶ 📧 Click the Subscribe button; the Subscribe to Discussion Groups dialog appears. At the bottom of the dialog you will see the status as Netscape reads the list of newsgroups available at your ISP.

▶ When the list has finished loading, you can scroll through it to find a newsgroup you like. You'll see both newsgroups and folders, as illustrated in Figure 8-6. You can click the plus signs to reveal newsgroups in different categories. To expose everything, click the Expand All button. To collapse a category, click a minus sign. To collapse everything, click the Collapse All button.

▶ To subscribe to a newsgroup, click the name of the newsgroup to select it, then click the Subscribe button.

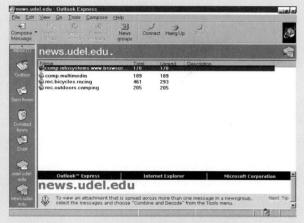

Figure 8-7 Outlook Express displays the news server menu.

▶ Outlook Express will download all of the available newsgroups and display them for you, as illustrated in Figure 8-8.

▶ To subscribe to a group, select it by clicking on it, and then click Subscribe.

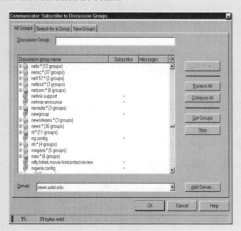

Figure 8-6 Netscape displays the list of available newsgroups.

▶ If you are already subscribed to a group, you can unsubscribe by clicking on its name to select it, then click Unsubscribe.

▶ To subscribe to a group you already know the name of, start typing the name of the group, and the list will shrink. When you see the newsgroup you want, select it by clicking on it, then click Subscribe.

▶ You can also search for newsgroups by key word. If you want to do this, click the Search for a Group tab, enter your key word(s) in the Search for field, and click the Search Now button.

▶ Click OK when you're done choosing newsgroups.

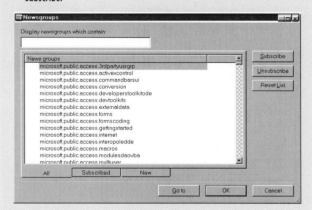

Figure 8-8 Outlook Express displays the list of available newsgroups.

▶ You can narrow the list by entering a subject in the box labeled *Display newsgroups which contain*. To get the full list back, just delete the word you entered.

▶ If you want to unsubscribe from a group, you can select it from this list and click Unsubscribe.

▶ To subscribe to a group you already know the name of, start typing the name of the group, and the list will shrink. When you see the one you want, select it by clicking on it, and then click Subscribe.

▶ Click OK when you're done choosing newsgroups.

In the list of newsgroups, you will see how the names of newsgroups are grouped by title using compound names such as rec.sport.basketball.college. Here, *rec* specifies recreational topics, *sport* specifies a subgroup of recreation, and so on.

READING A NEWSGROUP

Newsgroups are threaded. Each thread represents a different topic being discussed in the newsgroup. To read a newsgroup, you point and click on the topics and subtopics to navigate to the part of the newsgroup you want to read. Both Netscape Communicator and the Microsoft Internet Explorer keep track of what topics you have and have not read, so it's easy to tell whether you've already visited part of the newsgroup. It's also possible to display only new messages written to the newsgroup since the last time you read news. To read messages in a newsgroup, follow the steps in Table 8-3.

Table 8-3   How to Read a Newsgroup

Netscape Communicator	Microsoft Internet Explorer
▶ If the Message Center is not already on your screen, pull down the Netscape Communicator menu and choose Collabra Discussion Groups; the Netscape Message Center appears.	▶ In Outlook Express, click the Newsgroups icon to reveal the list of newsgroups to which you are subscribed.
▶ In the directory listing, double-click the News icon or the name of your news server to reveal the list of newsgroups to which you are subscribed.	▶ Double-click the name of the newsgroup you want to read. If the name of the newsgroup you want is not listed, follow the instructions in Table 8-2, which tells how to choose a newsgroup.
▶ Double-click the name of the newsgroup you want to read. If the name of the newsgroup you want is not listed, follow the instructions in Table 8-2, which tells how to choose a newsgroup.	▶ Your computer will contact your ISP and download a directory of the messages in the newsgroup; then the directory of messages will appear on screen.
▶ Your computer will contact your ISP and download a directory of the messages in the newsgroup; then the directory of messages will appear on screen.	▶ If a message has a plus sign alongside it, that means the message has a hierarchy of other messages beneath it; click the plus sign to reveal the hierarchy. Click the minus sign if you want to collapse the hierarchy.
▶ If a message has a plus sign alongside it, that means the message has a hierarchy of other messages beneath it; click the plus sign to reveal the hierarchy. Click the minus sign if you want to collapse the hierarchy.	▶ New messages that you haven't read yet will be printed in bold. To read a message, double-click it. Outlook Express will download the message and display it in a message window.
▶ New messages that you haven't read yet will be printed in bold. To read a message, double-click its title. Netscape will download the message and display it in a message window.	▶ To read the next message in the newsgroup, click the Next button.
▶ To read the next message in the newsgroup, click the Next button; if there are no more unread messages, the Next button will be inactive. For other options, right-click the Next button.	▶ To read the previous message, click the Previous button.
▶ Close the message window when you're done reading the message.	▶ Close the message window when you're done reading the message.
▶ To read another message in the newsgroup, double-click the title of the message you want to read.	▶ To read another message in the newsgroup, double-click the message title.
▶ To help you find your way through the newsgroup, Netscape lets you sort the messages in a variety of ways, as shown in Figure 8-9. To sort by subject, click the Subject button; to sort by the sender, click the Sender button; to sort by date, click the Date button.	▶ To help you find your way through the newsgroup, Outlook Express lets you sort the messages in a variety of ways, as shown in Figure 8-10. To sort by subject, click the Subject button; to sort by who sent the message, click the From button; to sort by date, click the Date button.

Click here
to sort by
the name of
the sender

Click here
to sort the
newsgroup
by date

Click here
to sort
according
to priority

Click here to reveal the
hierarchical structure of
the newsgroup

The plus sign means you can
click here to reveal additional
items under this one

Click a minus sign
to collapse the
directory listing

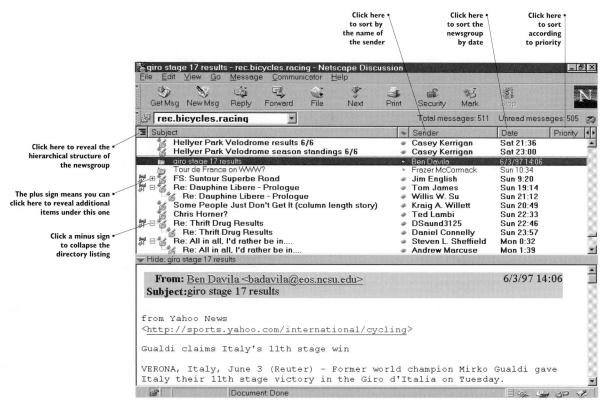

Figure 8-9 How Netscape Communicator lets you sort newsgroup messages.

Click here
to sort by
the name of
the sender

Click here
to sort the
newsgroup
by date

Click here
to sort by
file size

Click a minus sign
to collapse the
directory listing

The plus sign means you can
click here to reveal additional
items under this one

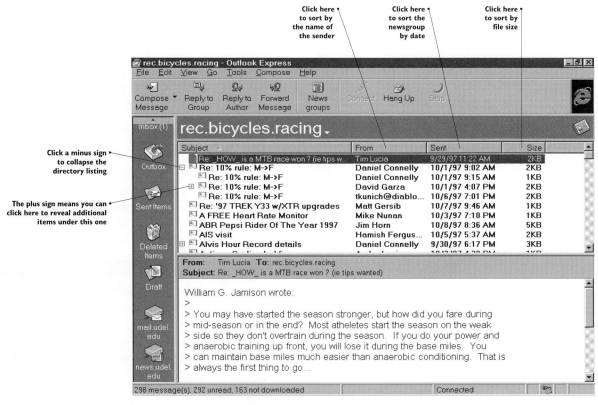

Figure 8-10 How Outlook Express lets you sort newsgroup messages.

RESPONDING TO A NEWSGROUP

Responding to a newsgroup is a lot like responding to an e-mail message. The main difference is that instead of being sent to an individual, your response gets posted to the newsgroup. Some newsgroups are moderated, meaning that someone looks over the messages you send to the newsgroup and makes sure the messages fit the purpose of the newsgroup before they get posted to the newsgroup. Many newsgroups are unmoderated, meaning that users can freely write messages without any form of review or censorship.

The rules of Netiquette dictate that when you are first learning how to use newsgroups, you should write your test messages in the newsgroup news.test. Subscribe to news.test now. If you have trouble, refer to the instructions in Table 8-2.

To learn how to respond to a message written in a newsgroup, follow the steps in Table 8-4.

Table 8-4 How to Respond to a Message in a Newsgroup

Netscape Communicator	Microsoft Internet Explorer
▶ While reading the message in the newsgroup to which you want to respond, click the Reply button.	▶ While reading the message in the newsgroup to which you want to respond, click the Reply to Group button. If you just want to reply to the author, click the Reply to Author button.
▶ A popout menu appears letting you choose to:	▶ The mail composition window appears with a blank message automatically addressed to the newsgroup.
▶ Post a Reply to the Newsgroup	▶ Complete the message as if you were creating an e-mail message.
▶ Reply Only to the Sender	▶ Click the Post Message button to send the message.
▶ Post a Reply to the Newsgroup and to the Sender	
▶ Reply to the Sender and the Recipients	
▶ When you choose how to reply, a Netscape Composition window appears with a blank message automatically addressed.	
▶ Complete the message as if you were creating an e-mail message.	
▶ Click the Send button to send the message.	

CREATING A NEW TOPIC IN A NEWSGROUP

While participating in a newsgroup, you may want to start a conversation on a new topic. To create a new topic in a newsgroup, follow the steps in Table 8-5.

Table 8-5 How to Create a New Topic in a Newsgroup

Netscape Communicator	Microsoft Internet Explorer
▶ Enter the newsgroup in which you want to create a new topic of conversation. (The first three steps of Table 8-3 told how to enter a newsgroup.)	▶ Enter the newsgroup in which you want to create a new topic of conversation. (The first three steps of Table 8-3 told how to enter a newsgroup.)
▶ Click the New Msg button; a Netscape Composition window opens with a blank message automatically addressed to the newsgroup.	▶ Click the Compose Message button; a composition window opens with a blank message automatically addressed to the newsgroup.
▶ Complete the message as if you were sending e-mail.	▶ Complete the message as if you were sending e-mail.
▶ Click the Send button to send the message.	▶ Click the Post Message button to send the message.

The next time you read the newsgroup, you should find your new topic listed in the newsgroup's hierarchy. If your topic is not there yet, it is possible that the server has not yet processed it, or in the case of a moderated newsgroup, the newsgroup's owner may have disallowed the topic. Netiquette calls for the newsgroup's moderator to send you an e-mail message if your posting gets rejected, to let you know why your message was not accepted into the newsgroup.

DELETING A MESSAGE FROM A NEWSGROUP

Two rules govern the deleting of messages from a newsgroup. First, you can only delete messages that you write. You cannot delete messages written by other users. Second, you should only delete messages to which no one has responded yet. If another user has written a reply in the newsgroup to one of your messages, deleting your message will interrupt the flow of the conversation. To delete a message in a newsgroup, follow the steps in Table 8-6.

Table 8-6   How to Delete a Message in a Newsgroup

Netscape Communicator	Microsoft Internet Explorer
▶ Enter the newsgroup in which you want to delete a message.	▶ Enter the newsgroup in which you want to delete a message.
▶ In the hierarchical listing of messages in the newsgroup, select the message you want to delete by clicking it once.	▶ In the hierarchical listing of messages in the newsgroup, select the message you want to delete by clicking it once.
▶ Press the Delete key on your computer keyboard, or pull down the Edit menu and choose Cancel Message.	▶ Pull down the Compose menu and choose Cancel Message. This option will only be active if you are the author of the message.
▶ If Netscape cannot delete the message, you will be told why not; otherwise, the message will be deleted from the newsgroup.	▶ If Outlook Express cannot delete the message, you will be told why not; otherwise, the message will be deleted from the newsgroup.

Be aware that when you delete a message from a public newsgroup, this won't necessarily prevent it from going around the world, because newsgroups get copied from node to node as they make their way over the Internet. When you delete a message, it gets deleted from your ISP's copy of the newsgroup, but that may be too late to keep it from going around the world. Your cancel message will go around the world to the servers that received it, but some servers do not honor cancel messages, because some people have abused them by canceling other people's messages.

FINDING NEWSGROUPS IN YOUR PROFESSION

CYBERFIBER® NEWSGROUPS

If you follow the links to CyberFiber at the Interlit Web site, you'll get a comprehensive listing of Usenet newsgroups. Click the subject you're interested in, and an outline of the newsgroups devoted to that topic will appear. To join a newsgroup, just click it, and your Web browser will automatically subscribe you and take you there.

Another way to find out about newsgroups in your profession is to use the DejaNews search engine, which can perform full-text searches of the Internet's newsgroups. Chapter 11 provides detailed information on how to use DejaNews to find out about information written in newsgroups. When you find the information you're looking for, DejaNews will identify the name of the newsgroup it came from. Then you can subscribe to that newsgroup to explore more of the information it contains. As illustrated in Figure 8-11, DejaNews rank-orders the newsgroups it finds according to how confident it is that what was found will fit your interests.

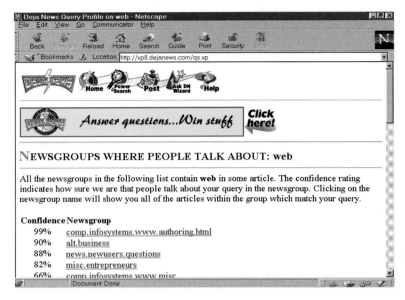

Figure 8-11 You can do a key word search for newsgroups on any topic at http://www.dejanews.com.

E X E R C I S E S

1. Subscribe to the newsgroups news.newusers.questions and news.announce.newusers and read the articles you will find there to learn about newsgroup technique and Netiquette before you begin posting your own messages to any newsgroups. If you have trouble using newsgroups, you can ask questions in news.newusers.questions, but read the introduction first before you write messages of your own.

2. Browse to http://www.cen.uiuc.edu/cgi-bin/find-news and perform a search of newsgroups based on topics that interest you. If you're a student, search topics dealing with your major program of study. If you're employed, search on topics related to your line of work. Subscribe to three of the newsgroups and lurk in them for a while. Remember that before you begin to participate in a newsgroup, you should first read a representative selection of articles for a few days before posting your own messages. Your chosen newsgroup may have its own set of accepted guidelines for what constitutes an appropriate posting; you should study those guidelines before posting messages. If you are unable to subscribe to the newsgroup, the reason may be that your ISP does not support it. Ask your ISP to help you subscribe to it.

3. Of the three newsgroups you joined in exercise 2, which one is most valuable? Why?

4. Following the instructions in Table 8-4, write a response to one of the topics that already exist in your favorite newsgroup. An hour or so later, go back into the newsgroup to find out if your message now appears there for the entire world to see. Since the whole world can see your message, make sure it makes sense in the context of the topic you write it on.

5. Following the instructions in Table 8-5, create a new topic in the newsgroup of your choice. Sometime later, go back into the newsgroup to find out if your new topic now appears in the newsgroup's hierarchical listing of topics. Since the whole world can see your new topic, make sure the topic and the message you wrote to initiate it make sense in the context of the conversation going on in the newsgroup.

6. Remember that anything you write in a newsgroup will probably remain on the Internet forever. Never write anything in a newsgroup that may embarrass you later on. In Chapter 11, you will learn how prospective employers can use DejaNews to search newsgroups for things written by job applicants. Writing stupid stuff in newsgroups now could reduce your chance of getting a good job later on.

9 Communicating in Real Time

After completing this chapter, you will be able to:

- **Understand how Internet Relay Chat (IRC) organizes conversations into channels.**

- **Download an IRC chat-room client and install it on your computer.**

- **Enter chat rooms on the Internet and engage other users in meaningful real-time conversations over IRC channels.**

- **Download Microsoft's NetMeeting software and use it to share data and make entries on a whiteboard shared with conference members over the Internet.**

- **Learn how to equip your PC for videoconferencing for as little as $249.**

- **Look in on videoconferences hosted on CU-SeeMe sites on the Internet, whether or not you have videoconferencing hardware.**

- **Understand the purposes of and the distinctions between a MUD, a MOO, and a MUSH.**

- **Experience real-time audio/video streaming technology that will one day permit chat rooms to be multimedia encounters.**

-MAIL, listserv, and newsgroups are great ways to communicate, but all three suffer from the lack of real-time interaction between you and the person with whom you're communicating. Historically, real-time communication has occurred either in face-to-face conversation or over the telephone. Now it is also possible to converse in real time over the Internet. If the person you're talking to has a video capture card, you can even see the other person on screen.

This chapter covers four kinds of environments used to communicate in real time over the Internet: chat rooms, whiteboards, videoconferencing, and MUDs (Multi User Dimension).

ONLINE CHAT

Chat rooms offered by online services such as America Online and CompuServe are becoming increasingly popular. Chat rooms are places on the Internet where you can go to talk with other users in real time. Following the metaphor for which this technology is named, you imagine yourself entering a room in which you can converse with other users you will find there. You can see on screen what each user is typing into the conversation, and when you type something, the other users in the room can see your message as well.

Internet Relay Chat (IRC)

The most prevalent chat-room technology is called Internet Relay Chat (IRC), which consists of several networks of IRC servers that support chat on the Internet. The largest IRC networks are EFnet (the original IRC net, often having more than 15,000 people chatting at once), Undernet, IRCnet, DALnet, and NewNet.

In order to connect to an IRC server, you must run an IRC client program. The two most popular clients for Windows are mIRC and PIRCH. On the Macintosh, the IRC clients are Ircle and MacIRC. Figures 9-1 and 9-2 provide a side-by-side comparison of the mIRC and MacIRC chat clients. You can download the client of your choice by following the links to IRC at the Interlit Web site. It's also possible to enter IRC chat rooms through Web pages containing Java-based IRC clients. Figure 9-3 shows a Web page on which an IRC chat is in progress.

IRC conversations are organized into channels. You can join one or more communication channels and converse with other users who are subscribed to the same channel. On EFnet, there often are more than 5,000 channels. Conversations may be public, allowing everyone in a channel to see what you type, or private between only two people, who may or may not be on the same channel.

IRC is not a game. The users you will meet there are real people, and you should treat them with the same courtesy as if you were talking to them in person. You should be aware that it is possible, however, for robots to enter chat rooms and lead you to believe they are human.

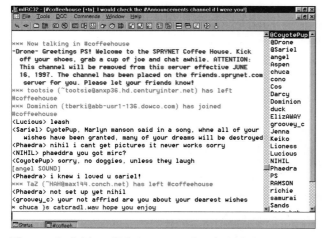

Figure 9-1 The mIRC chat-room client for Windows.

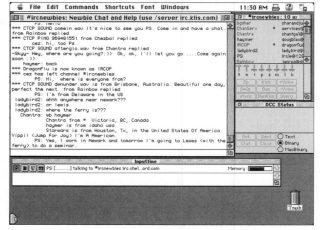

Figure 9-2 The MacIRC chat-room client for the Macintosh.

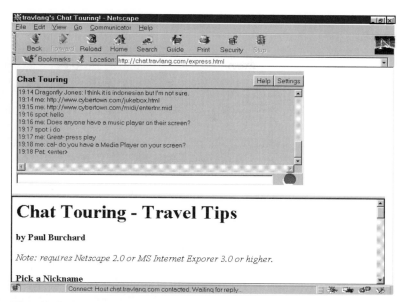

Figure 9-3 An IRC chat in progress on a Web page.

On the Web, there is an IRC Help site. One of its subsites is an IRC Prelude site for people new to chat rooms. Before you begin using Internet Relay Chat, you should follow the links to the IRC Help site and the IRC Prelude site and learn the rules of the road and the principles of IRC Netiquette you will find there.

Avatar-Based Chat

As you learned in Chapter 5, an avatar is an icon or representation of a user in a shared virtual reality. In avatar-based chat, you take on the identity of a graphical character in a 3-D world. As with text-based chat, you type to communicate, but you can also use your mouse to move your character around in a virtual universe. Two examples of avatar-based chat you'll find linked to the Interlit Web site include The Palace and Microsoft Chat. Figures 9-4 and 9-5 show avatar-based chats in progress.

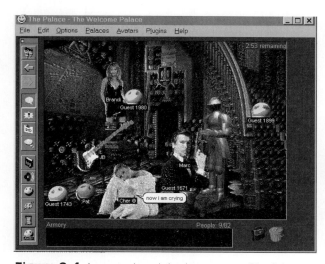

Figure 9-4 An avatar-based chat in progress at The Palace.

Figure 9-5 The Microsoft Chat site in action.

WHITEBOARDS

It's not always enough just to see what the other users are typing in a conversation. Sometimes you want to see other information that's on their screen as well. For example, a group of professionals collaborating on an economic model might want the conversants to be able to see a spreadsheet, play what-if games, and work together to evolve the best business plan. Distance-learning students collaborating on a scientific research project could similarly benefit from being able to contribute data from remote locations and view the results on a screen shared across the network. A computer program that enables remote users to share a common screen across the network is called **whiteboard** software.

NetMeeting

Microsoft's NetMeeting is a real-time communications client that supports multiuser conferencing and application sharing over the Internet. In addition to allowing users to chat with one another as in a chat room, NetMeeting also supports the sharing of voice, data, and computer files. Figure 9-6 shows how NetMeeting's whiteboard gives the conference members a common scratchpad to write on and share ideas. Figure 9-7 shows users collaborating on information in a spreadsheet. It's also possible to do videoconferencing with NetMeeting.

Best of all, NetMeeting is free. You can download it by clicking the NetMeeting icon at the Interlit Web site.

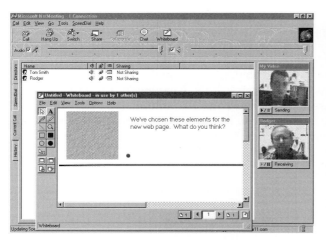

Figure 9-6 Microsoft's NetMeeting software has a whiteboard feature that lets conference members write on and exchange ideas on a common scratchpad.

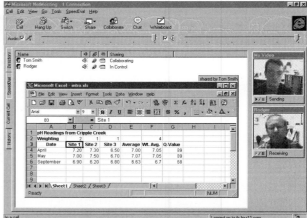

Figure 9-7 NetMeeting allows users to collaborate by sharing applications across the network.

VIDEOCONFERENCING

Videoconferencing enables you to see and hear the people you are conversing with over the Internet. Each person's PC has a video camera and a microphone attached to video and audio adapters that digitize what the camera sees and the microphone hears. Since digital video transmissions contain many more bits of information than textual communications, you need a faster connection to the Internet for video than is required for text. There is a lot of research and development being done on compressing video to make it require less bandwidth, however, and hopefully videoconferencing will become more widespread when the cost of transmitting it decreases.

Videoconferencing Hardware

The cost of equipping a multimedia PC for videoconferencing has dropped to less than $250, thanks to the availability of cameras with built-in computer interfaces. Figure 9-8 shows such a setup that uses the Color QuickCam, which has been recommended by *c|net* as the best-valued camera for videoconferencing, voted Best of What's New by the editors of *Popular Science* magazine, and awarded *NetGuide's* Best Internet Peripheral award. Instead of requiring an expensive video board to be added to your computer, Color QuickCam attaches to your computer's parallel port. And it works with Microsoft's NetMeeting software. For more information, follow the links to "Connectix" at the Interlit Web site.

CU-SeeMe

One of the first videoconferencing applications on the Internet is CU-SeeMe. CU stands for Cornell University, where the software was developed. CU-SeeMe 3.0 Video Chat Software has a directory for locating other CU-SeeMe users, 12 of whom can be viewed on screen simultaneously. To conserve bandwidth, you push a button in the software when you want to talk, and your video camera transmits a live picture to the other users. Figure 9-9 shows a CU-SeeMe videoconference in which five persons are on camera.

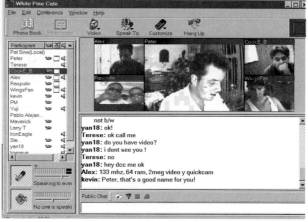

Figure 9-8 A multimedia PC equipped for videoconferencing by way of a $250 color camera with a built-in computer interface.

Figure 9-9 A CU-SeeMe videoconference in progress. Five of the people in the conference are on camera.

Because video is high-bandwidth, CU-SeeMe uses a network of Internet reflector sites that handle routing and trafficking problems. The frame rate depends on traffic, and rarely do you get the smooth, full-motion video you're used to on TV, but a new frame comes often enough to give you a good idea of the other person's appearance and body language.

To learn more, follow the links to CU-SeeMe at the Interlit Web site, or to check out the commercial version, follow the links to "White Pine Software."

Intel ProShare

Intel's ProShare lets anyone with a Pentium-based PC make person-to-person video phone calls over standard telephone lines. Intel is bringing the ProShare technology to the Internet with a product called Intel Internet Video Phone. After you register with one of the Internet white pages directory services, you can make and receive calls with other people currently connected to the Internet. The Intel Internet Video Phone is one of the first products to support the new H.323 video telephony standard for placing video phone calls over computer networks. If you purchase a video telephony product, you should make sure it's H.323 compliant. For more information, follow the Interlit Web site links to "Intel Internet Video Phone" and the H.323 video telephony standard.

MUDs, MOOs, AND MUSHes

The term MUD has evolved from its earlier game-related meaning of Multi User Dungeon to the more general concept of a Multi User Dimension. MUDs are synchronous multiuser communication environments that enable participants to take on a persona and create virtual worlds out of their own imaginations. In other words, you invent a character (which could be yourself) and interact with the characters created by other users you will encounter in the MUD. MUDs are anonymous, meaning that you cannot know for sure who owns the characters you will encounter. Thus, MUDs provide environments for playing out fantasies that you could never enact in real life. As in chat rooms, you communicate by typing, creating a textual world. The major advantage of a MUD over a chat room is that the participants have a chance to build a virtual world in which the location, participants, and objects in the environment can all be described, visited, and interacted with.

MUSH stands for Multi User Shared Hallucination. The acronym MUSH was chosen because this kind of environment is thought to be more squishy than a MUD. MUSHes are situated MUDs used for role-playing games that simulate worlds from books and movies or completely original environments.

MOO stands for MUD, Object-Oriented. The term object-oriented refers to a style of programming in which applications are constructed from reusable code segments known as objects that several programs can share. MOOs enable users to share code segments from one another's characters.

From a technical standpoint, MUDs, MOOs, and MUSHes are programs that run on one of the servers connected to the Internet. You enter the multiuser environment via the Internet's telnet protocol, which enables you to log on to the server that hosts the MUD. You will learn how to use telnet in Chapter 10. There are also MUD clients, such as zMUD, which establish the telnet session for you and provide pull-down menus containing features that make it easier to use the MUD. For example, Figure 9-10 shows how zMUD lets you record the path to a location in the MUD. In subsequent sessions, you can use that path to return to the location automatically, instead of having to navigate there step by step again.

Because MUDs, MOOs, and MUSHes originated in game-playing, many schools prohibit their use during peak operating hours. Academic work is beginning to be done in MUDs and MOOs, however, as educators discover their potential for distance education, cooperative learning, and collaboration.

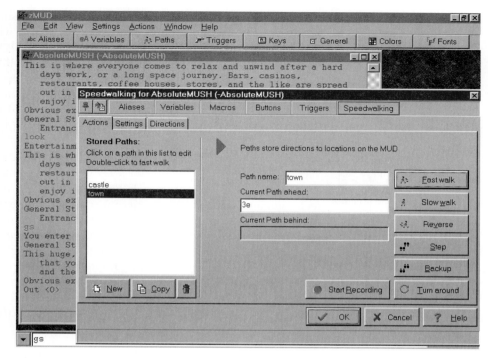

Figure 9-10 zMUD enables you to record paths to locations in MUDs.

To learn more about MUDs, MOOs, and MUSHes, follow the links at the Interlit Web site. "Ventana's Internet Virtual Worlds Quick Tour Online Companion" links to a number of MOOs and MUDs on the Internet. See also the societal issues discussion in Chapter 25 about how stalking and unwanted sexual advances can occur in MUDs.

STREAMING AUDIO AND VIDEO

As you will learn in Chapter 26, on emerging technology, a lot of research and development is underway to increase bandwidth and decrease the size of audio/video transmissions so more audio and video can be used in real-time conversations over the Net. Some streaming audio/video products already on the market are discussed here.

RealAudio and RealVideo

RealAudio and RealVideo are technologies that enable the Internet to transmit real-time audio/video streams. RealAudio transmits audio only, while RealVideo transmits both audio and video simultaneously. Because RealAudio and RealVideo are not interactive, they probably don't really belong in this chapter, but they're being mentioned here so you can get some experience with the progress researchers are making in figuring out how to compress real-time audio/video streams so that the Internet can handle them. Someday, these real-time audio/video technologies will probably become an everyday feature of multiuser communications on the Internet.

If you have a multimedia PC and would like to hear some RealAudio, follow the RealAudio links at the Interlit Web site. There you will find a broad range of RealAudio channels that you can hear. To see some RealVideo, follow the RealVideo links. Be sure to watch the short film by Spike Lee. If your computer does not already have the RealPlayer installed, you will first need to download and install the RealPlayer, which is the plug-in that handles RealAudio and RealVideo. To download the RealPlayer, follow the download link in the "RealPlayer" section of the Interlit Web site.

StreamWorks

Xing Technology Corporation is another leader in audio/video compression technologies that may one day permit real-time interactive communication over the Web. Xing's compression engine is called StreamWorks, which can deliver real-time and on-demand audio/video streams over the Internet and other networks. NBC and Reuters news services are using StreamWorks to Webcast financial news programming. Xing hopes to enable Internet service providers to get into the cable TV business via the Web. To learn more about Xing, follow the links to "Xing" at the Interlit Web site, which enables you to download the StreamWorks player and tune in to streaming audio/video programs listed in Xing's current programming guide.

VDOLive and VDOPhone

VDOnet Corporation is another source of real-time technologies for the Internet. Its investors include Microsoft Corporation, U S WEST Media Group, NYNEX, and Battery Ventures. VDOLive is one of the leading Internet video broadcasting solutions used by hundreds of companies around the world, including CBS News, CBC, MTV, PBS, Preview Media, and many corporate Intranet users. The award-winning VDOPhone is a full-color video telephone for either the Internet or regular phone lines. VDOPhone is available both as a standalone commercial product and bundled with products offered by Packard Bell and Diamond Multimedia. For more information, follow the links to VDOLive and VDOPhone at the Interlit Web site.

EXERCISES

1. Go to the Interlit Web site, click the IRC Prelude icon, and familiarize yourself with Internet Relay Chat terminology and Netiquette. This will prepare you for the next exercise.

2. Click the IRC icon at the Interlit Web site, and download the IRC client appropriate for your computer. Run the client, connect to an IRC server, list the channels of conversation, and pick one that interests you. Lurk until you get used to the conversation that is in progress. Then join in and participate. How does this form of communication differ from face-to-face communication? What are the advantages and disadvantages of IRC as compared to face-to-face communication?

3. Click the NetMeeting icon at the Interlit Web site, and download Microsoft's NetMeeting software. Use it to conference with one of your fellow classmates or coworkers. What do you see as the advantages of the NetMeeting software? Are there any disadvantages?

4. Click the CU-SeeMe icon at the Interlit Web site and go to one of the CU-SeeMe sites. Depending on Internet traffic and the speed of your Internet connection, the quality of the video you get may vary. Do you see a smooth video stream, or is it jerky? About how often would you say the frame rate is refreshing? (For comparison purposes, the frame rate of a television program on American TV is 30 frames per second.)

5. If your computer is equipped with a video camera and computer interface, join one of the CU-SeeMe conferences, and ask your fellow conversants how well they can see you. Does being on camera cause you to want to alter or improve your appearance in any way?

6. Go to the RealAudio site at www.real.com and download and install the RealPlayer. Then select one of the RealAudio sites, such as National Public Radio (NPR). What do you think about the quality of the audio? Does it meet your expectations?

7. Go to the RealVideo site at www.real.com. You will need at least a 28.8 Kbps modem in order to receive RealVideo. If you have not already downloaded and installed the RealPlayer, do so now. Then select one of the RealVideo sites, such as the Spike Lee videos. What do you think about the quality of the video you see? How does it need to be improved? What is the significance of the Internet's ability to host real-time video streams like this? What might be the implications of RealVideo technology for the future of television?

8. Go to the Xing Technology Corporation site at www.xingtech.com. Is StreamWorks being used in new applications or industries that were not mentioned in this chapter? If so, describe how Xing is branching out to apply real-time audio/video streaming to new communities of users on the Internet.

10 Telnet

After completing this chapter, you will be able to:

- **Use telnet to connect to remote host computers on the Internet.**

- **Configure your Web browser to launch telnet sessions.**

- **Understand how telnet helps you avoid paying long-distance telephone charges when you connect to remote host computers in other cities or countries.**

- **Find and connect to remote host computers that provide useful Internet resources via telnet.**

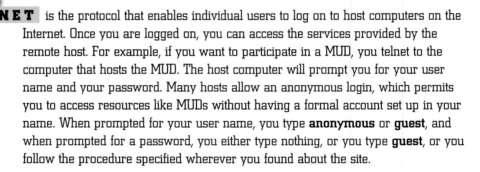 **ELNET** is the protocol that enables individual users to log on to host computers on the Internet. Once you are logged on, you can access the services provided by the remote host. For example, if you want to participate in a MUD, you telnet to the computer that hosts the MUD. The host computer will prompt you for your user name and your password. Many hosts allow an anonymous login, which permits you to access resources like MUDs without having a formal account set up in your name. When prompted for your user name, you type **anonymous** or **guest**, and when prompted for a password, you either type nothing, or you type **guest**, or you follow the procedure specified wherever you found about the site.

Telnet can save money on long-distance telephone charges. Suppose you live in Philadelphia, and you want to join a MUD hosted on a computer in Los Angeles. Instead of dialing up to the remote host in Los Angeles, you can telnet there instead to avoid the cost of the long-distance telephone call. You pay only for your existing Internet connection that you got from your Internet service provider.

RUNNING A TELNET CLIENT

The software that enables your computer to telnet to other computers on the Internet is known as a telnet client. Your computer may already have a telnet client program installed on it. For example, all Windows 95 users have a telnet client program called *telnet.exe*. To run it, you click the Start button, choose Run, type **telnet** and press ⌷Enter⌷. If your computer does not have a telnet client, contact your ISP, who should be able to tell you how to get a telnet client for your computer at little or no cost. If you have a Macintosh, for example, you can download the

NCSA Telnet client for free by following the Interlit Web site links to NCSA Telnet. If you have Windows 3.1, you can download the Ewan telnet client by following the Ewan links at the Interlit Web site.

TELNETTING TO REMOTE HOST COMPUTERS

Once you have the telnet client running on your computer, you can telnet to any other computer on the Internet. All you need to know is the computer's IP address or domain name. If the remote host does not support anonymous login, you will also need an account (i.e., user name) and password to log on.

For example, suppose you want to telnet to the Cleveland FreeNet and explore the resources available there. Follow the steps in Table 10-1.

Table 10-1   How to Telnet to the Cleveland FreeNet

Windows	Macintosh
▶ Get your telnet software running. If you have Windows 95, for example click the Start button, choose Run, type **telnet**, and press ⌈Enter⌋.	▶ Double-click the icon of your telnet software to launch it. If the icon isn't visible, refer to Table 13-5 for help running a program when you can't see its icon.
▶ In your telnet software, look for a menu choice that enables you to connect to a remote host. If you have the Microsoft Telnet client, for example, pull down the Connect menu, and choose Remote System; the Connect dialog appears as shown in Figure 10-1.	▶ In your telnet software, look for a menu choice that enables you to connect to a remote host. If you have the NCSA Telnet client, for example, pull down the File menu, and choose Open Connection; the Open Connection dialog appears as shown in Figure 10-2.

Figure 10-1 The Microsoft Telnet program's Connect dialog.

Figure 10-2 The NCSA Telnet program's Open Connection dialog.

Windows	Macintosh
▶ In the Host Name field, type the IP address or the domain name of the computer to which you want to connect. In this example, type **freenet-in-c.cwru.edu**	▶ In the Host/Session field, type the IP address or the domain name of the computer to which you want to connect. In this example, type **freenet-in-c.cwru.edu**
▶ Leave the Port field set to telnet, and leave the Term Type field set to vt100. (Term Type stands for Terminal Type, and vt100 stands for Video Terminal 100, which is the most prevalent terminal standard on the Internet.)	▶ You can enter a name for the window or leave it blank. Leave the Terminal field set at <default>.
▶ Click the Connect button to connect to the remote host.	▶ Click the Connect button to connect to the remote host.
▶ When the remote host responds, it will provide instructions telling how to proceed.	▶ When the remote host responds, it will provide instructions telling how to proceed.

ACCESSING REMOTE RESOURCES

There's a broad range of resources available via telnet. For example, you can telnet to the national weather underground at rainmaker.wunderground.com to find out about the weather. There's an InterNIC telnet site at ds.internic.net where you can look up the e-mail addresses of people on the Net. At the Geographic Name Server at martini.eecs.umich.edu, you can find out demographic information about cities that interest you.

As the Web increases in popularity, however, telnet is becoming less important as a way to find information, because it's easier to query databases using graphical tools on the Web than it is to type commands at a telnet prompt. Nevertheless, telnet remains an essential Internet resource, especially for programmers and developers who use telnet to log on remotely and perform operational tasks needed to manage Web sites and keep servers running properly.

SETTING THE LOCAL ECHO OPTION

When you visit a telnet site, it's possible that you might not see printing on your screen when you type keys on your computer keyboard. This happens when telnet sites do not echo the keys you type. To solve this problem, pull down your telnet client's Preferences or Settings menu, and choose the Local Echo option.

TELNETTING FROM THE WEB

It's possible to launch telnet sessions from the Web. If an item linked to a Web page begins with *telnet:* instead of with *http:*, your Web browser will attempt to launch a telnet session. To demonstrate this, the telnet section of the Interlit Web site contains a table full of useful telnet links. Each resource is linked to a URL beginning with *telnet.* For example, the Columbia University Lawnet item is linked to the URL telnet:// lawnet.law.columbia.edu. Clicking Columbia University Lawnet will make your Web browser launch a telnet session to lawnet.law.columbia.edu. If you're using Netscape Navigator, and your Web browser tells you that it cannot launch the telnet session, follow the steps in Table 10-2 to configure your browser for telnetting.

FREEING UP THE REMOTE CONNECTION

When you are finished using the remote computer, you should close your telnet connection to free up resources for other users who may want to connect there. To close a telnet session, type **logout** (or **quit**, **exit**, or **bye**, depending on the conventions followed at the telnet host) and press ⎡Enter⎤.

Table 10-2 Configuring Netscape Navigator for Telnet

▶ Pull down the Edit menu, choose Preferences, and under Navigator, choose Applications; the helper Applications list box appears as shown in Figure 10-3.

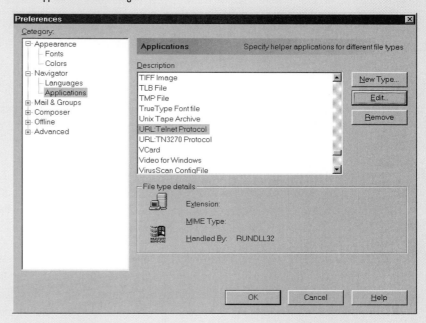

Figure 10-3 The Supporting Applications tab of the Preferences dialog.

▶ In the list box, scroll down to *URL: telnet protocol.* Click once on the telnet protocol to select it, then click the Edit button to make the Edit Type dialog appear, as shown in Figure 10-4.

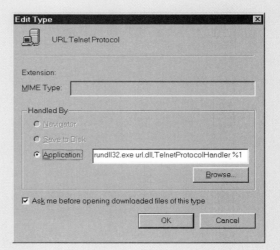

Figure 10-4 The Edit Type dialog.

▶ Click the Browse button, and browse to your telnet program. If you have Windows 95, for example, you'll find *telnet.exe* in your windows folder. Click Open to select the telnet program.

▶ The complete path/filename of the telnet program now appears in the Telnet field. Click OK to close the Edit Type dialog, then click OK to close the Preferences dialog.

▶ From now on, whenever Netscape encounters a telnet address, it will launch your telnet program and connect you to the remote host computer at the telnet address.

E X E R C I S E S

1. If your computer does not already have a telnet client installed, download one from the Interlit Web site. Remember that if you have Windows 95, you already have the Microsoft Telnet client, which is called *telnet.exe*.

2. Use your telnet client to telnet to the following remote host:

   rainmaker.wunderground.com

This host does not echo the keys you type on your computer keyboard. Pull down your telnet program's Terminal menu, choose Preferences, turn on the Local Echo option, and click OK. Explore the menu options that the Rainmaker site will provide, and see what you can find out about your weather conditions. Are there any earthquakes happening in the world today?

3. Click the Telnet icon at the Interlit Web site to go to an index of telnet sites. Click the site of your choice, and explore the resources you find there. If your Web browser tells you it doesn't know how to handle telnet, follow the steps in Table 10-2, which shows how to configure your Web browser to launch telnet sessions.

4. Using telnet enables you to avoid long-distance telephone charges that you would otherwise have to pay in order to connect to a remote host computer. Do you think it is fair to the telephone companies that the Internet enables you to avoid paying long-distance charges? Why do you feel this way? In some states, ISPs are being taxed to make up for the loss of revenues that the state formerly collected from taxing long-distance telephone companies.

Part Four

Finding Things on the Internet

The Internet is the richest source of information on the planet. Just about anything you could ever want to know is available online. Especially for students and scholars conducting research, the Internet is a fantastic resource for finding out what's been done in your field. This part of the book focuses on helping you find things on the Internet.

11 Searching for Information

After completing this chapter, you will be able to:

- Conduct subject-oriented searches using Yahoo, Magellan, and Lycos A2Z.

- Perform full-text key word searches using AltaVista, Excite, InfoSeek, and Lycos.

- Use the advanced search syntax to find what you're looking for efficiently.

- Perform concept searches based on ideas instead of specific key words.

- Use metasearching to search several search engines at once.

- Know how to get online help from human beings you can pay to conduct searches on your behalf.

- Conduct scholarly searches across a broad range of academic disciplines.

- Use multimedia search engines to find pictures, audio, and video, in addition to text.

- Search Usenet newsgroups to find information in discussions of current research topics.

- Learn how to find people using Switchboard and Four11.

 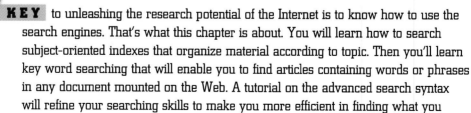 **HE KEY** to unleashing the research potential of the Internet is to know how to use the search engines. That's what this chapter is about. You will learn how to search subject-oriented indexes that organize material according to topic. Then you'll learn key word searching that will enable you to find articles containing words or phrases in any document mounted on the Web. A tutorial on the advanced search syntax will refine your searching skills to make you more efficient in finding what you want on the Internet.

You will also learn how to do concept-oriented searching using search engines that can expand an idea into related topics and search them automatically. Meta-searching will enable you to use one search engine to search several other search engines for the information you seek, collate the results of the searches, and return the results in a single organized report. You will also learn about human search services that use human beings to conduct searches. If you have trouble finding something on your own, you can pay a small fee, and a human being skilled at searching will conduct the search for you.

Some disciplines are ahead of others in terms of providing full-text source materials online, but online indexes make it quick and easy to create bibliographies of material related to topics in any field. This chapter will enable you to use discipline-based academic search engines. You will also learn how to do multimedia searches that can find pictures, audio, and video, in addition to plain text. You will even learn how to search Usenet newsgroups, which provide a rich source of information about current research in many fields.

SUBJECT-ORIENTED SEARCHING

When you research a topic, it is wise to begin by conducting a subject-oriented search. This will tell you how much information is available about your topic as a subject that others have written about. The subject-oriented search engines use a combination of human beings and robots (known as spiders) that search the Web continually, organizing what's found into a hierarchical index of topics. When you conduct a subject-oriented search, the search engine searches this index and provides you with a list of items related to your topic. To retrieve the item, you simply click it with your mouse.

Yahoo

As this book goes to press, Yahoo is the most popular subject-oriented search engine. Its Web address is www.yahoo.com. There is also a version for kids at www.yahooligans.com, which prevents access to materials unsuitable for children. To perform a Yahoo search, follow the steps in Table 11-1.

Table 11-1   How to Perform a Yahoo Search

- ▶ Point your Web browser at http://www.yahoo.com—the Yahoo home page appears.
- ▶ If you want to search all of Yahoo, type your search term(s) into the blank search field and click the Search button.
- ▶ If you want to search within a Yahoo subject area, scroll down through the subjects listed on the Yahoo home page, and click on the subject area you want—the Yahoo subject area page appears.
- ▶ If subtopics are listed on the subject area page, scroll down through the subtopics, and select the one you want. Repeat this process until you have narrowed the subject area of your search.
- ▶ When you are ready to conduct a search, type your search term(s) into the blank search field.
- ▶ Click the option to search all of Yahoo, or just the subject area you have chosen.
- ▶ Click the Search button; Yahoo will perform the search and display the items that match your search terms.
- ▶ Scroll down through the matches to see what Yahoo found. All of the matches are hotlinked; to see an item, click on a highlighted word.
- ▶ If there are more matches to be displayed, you will find "Next 25 matches" printed at the bottom of the search results. Click "Next 25 matches" if you want to see more.

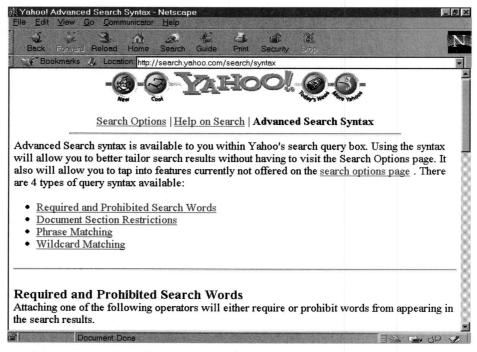

Figure 11-1 The advanced search options screen in Yahoo.

By default, Yahoo combines your search terms with the Boolean AND which means that you will get a match only when all of the search terms are found together in an item. If you want a Boolean OR done instead, click the word *Options* that you will see printed next to the Search button, and the advanced search screen appears, as shown in Figure 11-1. In addition to letting you set the Boolean OR option, the advanced options let you choose whether to search Usenet newsgroups, e-mail addresses, or the Yahoo index. You can specify whether search terms are considered to be substrings, which means that if the search term appears as part of a larger word, you want Yahoo to consider that a match. You can also change the number of entries that Yahoo will return on each Web page of your search results; the default number is 25 entries per page.

MAGELLAN Magellan

In the spirit of exploring and charting new worlds, the Magellan search tool is named after Ferdinand Magellan, a Portuguese explorer who navigated the Strait of Magellan in 1520. As an online guide to the Internet, Magellan includes original editorial content, a directory of rated and reviewed Internet sites, a database of yet-to-be-reviewed sites, and a search engine that helps you find what you're looking for. The Magellan database includes Web sites, FTP and gopher servers, newsgroups, and telnet sessions. Instead of using AND and NOT like other search engines, Magellan has you type a minus sign to exclude a term, or a plus sign to do an AND.

Magellan sites have ratings, on a scale from 1 to 10, that indicate how good the Magellan reviewers think the resources are. The ratings are determined by the criteria listed in Table 11-2.

Table 11-2 Magellan Rating Criteria

Criteria	Interpretation
Depth	Is the resource comprehensive and up-to-date?
Ease of Exploration	Is it well-organized and easy to navigate?
Net Appeal	Is it innovative? Does it appeal to the eye or the ear? Is it funny? Is it hot, hip, or cool? Is it thought-provoking? Does it offer new technology or a new way of using technology?

Lycos A2Z

A2Z is a subject-oriented index to the World Wide Web from the makers of Lycos. Its easy subject directory offers quick access to the most popular 10% of the Web. You'll find A2Z on the Web at http://a2z.lycos.com. It's also linked to the Interlit Web site, as are all of the search engines covered in this chapter.

KEY WORD SEARCHING

Like subject-oriented search engines, key word search engines have "spiders" that are constantly combing the Web and feeding information into a database. Instead of organizing the Web according to subject areas, however, key word search engines let you search for key words in documents, regardless of the "subject" of the documents. Therefore, key word search engines are likely to find more than subject-oriented search engines, but what's found may not be as relevant to your subject.

AltaVista

AltaVista is a search engine created by the Digital Equipment Corporation. Its Web address is http://www.altavista.digital.com. When this book went to press, AltaVista indexed 30 million Web pages found on 225,000 servers, and 3 million articles from 14,000 Usenet newsgroups. According to Digital, AltaVista is accessed over 10 million times daily.

Because you're likely to get thousands of hits when you search AltaVista for a key word, AltaVista sorts the hits according to the relevance or level of importance of the information found. A recent addition to AltaVista is a LiveTopics button that organizes pages with similar content into groups, thereby providing a sense of structure and meaning to the results of the search. LiveTopics creates its topics dynamically using statistical analysis rather than relying on a group of predefined categories.

Users have noticed a clever advertising scheme at the AltaVista site—the commercial ads that appear on screen often relate to the key words for which you're searching.

Advanced Search Syntax

To make the most effective use of key word search engines like AltaVista, you need to know how to do an advanced search that enables you to combine key words with logical operators such as AND, OR, NOT, and NEAR to narrow the scope of your search. To perform an advanced search with AltaVista, follow the steps in Table 11-3.

Table 11-3   How to Perform an Advanced Search with AltaVista

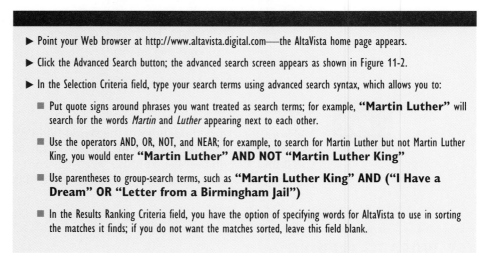

▶ Point your Web browser at http://www.altavista.digital.com—the AltaVista home page appears.

▶ Click the Advanced Search button; the advanced search screen appears as shown in Figure 11-2.

▶ In the Selection Criteria field, type your search terms using advanced search syntax, which allows you to:

■ Put quote signs around phrases you want treated as search terms; for example, **"Martin Luther"** will search for the words *Martin* and *Luther* appearing next to each other.

■ Use the operators AND, OR, NOT, and NEAR; for example, to search for Martin Luther but not Martin Luther King, you would enter **"Martin Luther" AND NOT "Martin Luther King"**

■ Use parentheses to group-search terms, such as **"Martin Luther King" AND ("I Have a Dream" OR "Letter from a Birmingham Jail")**

■ In the Results Ranking Criteria field, you have the option of specifying words for AltaVista to use in sorting the matches it finds; if you do not want the matches sorted, leave this field blank.

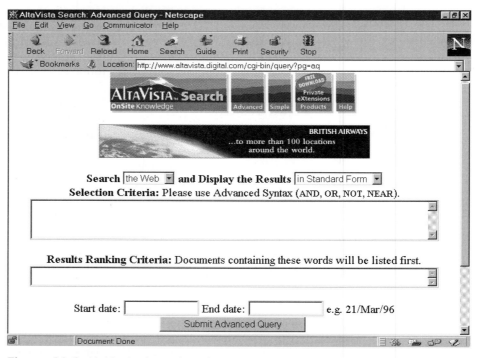

Figure 11-2 AltaVista's advanced search screen.

Almost anything in the world that you want to know is retrievable once you develop skill at using the advanced search syntax. The exercises at the end of this chapter will help you develop this skill. For more information about advanced searching, click Selection Criteria on the AltaVista advanced search screen.

Lycos

Another popular key word search engine is Lycos, which searches Carnegie Mellon University's Worldwide Internet Catalog. Lycos is located at http://www.lycos.com. In addition to searching Web pages, Lycos has a special section that lets you search for pictures and sounds as well.

WebCrawler

WebCrawler is the Global Network Navigator search engine licensed by America Online. Whether or not you subscribe to AOL, you can use WebCrawler, which you will find at http://www.webcrawler.com.

As its name suggests, WebCrawler searches the World Wide Web. When you use WebCrawler, however, you are actually searching an index of the Web rather than the Web itself. The index is updated daily to keep up with the rapid growth of the Web.

CONCEPT SEARCHING

Some users are better at key word searching than others. Finding the right combination of key words and logical operators (AND, OR, NOT) to get a search engine to find the kind of information you seek can be time-consuming and tedious. Concept-oriented search engines can help users who have difficulty with key word searching.

Excite

Excite is a search engine that you will find on the Web at http://www.excite.com. In addition to performing key word searches, Excite enables you to conduct concept-oriented searches. But Excite is much more than a search engine. There are also Excite Reviews of the more interesting Web sites; Excite Live!, which creates personalized news, sports, weather, financial, and lifestyle reports on topics you care about; ExciteSeeing Tours of the more interesting Web sites; Excite Reference, a quick way to look up people, businesses, and e-mail addresses; and Excite City.Net, a world guide to geography and travel destinations.

InfoSeek

Located at http://www.infoseek.com, InfoSeek is a search engine that includes a streamlined key word search called Ultraseek, and a concept-oriented search called Ultrasmart. Ultrasmart is especially good if you have a general idea of what you're after but you can't be very specific. In addition to finding sites that match your query, Ultrasmart offers Related Topics and Related News. Related Topics are other areas in the Directory that are relevant to your query, and Related News contains news stories that apply to your search.

In addition to the search engine, InfoSeek also includes a subject index, news center, and yellow pages directory of people and businesses. *PC Week* rates InfoSeek as "the most fully equipped search site" (*PC Week* 11 Dec 96). To find out more, follow the links to InfoSeek at the Interlit Web site.

METASEARCHING

By now you may be getting overwhelmed by the number of different search engines and the subtle distinctions in how they work. Metasearching provides an alternative to trying many individual search engines to find the information you seek. Metasearching means to use a search engine that invokes the other search engines automatically, conducting different kinds of searches for you, collating the results into one list of hits, and reporting back to you.

MetaCrawler™ ### MetaCrawler

MetaCrawler conducts searches by sending your queries to several Web search engines, including Lycos, WebCrawler, Excite, AltaVista, Yahoo, HotBot, and Galaxy. MetaCrawler organizes the results into a uniform format and displays them in the order of the combined confidence scores given to each reference by the services that return it. You also have the option of scoring the hits, enabling what's found to be sorted in a number of different ways, such as by date, locale, and organization. MetaCrawler supports the advanced search syntax, which was explained previously in Table 11-3. MetaCrawler is on the Web at http://www.metacrawler.com.

Dogpile

Research attorney Aaron Flin created Dogpile when he got frustrated finding too few results with subject-oriented indexes like Yahoo, and then trying key word search engines like AltaVista that returned 30,000 or more documents in response to the same query. Dogpile is a metasearch engine that sends your Web queries to Yahoo!, Lycos A2Z, Excite Guide, World Wide Web Worm, WWW Yellow Pages, What U Seek, Lycos, WebCrawler, InfoSeek, OpenText, AltaVista, Excite, and HotBot. You can find Dogpile on the Web at www.dogpile.com.

HUMAN SEARCHING

When you don't have time to wade through the tens of thousands of documents that a key word search engine can return in response to a search, you may wish to consider using a human search service. A person skilled in searching published information sources, proprietary databases, and the Internet will find an answer and e-mail you the results.

answers.com

Answers.com is a human search service on the World Wide Web. When you first sign up at answers.com, you get your first $5 worth of questions answered for free. After that, you must provide either a billing address or a credit card number. The fee varies, based on whether your question is considered to be easy ($1.79), medium ($5), or hard ($11.99).

Ask an Expert

There is a directory of "experts" who will answer your questions for free at the Pitsco Ask an Expert Web site. You can ask questions in 12 different categories, including Science/Technology, Career/Industry, Health, Internet/Computer,

Recreation/Entertainment, Education/Personal Development, International/ Cultural, Resources, Money/Business, Arts, Law, and Religion. The Ask an Expert site is on the Web at http://www.askanexpert.com/askanexpert.

SCHOLARLY SEARCHES

One of the problems with searching for information on the Internet is that the Web is a public resource. Anyone can create a Web page about any topic, regardless of how much the Web page author knows. When you use a search engine like AltaVista to find information about that topic, the results will contain a mix of pages written by people who know a lot about what they're talking about, as well as people who may not know much and may even write misleading or false information.

One way of filtering out the bad information is to use one of the search engines that restrict themselves to so-called scholarly information that has been published in refereed journals.

ERIC

ERIC stands for Educational Resources Information Center. It searches education journals and other scholarly documents, including books, conference proceedings, symposia, studies, and tests. Found on the Web at http://www.aspensys.com/ eric, ERIC corresponds to two printed publications: *Resources in Education (RIE)*, and *Current Index to Journals in Education (CIJE)*.

ABI/INFORM

Updated monthly, ABI/INFORM provides references and abstracts for articles from over 800 business and management journals. Subject areas include accounting and auditing; banking; data processing; economics; finance; human resources; insurance; laws and taxation; management science; and marketing and advertising. ABI/INFORM is not available for free; rather, your institution or ISP must license the database from Ovid Technologies to make it available on your network. For licensing information, go to http://www.ovid.com.

Information Access
COMPANY

Expanded Academic ASAP

Expanded Academic ASAP indexes and abstracts 1,580 scholarly and general-interest periodicals. Online is the full text of articles from more than 520 scholarly journals for the past three years plus the current year. The index also includes the most current six months of *The New York Times*.

Expanded Academic ASAP is not free; rather, your institution or ISP must license it from the Information Access Company, which you can find on the Web at http:// www.iacnet.com.

Ei CompendexWeb

CompendexWeb is an interdisciplinary engineering database that indexes and abstracts 2,600 engineering journals, conferences, and reports. All branches of engineering are included. CompendexWeb is not free; rather, your institution or ISP must license it from Engineering Information Inc., which you can find on the Web at http://www.ei.org.

Britannica Online

Britannica Online is a fully searchable and browsable electronic version of the *Encyclopaedia Britannica.* The obvious advantage of the online version is that you have access to all the latest information at once, without needing to conduct separate searches through the printed volumes of the *Micropaedia,* the *Macropaedia,* and the annual *Book of the Year.* The online version also includes hundreds of articles not found in the printed encyclopedia, *Merriam-Webster's Collegiate Dictionary* (Tenth Edition), and thousands of links to Web sites selected by Britannica editors.

For information on how to purchase a license to access the online version, go to http://www.britannica.com, where you will find out about a seven-day free-trial offer.

Discipline Databases Across the Curriculum

While it is beyond the scope of this book to cover search engines in specific academic disciplines, you should know that a wide range of databases exist across the curriculum. For example, if you follow the Interlit Web site links to the University of Delaware Library Databases, you will see how UD provides online access to discipline databases in fields as diverse as agriculture, aquatic sciences, biology, business, chemistry, cinema, clothing, computer science, economics, environmental sciences, government, health, medicine, modern languages, nursing, psychology, sociology, statistics, and the U.S. government. Unless you are a University of Delaware faculty member or student, you will not be able to access most of the databases listed here, but you can peruse the list of what's available.

If you find something interesting and you're denied access, check to see whether the database is available at your institution or ISP. If not, ask your school or ISP to subscribe and provide you with online access.

MULTIMEDIA SEARCHES

Although most of the search engines on the Internet deal exclusively with document retrieval, there are a couple of search engines that can locate multimedia objects.

Lycos

At the Lycos Web site at www.lycos.com, you can click the Pictures and Sounds button to conduct searches for multimedia objects. As illustrated in Figure 11-3, you enter your key words, press the Search button, and the Lycos search engine will return a list of pictures or sounds dealing with your topic. Then you preview the objects and download the ones you want, as illustrated in Figure 11-4.

If your intended use of a picture or a sound found on the Internet is not a fair use, you will need to seek copyright permission by contacting the administrator of the Web site where the object was found. Chapter 25 provides detailed information and guidelines regarding the fair use of multimedia.

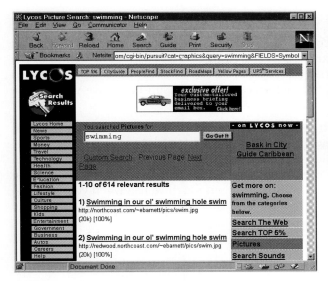

Figure 11-3 The result of searching for pictures of swimming at the Lycos Pictures and Sounds site.

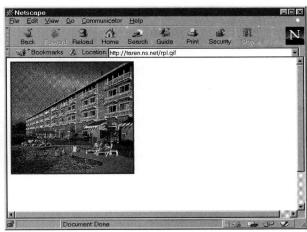

Figure 11-4 Previewing a picture at the Lycos Pictures and Sounds site.

Archive.edu

If you're an educator or a student, a bountiful site for finding royalty-free pictures, sounds, and videos is the University of Houston's Archive.edu. At this site, you'll find a broad range of multimedia materials that educators want to share. The materials can be used as is, or you can customize them into other instructional projects. You can find Archive.edu on the Web at http://www.coe.uh.edu/archive.

Please note that the materials at Archive.edu are free only for nonprofit educational purposes. If you're making a profit or using the materials for noneducational purposes, you need to seek permission. For further details, follow the links to Archive.edu at the Interlit Web site.

Publishers Depot

Created by Picture Network International, Publishers Depot is a virtual warehouse where you can find, buy, and download professional digital media, including photography, illustrations, line art, fonts, and maps. New content and information is always being added to the database, which contains more than 100,000 images. License fees start as low $30. Delivery options include free online delivery or images on CD-ROM delivered overnight.

Publishers Depot is on the Web at http://www.publishersdepot.com.

NEWSGROUP SEARCHES

Newsgroups are a rich source of information about current research in progress. Most disciplines have active newsgroups where current research topics are discussed. Some of the key word-oriented search engines discussed earlier in this chapter have options you can choose to search newsgroups as well as Web pages. For example, AltaVista, Excite, and InfoSeek provide a newsgroup search option. In addition, the DejaNews search engine is devoted to searching for news.

DejaNews

At http://www.dejanews.com you can perform key word searches of information written in Usenet newsgroups. The search terms can include the names of the people who wrote the messages. You can also search only on a name, to get an index of all of the topics and messages a given person may have written in a newsgroup.

Some users have expressed surprise upon learning that it's now possible for other users to search through newsgroups and find out what has been written by specific people about specific topics. Some consider this to be a retroactive invasion of privacy. If you want to prevent messages you write in newsgroups from being visible to search engines, you must set the x-no-archive flag when you write the message. You can set this flag by making the first line in the body of your message read as follows:

```
x-no-archive: yes
```

The DejaNews site also has free want ads. For more information, follow the links to DejaNews at the Interlit Web site.

FTP SEARCHES

As you learned in Chapter 1, FTP stands for File Transfer Protocol. There are millions of files on the Internet that you can FTP to your computer. Many of these files are Web pages that you can find with the Web-based search engines discussed earlier in this chapter. There are other kinds of files, however, that are not in Web page format. To find these other kinds of files, you need to use a search engine that can do FTP searches. Archie is such a search engine.

Archie

Archie is a search tool for FTP servers. The name Archie is easy to remember because it's very close to the word *archive,* which refers to the collection of files in the FTP database. Archie searches this archive, which consists of the millions of files that are available on anonymous FTP sites.

If you follow the links to Archie at the Interlit Web site, you'll find several Web sites that make it easy for you to conduct Archie searches.

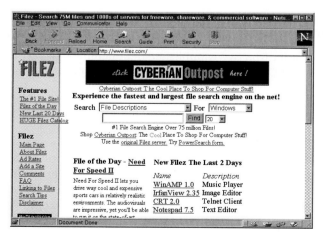

FILEZ

There are a lot of commercial files out on the Internet, such as shareware programs, that Archie may not find. Filez is a commercial file search site that you'll find at http://www.filez.com. In addition to searching for files by name, Filez lists the new files of the day, or you can see a list of files added in the past 20 days. Figure 11-5 shows the Filez home page.

Figure 11-5 The Filez search engine.

HOW TO FIND PEOPLE

In addition to helping you find Web pages, newsgroups, and scholarly documents, the Internet can also help you locate people.

Bigfoot

Located at http://www.bigfoot.com, Bigfoot offers a huge catalog of e-mail addresses and white page directories. As illustrated in Figure 11-6, you can search for someone's e-mail address, or street (i.e., white page) address, or both.

Figure 11-6 Bigfoot enables you to search for a person's e-mail address, or street address, or both.

WhoWhere

WhoWhere, located at http://www.whowhere.com, lets you look up more than 10 million e-mail addresses, 80 million U.S. residential listings, toll-free 800 numbers, and 14 million businesses, with maps and directions.

Switchboard

Switchboard is a white pages service that enables you to find people and businesses. As one of the Web's most popular sites, Switchboard handles more than 5 million look-ups for people and businesses each week. You'll find Switchboard at http://www.switchboard.com.

Four11

Four11 is a free online white pages search and listing service. The Four11 database contains more than 10 million listings. You can search by the person's name, company or organization, city, state, or domain name to find out the person's e-mail address or street address. There's also a government directory, and even a celebrity directory. You can look someone up at Four11 by going to http://www.four11.com.

INDEX OF COLLECTED SEARCH ENGINES

Search engines are undergoing a lot of research and development on the Internet. By the time you read this, new search engines will be announced that were not available when this book went to press. You can use Yahoo to find out the latest information about new search engines and what they do. At http://www.yahoo.com, go to the section on Computers and Internet, and do a search for the key word *search*.

E X E R C I S E S

1. Use your Web browser to go to http://www.yahoo.com. Set a bookmark there. In the future, whenever you want to go to Yahoo, you can get there quickly via the bookmark.

2. Use Yahoo to conduct a subject-oriented search for the topic "Martin Luther King" and make a note of the number of items found. You will need this number to conduct the comparison in exercise 4.

3. Use your Web browser to go to http://digital.altavista.com. Set a bookmark there. In the future, whenever you want to go to AltaVista, you can get there quickly via the bookmark.

4. Use AltaVista to conduct a subject-oriented search for the topic "Martin Luther King" and make a note of the number of items found. How does this compare to the number of hits you got when you searched Yahoo in exercise 2? Why did AltaVista find so much more than Yahoo?

5. At the Interlit Web site, follow the links to the people-finder search engines listed in the section on how to find people. Look yourself up in the different directories. Does Bigfoot find you? How about WhoWhere? Do you find yourself listed in Switchboard and Four11? How do you feel about being included or excluded from these people finders? If you're not included, and you'd like to be, scroll down and you'll find instructions for getting listed.

6. Use Yahoo to get driving instructions to Planet Hollywood in New York City. Then try getting driving instructions to your home. Does Yahoo know where you live?

7. Use the Web's Yahoo search engine to find out how many new online shopping services have been created since this book was printed. You will find the list of online malls at http://www.yahoo.com/Business_and_Economy/Companies/Shopping_Centers/Online_Malls. When this book went to press, about 650 malls were listed there.

8. Use AltaVista to perform the following searches. How many matches does each search find? Can you explain why these particular searches find progressively fewer matches?

   ■ "Martin Luther" AND NOT "Martin Luther King"

   ■ "Martin Luther King" AND ("I Have a Dream" OR "Letter from a Birmingham Jail")

   ■ "Martin Luther King" AND "Letter from a Birmingham Jail"

12 Commonly Found Internet File Types

After completing this chapter, you will be able to:

- Recognize the commonly found Internet file types.

- Explain why MIDI files occupy so much less file space than waveform audio files.

- Understand the concept of a markup language.

- Know the difference between the GIF and JPEG graphics formats.

- Understand why the audio/video interleave (AVI) file format was designed to give audio the priority when a computer does not have enough processing time to show all of the frames of a movie.

- Explain the difference between lossy and lossless compression methods.

- Understand how animated GIFs can bring a Web page to life.

- Explain the concept of a JavaScript.

- Understand the purpose of Adobe's Portable Document Format.

- Visit virtual reality Web sites that use VRML files to present the user with exciting 3-D worlds to explore.

 **HEN** you use an Internet search engine to find something, the information is almost always returned in the form of a file. The way in which the file is organized is known as its format. File formats vary according to the kind of information being transmitted and its intended use. It is important for you to recognize the commonly found Internet file types, for two reasons. First, you will want to know what the file contains, whether it's text, image, audio, video, animation, or data. Second, knowing the file type enables you to make the right choice in choosing a tool to view, manipulate, interpret, or modify the contents of the file.

TEXT FORMATS

There are three families of text formats: plain text, hypertext, and word processor files. Plain text means just that—the text and nothing but the text. Hypertext contains the text intermingled with special codes that define how certain words in the text serve as triggers that launch things when clicked. Word processors like

Microsoft Word and WordPerfect use proprietary formatting to encode the text and its properties, including font, size, margins, borders, headings, and pagination.

TXT (Plain Text)

Plain text files are identified by the filename extension *.txt.* When you see a filename such as *history.txt,* you know that it is a plain text file because of its *.txt* filename extension. In computer jargon, plain text files are known as ASCII files. ASCII (pronounced *askey*) stands for *American Standard Code for Information Interchange.* Every text editor and word processor has an option for reading and writing files in ASCII format. Sometimes the format is called "plain text" or "DOS text" instead of ASCII text.

Because plain text files are so common on the Internet, every Web browser needs to be able to display them. Both Netscape Communicator and Microsoft Internet Explorer have this ability built in. For more information about ASCII files, follow the links to ASCII at the Interlit Web site.

HTML (Hypertext)

HTML stands for hypertext markup language. Files in HTML format have the filename extension .html or .htm. HTML is the most prevalent file format on the World Wide Web, because almost every Web page is encoded in HTML. True to its name, an HTML file contains the text that gets displayed on a Web page, along with special codes known as **markup** that define (1) how the text should appear on screen, (2) which words in the text are hyper, and (3) what gets triggered when the user clicks the hypertext. For example, Figure 12-1 shows how a Web page displays the file *HGMPSHomePage.html*, and Figure 12-2 shows how the same file appears when viewed with a text editor. The codes inside <brackets> are the markup that tells the Web browser how to interpret the text. You will learn more about the HTML codes in the Web page creation tutorial in Part Five of this book. To visit the official Web site where the latest HTML specification is found, follow the links to HTML at the Interlit Web site.

DOC (Microsoft Word) and WPD (WordPerfect)

There are many word processor formats. The most common are Microsoft Word's DOC format, and WordPerfect's WPD format. DOC stands for document, and WPD stands for WordPerfect document. Web browsers do not usually contain built-in support for word processor file formats. Instead, you define a so-called Helper application that your browser calls upon to display the file upon demand. You will learn more about Helper applications in Chapter 23.

IMAGE FORMATS

The computer industry has produced so many graphics formats (more than 30 at last count) that there is no true standard across the industry. Table 12-1 lists a few of the more popular graphics file formats and describes what they are used for. On the Web, however, there are only two file formats that every Web browser can be guaranteed to support: GIF and JPEG.

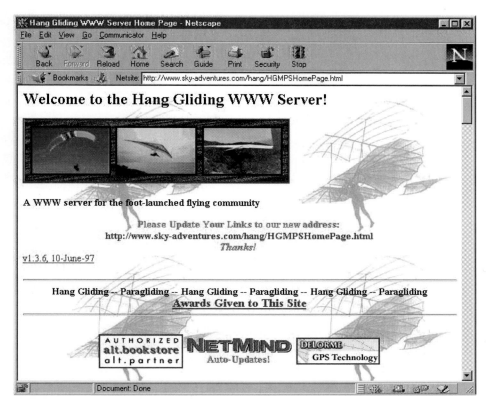

Figure 12-1 How the file *HGMPSHomePage.html* appears when viewed with a Web browser.

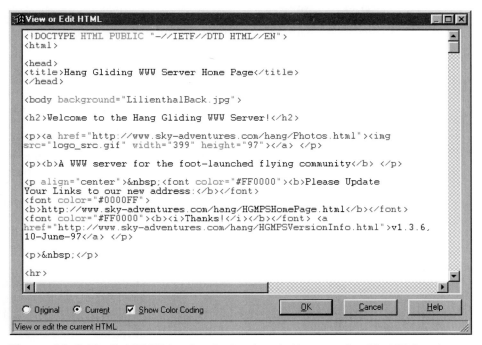

Figure 12-2 The file *HGMPSHomePage.html* as viewed with a text editor. The HTML codes have been colorized to facilitate comparing this screen to the Web page in Figure 12-1.

Table 12-1   The Most Common Computer Graphics Formats

Filename Extension	Intended Purpose
.bmp	Windows bitmap. The *.bmp* file is the most efficient format to use with Windows.
.dib	Windows device-independent bitmap; used to transfer bitmaps from one device or process to another.
.gif	Graphics Interchange Format. Invented by CompuServe for use on computer networks, GIF is the most prevalent graphics format for images on the World Wide Web.
.pcd	Kodak's Photo CD graphics file format; contains five different sizes of each picture, from "wallet" size to "poster" size.
.mac	Macintosh MacPaint format.
.jpg	JPEG image, named for the standards committee that formed it: Joint Photographic Experts Group. Intended to become a platform-independent graphics format.
.pic	PC Paint graphics format.
.pcx	Zsoft Paintbrush graphics format; popular in the DOS world.
.tga	Truevision Targa format; *tga* stands for Targa, which is a video capture board.
.tif	TIFF file; stands for Tagged Image File Format. Known as "the variable standard" because there are so many kinds of TIFF subformats.
.wpg	WordPerfect graphics format.

GIF

GIF stands for Graphics Interchange Format. Invented by CompuServe for use on computer networks, GIF is highly efficient. Instead of containing the RGB (red, green, blue) value of every pixel (picture element) in the image, a GIF file contains a table defining the different pixel patterns found in the image, with pointers into the table indicating where the patterns go on screen. It is important to understand that although GIF files are compressed, none of the original information in the graphic gets lost in the compression process. The decompressed image you see on screen is exactly the same as the one that got compressed into the GIF file. This process is known as lossless compression. GIF files are limited to a palette of 256 colors, however; if you need more than 256 different colors in a picture, you should use the JPEG format (see below). For more information about how GIF compression works, follow the links to "GIF" at the Interlit Web site.

JPEG

JPEG (pronounced *Jay-peg*) stands for Joint Photographic Experts Group, which is the name of the international standards committee that created it. JPEG is intended to become a platform-independent graphics format. JPEG images can contain millions of colors, whereas GIF images are limited to a palette of 256 colors.

PNG

The World Wide Web consortium is working on a new graphics format called PNG, which stands for Portable Network Graphics. The goal is to create a fast, lossless, patent-free file format that can handle pictures containing up to 48 bits of color information per pixel. You can monitor the progress of the creation of this new file format by following the links to "PNG" at the Interlit Web site.

WAVEFORM AUDIO FORMATS

Every sound has a waveform that describes its frequency, amplitude, and harmonic content. Waveform audio digitizers capture sound by sampling this waveform thousands of times per second; the samples are stored in a computer file. Figure 12-3 shows a waveform in the process of being sampled, and Figure 12-4 shows the samples from the corresponding waveform audio file. When such a file gets transmitted to your computer over the Internet, the samples play back through your computer's sound chip, and you hear the waveform audio. There are several file formats in which waveform audio can be transmitted over the Net.

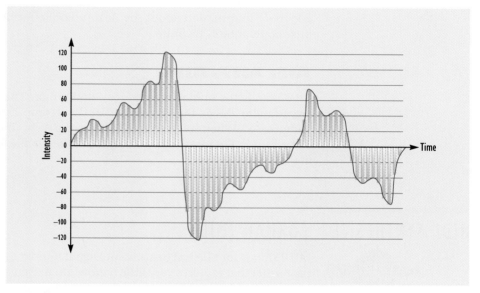

Figure 12-3 A waveform in the process of being sampled; the vertical lines show the points at which samples are taken.

0	33	80	−122	−56	−21	40	−43
15	47	96	−96	−47	−15	43	−40
21	56	122	−80	−33	0	47	−46
24	52	117	−84	−26	10	42	−66
34	48	85	−78	−24	35	18	−74
32	55	0	−55	−32	74	−18	−35
24	78	−85	−48	−34	66	−42	−10
26	84	−117	−52	−24	46	−47	0

Figure 12-4 Samples taken from the waveform shown in Figure 12-3.

WAV

On multimedia PCs, the most common waveform audio filename extension is *.wav,* which stands for waveform. When the Web started, you needed helper applications to play audio, because the browsers lacked built-in support for *.wav* files. Happily, both Netscape Communicator and Microsoft Internet Explorer now contain native support for playing *.wav* files. For more information about the WAV format, follow the links to "Waveform Audio" at the Interlit Web site.

AU and SND

High-end workstations, such as Sun and NeXT, create audio files in the AU and SND formats. These formats are essentially the same, except that *.au* files do not have file headers to specify different sampling rates and compression formats. Thus, an *.au* file gets recorded and played back at a "standard" rate, while *.snd* files can have different settings, depending on the nature of the sound and the purpose of the recording. For more detail, follow the links to "Sun Audio Format" at the Interlit Web site.

RA and RAM

Real-time audio streaming used in Internet radio broadcasts requires a special file format optimized for real-time transmission over the Internet. The RealAudio filename extensions are *.ra* and *.ram,* which stands for RealAudio metafile. A RealAudio metafile is a text file that contains the Web address (URL) of a RealAudio file. RealAudio files cannot be referenced directly by the Web page because this would cause them to be downloaded in their entirety before playback. In order for a RealAudio file to be played in real time, it must be played through a RealAudio player, and served by a RealAudio server. To accomplish this, there must be a link between the Web server and the RealAudio server. The link is contained in the metafile.

For more information about the RealAudio file formats, follow the "RealAudio" links at the Interlit Web site.

AIF, AIFF, AIFC

AIFF stands for Audio Interchange File Format. This is the file format used to create audio files on the Macintosh. AIFC is a compressed version; the C stands for compressed. When you find an AIF file on the Web, chances are it was recorded on a Macintosh. For more information about the AIF file formats, follow the AIF links at the Interlit Web site.

MIDI SYNTHESIZER FORMAT (MID)

MIDI stands for Musical Instrument Digital Interface. MIDI is a music synthesizer file format that requires very little bandwidth to transmit, because the sound chip inside your multimedia PC does the work of generating the waveform you hear. What gets transmitted is the performance information required for your computer's sound chip to play the music. Accordingly, a MIDI file consists of a stream of codes that tells your computer when to turn notes on and off, how loud to make them, what instrument should make the sound (such as trumpet, flute, or drums), and whether to bend the notes or add other special effects. Compared to the amount of storage required for waveform audio recordings, MIDI takes up so little space that it is a very popular format for transmitting music over the Internet. MIDI files have a *.mid* file extension.

There are some incredible indexes of MIDI files that you can listen to at the Interlit Web site. Follow the links to the MIDI archives, and you will get a list of indexes that contain thousands of songs in a wide variety of styles, ranging from classical to modern, and funk to rock. You will also find music listed by artists, from Abba to Frank Zappa.

VIDEO FORMATS

In the early 1990s, many PCs were too slow to play digital video satisfactorily. Unless your computer happened to have a digital video playback card, you had to settle for a picture the size of a postage stamp in which the video played at less than 15 frames per second. Now it is impossible to purchase a new multimedia PC that cannot play back full-screen, full-motion video.

AVI

The most common video format in the Windows world is Microsoft's Video for Windows, which uses the filename extension *.avi.* AVI stands for audio/video interleave, which describes a clever scheme in which audio frames are interleaved with the video. The sound track plays without interruption because the audio always takes priority. Then your computer shows as many frames of video as it has time to process. If it is too late to show a given frame, Video for Windows just skips it and goes on to the next frame.

Because the audio has priority, you get the aural illusion of uninterrupted playback, even though video frames may get dropped in the process, resulting in a jerky motion on the screen. Table 12-2 shows how many frames per second different processors can display, depending on the size of the playback window. The faster your processor, the smoother the motion. For more information, follow the links to "Video for Windows" at the Interlit Web site.

Table 12-2 Video Playback Frame Rates for Different Microprocessors

Processor	Full Screen	1/4 Screen	1/16 Screen
i386 SX-25	0 fps*	5 fps	10 fps
i386 DX-33	0 fps	10 fps	20 fps
i486 SX-25	5 fps	15 fps	30 fps
i486 DX2-66	10 fps	30 fps	30 fps
Pentium 75	20 fps	30 fps	30 fps
Pentium 130	30 fps	30 fps	30 fps

*fps = frames per second

MOV and QT

One of Apple Computer Corporation's greatest gifts to the field of multimedia is the QuickTime audio/video format. QuickTime is so robust and popular that it exists in both Macintosh and Windows formats. Because of its cross-platform capabilities, QuickTime has become very popular on the Internet. The filename extensions of QuickTime movies are *.qt* and *.mov.* For the latest information, follow the "QuickTime" links at the Interlit Web site.

MPG, MPEG, and MPE

MPEG is emerging as the new digital video standard for the United States and most of the world. MPEG stands for Motion Picture Experts Group, the name of the International Standards Organization committee that created it. Endorsed by more than 70 companies, including IBM, Apple, JVC, Philips, Sony, and Matsushita, MPEG compresses video by using a discrete cosine transform algorithm to eliminate redundant data in blocks of pixels on the screen. MPEG compresses the video further by recording only changes from frame to frame; this is known as **delta-frame encoding**. MPEG is expected to become the digital video standard for compact discs, cable TV, direct satellite broadcast, and high-definition television (HDTV).

Four versions of MPEG have been worked on:

- **MPEG-1** is the noninterlaced version designed for playback from CD-ROMs.

- **MPEG-2** is the interlaced version intended for the all-digital transmission of broadcast-quality TV. Adopted by the United States Grand Alliance HDTV specification, the European Digital Video Broadcasting Group, and the Digital Versatile Disc (DVD-ROM) consortium, MPEG-2 does surround sound. RCA's DirecTV service uses MPEG-2.

- **MPEG-3** was to be the HDTV version of MPEG, but then it was discovered that the MPEG-2 syntax could fulfill that need by simply scaling the bit rate, obviating the third phase.

- **MPEG-4** is a low-bit-rate version of MPEG that is being invented for transmitting movies over mobile and wireless communications.

For more information on MPEG, follow the links to MPEG at the Interlit Web site, which include the MPEG FAQ and the MPEG organization site at http://www.mpeg.org.

RM

One of the greatest challenges on the Internet is to deliver to your PC full-motion video in an uninterrupted real-time data stream. First to market with a product that does that is Progressive Networks, which is the same company that brought you the RealAudio technology discussed earlier in this chapter. The name of the product is RealVideo, and the filename extension is *.rm*.

RealVideo follows the industry-standard real-time streaming protocol (RTSP) that has been invented for streaming audio and video over the Internet. To read about this and other technical details, follow the links to the "RealVideo Technical White Paper" at the Interlit Web site.

ANIMATION FORMATS

Web pages that move are known as active Web pages. There are several ways to animate Web pages. Discussed here are four methods that progress in order from simple to complex.

Animated GIFs

Animated GIFs are a special kind of GIF file (known as GIF89a) that may contain multiple images intended to be shown in a sequence at specific times and locations on the screen. A looping option causes your Web browser to keep showing the frames in the GIF file continually, and as a result, you see an animation on screen.

Animated GIFs are very efficient, because they are only downloaded once, then cached from your hard drive as your browser loops the images. Some users don't like the constant disk chatter. You can be the judge by clicking the animated GIF icon at the Interlit Web site, which will take you to some neat examples of animated GIFs.

You can create animated GIFs with Microsoft GIF Animator or the GIF Construction Set, which you can download by following the links to animated GIFs at the Interlit Web site. The Interlit Web site also links to a tutorial on creating animated GIFs.

JavaScript

As noted earlier, Java is a programming environment used to create little applications known as applets that can be downloaded along with a Web page. One of the main uses of applets is to make Web pages become active. Ordinarily, it requires a high level of programming skill to create an applet in Java. Netscape invented a scripting language called JavaScript, however, that greatly simplifies the process. Instead of writing native Java code, you call scripts which can perform some of the same functions as a Java applet with much simpler coding. For a demonstration of the kinds of animations that JavaScript can create, follow the "JavaScript" links at the Interlit Web site. You will also find links to more information about JavaScript, including a tutorial on using JavaScript, and a comparison of Java and JavaScript, between which the differences are considerable.

QuickTime

Apple Computer Corporation has created a plug-in whereby QuickTime movies can be imbedded as animation objects on Web pages. Both Netscape Communicator and Microsoft Internet Explorer support this plug-in. To see some examples of Web pages containing QuickTime animations, follow the links to "QuickTime" at the Interlit Web site.

Shockwave

Macromind's Director is the undisputed leader in multimedia animation. Breakthrough products such as Brøderbund's *Living Books* series of animated storybooks, and the recording artist Sting's fantastic double CD-ROM *All This Time*, were created with Director. Shockwave is a Macromind product that enables animations created with Director, Authorware, and Flash to plug in to Web pages. For a demonstration, follow the "ShockWave" links at the Interlit Web site. Note, however, that you will need to download the ShockWave player in order to view Shockwave animations with your Web browser.

PORTABLE DOCUMENT FORMAT (PDF)

There is a huge amount of printed text that is not accessible on the Web yet. To provide a way to digitize printed text into a format that can be viewed on any computer platform, Adobe created the Portable Document Format, for which the filename extension is *.pdf*. PDF files are created by scanning printed documents into bitmaps that work like photographs of the printed pages.

You view PDF files with the Adobe Acrobat Reader, which you download from the Adobe Web site. If you configure the Acrobat Reader as the "helper" application for viewing PDF files in your Web browser, then your browser will launch Acrobat automatically whenever you follow a link to a PDF file. You will learn how to configure helper apps in Chapter 23.

You'll make some pretty amazing discoveries when you use the Adobe Acrobat Reader to view a PDF document. Because you're looking at what appears to be picture of the original document, you don't expect to be able to select, copy, paste, and search for text as you could on a regular Web page. You'll be pleasantly surprised to find, however, that all of these functions are available. Perhaps your biggest surprise will come when you choose to print the document. Instead of printing the bitmap version of the image you see on screen, Acrobat prints the document using the fonts on your printer. As a result, the printed version appears better than the original.

To learn more about the PDF file format, and to see some examples of *.pdf* files in action, follow the links to "Adobe Acrobat" and "Portable Document Format" at the Interlit Web site.

VIRTUAL REALITY FORMAT (VRML)

Web pages presented via the HTML file format are two-dimensional displays of text and graphics. In May 1994, at the First International Conference on the Web, Mark D. Pesce, Peter Kennard, and Anthony S. Parisi presented a paper entitled "Cyberspace" in which they argued that because human beings are used to working in a three-dimensional world, extending the Web with a third dimension would enable better ways of organizing the mass of information on the Net. After intense discussion hosted by a moderated listserv at *Wired* magazine, the Virtual Reality Modeling Language (VRML) standard was created. As illustrated in Figure 12-5, VRML enables Web page designers to add dimensions, texture, and lighting to Web sites.

To learn more about VRML, follow the VRML repository links at the Interlit Web site, where you will find out about viewers and authoring clients, mailing lists, newsgroups, documentation, and sample VRML worlds in architecture, art, astronomy, biomedical sciences, chemistry, commercial applications, computer science, entertainment, environmental science, history, maps, mathematics, music, physics, and scientific visualization. You'll also find the "Cyberspace" paper that led to the creation of the VRML file format.

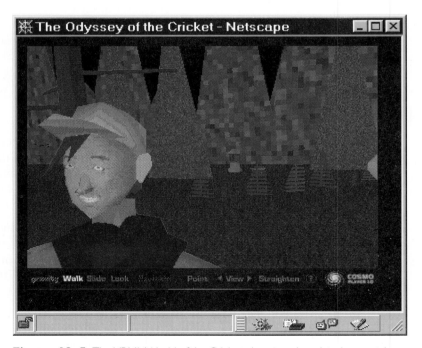

Figure 12-5 The VRML World of the Cricket places you in a virtual canoe trip on which you can look through the eye of the camera or the cricket. The address of this 3-D world is http://cicadaweb.com/vrml.

1. One of the most important concepts in the hypertext markup language (HTML) file format is the way it specifies how text and graphics flow with respect to each other, depending on the size and shape of the window in which the file is viewed. Follow the Interlit Web site links to Lewis Carroll's famous story *Through the Looking Glass,* and experiment with resizing your browser's window. Notice how the text and graphics of the story adjust themselves automatically to the size and position of the window.

2. Imagine a situation in which you have a waveform audio recording of a symphony orchestra playing a piece of classical music, and a MIDI file of the same composition. What will be the main difference you hear between the two files? Which file will take more time to transfer from the Web to your computer? To help you answer this exercise, there is a Waveform audio file and a MIDI file for you to compare at the Interlit Web site. Follow the links to "MIDI versus Wave," and listen to the two files. Both files are the same size, 17 kilobytes. Which one lasts longer? How do you explain the difference in the length of the music you hear, when the file size is the same? Which example sounds better to you?

3. Give one example of when you might use each one of the following techniques to animate a Web page. Make sure the example you give is appropriate to the technique in terms of authoring time and visual effect.

Animated GIF

JavaScript

Shockwave

4. What is the most important difference between the document you view on screen when you use your Web browser to view an HTML file as opposed to a PDF file? Under what circumstances is it better to use a PDF file than an HTML file?

5. Visit some of the VRML sites linked to the Interlit Web site, and reflect on what the VRML sites are enabling you to do that ordinary HTML Web pages do not. Under what circumstances would you prefer to use the 3-D VRML user interface? For what purposes is HTML more appropriate?

13 Downloading from the Internet

After completing this chapter, you will be able to:

- Download text and graphics from the Internet.

- Download audio and video resources from the Internet.

- Download data files and software from the Internet.

- Make sure the downloaded file has the correct filename extension for the type of file it is.

- Install self-extracting archives that you download from the Internet.

N THE PAST, prior to the creation of the graphical user interface that is used in Web browsers like Netscape Communicator and Microsoft Internet Explorer, downloading files required you to know how to use a complicated set of commands for telnetting to the computer that hosts the file, and FTPing the file to your computer. These commands were so complicated that only technically inclined users were able to download files from the Internet. Happily, the graphical user interface has made it so easy to transfer files that you no longer need to know a single FTP command to download a file.

DOWNLOADING TEXT FROM THE INTERNET

The quickest way to download text from the Internet is to copy the text onto your Windows clipboard, from which you can paste the text into any other window on your screen. Both Netscape Communicator and the Microsoft Internet Explorer let you copy text onto your Windows clipboard. To download text this way, follow the steps in Table 13-1.

Table 13-1   How to Download Text via the Clipboard

Windows	Macintosh
▶ Use your browser to display the text you want to download.	▶ Use your browser to display the text you want to download.
▶ Drag your mouse over the text you want to copy; the selected text will appear highlighted. Or, if you want to select all of the text on the Web page, pull down the browser's Edit menu and choose Select All.	▶ Drag your mouse over the text you want to copy; the selected text will appear highlighted. Or, if you want to select all of the text on the Web page, pull down the browser's Edit menu and choose Select All.
▶ Press the Windows copy keys Ctrl-C or pull down the Edit menu and choose Copy.	▶ Press the Macintosh copy keys ⌘-C or pull down the Edit menu and choose Copy.
▶ If the application into which you want to paste the text is not already running, get it running now.	▶ If the application into which you want to paste the text is not already running, get it running now.
▶ Position your cursor at the spot in the window to which you want to want to paste the text.	▶ Position your cursor at the spot in the window to which you want to paste the text.
▶ Press the Windows paste keys Ctrl-V or pull down the application's Edit menu and choose Paste.	▶ Press the Macintosh paste keys ⌘-V or pull down the application's Edit menu and choose Paste.

DOWNLOADING IMAGES FROM THE INTERNET

The quickest way to download an image from the Internet is to use your Web browser's option for saving the image to a file. When you save the image to a file, you will have the option of changing its name. If you change the filename, make sure that you keep the filename extension the same as the original filename's. For example, if the image you're saving is in GIF format, make sure the filename extension on the file to be saved is *.gif*. If the image you're saving is in JPEG format, make sure the filename extension on the file to be saved is *.jpg*. Saving a GIF-formatted file with a *.jpg* filename extension does not change the format of the file. If you want to change the format of the file, you must use a file-conversion program such as Paint Shop Pro, which you will learn how to use in Chapter 19. To download an image from the Internet, follow the steps in Table 13-2.

Table 13-2   How to Download an Image from the Internet

▶ Use your browser to display the image you want to download.
▶ Click your right mouse button on the image you want to download.
▶ A popout menu will provide you with options you can do with the image; choose the option to "Save image as..." or "Save picture as..." The Save As dialog appears.
▶ In the Filename field, you will see the name of the file that this image has on the Internet. You can change the name if you want, but make sure you leave the filename extension the same as in the original.
▶ You can use the Save As dialog to navigate to a different drive or folder on your computer, or you can type a complete path onto the beginning of the filename, to specify exactly where you want the image file to be saved on your computer.
▶ Click the Save button when you are ready to save the file.

DOWNLOADING AUDIO AND VIDEO FROM THE INTERNET

Downloading audio and video is similar to downloading graphics. You right-click instead of left-click on the link that triggers the audio or video, and the Save As dialog appears. Detailed instructions are provided in Table 13-3.

Table 13-3   How to Download Audio and Video from the Internet

> ▶ Use your browser to display the link that triggers the audio or video you want to download.
>
> ▶ Click your right mouse button on the trigger. A popout menu will provide you with options you can do with the object linked to the trigger; choose the "Save link as" or "Save target as" option to make the Save As dialog appear.
>
> ▶ In the Filename field, you will see the name of the file that this object has on the Internet. You can change the name if you want, but make sure you leave the filename extension the same as in the original.
>
> ▶ Click the Save button when you are ready to save the file.

DOWNLOADING SOFTWARE AND DATA FROM THE INTERNET

To download software and data from the Internet, you should begin by reading any special instructions that might appear on screen explaining what will happen when you trigger the download. Almost all of these instructions fall into one of two categories: archived files and self-extracting archives. Each kind is discussed in turn as follows.

Archived Files

A popular method of distributing software and data over the Internet is via archived files. An archive is a container into which one or more files has been compressed to save space and packed into a single file that can be transmitted easily over a network. When you receive such a file, you need to use an extractor to unpack the archive and restore its contents onto your computer. Windows users unpack archived files with a product known as PKZIP for Windows; Macintosh users unpack them with Stuffit Expander. Each of these products is described as follows.

PKZIP FOR WINDOWS

PKWARE, Inc., is the industry leader in compression and decompression technology. Their product, PKZIP for Windows, takes its name from the *.zip* filename extension that archived files have on Windows-based machines. PKZIP for Windows makes it easy to zip and unzip files. After a Windows user downloads a zipped file from the Internet, you simply open it with PKZIP for Windows. As illustrated in Figure 13-1, PKZIP for Windows displays the contents of the zipped file. Then, following the instructions on the Web page from which you downloaded the zip file, you install the files to your computer by running the *install.exe* or *setup.exe* file listed in the contents.

PKZIP for Windows is shareware, meaning that you can download it for free, try it out for a limited time period (usually 30 to 60 days), and then, if you decide to keep using it, pay a reasonable fee (usually $29 to $69) to the vendor. To download a copy of PKZIP for Windows, follow the links to PKZIP at the Interlit Web site.

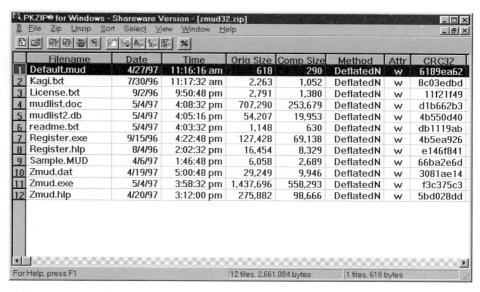

Figure 13-1 PKZIP for Windows displays the contents of the zipped file.

Figure 13-2 Stuffit Expander displays a status bar while it extracts archived files on the Macintosh.

STUFFIT EXPANDER FOR MACINTOSH

For Macintosh users, Aladdin Systems makes a product called Stuffit Expander. True to its name, Stuffit Expander can extract files from archives you download from the Internet. If you don't have Stuffit Expander, you can download it by following the Interlit Web site links to "Stuffit Expander."

When you ask Stuffit Expander to expand a file, it opens a new folder on the desktop and decompresses each file into that folder. While the files get expanded, a status bar shows the status of the decompression, as illustrated in Figure 13-2. When Stuffit Expander is done extracting the files, many applications will be ready to run by clicking their icon in the new folder. Others will create an install program which must be run separately to set up the application.

Self-extracting Archives

Another popular method of distributing software and data on the Internet is via self-extracting archives. A self-extracting archive is a compressed file into which the files that comprise an application or set of data have been packed. You download the archive file to your computer. Then you run the archive, which unpacks the files and stores them on your computer.

Archives work differently, depending on whether you have a Windows-based PC or a Macintosh. Follow the steps in Table 13-4 for your brand of computer.

Table 13-4   How to Download Software and Data in Self-Extracting Archives

Windows-based PC	Macintosh
▶ When you download a self-extracting archive, you need someplace to put it. Windows users typically put self-extracting archives into the *temp* folder on their hard drive. If your computer does not have a *temp* folder, follow the instructions in Table 6-9 to create a folder named *temp* on your hard drive.	▶ When you download a self-extracting archive, you need someplace to put it. Macintosh users typically put self-extracting archives into the *temp* folder on their hard drive. If your computer does not have a *temp* folder, follow the instructions in Table 6-9 to create a folder named *temp* on your hard drive.
▶ Use your browser to display the trigger to which the self-extracting archive has been linked. In this example, go to the Interlit Web site and follow the links to "PKZIP for Windows."	▶ Use your browser to display the trigger to which the self-extracting archive has been linked. In this example, go to the Interlit Web site and follow the links to "Stuffit Expander for the Macintosh."
▶ Click your right mouse button on the trigger. A popout menu will provide you with options you can do with the object linked to the trigger; choose the "Save link as" or "Save target as" option to make the Save As dialog appear.	▶ Click and hold your mouse button on the trigger. A popout menu will provide you with options you can do with the object linked to the trigger; choose the "Save link as" or "Download link to disk" option to make the Save As dialog appear.
▶ In the Filename field, you will see the name of the file that this object has on the Internet. In this example, the filename is *pk250w32.exe*. To save this file in the *temp* folder on your hard drive, click once at the beginning of the filename field to position your cursor there, and assuming your hard drive is C, make the field read **c:\temp\pk250w32.exe**	▶ In the Save As field, you will see the name of the file that this object has on the Internet. In this example, the filename is *stuffit_expander_installer.sea*. To save this file in the *temp* folder on your hard drive, use the menus to navigate to the *temp* folder's location on your hard drive.
▶ Click the Save button when you are ready to save the file.	▶ Click the Save button when you are ready to save the file.
▶ The Download dialog will show the progress as the file gets downloaded to your computer; do not proceed until this process is completed.	▶ The Save dialog will show the progress as the file gets downloaded to your computer; do not proceed until this process is completed.
▶ Run the self-extracting archive. (Refer to Table 13-5 if you need help running a file on your computer.)	▶ Run the self-extracting archive. (Refer to Table 13-5 if you need help running a file on your computer.)
▶ After the application installs itself, you can double-click its startup icon to launch it.	▶ After the application installs itself, you can double-click its startup icon to launch it.

This method of distributing applications in self-extracting archives is how all of the major vendors distribute software over the Internet. For example, both Netscape and Microsoft distribute the latest versions of their Web browsers in self-extracting archives. To conserve space on your computer's hard disk after you've run the self-extracting archive, you can delete it from your computer's *temp* folder.

Table 13-5   How to Start a Program If Its Icon Isn't Visible

Windows 3.1	Windows 95	Macintosh
▶ Pull down the Program Manager File menu and choose Run to make the Run dialog appear.	▶ Click the Start button, and choose Run to make the Run dialog appear.	▶ Click the Apple icon in the upper left corner of the screen to pull down the menu, then choose Find File.
▶ Click the Browse button; the Browse dialog appears.	▶ Click the Browse button; the Browse dialog appears.	▶ Set the two drop-down menus to "Name" and "Contains," if they don't say that already.
▶ Use the browse controls to select the filename of the program you want to run.	▶ Use the browse controls to select the filename of the program you want to run.	▶ In the blank field, type the name of the program you're looking for.
▶ Click OK to close the Browse dialog; the filename of the program to be run appears in the filename field of the Run dialog.	▶ Click Open; the filename of the program to be run appears in the Open field of the Run dialog.	▶ Press the Find button to make your computer find the file.
▶ Click OK to run the file.	▶ Click OK to run the file.	▶ Double-click the file to run it.

NOTE   It's possible for executable files (such as those with the filename extension .exe) to transmit viruses to your computer. Whenever you download files from the Internet, you should run a virus scan on your computer to make sure you have not received a virus. It's important to remove viruses promptly, because letting them remain on your computer can cause unwanted things to happen, such as files disappearing, unwanted messages appearing on screen, software acting strangely, and even your entire hard disk losing its contents. Make sure your virus scanner is fairly recent so it will recognize the latest viruses. Most producers of antivirus software have monthly updates available. For the latest information about viruses and how to remove them from your computer, follow the antivirus links at the Interlit Web site.

E X E R C I S E S

1. Get your favorite word processor or text editor running on your computer. If you do not have a word processor, follow the instructions in Table 6-10 to get a Notepad or a SimpleText editor running on your computer. Use your Web browser to display one of your favorite Web pages. Practice copying text from the Web page into your Notepad, word processor, or text editor window. If you have trouble, refer to the instructions in Table 13-1.

2. There are lots of interesting icons at the Interlit Web site. Use your Web browser to go to the Interlit Web site, and download one of the icons to your computer. If you have trouble, refer to the instructions in Table 13-2. If you change the filename before you save the file, make sure the filename extension of the file you save matches the filename extension of the original. Now get your favorite graphics program running. For example, run the Windows 3.1 *pbrush.exe* program, or the Windows 95 *mspaint.exe,* or the Paint Shop Pro (Windows) or Graphic Converter (Macintosh) software discussed in Chapter 19. Use the Paint program to open the image you downloaded. If the image appears properly, you have succeeded in learning how to download images to your computer.

3. There's a touchy-mood MIDI file at the Interlit Web site, provided courtesy of the Ensoniq Corporation, makers of some of the world's finest MIDI gear. To hear the song, click *touchy.mid.* Download this file onto your computer, so you can listen to it whenever you want, whether or not your Web browser is running. If you have trouble downloading the MIDI file, refer to the instructions in Table 13-3. Now get a program running that can play MIDI files, such as the Windows *mplayer.exe* program, or the Macintosh QuickTime MoviePlayer. Use this program to open and play the MIDI file you downloaded. If the song plays properly, you have succeeded in learning how to download audio files to your computer, as well as video files, which follow the same downloading process.

4. Depending on whether you're using a Netscape or a Microsoft browser, click either the Netscape or the Microsoft icon in the Chapter 13 exercises section of the Interlit Web site. This takes you to the Web site from which you can download new versions of your browser. Check to see if a new version is available. If so, download it to your computer. If you have trouble, refer to the instructions in Table 13-4 for downloading self-extracting archives to your computer. If you're a Netscape user, and you'd like to explore what life is like on the other side of the tracks, download the Microsoft browser and take it for a test drive. Likewise, if you're a Microsoft user, give Netscape a try. How do the two browsers compare? Which one do you like best? Why do you feel that way? How would you recommend that Netscape improve its browser? How could the Microsoft Internet Explorer be improved?

14 Bibliographic Style for Citing Internet Resources

After completing this chapter, you will be able to:

- **Explain the differences among APA, MLA, and CMS styles.**

- **Know when to use APA, MLA, or CMS style.**

- **Cite Internet resources in APA, MLA, or CMS style.**

- **Use the fair use guidelines to determine whether your use of a copyrighted work is fair.**

SCHOLARLY writing is not done in a vacuum. Instead of just writing about your thoughts on a topic, you conduct research to find out what other people have discovered and documented. When you write your paper, you refer to this research to support your assertions, or to compare them with another point of view.

To provide a standard way of presenting and documenting references to scholarly material, style guides have been created. This chapter demonstrates how to cite Internet resources according to the three most popular style guides.

APA, MLA, AND CMS STYLE GUIDES

The three most popular style guides are the American Psychological Association (APA) method, the Modern Language Association (MLA) style, and the Chicago Manual of Style (CMS). All three use in-text citations rather than footnotes at the bottom of the page to refer to scholarly references. Because Web documents are not paginated, in-text citations are particularly applicable to Web documents. Just imagine trying to print footnotes at the bottom of each screen of a Web document; it just wouldn't work, because due to different screen resolutions and font sizes, you could never be sure where the bottom of the screen would be, so you wouldn't know where to put the footnotes. Plus, the user can scroll a Web document to any position of any page, which would throw off the footnoting. It is fortunate, therefore, that the three most popular style guides use in-text citations appropriate for use on Web pages.

At the Interlit Web site, you will find examples of term papers written in APA, MLA, and CMS styles. When you write a term paper, you should emulate one of these styles. The APA style is normally used for papers written in psychology classes and the social sciences. The MLA style is often used for papers written in English courses and the humanities. The CMS style is used across a broad range of disciplines; this book, for example, is written in CMS style.

Unless your instructor, publisher, or employer tells you to use a specific style guide, it doesn't really matter whether you choose APA, MLA, or CMS style. What's important is that you follow an established style guide consistently to enable people who read your paper to locate the sources you cite.

CITING INTERNET RESOURCES IN APA STYLE

In the APA section of the Interlit Web site, you'll find resources related to APA style. Among them is a sample term paper written in APA style. If you study that term paper, you will notice that some of the references have been linked to other documents on the Web. When a reference that you cite is available online, you should link your citation of that reference to the online resource, to provide someone reading your article quick and easy access to the online reference. Printed here are the guidelines for citing Web documents in APA style. Other aspects of the APA style are documented in the *Publication Manual of the American Psychological Association*. To obtain a copy, follow the links to "APA Style Guidelines" at the Interlit Web site.

The source of the guidelines printed here is University of Vermont librarians Xia Li and Nancy Crane, who have written a book entitled *Electronic Styles: A Handbook for Citing Electronic Information*. For the latest information on the availability of the Li and Crane book, visit their Web site at http://www.uvm.edu/~ncrane/estyles.html. The guidelines provided here were adapted from the Li and Crane Web site in the section on citing World Wide Web resources in the APA style.

Individual Works

Author/editor. (Year). *Title* (edition) [Type of medium]. Producer (optional). Available Protocol (if applicable): Site/Path/File [Access date].

Example:

Pritzker, T. J. (No date). *An early fragment from central Nepal* [Online]. Available: http://www.ingress.com/~astanart/pritzker/pritzker.html [1995, June 8].

Parts of Works

Author/editor. (Year). Title. In *Source* (edition) [Type of medium]. Producer (optional). Available Protocol (if applicable): Site/Path/File [Access date].

Example:

Daniel, R. T. (1995). The history of Western music. In *Britannica online: Macropaedia* [Online]. Available: http://www.eb.com:180/cgi-bin/g:DocF=macro/5004/45/0.html [1995, June 14].

Journal Articles

Author. (Year). Title. *Journal Title* [Type of medium], *volume*(issue), paging or indicator of length. Available Protocol (if applicable): Site/Path/File [Access date].

Example:

Inada, K. (1995). A Buddhist response to the nature of human rights. *Journal of Buddhist Ethics* [Online], *2*, 9 paragraphs. Available: http://www.cac.psu.edu/jbe/twocont.html [1995, June 21].

Newspaper Articles

Author. (Year, month day). Title. *Newspaper Title* [Type of medium], paging or indicator of length. Available Protocol (if applicable): Site/Path/File [Access date].

Example:

Johnson, T. (1994, December 5). Indigenous people are now more combative, organized. *Miami Herald* [Online], p. 29SA(22 paragraphs). Available: gopher:// summit.fiu.edu/Miami Herald—Summit-Related Articles/12/05/95—Indigenous People Now More Combative, Organized [1995, July 16].

Other Forms of Online Communication

For other forms of online communication, such as newsgroups, Web sites, and listservs, provide as much of the following information as you can, in the order specified.

Author. (Year). *Title*. [Type of medium]. Available Protocol (if applicable): Site/Path/File [Access date].

Example:

Rithcie, Collin. *Emulating PRINT & COPY in a JAVA Applet.* [Newsgroup]. Available: news://msnews.microsoft.com/microsoft.public.java.visualj++ [1997, July 2].

CITING INTERNET RESOURCES IN MLA STYLE

In the MLA section of the Interlit Web site, you'll find resources related to MLA style. Among them is a sample term paper written in MLA style. If you study that term paper, you will notice that some of the references have been linked to other documents on the Web. When a reference that you cite is available online, you should link your citation of that reference to the online resource, to provide someone reading your article quick and easy access to the online reference. Printed here are the guidelines for citing Internet resources in MLA style. Other aspects of the MLA style are documented in the *MLA Handbook for Writers of Research Papers*. To obtain a copy, follow the links to "MLA Style Guidelines" at the Interlit Web site.

The source of the guidelines printed here is University of Vermont librarians Xia Li and Nancy Crane, who have written a book entitled *Electronic Styles: A Handbook for Citing Electronic Information.* For the latest information on the availability of the Li and Crane book, visit their Web site at http://www.uvm.edu/~xli/reference/ estyles.html. The guidelines provided here were adapted from the Li and Crane Web site in the section on citing World Wide Web resources in the MLA style.

Individual Works

Author/editor. *Title of Print Version of Work*. Edition statement (if given). Publication information (Place of publication: publisher, date), if given. *Title of Electronic Work*. Medium. Information supplier. Available Protocol (if applicable): Site/Path/File. Access date.

Example:

Pritzker, Thomas J. *An Early Fragment from Central Nepal*. N.D. Online. Ingress Communications. Available: http://www.ingress.com/~astanart/pritzker/ pritzker.html. 8 June 1995.

Parts of Works

Author/editor. "Part title." *Title of Print Version of Work.* Edition statement (if given). Publication information (Place of publication: publisher, date), if given. *Title of Electronic Work.* Medium. Information supplier. Available Protocol (if applicable): Site/Path/File. Access date.

Example:

Daniel, Ralph Thomas. "The History of Western Music." *Britannica Online: Macropaedia.* 1995. Online. Encyclopaedia Britannica. Available: http://www.eb.com:180/cgi-bin/g:DocF=macro/5004/45/0.html. 14 June 1995.

Journal Articles

Author. "Article Title." *Journal Title.* Volume.Issue (Year): paging or indicator or length. Medium. Available Protocol (if applicable): Site/Path/File. Access date.

Example:

Inada, Kenneth. "A Buddhist Response to the Nature of Human Rights." *Journal of Buddhist Ethics* 2 (1995): 9 pars. Online. Available: http://www.cac.psu.edu/jbe/twocont.html. 21 June 1995.

Newspaper Articles

Author. "Article Title." *Newspaper Title.* Date, Edition (if given): paging or indicator of length. Medium. Available Protocol (if applicable): Site/Path/File. Access date.

Example:

Johnson, Tim. "Indigenous People Are Now More Combative, Organized." *Miami Herald* 5 Dec. 1994: 29SA. Online. Available: gopher://summit.fiu.edu/Miami Herald—Summit-Related Articles/12/05/95—Indigenous People Now More Combative, Organized. 16 July 1995.

Other Forms of Online Communication

For other forms of online communication, such as newsgroups, Web sites, and listservs, provide as much of the following information as you can, in the order specified.

Author. *Title.* (Year). Medium. Available Protocol (if applicable): Site/Path/File. Access date.

Example:

Rithcie, Collin. *Emulating PRINT & COPY in a JAVA Applet.* 1997. Newsgroup. Available: news://msnews.microsoft.com/microsoft.public.java.visualj++. 2 July 1997.

CITING INTERNET RESOURCES IN CMS STYLE

In the CMS section of the Interlit Web site, you'll find resources related to CMS style. Among them is a sample term paper written in CMS style. If you study that term paper, you will notice that some of the references have been linked to other documents on the Web. When a reference that you cite is available online, you should link your citation of that reference to the online resource, to provide someone reading your article quick and easy access to the online resource.

Instead of issuing its own guidelines for citing electronic documents, the *Chicago Manual of Style* (1993:633–4) has adopted the International Standards Organization (ISO) system. Printed here are some examples of how to cite Internet resources in the ISO style. For complete documentation of the ISO style, follow the links to CMS/ISO at the Interlit Web site.

Individual Works

Author/editor. *Title*. Type of medium. Subordinate responsibility (optional). Edition. Publication information (Place of publication: publisher, date, date of update/revision). Date of citation. Series (optional). Notes (optional). Availability and access. Standard number.

Example:

Pritzker, T. J., *An early fragment from central Nepal*. Available from http://www.ingress.com/~astanart/pritzker/pritzker.html [cited 8 June 1995].

Parts of Works

Author/editor (of host document). Title (of host document). Type of medium. Subordinate responsibility (of host document) (optional). Edition. Publication information (place of publication: publisher, date, date of update/revision), if given. Date of citation. Chapter or equivalent designation (of part). Title (of part). Location within host document. Notes (optional). Availability and access. Standard number.

Example:

Daniel, R. T., "The history of Western music." In Britannica online: Macropaedia [database online]. Available from http://www.eb.com:180/cgi-bin/g:DocF=macro/5004/45/0.html [cited 14 June 1995].

Journal Articles

Author. Article Title. *Journal Title*. Type of medium. Edition. Issue designations. Date of update/revision. Date of citation. Location within host document. Notes (optional). Availability and access. Standard number.

Example:

Inada, L., "A Buddhist Response to the Nature of Human Rights," *Journal of Buddhist Ethics* [journal online], vol. 2, 9 paragraphs. Available from http://www.cac.psu.edu/jbe/twocont.html [cited 21 June 1995].

Other Forms of Online Communication

For other forms of online communication, such as newsgroups, Web sites, and listservs, provide as much of the following information as you can, in the order specified.

Author. Title. Type of Medium. Date of citation. Available Protocol (if applicable): Site/Path/File.

Example:

Rithcie, Collin, "Emulating PRINT & COPY in a JAVA Applet." In Visual J++ News [Newsgroup online]. [written 2 July, 1997; cited 18 Aug 1997]. Available from news://msnews.microsoft.com/microsoft.public.java.visualj++.

FAIR USE GUIDELINES FOR INTERNET RESOURCES

The Internet is a brave new world in which debates about copyright and fair use are ongoing. Suppose you find a diagram or an illustration on the Internet that you'd like to include in your term paper. Are you permitted to put the picture on your Web page? What about poems and songs, animations and movies that you find on the Internet—are you permitted to include them in your term paper?

To provide guidance in what's fair, the Consortium of College and University Media Centers (CCUMC) has issued a set of guidelines for the educational fair use of new media. These guidelines have been endorsed by a broad range of publishers and educational institutions. The recommendations provided here are based on the CCUMC guidelines. The full text of the guidelines is available at the Interlit Web site; follow the links to the *"Fair Use Guidelines for Educational Multimedia."*

Downloading

According to the CCUMC guidelines, students are permitted to download into term papers certain portions of copyrighted works. These portions include:

- Up to 10% or 1,000 words of a text, whichever is less. Special rules apply to poetry; see section 4.2.2 of the guidelines for details.

- Not more than five images by an individual artist or photographer; for anthologies, not more than 10% or 15 images, whichever is less.

- Up to 10% but never more than 30 seconds of music, lyrics, and music video.

- Up to 10% of motion media or three minutes, whichever is less.

- Up to 10% or 2,500 fields or cell entries, whichever is less, from a copyrighted database or data table.

If you are not a student or an educator, however, or if you are engaging in a profit-making activity, you may not qualify for fair use. Refer to the CCUMC guidelines for detailed information on who qualifies. When in doubt, always request permission from the person or agency holding the copyright to the resource you wish to include.

Whenever you include a portion of a copyrighted work, you should always document the source with an in-text reference at the point where the object appears in your paper, and you must include a bibliographic citation at the end of the paper. If an image includes a copyright notice that is part of the bitmap of the image, it is unethical to remove the copyright notice from the image.

Linking

An alternative to downloading an Internet resource into your term paper is to link to its URL instead. For example, suppose you want a picture of the Mona Lisa to appear as an illustration in your term paper. There's a beautiful image of the Mona Lisa at the Louvre at http://mistral.culture.fr/louvre/images/ipeint01.jpg. Instead of downloading the image to your computer and making it part of your term paper locally, you could link to the image's URL, thereby saving disk space on your computer. This could cause problems, however, if the Louvre Web site is down when someone's reading your paper, or if the Louvre changes the URL of the Mona Lisa's picture.

When you include portions of Internet resources in a term paper, therefore, you will probably want to download those portions to your computer and put them into the same folder your term paper is in, so you can work with local resources that you control, instead of running the risk that if something happens to prevent the original copy from being found, a hole will appear in your term paper. Figures 14-1 and 14-2 show the icons Web browsers display when images on a Web page cannot be found.

▸ This icon appears in the place of the missing image   ▸ This icon appears in the place of the missing image

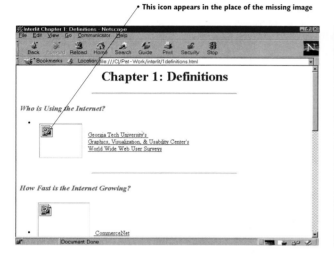

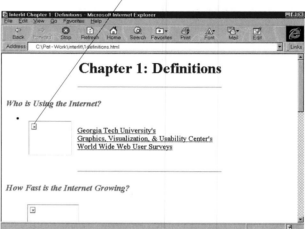

Figure 14-1 How Netscape Communicator handles the case of missing images on a Web page.

Figure 14-2 How Microsoft Internet Explorer handles the case of missing images on a Web page.

E X E R C I S E S

1. Go to http://www.usatoday.com and find a newspaper article that interests you. Following the style guidelines presented in this chapter, write a bibliographic reference to the article in APA, MLA, and CMS styles. Which style do you prefer? Why do you like it better than the others?

2. Imagine yourself applying for a job and wanting to send your employer a copy of a multimedia term paper you wrote as a student. Suppose the term paper contains a copyrighted picture that you included as a fair use. Do the fair use guidelines permit you to include the copyrighted picture when you submit the paper as a writing sample while applying for a job? To find out, go to the bibliographic style chapter's section at the Interlit Web site, and follow the links to the *"Fair Use Guidelines for Educational Multimedia."*

3. Section 6.2 of the *Fair Use Guidelines for Educational Multimedia* warns that some copyrighted works may have been uploaded to the Internet without the permission of the copyright holder. You cannot assume, therefore, that every work on the Internet which does not bear the copyright symbol © is free of copyright. Some people believe that since public funds were used to create the Internet, everything mounted on the Internet is free of copyright. Have you ever met someone who believes that everything on the Internet is in the common domain? (For a work to be in the common domain means that it is publicly available and free of copyright restrictions.)

Part Five

Creating Web Pages

This tutorial on creating World Wide Web pages has a topic that will interest almost everyone: creating a résumé that you can use to apply for a job. Creating a résumé on the Web may provide you with a strategic advantage because you will be able to give prospective employers the World Wide Web address of your résumé. This shows you have network savvy that can benefit an employer in an information society.

On the Web, your résumé will be presented in color with hypertext links that make it quick and easy to read and to find information. You will be able to print your résumé from the Web; the printed version will be neatly typeset with professional-looking fonts, headings, graphics, and bulleted lists of your qualifications and accomplishments.

You will also learn how to create your "home page," which is the Web page that establishes your identity on the Web. By linking things to your home page, you will create a hierarchy that makes it easy for people to access resources you put on the Web. For example, one of the things you will link to your home page is your Web page résumé. Later on, you'll be able to link multimedia term papers that you write on the Web. Thus, your home page will provide potential employers with convincing examples of your online writing skills, and your term papers will contribute to the world of interconnected scholarship.

15 Web Page Creation Strategies

After completing this chapter, you will be able to:

- **Explain the three basic approaches to creating Web pages.**

- **Know when to use an HTML editor, a WYSIWYG tool, or an HTML translator.**

- **Understand how HTML editors work, and be able to find HTML editors on the Web.**

- **Recognize the names of the most popular WYSIWYG editors, and know how to find out more about them.**

- **Realize how HTML translators can save time when you need to create a Web page from a word-processed document, a spreadsheet, a database, or a presentation.**

- **Understand the concept of an applet, and know where to find tools for creating active Web pages.**

- **Define what is meant by the common gateway interface, and understand the server side of Web page development.**

HERE are three ways to create Web pages. First, you can use an HTML editor to create a Web page by working directly with the hypertext markup language, in which all Web pages are encoded. This method provides you with a good understanding of how HTML works, but it is technical. Second, you can use a what-you-see-is-what-you-get (WYSIWYG) editor to create Web pages through a graphical user interface that lets you enter text and graphics directly onto the screen exactly as you want them to appear. As you create the screen, the WYSIWYG editor automatically generates the HTML codes that make the Web page. Third, you can use converters that create Web pages by translating word-processed documents into HTML. This is the most productive way to create Web pages from term papers and other forms of scholarly writing.

This chapter provides an overview of some of the more popular HTML editors, WYSIWYG on-screen editors, and HTML translators. Then it covers tools you can use to create active Web pages that spring to life with sound, video, and animations.

HTML EDITORS

As you learned in the previous chapter, Web pages are encoded in the hypertext markup language (HTML). This language consists of the text of the Web page, plus special codes called **tags** that mark up the text. The tags determine how the text will flow onto the screen, whether it will contain pictures and where they will appear, and what will happen when the user triggers items linked to the document. An editor that lets you create Web pages by working directly with the HTML tags is known as an **HTML editor**. The advantage of creating Web pages with an HTML editor is that it gives you more control over the Web page than WYSIWYG editors and HTML translators, which create the HTML for you. The disadvantage is that for less technically inclined authors, editing HTML tags can seem tedious and time-consuming.

WebEdit

WebEdit is a popular HTML editor for creating Web pages under the Windows operating system. As shown in Figure 15-1, WebEdit lets you edit the HTML in one window and view how it will appear on the Web in another. There is a WebEdit tutorial in the textbook *Multimedia Literacy,* which comes with a multimedia CD-ROM with tutorials and "Show Me" movies that show how to use WebEdit. For more information, follow the links to *Multimedia Literacy* at the Interlit Web site.

HoTMetaL

HoTMetaL is one of the most popular HTML editors. It's cross-platform, meaning that it runs under both Windows and Macintosh operating systems. As illustrated in Figure 15-2, HoTMetaL displays borders around the HTML tags to make it easy for the Web page author to inspect an HTML file and quickly see where the tags are.

Other HTML Editors

There are dozens of other HTML editors that let you create Web pages by working directly with HTML tags. For information about the others, follow the links to the Yahoo list of HTML editors at the Interlit Web site.

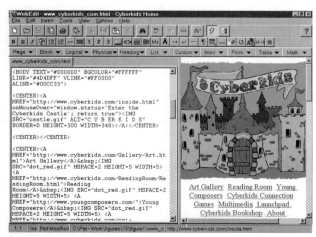

Figure 15-1 WebEdit lets you simultaneously edit the HTML source code in the window on the left and view how it will appear on the Web in the window on the right.

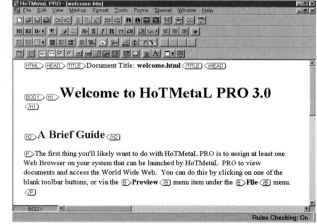

Figure 15-2 HoTMetaL draws borders around the HTML tags to make them easy to find.

WYSIWYG EDITORS

WYSIWYG editors let you create Web pages by typing your text directly on screen, where it appears exactly as it will look on the Web. To change a font, size, color, or other text attribute, you select the text you want to change, then click a button or icon that makes the change. Never do you see the HTML tags, which the WYSIWYG editor inserts into the document automatically, depending on what you do with the WYSIWYG controls. For authors who are less technically inclined, using WYSIWYG tools is preferred to using HTML editors. There are two disadvantages, however, that you need to be aware of. First, when you work with WYSIWYG tools, you do not have as much control over the appearance of the Web page as when you work directly with the HTML tags. Second, WYSIWYG tools normally don't support newly invented tags, which require the use of an HTML editor to insert into a Web page.

Netscape Composer

Netscape Composer is the name of the WYSIWYG Web page editor that comes as part of the suite of tools in Netscape Communicator. When you create a Web page with Netscape Composer, you work on a screen that makes what you create appear just as it will when viewed in the Netscape Web browser. Hence the term, what you see is what you get (WYSIWYG). Chapter 18 will teach you how to create WYSIWYG Web pages with Netscape Composer.

Microsoft FrontPage and FrontPage Express

Microsoft FrontPage Express, formerly known as FrontPad, is a WYSIWYG Web page editor that comes with Microsoft Internet Explorer, and Microsoft FrontPage is a more fully featured Web site creation and management tool that's part of Microsoft Office 97. The tutorial in Chapter 18 will teach you how to create Web pages with Microsoft FrontPage Express. Later, if you decide to upgrade to Microsoft FrontPage, what you learn about FrontPage Express will carry forward.

Adobe PageMill

Another popular WYSIWYG Web page editor is Adobe PageMill. Adobe claims that no matter whether you're just developing individual home pages or an entire corporate Intranet Web site, PageMill makes it as easy as creating an e-mail message. Whether or not this claim is true, Adobe PageMill is the tool of choice for many professional Web site developers. To learn more, follow the links to Adobe PageMill at the Interlit Web site.

Claris Home Page

Another popular WYSIWYG Web page editor is Claris Home Page. Claris claims that whether you're a novice or an expert, Home Page gives you the ability to create dynamic Web pages that look great. To learn more about Claris Home Page, follow the Claris Home Page links at the Interlit Web site.

HTML TRANSLATORS

If you've got an existing document that you want to turn into a Web page, the most efficient way to create the page is with an HTML translator. There are HTML translators for WordPerfect, Microsoft Word, Excel, Access, and Power-Point. The translators are free, and you can download them by following the links to HTML translators at the Interlit Web site. Once you install a translator, you can convert documents to Web pages automatically. Simply open the document you want to translate, pull down the File menu, choose Save As, and select the option to save as HTML.

WordPerfect

The WordPerfect HTML translator is called WP Internet Publisher. You can download it for free by following the links to WordPerfect at the Interlit Web site.

Internet Assistant for Microsoft Word

The Microsoft Word translator is called the Internet Assistant for Microsoft Word. If you have Word 6.0 or Word for Windows 95, you can download the Internet Assistant for free by clicking the Microsoft Word icon at the Interlit Web site. If you have Word for Windows 97 or later, the Internet Assistant is built in; when you install Word, however, you need to choose the option to install the Web page creation tools.

Internet Assistant for Microsoft Excel

Excel is the name of Microsoft's premier spreadsheet software. The Microsoft Excel translator is called the Internet Assistant for Microsoft Excel. You can download it for free by following the links to Microsoft Excel at the Interlit Web site. If you have Excel for Windows 97 or later, the Internet Assistant is built in; when you install Excel, however, you need to choose the option to install the Web page creation tools.

Internet Assistant for Microsoft Access

Access is the name of Microsoft's database software. The Microsoft Access translator is called the Internet Assistant for Microsoft Access. You can download it for free by clicking the Microsoft Access link at the Interlit Web site. If you have Access for Windows 97 or later, the Internet Assistant is built in; when you install Access, however, you need to choose the option to install the Web page creation tools.

Internet Assistant for PowerPoint

Microsoft's presentation software is called PowerPoint. The Microsoft PowerPoint translator is called the Internet Assistant for Microsoft PowerPoint. You can download it for free by following the Microsoft PowerPoint link at the Interlit Web site. If you have PowerPoint for Windows 97 or later, the Internet Assistant is built in; when you install PowerPoint, however, you need to choose the option to install the Web page creation tools.

ACTIVE TOOLS

Active tools are so named because they bring Web pages to life. There are several approaches to creating active Web pages. Some are very easy, while others are quite complex.

Animated GIFs

The simplest way to get motion on a Web page is to create an animated GIF, which is a special kind of GIF file containing multiple images intended to be shown in a sequence at specific times and locations on the screen. A looping option causes your Web browser to keep showing the frames continually, and you see an animation.

 Windows users can create animated GIFs with a shareware package called GIF Construction Set. To download it, click the GIF Construction Set icon at the Interlit Web site.

 Macintosh users can create animated GIF images with GifBuilder. To download it, follow the Interlit Web site links to GifBuilder.

Java

Java is an object-oriented programming language invented by Sun Microsystems. Its main advantage over other programming languages is machine independence. Instead of creating code that can only run on a specific machine (such as a Macintosh or a Windows PC), Java creates an intermediate code, which can run on any computer that knows how to interpret it. As a result, Java runs under Windows, Macintosh, Unix, and many other operating systems, such as the OS9 system used to program settop boxes for the Internet. Machine independence has made Java the hottest new language on the planet. For more information about the Java programming language, click the Java icon at the Interlit Web site.

applets ### JAVA APPLETS

Java can be used to create little applications, called **applets**, that can be transmitted over the Internet as part of a Web page. Applets can bring Web pages to life in several ways. For example, scrolling tickers can move information across the screen. You can use a mouse to rotate three-dimensional objects that would otherwise appear flat on a static Web page. Active spreadsheets let users manipulate Web page data right on the Web page. Web pages can contain games, such as Hangman or Tic-Tac-Toe, or more-complex simulations. Interactive tutorials can enable users to interact with economic models. With Java, Web pages can even contain graphics editors that enable users to create their own graphics.

To explore Web pages that use Java, follow the Interlit Web site links to Java-enabled Web pages. Make sure you try running the Tokamak reactor at the Princeton Nuclear Physics Laboratory.

JAVASCRIPT

Developing applets in Java is time-consuming and requires advanced programming skills. Does this mean that creating active Web pages is beyond the scope of the typical Web page author? No, thanks to JavaScript. Netscape developed JavaScript so you can make active Web pages without having to become a Java programmer. Instead of having to compile Java code, JavaScript lets you include a sequence of computer commands (called a *script*) directly on the Web page.

The Interlit Web site contains links to Web pages that use JavaScript. These pages illustrate how JavaScript can be used to perform (1) simple tasks such as selecting the image displayed on a Web page or manipulating foreground and background colors dynamically; (2) numerical computations such as computing your grade-point average; and (3) more-complex tasks such as filling out an income tax form.

It is beyond the scope of this book to provide a tutorial on JavaScript. After you complete the Web page tutorial in this book, if you are interested in learning how to use JavaScript, you can find an excellent tutorial online by following the links to Netscape's JavaScript Resources Web site.

JavaScript is supported both by Netscape—its inventor—and by the Microsoft Internet Explorer.

ActiveX

ActiveX was begun by Microsoft as a way to create and distribute information over the Internet using existing software applications and data. At first, developers were somewhat reluctant to embrace the ActiveX technology, however, because it was not an open standard, as was Java. In 1996, Microsoft released ActiveX to the Open Group, an industry consortium experienced in promoting cross-platform technologies.

ActiveX involves three concepts—controls, scripts, and documents. ActiveX controls enable a wide variety of applications and content to be embedded in HTML documents. Utilizing Microsoft's object linking and embedding technology, ActiveX controls enable you to incorporate any supported data type directly into the window of an ActiveX-enabled Web browser such as the Microsoft Internet Explorer. More than a thousand ActiveX controls are available, from multimedia sound and video players, to spreadsheets, charts, graphs, calculators, and paint programs. The Microsoft Internet Explorer itself is an ActiveX control that can be embedded inside other applications.

Active Scripts work in conjunction with ActiveX controls, enabling the user to manipulate and interact with data displayed by ActiveX controls. HTML documents that make use of ActiveX controls and scripts are known as ActiveX documents.

For more information about ActiveX controls, follow the links to ActiveX at the Interlit Web site.

Shockwave

Macromedia Director is the state-of-the-art animation program for creating multimedia applications. Best-selling CD-ROMs such as the *Living Books, Myst,* and Sting's *All This Time* were produced with Director. Shockwave is the name of Macromedia's Director plug-in for Web browsers. Like Java, Shockwave code gets downloaded and runs on your computer when you view a Web page with a Shockwave-enabled browser. Both Netscape Communicator and Microsoft Internet Explorer support Shockwave. For the latest information, or to download a free copy of Shockwave, follow the links to Shockwave at the Interlit Web site.

Supercard with Roadster

Supercard is a popular cross-platform multimedia tool for creating hypermedia presentations. Roadster is the name of the plug-in that makes it possible for Supercard applications to be distributed via Web pages. For more information, and to download the Roadster player, follow the links to Supercard at the Interlit Web site.

SERVER-SIDE TOOLS

Viewing a Web page on the Internet always involves a client (the browser that requests, downloads, and displays the Web page) and a server (the computer that serves the Web page to the client). After the browser receives the requested Web page from the client, your computer does the work of displaying the text and graphics and enables you to scroll up and down to view the content of the page. No other computer is involved.

There are times, however, when another computer must get involved to help a browser process a Web page. Consider the example in Figure 15-3, which displays a Web page with a form that the user fills out to order a book from amazon.com using a credit card. When the user enters a password and clicks the Submit button to process the information, the browser must ask another computer on the Internet to validate the password. For transactions like this between a browser and another computer on the Internet, there is a standard protocol known as the common gateway interface (CGI).

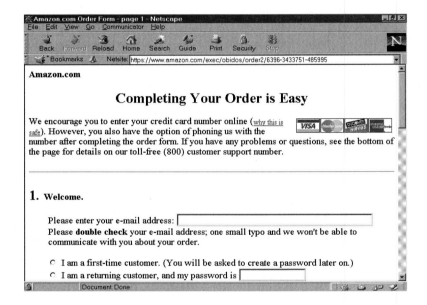

Figure 15-3 Ordering a book via credit card at amazon.com.

Common Gateway Interface (CGI) Programs

The common gateway interface enables the Web page author to link CGI programs to the triggers on a Web page. When the user triggers a link to a CGI program, your Web browser tells the appropriate computer on the Internet to run the CGI program, which processes the request and returns the information requested. CGI programs can be written in any computer language, such as C, COBOL, or BASIC. CGI programs can also be written as **batch files**, which are lists of operating system commands run in sequence to accomplish a given task. On servers that run the Unix operating system, batch files are called **scripts**. CGI programs that are Unix scripts are also called **CGI scripts**.

Perl

Perl is a machine-independent scripting language developed by Larry Wall, the author of *rn*, which is a popular Unix newsgroup reader. You can create and run Perl scripts under Unix (where it was originally developed), as well as under DOS,

OS/2, Macintosh, Amiga, and Windows. There is a large public-domain library of Perl scripts that you can download and use for free at your own Web site. The popularity of Perl has also led to the creation of many tools for creating new Perl scripts. For more information about Perl, follow the links to Perl at the Interlit Web site. There's also a Usenet newsgroup named comp.lang.perl.

CLIENT-SIDE TRENDS

As HTML continues to evolve and improve, it is becoming possible for Web page authors to handle tasks on the client side that formerly required CGI calls to other computers on the Internet. Image maps are a good example. An image map is an invisible layer of rectangular triggers placed over an image on the screen. When the user clicks inside one of the invisible rectangles, your Web browser triggers the object of the link. In earlier versions of HTML, using image maps required the use of a CGI call. When the user clicked a trigger in an image map, the browser sent the coordinates of the mouse click to a CGI program on a server, which told the browser what to do in response to the click. In the latest version of HTML, it is possible to process image maps locally within the document, instead of having to call upon a CGI program for help in handling the mouse click.

This trend to move server-side tasks to the client simplifies Web page development and makes authors less dependent on CGI servers.

E X E R C I S E S

1. In your own words, describe when it's best to use an HTML editor, a WYSIWYG tool, or an HTML translator to create a Web page.

2. There's a lot of competition between companies like Netscape, Microsoft, and Sun Microsystems to come up with the most popular way of distributing applications over the Web. This competition results in requiring you to install support for multiple technologies if you want to take advantage of neat new stuff happening at different sites out on the Web. A good example is the difference between Java and ActiveX. Do you think this kind of competition is good for the industry? Or would it be better for the government to require that companies work together and embrace common standards from the get-go?

3. Several companies are competing for market share in multimedia. The plug-ins these companies create to enable multimedia applications to become part of Web pages are not compatible with one another. For example, you need a plug-in called Shockwave to do Macromedia Director over the Web. Toolbook requires a plug-in called Asymetrix Neuron. Supercard's plug-in is Roadster. Apple's Cocoa uses yet another format. Do you think this competition among competing standards is good, or do you think it clutters your computer to have to install so many different plug-ins to get multimedia content over the Web? Should the vendors be forced into cooperating on a single standard for multimedia? Or is it still too soon for multimedia standards?

4. Comment on the trend to enable Web clients such as Netscape Navigator and the Microsoft Internet Explorer to handle features that formerly required server-side CGI calls. Do you hope the clients become so powerful that you'll never need to run your own Web server? Or do you think that you might some day want to run your own server so you can have direct control over the materials you publish on the Web?

16 Web Page Design

After completing this chapter, you will be able to:

- Identify the basic elements that constitute a **Web page**.

- Explain the uses and general appearance of the elements of a **Web page**.

- Begin thinking about the design of your **Web page** résumé and how to make it engaging and informative.

- Arrange text in the proper size, color, and font on a **Web page**.

- Choose an appropriate background color and understand how foreground text colors interact with background screen colors.

- Arrange pictures on the screen either as background images or design elements for text to flow around.

- Make text stand out against a background photo.

- Adopt a common look and feel for your **Web pages**.

HERE are two primary factors to consider in World Wide Web page design: how the page will look, and how the user will interact with it. This chapter presents the elements you will use to design your Web page résumé.

WEB PAGE ELEMENTS

World Wide Web pages consist of elements defined in the HTML language that is used to create Web pages. As illustrated in Figures 16-1 to 16-9, these elements include:

- headings
- paragraphs
- horizontal rules
- lists
- images
- backgrounds

- targets
- links
- special characters
- tables
- frames

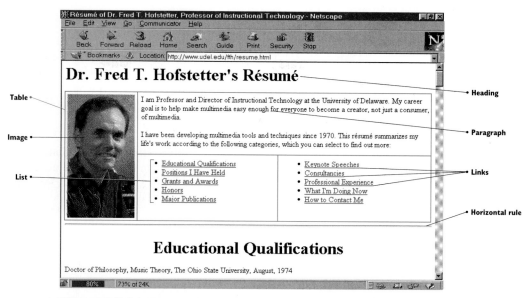

Figure 16-1 Web page elements in action on the author's Web page résumé.

Headings

As illustrated in Figure 16-2, there are six heading styles, numbered from H1 to H6. The smaller the number, the bigger the heading. H1 is the biggest or most important heading, and H6 is the smallest. Headings can be left justified, centered, or right justified.

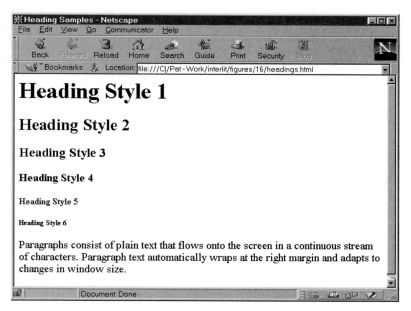

Figure 16-2 Heading styles and paragraphs.

Paragraphs

Paragraphs consist of plain text that flows onto the screen in a continuous stream of characters. Paragraph text automatically wraps at the right margin and adapts to changes in window size.

Horizontal Rules

Horizontal rules are a design element used to create dividers between sections of a Web page. Horizontal rules appear with a neat three-dimensional effect. It is possible to vary the length, thickness, and shading of a horizontal rule, but the default settings look pretty good.

Lists

Lists can be ordered or unordered. In an ordered list, the items are numbered automatically; in an unordered list, the items are bulleted.

Images

Images enhance the visual appeal of Web pages. Images can be left justified, right justified, or centered on the screen. Text can be made to flow around the left or the right side of an image, as illustrated in Figure 16-4.

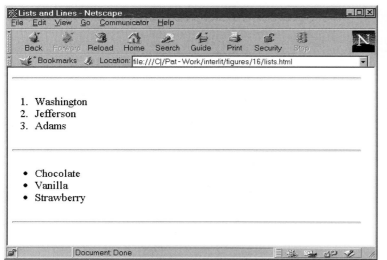

Figure 16-3 Horizontal rules and lists help organize and delimit information on a Web page.

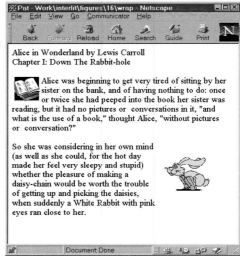

Figure 16-4 Text can flow around the left or the right side of an image.

Backgrounds

Backgrounds can be filled with a solid color, or you can tile a bitmap into the background to create a textured appearance. It is important to choose a background that does not detract from the readability of the text. For this reason, black text on a white background is the most popular color choice on the Web.

In many browsers the default background color is gray. When the default black text color displays on a gray background, the screen is not as readable as black text on a white background, which provides better contrast. Figure 16-5 compares the default black-on-gray color combination to the more readable black-on-white color scheme.

Targets

To provide the user with a quick way to jump around among the various topics in your Web page, you can insert targets. For example, you might set a target named

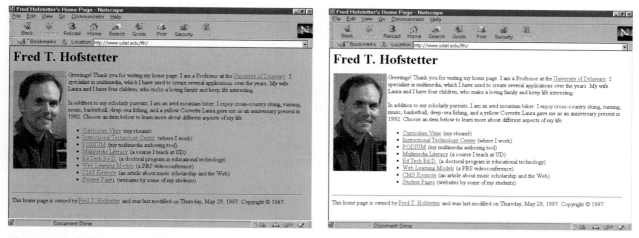

Figure 16-5 Comparison of the default black-on-gray color combination to a black-on-white color scheme.

Click here to jump to a target further down on this Web page

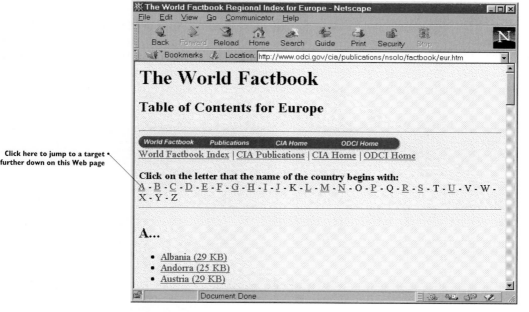

Figure 16-6 Targets work like bookmarks to provide easy access to sections within a Web page.

"education" at the start of the education section of your résumé. In your résumé's bulleted table of contents, you would link the education bullet to the target named "education" to provide a quick way of jumping to your educational qualifications.

Links

Links are the most essential element in Web design, because links create webs. Without links, there would be no webs! On World Wide Web pages, links can be textual or pictorial. Any word or picture on the screen can be linked to any resource on the Web. Most links connect you to other Web pages or bookmarks on the current Web page, as shown in Figure 16-6. However, as you will learn in Chapter 23, any multimedia file or application can be the object of a link on the World Wide Web. For example, your term papers, scholarly publications, software, and multimedia applications can all be mounted on the World Wide Web and linked to your résumé so potential employers can review samples of your work.

Special Characters

Web pages can contain special symbols such as the Greek characters used in scientific notation, as well as mathematical functions, operators, delimiters, accents, arrows, and pointers.

Tables

Normally, the text of a Web page flows evenly onto the screen, aligning itself automatically with the left and right edge of your browser's window. Tables provide a way of dividing the screen into rectangular regions. Text flows inside the rectangles, creating a columnar appearance, much like the columns of text that appear in printed newspapers. Graphics can also be made to flow into tabular columns. The border of the rectangles in the table can be visible, creating on-screen dividing lines between the table elements, as shown in Figure 16-7, or the border can be invisible, as illustrated in Figure 16-8.

When HTML was invented, there was no support for tables, and Web pages looked pretty much the same in terms of design and layout. Today, tables are the most powerful way of positioning items on a Web page to create many interesting designs. In Chapter 20, you will get a lot of practice using tables to lay out Web pages.

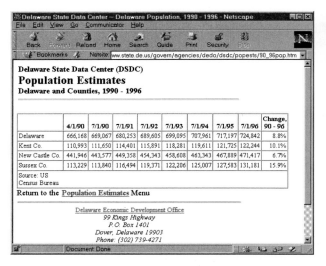

Figure 16-7 Making the borders of the table visible helps the user follow data across the table.

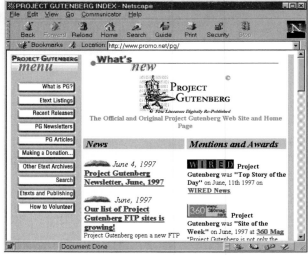

Figure 16-8 Invisible borders permit a table to govern subtly the positioning of Web page elements.

Frames

Have you ever seen a TV that supports a feature called "picture in a picture"? While viewing one television program full-screen, you can watch another program in a smaller on-screen window. On Web pages, frames serve a similar purpose. The term **frame** refers to the border that appears around windows on your screen. When you learned how to resize your Web browser in Chapter 4, you did so by clicking and dragging its window frame. When Web pages contain frames, more than one window appears on your Web page, and you can interact with the information in the windows independently.

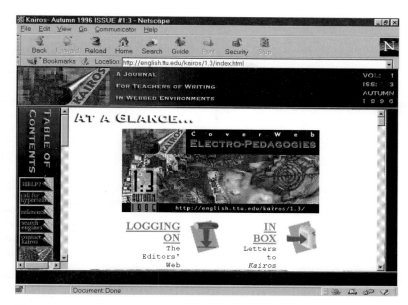

Figure 16-9 The *Kairos* Web site is an excellent example of the use of frames on Web pages.

Some users find frames confusing and prefer not to use them. That's why Web pages with frames often allow the user to turn the frames off. There's a great example of the use of frames at the *Kairos* Web site, where you will find the electronic journal *Kairos* presented with frames. As illustrated in Figure 16-9, one frame enables you to scroll through the site's contents, while another frame displays the article chosen. To try the frames yourself, follow the Interlit links to *Kairos*. Notice how the *Kairos* Web site provides an option to turn the frames on or off, depending on whether you like using frames.

HoTMetaL Pro contains tools for creating frames. For more information, follow the links to HoTMetaL at the Interlit Web site.

SCREEN DESIGN PRINCIPLES

The hands-on tutorial in this part of the book teaches you how to create a Web page résumé. You will learn how to flow text onto the screen, create bulleted lists, and link items in the list to the different parts of your résumé. Then you will learn how to put pictures on the screen, either as backgrounds that appear behind the text or as design elements around which text flows. Before you begin, it is important to understand a few principles of Web page design that will help you make screens that have a good layout.

Layout

As you learned earlier in this chapter, Web pages consist of several design elements, including headings, paragraphs, horizontal rules, lists, images, backgrounds, bookmarks, links, special characters, tables, and frames. The relationship between these elements on the screen is called *layout*. When you create a Web page, you should plan its layout so your content gets presented with good balance. Think of dividing the screen into regions, of which some will be pictorial, with others consisting of blocks of text. You must also think about how the user will interact with your screen, and include the appropriate navigational buttons and hypertext links.

Figures 16-10 through 16-15 analyze the screen layouts of some example Web pages. Notice how some rely heavily on text, while others are more graphical. All of the sample screens provide intuitive ways to navigate that make these Web pages user-friendly.

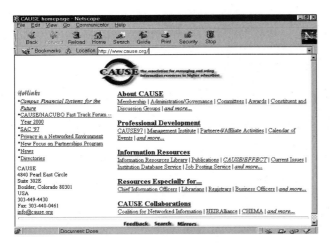

Figure 16-10 Textual screen design.

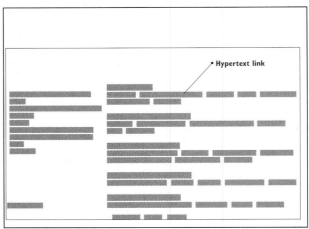

Figure 16-11 Layout analysis of Figure 16-10.

Figure 16-12 Graphical screen design.

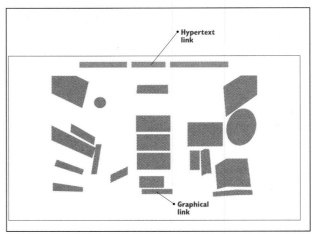

Figure 16-13 Layout analysis of Figure 16-12.

Figure 16-14 Mixed screen design.

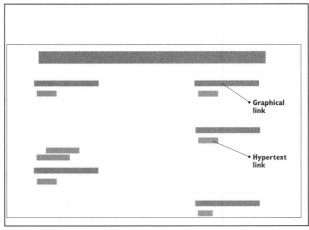

Figure 16-15 Layout analysis of Figure 16-14.

In Chapter 20, you will learn how to use tables to lay out Web pages in rectangular regions such as these.

Font Selection

Most Web browsers support the fonts listed in Figure 16-16. Web pages can either set these fonts specifically or leave the choice of the font up to the user. When no font is specified, the browser displays text in the default font. Most users have the default font set to Times New Roman. Note that in order for a font to appear on a Web page, that font must be installed on your computer.

Times New Roman   ABCDEFGabcdefg123456789
Courier New   ABCDEFGabcdefg123456789
Arial   ABCDEFGabcdefg123456789

Figure 16-16   Fonts used on the Web.

All of the fonts illustrated in Figure 16-16 are proportionally spaced except for Courier. Proportional spacing means that fat letters like *m* and *w* take up more space than thin letters like *l* and *i*. Normally you will want to use a proportional font, because proportional spacing is easier to read than nonproportional fonts. However, if you want to make columns of text line up precisely on the screen, such as in a spreadsheet, you will need to use the nonproportional Courier font. Figure 16-17 illustrates the difference between proportional and nonproportional spacing.

Times New Roman

For headings and paragraphs, proportional fonts are easiest to read. For preformatted text with vertical alignments, however, they are not appropriate:

Sales:	$100,000	$85,000	$43,614
Taxes:	54,521	3,425	6,921
Fees:	231,947	41	324
Total:	$386,468	$88,466	$50,859

Courier New

```
Nonproportional, or monospaced, fonts are
regimented and somewhat graceless, but
make vertical alignment much easier:

Sales:     $100,000     $85,000     $43,614
Taxes:       54,521       3,425       6,921
Fees:       231,947          41         324
Total:     $386,468     $88,466     $50,859
```

Figure 16-17 Comparison of proportional and nonproportional spacing.

The primary difference between the Times and Arial fonts is that Times has serifs, while Arial does not. A serif is a line stemming at an angle from the upper and lower ends of the strokes of a letter. Figure 16-18 compares a few characters from the Times and Arial fonts, pointing out the serifs in the Times font.

Text Sizing

Text size is measured in points, which tell how high the text is. In print media, a point is one seventy-second (1/72) of an inch. On a 640 × 480 computer screen, a point is about the height of a single pixel. Due to different-sized monitors, the actual size of the text will vary somewhat, depending on the physical height of the screen. Figure 16-19 illustrates different point sizes used on the Web.

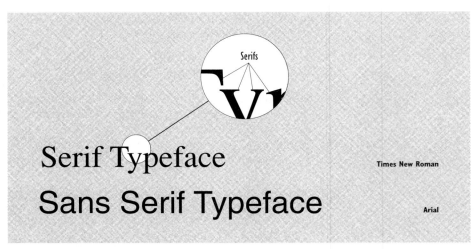

Figure 16-18 Comparison of Times New Roman and Arial fonts.

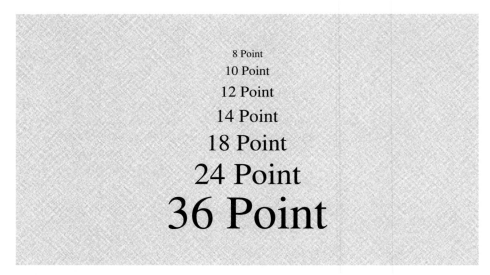

Figure 16-19 Comparison of different point sizes.

Foreground Versus Background Colors

You can select from a wide range of colors for the text and the background of a Web page. Some color combinations work better than others. Figure 16-20 illustrates recommended color combinations as well as colors to avoid.

There are sites on the Web where you can see what different color combinations look like. To explore different foreground/background combinations, follow the links to the InfiNet color index at the Interlit Web site.

Photographic Backgrounds

Exercise care when placing text on photographic backgrounds. Some photos are so busy that text placed atop them is difficult to read. Bolding can improve the readability of text placed on photographic backgrounds. Figure 16-21 illustrates text printed on top of a background photo in different colors and sizes, with and without bolding.

Background Color	Recommended Foregrounds	Foregrounds to Avoid
White	Black, DarkBlue, Red	Yellow, Cyan, LightGray
Blue	White, Yellow, Cyan	Green, Black
Pink	Black, White, Yellow, Blue	Green, Red, Cyan
Red	Yellow, White, Black	Pink, Cyan, Blue, Green
Yellow	Red, Blue, Black	White, Cyan
Green	Black, Red, Blue	Cyan, Pink, Yellow
Cyan	Blue, Black, Red	Green, Yellow, White
LightGray	Black, DarkBlue, DarkPink	Green, Cyan, Yellow
Gray	Yellow, White, Blue	DarkGray, DarkCyan
DarkGray	Cyan, Yellow, Green	Red, Blue, Gray
Black	White, Cyan, Green, Yellow	DarkRed, DarkCyan
DarkBlue	Yellow, White, Pink, Green	DarkGreen, Black
DarkPink	Green, Yellow, White	Black, DarkCyan
DarkRed	White, LightGray, Yellow	Black, DarkBlue
Brown	Yellow, Cyan, White	Red, Pink, DarkGreen
DarkGreen	Cyan, White, Yellow	DarkBlue, DarkRed
DarkCyan	White, Yellow, Cyan	Brown, Blue, Gray

Figure 16-20 Recommended color combinations and colors to avoid.

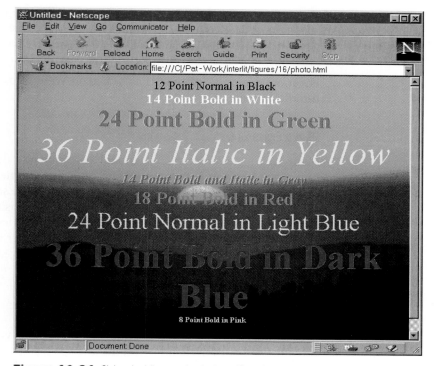

Figure 16-21 Sizing, bolding, and coloring affect the readability of text on a photographic background.

Tiled Backgrounds

Tiled backgrounds are created when a bitmap smaller than the screen is drawn repeatedly up, down, and across the screen until all of the screen surface has been covered. As illustrated in Figure 16-22, a tiled background can create a special effect on a Web page. You must be careful, however, to select a tile that does not interfere with the readability of the text printed on top of it.

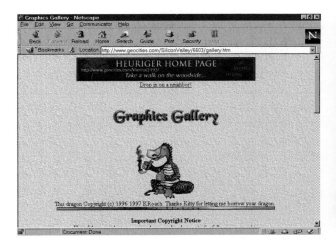

Figure 16-22 Example of a seamless tile in the background of a Web page. The tile image is:

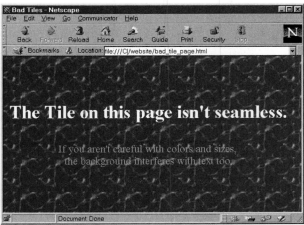

Figure 16-23 A bad tile that is not seamless and interferes with the readability of the text. The tile image is:

Tiles should be seamless, meaning that when the bitmap replicates itself up and down the screen, you cannot perceive the edges of the bitmap or detect a regular interruption in the pattern caused by the edges of the bitmap not fitting against each other smoothly. Figure 16-23 shows an example of a bad tile, in which you can clearly see a rectangular interruption around the edges of the bitmap. It is also difficult to read the text on top of this tile, making it a doubly bad choice on a Web page.

For more examples of good tiles to use on Web pages, click the tile icon at the Interlit Web site.

Navigational Icons

Many Web pages contain navigational icons that give the user the option to page forward or backward, go to a menu, or return to a home page. Navigational icons normally work best when they appear lined up in the same region of the screen, instead of being scattered about the screen. Try to position the icons in a logical order. For example, it is logical to place the page-back icon in the lower left corner of the screen, and the page-forward icon in the lower right. Here is a suggested sequence of icons that gives the user the option to page back, return to the menu, go to a home page, or page forward:

Figure 16-24 shows a Web page that makes a simple, yet effective use of icons to provide users with navigation options through a large Web site. To visit this page, click the navigation icon at the Interlit Web site.

Scrolling

When you design a Web page, keep in mind that the user can scroll up and down through the information that is in it. Imagine what the user will see on each screen of your Web page document, and plan the layout accordingly. If your document is long, you will want to provide navigation options periodically in the midst of the document, instead of only putting them at the end. Otherwise, the user will have to scroll all the way down to find out what the navigation options are.

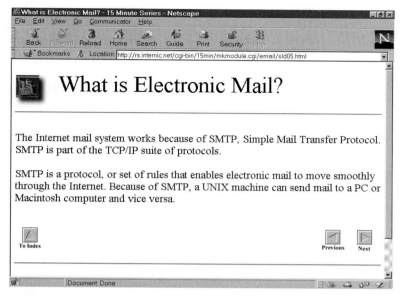

Figure 16-24 A simple, yet effective use of navigation icons.

When you have a long document, it's best to organize it into sections divided by horizontal rules, and put the navigation options at the end of each section. You will learn how to do this in Chapter 18, in which you will provide navigation options at the end of each section of your Web page résumé.

User Friendliness

It is important that Web pages be easy to use. When you plan your layout and decide where you will place pictures and text on your screen, make sure you include navigational buttons, icons, or hypertext to clarify what the navigational options are and where the user should click to navigate.

Word your hypertext links to make it clear what will happen when the user triggers them. Descriptive phrases are better than single words. A descriptive phrase such as "go to the table of contents" tells what will happen when the user clicks it. The *Kairos* journal contains guidelines for writing hypertext in such a way that the user knows what the links will trigger; to review these guidelines, follow the Interlit links to Informed Linking.

Iconic navigation is often more effective than words, takes up less screen space, and works better with international audiences because the icons can be understood regardless of what language the user speaks.

Be consistent. If you adopt navigational icons, use them consistently throughout your Web site. If you use hypertext navigation, be consistent in how you word the directions.

Consistency

Avoid the temptation to demonstrate every trick you know when you design a Web page. Keep it simple. Do not make every screen look and work a different way. Rather, adopt a common look and feel so the user will be able to navigate through your Web site intuitively.

It is frustrating to use a Web page that mixes metaphors and changes what icons mean on different screens. Be consistent.

LAYOUT ANALYSIS OF A WEB PAGE RÉSUMÉ

Figure 16-25 contains a layout analysis of a Web page résumé. Notice how the use of text, fonts, sizes, and colors enhances the readability of the text. Each item in the menu serves as a hypertext that links to different sections of the résumé. The navigation options at the end of each section make it clear how to move around on the page. The common look and feel of each section makes it easy for a prospective employer to find out about your job skills and work experience.

Figure 16-25 Layout analysis of a Web page résumé.

E X E R C I S E S

1. Using the design elements presented in this chapter, plan the layout of your Web page résumé. Think about the menu choices you will want to provide prospective employers who visit your Web page to find out about your experience and qualifications. Include this menu as one of the design elements in your résumé. Possible menu items include:

- Educational Qualifications
- Work Experience
- Computer Skills
- Grants and Awards
- Honorary Societies

- Professional Association Memberships
- Publications
- Software
- Presentations
- How to Contact Me

2. Since it is possible to link any document, audio, picture, movie, or software application to your Web page, you will be able to link your résumé to examples of your work to prove your worth to a prospective employer. What examples would you like to link to your résumé? Include these links in the design of your résumé.

3. There's a knack to writing hypertext in such a way that the wording makes it clear what will happen when the user triggers the link. List three different ways you could write a hypertext instruction on the screen which, when clicked, takes the user to your home page.

4. Draw three different ways of providing an icon that moves forward to the next screen of an application.

17

How HTML Works

After completing this chapter, you will be able to:

- **Explain the concept of a markup language.**

- **Realize that different Web browsers may display the same HTML somewhat differently.**

- **Understand the two HTML tag formats.**

- **Define the families of HTML tags.**

- **Understand the HTML tags used in creating a résumé.**

- **Describe how HTML evolved and still is emerging.**

- **Understand the elements of a URL.**

TML is the markup language used to create hypertext documents for the World Wide Web. HTML stands for *h*yper*t*ext *m*arkup *l*anguage. The key to understanding how HTML works is to know what it means to mark up a text. This chapter explains the concept of a markup language, defines the families of HTML tags, and identifies the tags that you will use in creating your Web page résumé.

If you are not a technical person, you may be concerned that learning these tags is too complicated, and you'll never be able to create a Web page on your own. Do not worry about this. You do not need to memorize the tags presented in this chapter. When you create your Web page résumé in the next chapter, you'll be using a WYSIWYG tool that inserts the tags automatically for you. Why then, you may ask, do you need to know about the tags at all? Because sometimes you do need to work at the level of the HTML code to create a special effect or to insert a command that a certain tool may not yet handle.

UNDERSTANDING MARKUP

To mark up a text means to insert special codes called **tags** into the text. The tags control how the text appears on a Web page. For example, compare Figures 17-1 and 17-2. In Figure 17-1, you see how a text appears on a Web page; notice the different-sized headings, the paragraphs, and the list of bulleted items. In Figure 17-2, you can see the HTML tags that mark up the text. By comparing these two figures, you can begin to understand how HTML controls the appearance of text on the Web. Notice how the HTML tags always appear <inside> brackets.

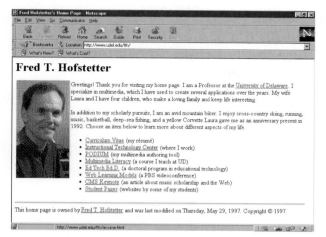

Figure 17-1 How the author's home page appears on the Web.

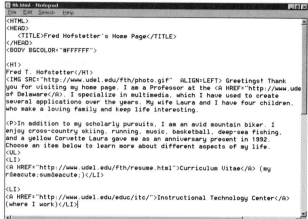

Figure 17-2 The HTML source code that creates the author's home page. The codes in <brackets> are the HTML tags that "mark up" the text.

HTML TAG FORMATS

There are two HTML tag formats: paired tags and single tags.

Paired tags come in pairs, which consist of a start tag and a stop tag. Headings are an example of paired tags. For example, to make the words *Internet Literacy* appear in the largest style of heading, you would mark them up as follows:

```
<H1>Internet Literacy</H1>
```

<H1> is the start tag, and </H1> is the stop tag. The words between them will appear in heading style H1, which is the largest of the six heading styles. You can tell a start tag from a stop tag because the stop tag always has a slash, as in </H1>.

Single tags function on their own with no stop tag. For example, the tag <HR> makes a line known as a "horizontal rule" appear on your Web page; there is no stop tag for a horizontal rule.

TAXONOMY OF HTML TAGS

There are more than a hundred HTML tags. Learning that many tags may seem like a foreboding task. You can simplify the process, however, if you realize that the tags can be thought of in families devoted to accomplishing similar tasks. The following taxonomy, which was created by Ken Nesbitt as a way of organizing the tools in his WebEdit software, groups the HTML tags into 13 families:

- **Page structure tags** provide a framework for the document as a whole. They identify that the document is encoded in HTML and provide titling, framing, and header information that defines the structure of the file.

- **Block-style tags** control the flow of text into blocks on the screen. The most common block style is the paragraph.

- **Logical font-style tags** include styles for abbreviations, acronyms, citations, and quotations.

- **Physical font-style tags** let you create text that is blinking, bold, italic, subscripted, superscripted, or underlined.

■ **Heading tags** let you create headings in six different levels or sizes of importance.

■ **Lists and miscellaneous tags** let you create ordered lists (i.e., numbered lists), unordered lists (i.e., bulleted lists), menus, directories, horizontal rules (i.e., dividing lines), and line breaks.

■ **Form tags** let you create input fields, buttons, and selection boxes for gathering information from the user.

■ **Table tags** let you define tables that present data in neat rows and columns.

■ **Math tags** provide a wide range of special symbols used in scientific notation.

■ **Anchor/link tags** let you create bookmarks, hypertext, and hyperpicture triggers and link them to any resource or file on the World Wide Web.

■ **Image tags** let you insert figures, center or align pictures with the left or right margin, flow text around images, or place little icons inline in the midst of your text.

■ **Server side includes (SSI) tags** provide a simpler way of adding database access to your Web pages than the old method of writing CGI (common gateway interface) scripts to interact with database programs on a server.

■ **Java tags** provide a means for defining a way to interact with Java applets, which are little applications that get downloaded to your computer along with a Web page.

TAGS USED IN THE WEB PAGE CREATION TUTORIAL

Table 17-1 defines the HTML tags used in this book. These are all a standard part of HTML, and they will work with almost any Web browser, including both Netscape Communicator and the Microsoft Internet Explorer.

Table 17-1   HTML Tags Used in the Web Page Creation Tutorial

HTML Tag Syntax	Use on Web Page
<HTML> and </HTML>	These tags define the beginning and end of an HTML document. Your Web pages will always begin with the <HTML> start tag and end with the </HTML> stop tag.
<HEAD> and </HEAD>	The headers of your HTML file will appear between these tags.
<TITLE> and </TITLE>	The title of your HTML file goes between these tags, which in turn go between the header tags.
<BODY> and </BODY>	The body of your HTML file goes between these tags.
<H1> and </H1>	You will use the H1 heading tags at the beginning of your résumé to make your name appear in the most important heading style.
<P> and </P>	The <P> tag marks the beginning of a new paragraph. The stop tag </P> is optional. The <P> tag will always begin a new paragraph, whether or not a </P> tag marks the end of the paragraph.
<UL> and </UL>	These unordered list tags will mark the beginning and end of the table of contents in your résumé.
<LI>	The list item tag will mark the beginning of each item in your table of contents. There is no "end of list item" tag.

Table 17-1   *(Continued)*

HTML Tag Syntax	Use on Web Page
`<HR>`	The horizontal rule tag makes the neat three-dimensional dividing lines on Web pages.
`<A NAME="name">`	A stands for *anchor*. The anchor name tag creates names for the bookmarks in your résumé.
`<A HREF="url"> </A>`	HREF stands for *hypertext reference*. The anchor HREF tag creates hypertext links to the URLs of resources on the Web.
`<IMG SRC="filename">`	The image tag places pictures on your Web page.
`<BODY BACKGROUND="filename"> </BODY>`	The background body tag tiles an image into the background of your Web page to give your résumé a sophisticated look.
`<TABLE> and </TABLE>`	Table cells go between these tags.

VERSIONS OF HTML

The World Wide Web is an emerging technology, and new HTML tags get invented constantly. When this book was printed, HTML was in its third version. By the time you read this, HTML will probably have advanced beyond version 3. Happily, new versions of HTML are backwards compatible, meaning that Web pages you create with today's version will continue to work with future versions.

 Sometimes the hottest new features of HTML are not supported by all browsers. For example, Netscape's latest HTML features may not work in Microsoft's browser, and vice versa. The World Wide Web Consortium (W3C) is the standards body that officially registers new features into HTML. All of the major computing vendors and network companies belong to the W3C. To learn more about the consortium, follow the Interlit links to W3C.

E X E R C I S E S

1. Compare the advantages and disadvantages of the evolutionary nature of HTML. What is good about designing the language so new HTML tags can be added to it? Are there disadvantages to developing a language this way?

2. Think about the taxonomy of HTML tags provided in this chapter. What capabilities do you think the World Wide Web should have that are not included in this taxonomy?

3. Follow the links to W3C at the Interlit Web site, and read how the consortium oversees the continued evolution of HTML. What mechanism is provided by the W3C for you to request new features to be added to HTML?

18 Creating Your Web Page Résumé

After completing this chapter, you will be able to:

☐ **Create a file folder for your Web pages.**

☐ **Use Netscape Composer or Microsoft FrontPage Express to create a new HTML file.**

☐ **Enter your own content into the Web page.**

☐ **Create new paragraphs on a Web page.**

☐ **Make lists on a Web page.**

☐ **Put pictures on a Web page.**

☐ **Tile a background onto a Web page.**

☐ **Create named targets on a Web page.**

☐ **Create links to targets.**

☐ **View the Web page with your favorite Web browser.**

 that you know how HTML works, you are ready to put your new knowledge to work. This chapter takes you through all the steps needed to build your own online résumé with text, graphics, and links to other Web pages.

MAKING A FILE FOLDER FOR YOUR WEB PAGES

When you create a World Wide Web page, you begin by creating the file folder in which the Web page will reside. The name of the folder for this tutorial is *website*; you should create the *website* folder now. Follow these steps:

▶ If you have Windows 3.1, pull down the File Manager's File menu, choose Create Directory, type **c:\website**, and press ⏎Enter.

▶ If you have Windows 95, click the Start button, choose Programs, open the Explorer, navigate to the root of your hard drive, pull down the Explorer's File menu, choose New/Folder, type **website**, and press ⏎Enter.

▶ If you have a Macintosh, select File from the menu bar, then select New Folder. The folder will be created with the name *untitled folder*. Select the name by clicking it once, then type the new name, and press ⏎Enter.

SELECTING A WEB PAGE CREATION TOOL

The Web page creation tutorial in this part of the book can be completed with either Netscape Composer or Microsoft FrontPage Express (formerly known as FrontPad). Netscape Composer is part of Netscape Communicator, and Microsoft FrontPage Express comes with Microsoft Internet Explorer. If you're using Netscape as your Web browser, you'll probably want to use Netscape Composer as your Web page creation tool. Microsoft FrontPage Express is a good choice if you're using the Microsoft Internet Explorer.

RUNNING THE WEB PAGE CREATION SOFTWARE

The first step in creating a new Web page is to get your Web page creation software running. Follow the steps in Table 18-1.

Table 18-1 How to Start Your Web Page Creation Software

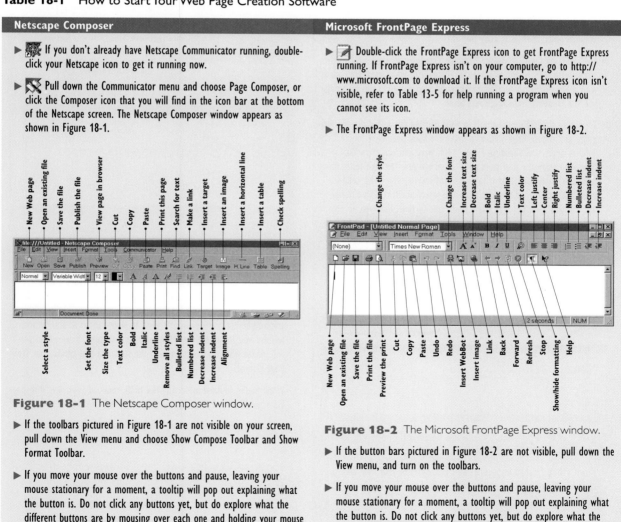

Netscape Composer	Microsoft FrontPage Express
▶ If you don't already have Netscape Communicator running, double-click your Netscape icon to get it running now.	▶ Double-click the FrontPage Express icon to get FrontPage Express running. If FrontPage Express isn't on your computer, go to http://www.microsoft.com to download it. If the FrontPage Express icon isn't visible, refer to Table 13-5 for help running a program when you cannot see its icon.
▶ Pull down the Communicator menu and choose Page Composer, or click the Composer icon that you will find in the icon bar at the bottom of the Netscape screen. The Netscape Composer window appears as shown in Figure 18-1.	▶ The FrontPage Express window appears as shown in Figure 18-2.

Figure 18-1 The Netscape Composer window.

▶ If the toolbars pictured in Figure 18-1 are not visible on your screen, pull down the View menu and choose Show Compose Toolbar and Show Format Toolbar.

▶ If you move your mouse over the buttons and pause, leaving your mouse stationary for a moment, a tooltip will pop out explaining what the button is. Do not click any buttons yet, but do explore what the different buttons are by mousing over each one and holding your mouse still to pop out the tooltip.

Figure 18-2 The Microsoft FrontPage Express window.

▶ If the button bars pictured in Figure 18-2 are not visible, pull down the View menu, and turn on the toolbars.

▶ If you move your mouse over the buttons and pause, leaving your mouse stationary for a moment, a tooltip will pop out explaining what the button is. Do not click any buttons yet, but do explore what the different buttons are by mousing over each one and holding your mouse still to pop out the tooltip.

STARTING A NEW PAGE

Now that you have your Web page creation software running, you can start creating a Web page. Follow the steps in Table 18-2.

Table 18-2   How to Start a New Web Page

Netscape Composer	Microsoft FrontPage Express

▶ 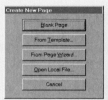 Click the New Page button; the Create New Page dialog appears as shown in Figure 18-3.

Figure 18-3 The Create New Page dialog.

▶ Click the Blank Page button. This creates a new page and enters a minimal amount of HTML code into it.

▶ You can't see the HTML in the Netscape Composer window, which only shows what will appear on screen when the user views your Web page with a browser. Since you haven't entered anything onto the Web page yet, the Composer screen appears blank.

▶ To inspect the HTML code that's in your page so far, pull down the View menu and choose Page Source to make the View Document Source window appear, as shown in Figure 18-4. Here you can see what happened when the new page got created for you. The nice thing about a WYSIWYG editor is that it takes care of creating the HTML code for you automatically, so you don't need to worry about it. This tutorial will ask you to inspect the HTML from time to time, however, so you will realize what's going on behind the scenes as you create your Web page résumé.

The tags **<HTML>** and **</HTML>** indicate the beginning and end of the document

<HEAD> and **</HEAD>** mark the document's heading

<BODY> and **</BODY>** frame the body of the document

** ** is a nonbreaking space

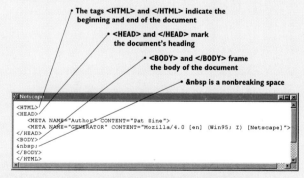

Figure 18-4 A new Web page displayed in the View Document Source window.

▶ When you're finished inspecting the HTML codes of your new Web page, close the View Document Source window, and read on.

▶ 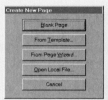 FrontPage Express automatically starts a new page. If you ever need to create another one, click the New Page button.

▶ Each new page created by FrontPage Express contains a minimal amount of HTML code. You can't see the HTML in the FrontPage Express window, which only shows what will appear on screen when the user views your Web page with a browser. Since you haven't entered anything onto the Web page yet, the screen appears blank.

▶ To inspect the HTML code that's in your page so far, pull down the View menu and choose HTML. The View or Edit HTML window appears, as shown in Figure 18-5.

The tags **<HTML>** and **</HTML>** indicate the beginning and end of the document

<HEAD> and **</HEAD>** mark the document's heading

<BODY> and **</BODY>** frame the body of the document

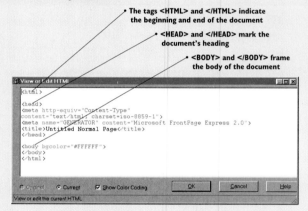

Figure 18-5 A new Web page displayed in the View or Edit HTML window.

▶ The View window shows what went on behind the scenes when FrontPage Express created the new page for you. The nice thing about a WYSIWYG editor is that it takes care of creating the HTML code for you automatically, so you don't need to worry about it. This tutorial will ask you to inspect the HTML from time to time, however, so you will realize what's going on behind the scenes as you create your Web page résumé.

▶ When you're finished inspecting the HTML codes of your new Web page, close the View or Edit HTML window, and read on.

CREATING THE PAGE TITLE AND KEYWORDS

The page title is the name that will appear in the browser's title bar when people visit your Web page on the Internet. The title is also used by many Web search engines, so you will want to make sure the title identifies the primary purpose of your Web page by including keywords you want search engines to find. To create the page title and keywords, follow the steps in Table 18-3.

Table 18-3 How to Create the Page Title and Keywords

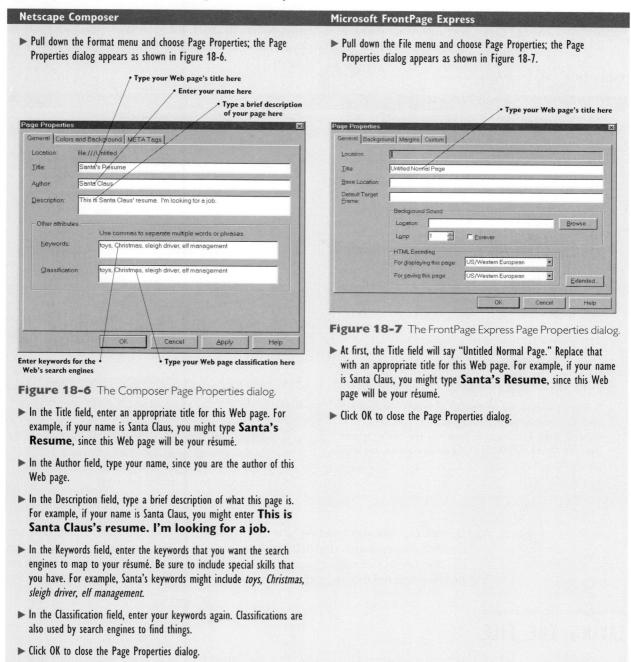

Netscape Composer	Microsoft FrontPage Express
▶ Pull down the Format menu and choose Page Properties; the Page Properties dialog appears as shown in Figure 18-6.	▶ Pull down the File menu and choose Page Properties; the Page Properties dialog appears as shown in Figure 18-7.

Figure 18-6 The Composer Page Properties dialog.

Figure 18-7 The FrontPage Express Page Properties dialog.

Netscape Composer steps:

▶ In the Title field, enter an appropriate title for this Web page. For example, if your name is Santa Claus, you might type **Santa's Resume**, since this Web page will be your résumé.

▶ In the Author field, type your name, since you are the author of this Web page.

▶ In the Description field, type a brief description of what this page is. For example, if your name is Santa Claus, you might enter **This is Santa Claus's resume. I'm looking for a job.**

▶ In the Keywords field, enter the keywords that you want the search engines to map to your résumé. Be sure to include special skills that you have. For example, Santa's keywords might include *toys, Christmas, sleigh driver, elf management.*

▶ In the Classification field, enter your keywords again. Classifications are also used by search engines to find things.

▶ Click OK to close the Page Properties dialog.

Microsoft FrontPage Express steps:

▶ At first, the Title field will say "Untitled Normal Page." Replace that with an appropriate title for this Web page. For example, if your name is Santa Claus, you might type **Santa's Resume**, since this Web page will be your résumé.

▶ Click OK to close the Page Properties dialog.

The name you gave your Web page should now appear in the title bar at the top of your window. If you pull down the View menu and choose Page Source (Netscape) or HTML (FrontPage Express) to inspect your HTML code, you will see how the page title has been added to the <HEAD> section of your Web page.

Now it's time to enter some text onto your Web page. Close the View window, and read on.

WRITING THE HEADING

Since this Web page is your résumé, you'll want to start it with a heading that includes your name in big, bold letters at the top of the Web page. The largest heading style is the <H1> style. To create a heading, follow the steps in Table 18-4.

Table 18-4   How to Write a Heading

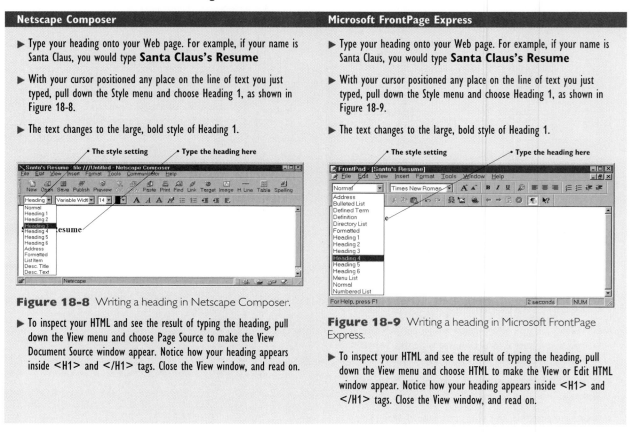

Netscape Composer	Microsoft FrontPage Express
▶ Type your heading onto your Web page. For example, if your name is Santa Claus, you would type **Santa Claus's Resume**	▶ Type your heading onto your Web page. For example, if your name is Santa Claus, you would type **Santa Claus's Resume**
▶ With your cursor positioned any place on the line of text you just typed, pull down the Style menu and choose Heading 1, as shown in Figure 18-8.	▶ With your cursor positioned any place on the line of text you just typed, pull down the Style menu and choose Heading 1, as shown in Figure 18-9.
▶ The text changes to the large, bold style of Heading 1.	▶ The text changes to the large, bold style of Heading 1.

Figure 18-8 Writing a heading in Netscape Composer.

▶ To inspect your HTML and see the result of typing the heading, pull down the View menu and choose Page Source to make the View Document Source window appear. Notice how your heading appears inside <H1> and </H1> tags. Close the View window, and read on.

Figure 18-9 Writing a heading in Microsoft FrontPage Express.

▶ To inspect your HTML and see the result of typing the heading, pull down the View menu and choose HTML to make the View or Edit HTML window appear. Notice how your heading appears inside <H1> and </H1> tags. Close the View window, and read on.

Do not confuse the heading you just entered with the document title that you entered earlier in this tutorial. The heading will appear on your Web page, while the document title will appear in the Web browser's title bar. It is OK for both the heading and the title to be the same, such as *Santa Claus's Résumé.*

SAVING THE FILE

Whenever you make a change to a file that you want to keep, you should save the file. Do so now by following the steps in Table 18-5.

Table 18-5 How to Save a Web Page File

Netscape Composer	Microsoft FrontPage Express
▶ 💾 Click the Save button, or pull down the File menu, and choose Save.	▶ 💾 Click the Save button, or pull down the File menu and choose Save.
▶ The first time you save a file, the Save As dialog appears, which you use to choose a folder and give the file a name. Save this file in the *website* folder that you created at the beginning of this chapter. Since this file is your résumé, you should name it *resume.htm*. Thus, assuming your hard drive is C, the filename will be *c:\website\resume.htm*.	▶ The first time you save a file, the Save As dialog will appear. As illustrated in Figure 18-11, you can save the file to the Web, or you can save it as a local file.
	▶ Click the As File button to save the page as a local file; you'll mount the page on the Web later. The Save As File dialog appears.
▶ If a long period of time passes during which you haven't saved your file, Netscape will ask if you want to save it. Figure 18-10 shows the AutoSave dialog that will appear when Netscape asks you about this. If you do not want this dialog popping out automatically, you can disable it by clicking the Cancel button. If you disable this reminder, however, make sure you remember to save your file from time to time. If a power failure or some other accident occurs before you save the file, you will lose all the work you did since the last time you saved the file.	▶ Save this file in the *website* folder that you created at the beginning of this chapter. Since this file is your résumé, you should name it *resume.htm*. Thus, assuming your hard drive is C, the filename will be *c:\website\resume.htm*.

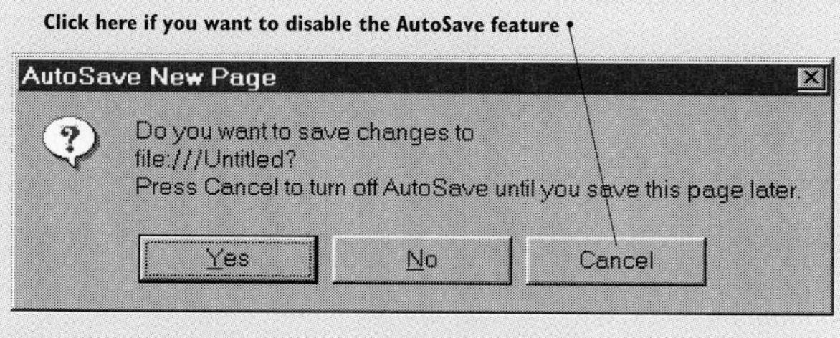

Click here if you want to disable the AutoSave feature ▸

Click the As File button ▸

Figure 18-10 Netscape Composer's AutoSave dialog.

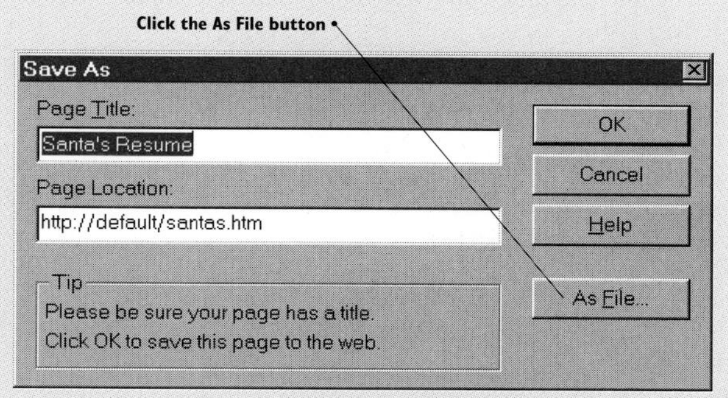

Figure 18-11 The FrontPage Express Save As dialog.

INSPECTING YOUR NEW WEB PAGE WITH A BROWSER

While you are creating a new Web page, you'll want to have a look at it with a Web browser from time to time so you can see how it's going to appear on the Web. Follow the steps in Table 18-6.

Table 18-6 How to Preview a Web Page with a Browser

Netscape Composer	Microsoft FrontPage Express
▶ 🌼 Click the Preview button.	▶ Get Microsoft Internet Explorer running.
▶ If the file has not been saved, Netscape will ask if you want to save it before you preview it. It's always a good idea to save the file first.	▶ Pull down the File menu and choose Open; the Open dialog appears.
▶ Click the Preview button now, to have a look at your Web page in the browser window. Notice how the title you entered appears in the browser's title bar, and the heading appears at the top of your Web page.	▶ [Browse…] Click the Browse button; the Open File dialog appears.
	▶ Use the controls to browse to the file you want to open, or type the filename into the File name field. For this exercise, the filename is *c:\website\resume.htm*.
▶ After you are done looking at your Web page with your Web browser, close the browser window; the Composer window will reappear.	▶ After you are done looking at your Web page with your Web browser, [Alt]-[Tab] back to FrontPage Express. Do not close your Web browser.
	▶ 🖼 As you continue creating this page with FrontPage Express, any time you want to view it with your browser, you can just [Alt]-[Tab] to the browser, and click the Refresh button. This makes your browser read the new version of the file without your having to pull down the File menu and open the file each time.

ENTERING A NEW PARAGRAPH

Now you're ready to type the first paragraph of your résumé. Mouse to the spot on the screen right after the heading on your Web page, and press Enter. If you mistakenly press Enter in the midst of the heading, instead of at the end of it, you can pull down the Edit menu and choose Undo to fix the mistake.

```
I am Professor and Director of
Instructional Technology at the
University of Delaware. My career goal
is to help make multimedia easy enough
for everyone to become a creator, not
just a consumer, of multimedia.
```

Figure 18-12 How the author began his résumé.

Now you're ready to type a few sentences about yourself, as an introduction to your résumé. Don't be bashful: a résumé should begin with a strongly stated summary of your professional qualifications and career goals. Figure 18-12 shows how the author began his résumé.

Repeat the steps in Table 18-6 to take another look at your Web page in the browser window. Notice how the paragraph you typed appears beneath the heading of your résumé.

STARTING A NEW PARAGRAPH

To make a new paragraph, follow the steps in Table 18-7.

Table 18-7   How to Start a New Paragraph

Netscape Composer	Microsoft FrontPage Express
▶ In the Composer window, position your cursor at the place you want the new paragraph to start, and press Enter twice. This creates white space that will appear between the two paragraphs.	▶ In the FrontPage Express window, position your cursor at the place you want the new paragraph to start, and press Enter. This creates white space that will appear between the two paragraphs.
▶ Now type another paragraph that summarizes what is in your résumé. Figure 18-13 shows how the author completed this task.	▶ Now type another paragraph that summarizes what is in your résumé. Figure 18-13 shows how the author completed this task.
▶ To inspect your HTML and see the result of typing the first two paragraphs of your résumé, pull down the View menu and choose View Source to make the View Document Source window appear. Notice how the tags appear in between the paragraphs. BR stands for "break." Each time you press Enter to start a new line on the screen, Netscape enters a code into your HTML.	▶ To inspect your HTML and see the result of typing the first two paragraphs of your résumé, pull down the View menu and choose HTML to make the View or Edit HTML window appear. Notice how the <p> tag appears at the beginning of each paragraph, and the </p> tag appears at the end. The <p> stands for paragraph, and </p> is the paragraph stop tag.
▶ Close the View Document Source window, and read on.	▶ Close the View window, and read on.

```
I am Professor and Director of Instructional Technology at
the University of Delaware. My career goal is to help make
multimedia easy enough for everyone to become a creator, not
just a consumer, of multimedia.

I have been developing multimedia tools and techniques since
1970. This résumé summarizes my life's work according to the
following categories, which you can select to find out more:
```

Figure 18-13 The first two paragraphs of the author's résumé.

CREATING A LIST

Now that you've created the two introductory paragraphs of your résumé, it's time to create the bulleted list that will serve as your table of contents. Follow the steps in Table 18-8.

Table 18-8 How to Create a Bulleted List

Netscape Composer	Microsoft FrontPage Express
► Position your cursor in the Netscape Composer window at the end of your second paragraph, and press (Enter) a couple of times to move down to the point where you want your résumé's bulleted table of contents to begin.	► Position your cursor in the Microsoft FrontPage Express window at the end of your second paragraph, and press (Enter) to move down to the point where you want your résumé's bulleted table of contents to begin.
► Click the Bullet List button; a bullet appears on screen. Type the first item in your résumé's table of contents.	► Click the Bulleted List button; a bullet appears on screen. Type the first item in your résumé's table of contents.
► To enter another item into the list, simply press (Enter) at the end of the first item, and type your next list item.	► To enter another item into the list, simply press (Enter) at the end of the first item, and type your next list item.
► Repeat this process to enter as many items as you want to list right now. You can always add more items to your résumé later on.	► Repeat this process to enter as many items as you want to list right now. You can always add more items to your résumé later on.
► To see how your bulleted list will appear in a browser, click the Preview button.	► To see how your bulleted list appears in a browser, (Alt)-(Tab) to your browser, and click the Refresh button. If you don't have your browser running, repeat the steps in Table 18-6 to inspect your Web page with a browser.

Figure 18-14 shows how the author typed his list into Netscape Composer, and Figure 18-15 shows the corresponding HTML code. Take a look at the HTML code for your bulleted list. If you forget how to inspect your HTML code, review the steps in Table 18-6.

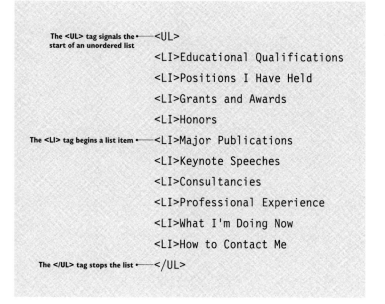

- Educational Qualifications
- Positions I Have Held
- Grants and Awards
- Honors
- Major Publications
- Keynote Speeches
- Consultancies
- Professional Experience
- What I'm Doing Now
- How to Contact Me

```
The <UL> tag signals the ────<UL>
start of an unordered list
                            <LI>Educational Qualifications
                            <LI>Positions I Have Held
                            <LI>Grants and Awards
                            <LI>Honors
The <LI> tag begins a list item ───<LI>Major Publications
                            <LI>Keynote Speeches
                            <LI>Consultancies
                            <LI>Professional Experience
                            <LI>What I'm Doing Now
                            <LI>How to Contact Me
The </UL> tag stops the list ───</UL>
```

Figure 18-14 How the author typed his résumé's bulleted table of contents.

Figure 18-15 How the table of contents appears in the HTML code of the author's résumé.

UNDO AND REDO

Whenever you make a mistake that you want to undo while editing a document, pull down the Edit menu and choose Undo. If you undo something that you want to redo, pull down the Edit menu and choose Redo.

 Microsoft FrontPage Express has icons for Undo and Redo; FrontPage Express users can click these icons instead of pulling down the Edit menu.

HORIZONTAL RULES

 As you learned in Chapter 16, horizontal rules create neat-looking dividing lines between different parts of a Web page. To insert a horizontal rule after the bulleted table of contents in your résumé, follow the steps in Table 18-9.

Table 18-9   How to Insert a Horizontal Rule

Netscape Composer	Microsoft FrontPage Express
▶ In the Netscape Composer window, position your cursor at the end of the list. Press ⎡Enter⎤ as if you were going to enter another list item.	▶ In the Microsoft FrontPage Express window, position your cursor at the end of the list. Press ⎡Enter⎤ as if you were going to enter another list item.
▶ Pull down the Styles menu and choose Normal. This ends the list, and puts you into normal text entry mode.	▶ Pull down the Styles menu and choose Normal. This ends the list, and puts you into normal text entry mode.
▶ Click the Horizontal Line button; the line will appear on your page.	▶ Pull down the Insert menu, and choose Horizontal Line.
▶ You can change the properties of the line if you want by double-clicking on the line after you enter it; this makes the Horizontal Line Properties dialog appear, as shown in Figure 18-16. The author recommends you choose the 3-D Shading option, unless you prefer a plain line instead.	▶ You can change the properties of the line if you want by double-clicking on the line after you enter it; this makes the Horizontal Line Properties dialog appear, as shown in Figure 18-17. The author recommends the default settings, which create a 3-D effect.

Height controls the thickness of the line   • Width controls the length of the line   • Choose 3-D shading for a special effect

Width controls the length of the line   •
Height controls the thickness of the line   •

Horizontal Line Properties

Dimensions
Height: 2 pixels
Width: 100 % of window

Alignment
○ Left
● Center
○ Right

☑ 3-D shading

Extra HTML...

☑ Save settings as default

OK   Cancel   Help

Horizontal Line Properties

Width
100 ● Percent of window
○ Pixels

Height
2 Pixels

Alignment
○ Left ● Center ○ Right

Color:
Default ☐ Solid line (no shading)

OK
Cancel
Extended...
Help

• You will probably want your line centered   • Check here to make these options become the default for future lines

• Use this menu to change the color of the line   • You will probably want your line centered   • Check this box for a solid line with no shading

Figure 18-16 The Netscape Composer Horizontal Line Properties dialog in Netscape Composer.

Figure 18-17 The Horizontal Line Properties dialog in Microsoft FrontPage Express.

Table 18-9 (Continued)

Netscape Composer	Microsoft FrontPage Express
▶ To see how the horizontal line will appear on the Web, click the Preview button.	▶ To see how the horizontal line will appear on the Web, Alt - Tab to your browser, and click the Refresh button. If you don't have your browser running, repeat the steps in Table 18-6 to inspect your Web page with a browser.
▶ To see how the line got inserted in your HTML, pull down the View window, and choose Document Source. There you will find the <HR> code, which stands for "Horizontal Rule."	▶ To see how the line got inserted in your HTML, pull down the View menu and choose HTML to make the View or Edit HTML window appear. There you will find the <HR> code, which stands for "Horizontal Rule."

It is easy to insert horizontal rules in your documents, and the dividing lines look nice. However, don't give in to the temptation to overuse them! Horizontal rules are best used to separate major sections of your document.

REMEMBER TO SAVE THE FILE

Remember to save your HTML file periodically to prevent accidental loss due to power failures or other accidents. To save the file, click the Save button or pull down the File menu and choose Save.

INSERTING A NEW HEADING

Every main section of your résumé should begin with a large-sized heading that identifies what that section is. It is common for Web pages to have a title displayed in the largest-sized heading, <H1>, and then use the next smaller size, <H2>, for subheads. For example, when you enter the educational qualifications section of your résumé, follow these steps to give it a heading:

▶ Position your cursor at the start of the education section of your résumé. This location will probably be right after the horizontal line you just inserted.

▶ Press Enter once or twice to create a little space after the line.

▶ Type the heading, which in this example will be **Educational Qualifications**

▶ Pull down the Style menu and choose Heading 2.

To begin a new paragraph after the heading, position your cursor at the end of the heading, press Enter, and begin typing.

CREATING TARGETS

As you create the different sections in your résumé, it will grow too long to fit on the screen all at once. To make it easy for the user to find the different parts of your résumé, you can insert named locations known as targets into your document. Then you can link each item in your résumé's bulleted list of topics to its corresponding target to make it quick and easy for the user to find that section. To create a target, follow the steps in Table 18-10.

Table 18-10 How to Create a Target on a Web Page

Netscape Composer	Microsoft FrontPage Express
▶ To create a target, use the mouse to position your cursor at the spot in the HTML window where you want it. In this example, position your cursor at the start of the Education section in your Netscape Composer window.	▶ To create a target, use the mouse to position your cursor at the spot in the HTML window where you want it. In this example, position your cursor at the start of the Education section in your FrontPage Express window.
▶ 🎯 Click the Insert Target button; the Target Properties dialog appears.	▶ Pull down the Edit menu and choose Bookmark; the Bookmark dialog appears. *Note:* In FrontPage Express, targets are called bookmarks.
▶ In the Name field, type **education**, as shown in Figure 18-18.	▶ In the Bookmark Name field, type **education**, as shown in Figure 18-19.
▶ Click OK; the target appears in your document.	▶ Click OK; the target appears in your document.

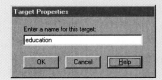

Figure 18-18
Creating the education target in the Target Properties dialog.

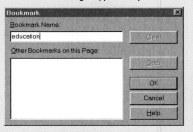

Figure 18-19
Creating the education target in the Bookmark dialog.

▶ To see how the target got inserted in your HTML, pull down the View window, and choose Document Source. In the View Document Source window, you will see the `<A NAME="education"></A>` tags that create the target in HTML. The word in quotes is the name of the target.

▶ To see how the target got inserted in your HTML, pull down the View menu, and choose HTML. In the View or Edit HTML window, you will see the `<a name="education"></a>` tags that create the target in HTML. The word in quotes is the name of the target.

LINKING TO TARGETS

To create a link to a target, follow the steps in Table 18-11.

Table 18-11 How to Create a Link to a Target

Netscape Composer	Microsoft FrontPage Express
▶ Use the mouse to highlight the text that you want to trigger the link; in this example, position the cursor in your bulleted list right before *Educational Qualifications* and drag your mouse over the words *Educational Qualifications* to select them.	▶ Use the mouse to highlight the text that you want to trigger the link; in this example, position the cursor in your bulleted list right before *Educational Qualifications* and drag your mouse over the words *Educational Qualifications* to select them.
▶ 🔗 Click the Insert Link button; the Character Properties dialog appears.	▶ 🔗 Click the Hyperlink button; the Create Hyperlink dialog appears.
▶ In the list box, click once on the target you want, which in this example is *education*.	▶ Click the Open Pages tab, on which the Bookmark field appears.
▶ The symbol *#education* automatically appears in the Link To... field.	▶ Click the arrow at the right end of the Bookmark field to pull down the menu, and select the target you want, which in this example is *education*.
▶ Click OK to complete the link.	▶ Click OK to complete the link.
▶ 🎨 Click the Preview button to see how your résumé will appear on the Web. Now the words *Educational Qualifications* should appear in color in your résumé's bulleted table of contents. The coloration denotes hypertext; clicking the colored text will trigger the link.	▶ 🖥 Alt-Tab to your browser, and click the Refresh button to see how your résumé will appear on the Web. Now the words *Educational Qualifications* should appear in color in your résumé's bulleted table of contents. The coloration denotes hypertext; clicking the colored text will trigger the link.
▶ To see how the link got inserted in your HTML, pull down the View window, and choose Document Source.	▶ To see how the link got inserted in your HTML, pull down the View window, and choose HTML.

In the View window, you will see how the Insert Link tool inserted the following HTML into your document:

```
<A HREF="#education">Educational Qualifications</A>
```

In this code, A stands for anchor, and HREF stands for hypertext reference. The word in quotes (*#education*) is the name of the target. In HTML, target names are always preceded by a pound sign (*#*).

Let's test the link. View your résumé with your Web browser. Click on the words *Educational Qualifications* in your résumé. If your browser jumped to the Educational Qualifications section of your résumé, congratulations! If not, repeat these steps, compare your HTML to the samples shown here, and keep trying until you get the named location link to work.

RETURNING TO THE TABLE OF CONTENTS

Web pages that use targets often provide a way for the user to return to the table of contents. This return-to-contents capability is created with another named location. First, you create a target at the start of the bulleted list to which you want the user to return; then you create a return link to that target at the end of each section in your document.

To create a return-to-contents link in the Education section of your résumé, follow the steps in Table 18-12.

Table 18-12   Creating a Return-to-Contents Link

Netscape Composer	Microsoft FrontPage Express
▶ Position the cursor in your Netscape Composer window at the start of the bulleted table of contents in your résumé.	▶ Position the cursor in your Microsoft FrontPage Express window at the start of the bulleted table of contents in your résumé.
▶ Create a target called *contents*—try to do this on your own, but if you need help, follow these steps: ▶ Click the Insert Target button; the Target Properties dialog appears. ▶ In the Name field, type **contents** ▶ Click OK; the target appears in your document.	▶ Create a bookmark target called *contents*—try to do this on your own, but if you need help, follow these steps: ▶ Pull down the Edit menu and choose Bookmark; the Bookmark dialog appears. ▶ In the Bookmark Name field, type **contents** ▶ Click OK; the target appears in your document.
▶ Position your cursor at the end of the Educational Qualifications section of your résumé. Insert a new paragraph that contains the text *Résumé Contents.*	▶ Position your cursor at the end of the Educational Qualifications section of your résumé. Insert a new paragraph that contains the text *Résumé Contents.*
▶ Link the words *Résumé Contents* to the *contents* bookmark—try to do this on your own, but if you need help, follow these steps: ▶ Drag your mouse over the words *Résumé Contents* to select them. ▶ Click the Insert Link button; the Character Properties dialog appears. ▶ In the list box, click once on the target you want, which in this example is *contents*. ▶ The symbol *#contents* automatically appears in the Link To... field. ▶ Click OK to complete the link.	▶ Link the words *Résumé Contents* to the *contents* bookmark—try to do this on your own, but if you need help, follow these steps: ▶ Click the Hyperlink button; the Create Hyperlink dialog appears. ▶ Click the Open Pages tab, on which the Bookmark field appears. ▶ Click the arrow at the right end of the Bookmark field to pull down the menu, and select the target you want, which in this example is *contents*. ▶ Click OK to complete the link.
▶ Click the Preview button to see how your résumé will appear on the Web.	▶ [Alt]-[Tab] to your browser, and click the Refresh button to see how your résumé will appear on the Web.

Test the link to make sure it works. Clicking on *Educational Qualifications* in the bulleted table of contents should jump to the education section of your résumé. At the end of that section, clicking on *Résumé Contents* should return you to the list of contents.

LINKING TO URLs

There are more than 50 million documents on the World Wide Web. You can link your résumé to any document for which you know the URL. For example, if the place where you work or go to school has a home page, you might want to provide a way for the user to navigate there. Follow the steps in Table 18-13:

Table 18-13   How to Create a Link to a URL

Netscape Composer	Microsoft FrontPage Express
▶ In your Netscape Composer window, drag your mouse to select the text that you want to link to some other Web page	▶ In your Microsoft FrontPage Express window, drag your mouse to select the text that you want to link to some other Web page.
▶ Click the Insert Link button; the Character Properties dialog appears.	▶ Click the Hyperlink button; the Create Hyperlink dialog appears.
▶ In the Link To... field, type the URL to which you want to link; for example, to link to the White House, you'd type **http://www. whitehouse.gov**	▶ Click the World Wide Web tab. If the Hyperlink type isn't already set to http:, then click the arrow to pull down the choices and select http:.
▶ Click OK to complete the link.	▶ In the URL field, type the URL to which you want to link; for example, to link to the White House, you'd type **http://www.whitehouse.gov**
	▶ Click OK to complete the link.

IDENTIFYING THE WEB PAGE OWNER

Netiquette (network etiquette) calls for Web pages to end with a few lines of text indicating who owns the page and how to contact the owner. To identify yourself as the owner of your Web page, follow these steps:

▶ Position the cursor in your Netscape Composer or Microsoft FrontPage Express window at the bottom of the document.

▶ Press Enter once or twice to create a little white space.

▶ Type the following words: **This web page is owned by [type your name here]. My e-mail address is [type your e-mail address here]**.

MAILTO LINKS

It is customary for Web page owners to include a **mailto** link to their e-mail address to make it easy for you to contact them. When you click such a link, an e-mail dialog appears, automatically addressed to the Web page owner.

For example, consider the Web page owner statement you put at the bottom of your home page. Your e-mail address appears there. To provide a mailto link to your e-mail address, follow the steps in Table 18-14.

Table 18-14　How to Create a Mailto Link

Netscape Composer	Microsoft FrontPage Express
▶ In your Netscape Composer window, drag the mouse over your e-mail address to select it.	▶ In your Microsoft FrontPage Express window, drag your mouse over your e-mail address to select it.
▶ *(icon)* Click the Insert Link button; the Character Properties dialog appears.	▶ *(icon)* Click the Hyperlink button; the Create Hyperlink dialog appears.
▶ In the Link To... field, type **mailto:** followed by your e-mail address; for example, if your e-mail address is SantaClaus@northpole.com, type **mailto:SantaClaus@northpole.com**	▶ Click the World Wide Web tab. Pull down the Hyperlink type menu and choose *mailto:*.
▶ Click OK to complete the link.	▶ In the URL field, type the URL to which you want to link; for example, if your e-mail address is SantaClaus@northpole.com, type **mailto:SantaClaus@northpole.com**
	▶ Click OK to complete the link.

E X E R C I S E S

1. This chapter got you started creating your Web page résumé. Now you should complete your résumé by adding all the sections you sketched when you designed your résumé at the start of this tutorial. If you have any trouble, refer back to the step-by-step instructions in this chapter for creating new paragraphs, headings, list items, and horizontal rules.

2. Each item in your bulleted table of contents should be linked to its corresponding section in your résumé. Insert bookmark targets at the beginning of each new section in your résumé. Then link each item in your table of contents to the corresponding target in your résumé. Test the links to make sure they work.

3. At the end of each section in your résumé, provide a way for the user to return to your table of contents.

19 Putting Images on Web Pages

After completing this chapter, you will be able to:

- **Download the shareware version of Paint Shop Pro for Windows or Graphic Converter for the Macintosh.**

- **Convert images into a file format suitable for display on Web pages.**

- **Resize and resample images to fit the layout of a Web page.**

- **Adjust colors for optimum display performance on Web pages.**

- **Understand the concept of a transparent GIF.**

- **Know how to download a utility for creating transparent GIFs.**

- **Paste an image onto a Web page.**

- **Tile an image onto a Web page.**

T HAS often been said that a picture is worth a thousand words. The ease with which you can paste pictures onto Web pages makes it possible to illustrate documents and use images as design elements in the layout of a Web page. Before you can paste a picture onto a Web page, however, you must get it into the proper format for display on a Web page. This chapter provides you with a utility that makes it easy to get images into the proper format. Then you will learn not only how to paste pictures onto Web pages, but also how to create special effects with techniques known as tiling and watermarking.

Kodak Let's assume that you have an image that you want to paste onto your Web page. Since you have created a Web page résumé, it would be natural to include your picture in the upper left corner of the résumé, so prospective employers can see what you look like. Many photo shops, such as Kodak, and mass-market retail stores, such as Wal-Mart, give you the option of having a floppy disk or a CD returned along with your prints when you have a roll of film developed. The diskette costs only a few dollars, while the CD costs $10.99 plus 69¢ per image. Both contain digitized bitmaps of the pictures on film. The diskette contains only one version of each bitmap, digitized at computer screen resolution. The CD, known more formally as a Kodak PhotoCD, contains five versions of each bitmap, sampled at resolutions ranging from a wallet-sized thumbnail to a poster version much larger than the size of your computer screen. For more information, follow the links to Kodak PhotoCD at the Interlit Web site.

EPSON If you happen to own a digital camera, you can avoid needing to have your pictures developed, because digital cameras take pictures as bitmaps, which can be downloaded from the camera to your PC. Epson, Apple, Kodak, and Olympus are just a few of the companies that make digital cameras. To find out what digital cameras are available and how their features compare, follow the links to Digital Cameras at the Interlit Web site.

On the other hand, if you prefer not to include your picture on your résumé, you may want to enhance its appearance by including some other graphics. There is a Web page full of general-purpose graphics at the Interlit Web site. You can download any image on this page by following the procedure you learned for downloading images in Chapter 13. To inspect these images, follow the links to general-purpose graphics at the Interlit Web site.

PREPARING IMAGES FOR A WEB PAGE

Before you can paste an image onto a Web page, you need to ask yourself a few questions:

- Is the image in the correct format for pasting onto a Web page? Images must be in either the GIF or JPEG file format. If the image is not in the correct format, you must convert it into the proper file format.

- Is the image the proper size for your Web page layout? If not, you must resize or resample it.

- What is the color format of the image? If the image is in 24-bit format, you may want to reduce it to an 8-bit color format, because that will make it appear three times faster on the Web.

Paint Shop Pro (for Windows)

A very popular graphics program that enables Windows users to do all these things is Paint Shop Pro, which is a Windows program for image capture, creation, viewing, and manipulation. Features include painting, photo retouching, image enhancement and editing, color enhancement, graphics format conversion, and color scanner support. Over 30 file formats are supported, including JPEG, TIFF, Kodak PhotoCD, BMP, and GIF. You can even browse images on your computer; Figure 19-1 shows how the images appear as thumbnails, which you can double-click to view full-screen.

Paint Shop Pro is **shareware**, which is software that you can try out before you buy. You can download it from the Web by following the links to Paint Shop Pro at the Interlit Web site. If you keep using the shareware version for more than 30 days, you should pay the license fee of $54.99, for which you will receive the retail version, which contains even more features.

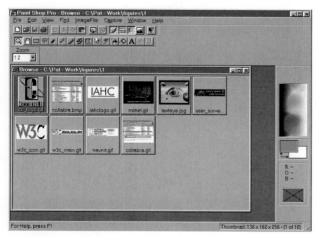

Figure 19-1 Paint Shop Pro contains an image browser and many powerful graphics tools.

Graphic Converter (for Macintosh)

Macintosh users can do all of the things covered in this chapter with a program called Graphic Converter. It's **shareware**, which means you can try it out before you buy it. You can download Graphic Converter from the Web by following the links at the Interlit Web site. If you decide to keep using the shareware version, you should pay the license fee, which is currently $35.

Converting Images

It's easy to convert images into the proper format for pasting onto Web pages. Follow the steps in Table 19-1.

Table 19-1   How to Convert Images into the Proper Format for Pasting onto Web Pages

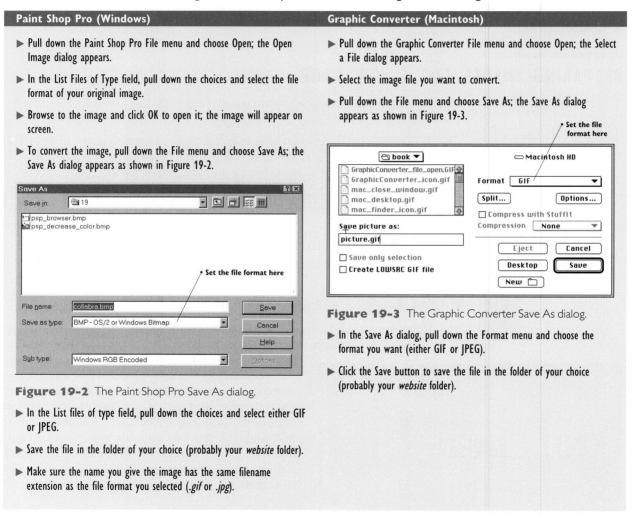

Paint Shop Pro (Windows)	Graphic Converter (Macintosh)
▶ Pull down the Paint Shop Pro File menu and choose Open; the Open Image dialog appears.	▶ Pull down the Graphic Converter File menu and choose Open; the Select a File dialog appears.
▶ In the List Files of Type field, pull down the choices and select the file format of your original image.	▶ Select the image file you want to convert.
▶ Browse to the image and click OK to open it; the image will appear on screen.	▶ Pull down the File menu and choose Save As; the Save As dialog appears as shown in Figure 19-3.
▶ To convert the image, pull down the File menu and choose Save As; the Save As dialog appears as shown in Figure 19-2.	

Figure 19-2 The Paint Shop Pro Save As dialog.

Figure 19-3 The Graphic Converter Save As dialog.

▶ In the List files of type field, pull down the choices and select either GIF or JPEG.

▶ In the Save As dialog, pull down the Format menu and choose the format you want (either GIF or JPEG).

▶ Save the file in the folder of your choice (probably your *website* folder).

▶ Click the Save button to save the file in the folder of your choice (probably your *website* folder).

▶ Make sure the name you give the image has the same filename extension as the file format you selected (*.gif* or *.jpg*).

When you select the file type for the converted file, choose either GIF or JPEG. The author recommends you choose GIF if your image has 256 or fewer colors. Use JPEG for images with more than 256 colors.

It is important that when you save the file, you save it in the same folder as the Web page for which it is intended. In this case, if you are making an image for your Web page résumé, save the converted image in your *website* folder. This will simplify the publication process when you transfer your files to the Web in Chapter 22.

Resizing Images

Images may be the wrong size for placement on your Web page. For example, the photo of the author that appears on his Web page résumé was a 640 × 480 image. This would have covered way too much screen space, spoiling the layout of the résumé. To resize an image, follow the steps in Table 19-2.

Table 19-2   How to Resize Images

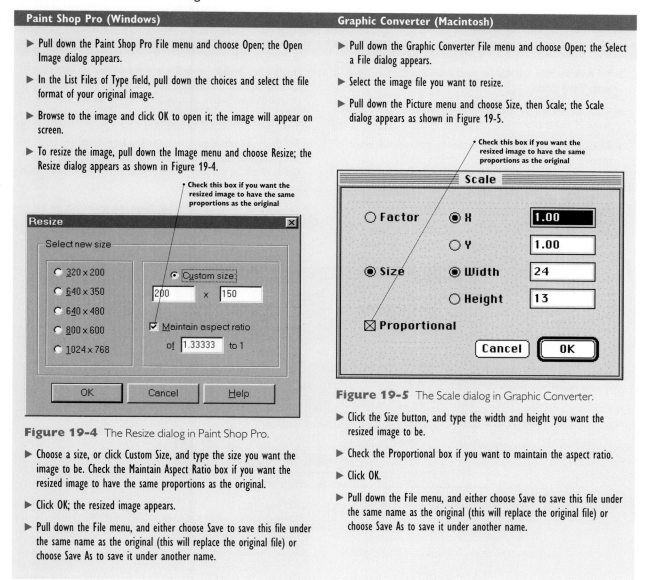

Paint Shop Pro (Windows)	Graphic Converter (Macintosh)
▶ Pull down the Paint Shop Pro File menu and choose Open; the Open Image dialog appears.	▶ Pull down the Graphic Converter File menu and choose Open; the Select a File dialog appears.
▶ In the List Files of Type field, pull down the choices and select the file format of your original image.	▶ Select the image file you want to resize.
▶ Browse to the image and click OK to open it; the image will appear on screen.	▶ Pull down the Picture menu and choose Size, then Scale; the Scale dialog appears as shown in Figure 19-5.
▶ To resize the image, pull down the Image menu and choose Resize; the Resize dialog appears as shown in Figure 19-4.	

Figure 19-4   The Resize dialog in Paint Shop Pro.

▶ Choose a size, or click Custom Size, and type the size you want the image to be. Check the Maintain Aspect Ratio box if you want the resized image to have the same proportions as the original.

▶ Click OK; the resized image appears.

▶ Pull down the File menu, and either choose Save to save this file under the same name as the original (this will replace the original file) or choose Save As to save it under another name.

Figure 19-5   The Scale dialog in Graphic Converter.

▶ Click the Size button, and type the width and height you want the resized image to be.

▶ Check the Proportional box if you want to maintain the aspect ratio.

▶ Click OK.

▶ Pull down the File menu, and either choose Save to save this file under the same name as the original (this will replace the original file) or choose Save As to save it under another name.

Make sure you save the resized file in the GIF or JPEG file format in the same folder as the Web page on which it will appear. If you are resizing an image for your Web page résumé, save the image in your *website* folder.

Resampling Images (Windows only)

Sometimes the Paint Shop Pro resize function doesn't work very well. Resizing an image that contains alphabetic characters, for example, can alter the shape of the characters. Increasing the size of a picture often exaggerates the pixels in the image, making curves and diagonal lines seem jagged instead of smooth.

Windows users can minimize these problems by resampling instead of resizing the image. Resampling uses an algorithm that rescales the image to avoid the jagged artifacts of resizing. To resample an image with Paint Shop Pro, follow the steps in Table 19-3.

Table 19-3   How to Resample Images with Paint Shop Pro

▶ Pull down the Paint Shop Pro File menu and choose Open; the Open Image dialog appears.

▶ In the List Files of Type field, pull down the choices and select the file format of your original image.

▶ Browse to the image and click OK to open it; the image will appear on screen.

▶ Before you can resample the image, you must increase its color depth to 16 million colors. Pull down the Colors menu, choose Increase Color Depth, and select 16 million colors (24-bit format).

▶ To resample the image, pull down the Image menu and choose Resample; the Resample dialog appears as shown in Figure 19-6.

▶ Choose a size, or click Custom Size, and type the size you want the image to be. Check the Maintain Aspect Ratio box if you want the resampled image to have the same proportions as the original.

▶ Click OK; the resampled image appears.

▶ Pull down the Colors menu, choose Decrease Color Depth, and select 256 colors (8-bit format). In the Decrease Color dialog, choose Optimized palette, and click the option to Include Windows Colors. Then click OK to close the dialog.

▶ Pull down the File menu, and either choose Save to save this file under the same name as the original (this will replace the original file) or choose Save As to save it under another name.

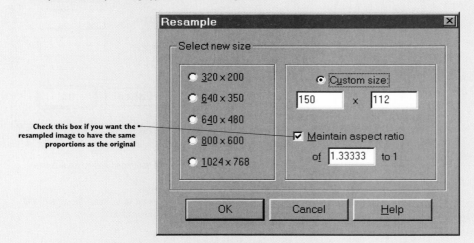

Figure 19-6 The Resample dialog in Paint Shop Pro.

Make sure you save the resampled file in the GIF or JPEG file format in the same folder as the Web page on which it will appear. If you are resizing an image for your Web page résumé, save the image in your *website* folder.

Color Adjustments

Unless you have a special reason for wanting to keep your images encoded in 16 million colors (24-bit format), you should convert the images to 256 colors (8-bit format), which will make them appear three times faster on your Web page. To convert a 24-bit image into an 8-bit image, follow the steps in Table 19-4.

Table 19-4 How to Reduce the Color Depth of an Image

Paint Shop Pro (Windows)	Graphic Converter (Macintosh)
▶ Pull down the Paint Shop Pro File menu, choose Open, and open the image, which will appear on screen.	▶ Pull down the Graphic Converter File menu, choose Open, and open the image, which will appear on screen.
▶ Pull down the Colors menu, choose Decrease Color Depth, and see if the 256-colors option is active. If it is not active, your image does not need to be reduced in color depth, so close the image and skip the rest of these instructions.	▶ Pull down the Picture menu, choose Colors, then Change to 256 Colors, as shown in Figure 19-8.
▶ If the 256-colors option is active, select it; the Decrease Color Depth dialog appears as shown in Figure 19-7.	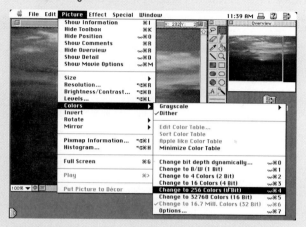
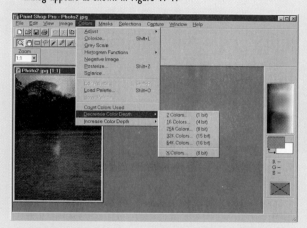 **Figure 19-7** The Decrease Color Depth dialog in Paint Shop Pro.	**Figure 19-8** Decreasing the color depth with Graphic Converter.
▶ Choose Optimized palette, and click the option to Include Windows Colors. Whether to choose Nearest Color or Error Diffusion is up to you. Click OK to close the dialog.	▶ Pull down the File menu, and either choose Save to save this file under the same name as the original (this will replace the original file) or choose Save As to save it under another name.
▶ Pull down the File menu, and either choose Save to save this file under the same name as the original (this will replace the original file) or choose Save As to save it under another name.	

Make sure you save the color-converted file in the GIF or JPEG file format in the same folder as the Web page on which it will appear. If you are converting an image for your Web page résumé, save the image in your *website* folder.

Creating Interlaced "Fade-in" GIFs

A special effect when an image appears on a Web page is to make it fade in with a Venetian blind effect. A file subformat known as GIF 89a Interlaced creates this effect. You can easily convert any image into the GIF 89a Interlaced format. Simply follow the steps in Table 19-1, which shows how to convert the file format of an image. When you save the file as a GIF image, Windows users should set the file subformat to Gif 89a Interlaced. Macintosh users should click Options, then click the radio buttons for Version 89a and Interlaced.

PASTING A PICTURE ONTO YOUR WEB PAGE RÉSUMÉ

You'll be happy to discover that pasting an image onto a Web page is a lot easier than preparing the picture to fit the Web page's layout. To paste an image onto a Web page, follow the steps in Table 19-5.

Table 19-5   How to Paste an Image onto a Web Page

Netscape Composer	**Microsoft FrontPage Express**
▶ Get Netscape Composer running and open the Web page on which you want to paste an image; if you are pasting the image onto your Web page résumé, click the Open File button and open the file *website\resume.htm*.	▶ Get Microsoft FrontPage Express running and open the Web page on which you want to paste an image; if you are pasting the image onto your Web page résumé, click the Open File button and open the file *website\resume.htm*.
▶ Position your cursor at the spot on the Web page where you want the picture to appear. For your résumé, position the cursor right before the heading at the top of the document.	▶ Position your cursor at the spot on the Web page where you want the picture to appear. For your résumé, position the cursor right before the heading at the top of the document.
▶ Click the Insert Image button; the Image Properties dialog appears as shown in Figure 19-9.	▶ Click the Insert Image button; the Image dialog appears as shown in Figure 19-10. Make sure the Other Location tab is selected.

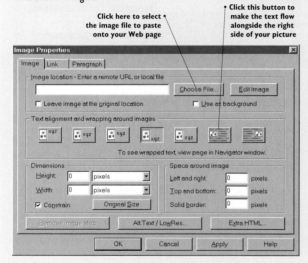

Click here to select
the image file to paste
onto your Web page

Click this button to
make the text flow
alongside the right
side of your picture

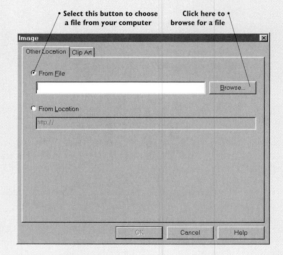

Select this button to choose
a file from your computer

Click here to
browse for a file

Figure 19-9 The Image Properties dialog.

Figure 19-10 The Image Properties dialog.

▶ Click the Choose File button; the Select Image File dialog will appear. Use it to select the image file you want to appear on your Web page, and click OK.	▶ Click the Browse button; the Image dialog will appear. Use it to select the image file you want to appear on your Web page, and click OK. The image now appears on your Web page.
▶ The filename information appears in the Image Properties dialog.	▶ To make the text flow alongside your image, so your picture appears in the upper left-hand corner of your résumé, double-click the image to make the Image Properties dialog appear.
▶ To make the text flow alongside your image, so your picture appears in the upper left-hand corner of your résumé, click the appropriate alignment button, as shown in Figure 19-9.	
	▶ Click the Appearance tab. Pull down the Alignment settings, and choose left.
▶ Click OK to close the Edit Image dialog. Your image should appear on screen. If you get an "Image Not Available" message, you did something wrong. Press the Undo button and repeat these instructions more carefully.	▶ Click OK to close the Image Properties dialog. The text should flow alongside your image. If it doesn't, you did something wrong. Press the Undo button and repeat these instructions more carefully.
▶ Press the Preview button to see how the image will appear on your Web page.	▶ Save the file, then open it in the Microsoft Internet Explorer to see how it will appear on the Web.
▶ To modify the properties of an image to make the text flow around it differently, or to change other image parameters, double-click on the image in the Netscape Composer window, and the Image Properties dialog will reappear to let you make any adjustments you want.	▶ To modify the properties of an image to make the text flow around it differently, or to change other image parameters, double-click on the image in the Microsoft FrontPage Express window, and the Image Properties dialog will reappear to let you make further adjustments.

TILING A BACKGROUND ONTO A WEB PAGE

As a final touch, let's add some pizzazz to your résumé. Most Web browsers, including both Netscape Communicator and Microsoft Internet Explorer, permit you to set a background bitmap that the browser uses to tile the background. Tiling means that the bitmap gets drawn repeatedly across and down the screen until the entire window has been covered. If the bitmap is designed in such a way as to hide the edges when tiled, you get a seamless appearance in the background.

The Interlit Web site has a page that contains a few bitmaps designed for tiling on Web pages. To see these bitmaps, click the tile icon at the Interlit Web site. To see what the different bitmaps look like when tiled onto a Web page, click them with your left mouse button. To download a tile to your computer, right-click a bitmap, and choose Save As to download the tile. Make sure you save the tile in your *website* folder. Then follow the steps in Table 19-6 to make one of the tiles fill the background of your résumé.

Table 19-6   How to Tile an Image onto a Web Page

Netscape Composer	Microsoft FrontPage Express
▶ Get Netscape Composer running and open the file *website\resume.htm*.	▶ Get Microsoft FrontPage Express running and open the file *website\resume.htm*.
▶ Pull down the Format menu and choose Colors and Background; the Page Properties dialog appears.	▶ Pull down the Format menu and choose Background; the Page Properties dialog appears.
▶ In the Background Image group, press the Choose File button; the Select Image File dialog will appear. Use it to select the image file you want to tile into the background of your Web page, and click OK. *Important:* The image file must be in the same folder as your Web page résumé. If that's not where it is, close the dialog, copy the image to your *website* folder, and go back to the previous step.	▶ Click the Background Image checkbox, then click the Browse button to select the image you want tiled into the background. *Important:* The image file must be in the same folder as your Web page résumé. If that's not where it is, close the dialog, copy the image to your *website* folder, and go back to the previous step.
▶ The filename information appears in the Page Properties dialog.	▶ The filename information appears in the Page Properties dialog.
▶ Click OK to close the Page Properties dialog.	▶ Click OK to close the Page Properties dialog.
▶ Press the Preview button to see how the image will tile onto the background of your Web page. If you do not see the tile when you press the Preview button, the image is probably not in your *website* folder. Move it there, then repeat these steps.	▶ The image appears tiled into the background of your Web page.
	▶ Save the page, and open it in Microsoft Internet Explorer to see how it will look out on the Web. If you do not see the tile in your browser window, the image is probably not in your *website* folder. Move it there, then repeat these steps.

Tiles are nice, but be careful that the pattern in your tiling does not obstruct or interfere with the text on the screen. A good tile provides a subtle backdrop texture that enhances readability. Bad tiles interfere and make the text harder to read. To conserve bandwidth, tiles should be small, like the ones at the Interlit Web site.

To see how the tile got inserted in your HTML, pull down the View window, and choose Document Source. In the View Document Source window, you will see how your document's <BODY> tag got modified. Now it reads <BODY BACKGROUND="*filename*.gif"> where *filename* is the name of your tile.

CREATING TRANSPARENT IMAGES

Transparency is a special effect in which one of the colors in a bitmap becomes translucent—instead of seeing that color, you see through it into the background color or image on the screen. Consider the example in Figure 19-11, which shows two images overlayed on a background. In the first image, there is no transparency, and the image looks rectangular. In the second image, the red pixels are transparent, enabling you to see through them into the background.

To create a transparent GIF image, follow the steps in Table 19-7.

No transparency   Transparent background

Figure 19-11 The image on the right has red set to be transparent, making that color invisible.

Table 19-7   How to Create a Transparent GIF Image

Paint Shop Pro (Windows)	Graphic Converter (Macintosh)
▶ Use Paint Shop Pro to open the image.	▶ Use Graphic Converter to open the image.
▶ ✏ Use the eyedropper tool to set the background color.	▶ ✎ Click once on the transparency icon to select it as your tool.
▶ Pull down the File menu and choose Save As; the Save As dialog appears.	▶ Click once on the image on the color you want to make transparent.
▶ Click Options, select the tab for GIF, then select "Set the transparency value to the background color."	▶ Pull down the File menu and choose Save As.
▶ Click OK to save the file.	▶ In the Save As dialog, pull down the Format menu and choose the GIF format.
	▶ Click the Save button to save the file in the folder of your choice (probably your *website* folder).

To paste the image onto your Web page, follow the steps in Table 19-5. The transparent color in the GIF image will be invisible.

CREATING ANIMATED IMAGES

A special feature of the GIF graphics format is its ability to contain animated images. Animated GIFs contain multiple images intended to be shown in a sequence at specific times and locations on the screen. A looping option causes your Web browser to keep showing the frames in the GIF file continually, and as a result, you see an animation on screen.

GIF Animator for Windows

Windows users can create animated GIFs with Microsoft GIF Animator or the GIF Construction Set, which you can download by following the links to animated GIFs at the Interlit Web site. The Interlit Web site also links to a tutorial on creating animated GIFs.

GifBuilder for Macintosh

If you have a Macintosh, you can create animated GIF images with GifBuilder. Follow the Interlit Web site links to GifBuilder. It's freeware, which means that it's copyrighted, but you don't have to pay anything to download and use it.

EXERCISES

1. Choose an image that has a lot of detail in it, such as a photograph, and make both GIF and JPEG versions of it. Compare the two images side-by-side, and see if you can perceive any difference in the appearance of the files. What difference is there, if any?

2. Take a small image, such as one of the icons found at the Interlit Web site, and resize it to 640 × 480. Notice how the resizing process caused the image to become jagged and pixilated. Now take the same small image, and resample it to 640 × 480. Does the result appear better than when you resized the image? If the image still appears distorted, try resampling it at smaller sizes. How large can you make it before the distortion renders the image unusable?

3. Take any image, and increase its color depth to 16 million colors (24-bit format). Inspect the file's size with the Windows Explorer or File Manager, or via the Macintosh Finder, and make a note of how large the file is. Now decrease the color depth to 256 colors (8-bit format). Inspect the file's size again. By what percentage has the size of the file decreased? Will this make the file appear more quickly when it gets downloaded from the Internet for display on a Web page?

4. Following the instructions in this chapter, paste your photo onto your Web page, or if you choose not to put your picture on the Web, select some other graphic from the clip-art library at the Interlit Web site. Experiment with making the text flow along the left or right side of the picture.

5. The Interlit Web site contains several images designed for use as tiles on Web pages. Download several of these images, and try tiling them onto your Web page résumé. Which tile appears best on your Web page résumé?

6. Both Paint Shop Pro (Windows) and Graphic Converter (Macintosh) contain special effects that can enhance considerably the appearance of an image on a Web page. Use Paint Shop Pro to open a photograph of your choice. Pull down the Colors menu, choose Adjust, and experiment with adjusting the brightness, contrast, and gamma settings. The gamma settings enable you to correct the difference in color balance between a printed photograph and a computer screen. With Graphic Converter, pull down the Picture menu and choose Brightness/Contrast. Use the Levels option to adjust the input and output levels of the image. You can adjust black, white, or both.

20 Using Tables for Advanced Web Page Layout

After completing this chapter, you will be able to:

- [ ] **Explain the role of tables in designing Web pages.**

- [ ] **Use tables to organize Web pages into rectangular regions called cells.**

- [ ] **Flow text and pictures into table cells.**

- [ ] **Recognize the HTML tags that create tables.**

COMPARE the design of the Web pages illustrated in Figures 20-1 and 20-2. How are they alike? Both contain pictures, and both contain text. How do they differ? Figure 20-1 treats the screen as one large column of information, while Figure 20-2 divides the screen into rectangular regions that position the text and graphics in different sections of the Web page. Although both screens convey the same information, you probably will agree that the sectional layout of Figure 20-2 creates a more interesting Web page. This chapter shows how to use tables to arrange information into rows and columns on the screen. In the next chapter, you will use tables to create a unique design for your home page on the Web.

NOTE   Tables became part of the HTML standard when Version 3.2 was released in 1996. Web pages produced before then were limited to a single column of information.

WHAT IS A TABLE?

A table is a design element that divides the screen into a grid consisting of rectangular regions called cells. Into each cell you can enter text or graphics, which will align with the boundaries of the cell's rectangle. The grid that forms the boundaries of the cells can be either visible or invisible. You normally make the grid visible when presenting a table full of technical information that would be hard to read without horizontal and vertical lines to help the user follow the data across the table. HTML provides control over border thickness, and you can use thinner or thicker grid lines, depending on the situation.

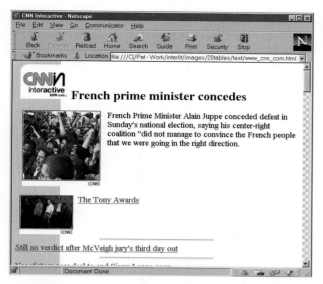

Figure 20-1 How a Web page appears without the use of tables to create rectangular regions on the screen.

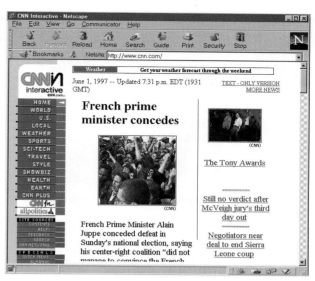

Figure 20-2 Tables create rectangular regions used as design elements in an advanced Web page layout.

WHY USE TABLES ON WEB PAGES?

There are two reasons for using tables on Web pages. The first reason is rather obvious—to present data neatly in rows and columns that help the user perceive the order or the relationships in the information. This book uses tables extensively to present complex information in an understandable manner. For example, consider the presentation of HTML tags in Table 17-1. Displaying the tags in column 1 followed by their description in column 2 provides an orderly presentation that enables the user to find a tag in column 1, then read across to its definition in column 2. The grid is visible to help the user read across the table to find the definitions of the different tags.

The second reason for using tables is to create advanced Web page layouts consisting of rectangular sections, into which you can flow blocks of text or insert graphics. Tables consist of one or more rows of one or more cells. You can adjust the width and height of the cells to create a wide variety of Web page layouts. You can even have more than one table on the page at once, which enables you to create many interesting designs. For example, consider the layout of the Web page shown in Figure 20-3. The layout analysis in Figure 20-4 shows how this page consists of several tables with varying numbers of rows and columns, and different cell heights and widths. Notice how the use of multiple tables adds interest to the design of this page.

CREATING A TABLE

It's easy to create a table. If you have Netscape Composer, follow the steps in Table 20-1. If you have Microsoft FrontPage Express, follow Table 20-2.

Figure 20-3 An advanced Web page design employing multiple tables with varying cell heights and widths.

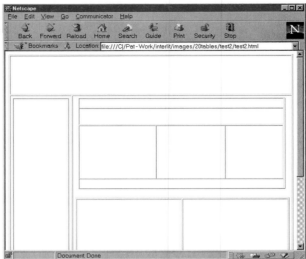

Figure 20-4 Layout analysis of the tables used to create the Web page in Figure 20-3.

Table 20-1 How to Create a Table on a Web Page with Netscape Composer

Netscape Composer

Use Netscape Composer to open the Web page on which you want to create a table. If this is your first time through these instructions, you'll be creating a table of the world's highest mountains, and you'll need a blank Web page to hold the table. Click the New Page button to create the blank Web page, then click the Save button and save the page in your *website* folder under the filename *highest.htm*. Then follow these steps:

▶ Position your cursor at the spot in the document where you want to insert a table.

▶ Click the Table button to insert a new table; the New Table Properties dialog appears as shown in Figure 20-5.

Figure 20-5 Netscape Composer's New Table Properties dialog.

▶ In the Number of rows field, enter the number of rows you want this table to have. For this example, enter 8.

▶ In the Number of columns field, enter the number of columns you want this table to have. For this example, enter 4.

▶ Click the Apply button to see how your table appears so far, but do not close the New Table Properties dialog yet.

▶ The controls inside the Attributes group enable you to modify certain table formatting parameters. After changing these parameters, you can click the Apply button at the bottom of the dialog to preview their effect on the table. You will also be able to modify these parameters later on, if you decide you want to change the appearance of the table:

  ▶ The Border line width field lets you define how wide you want the border around the table to be drawn, in pixels. If you do not want the table grid to be visible, set the border to 0. For this example, set the Border line width to 1.

  ▶ The Cell spacing field lets you specify how many pixels of blank space you want between the cells. If the grid is visible, this will increase the thickness of the grid. For this example, do not change the cell spacing, which you can adjust later on.

  ▶ The Cell padding field lets you specify how many pixels of blank space will appear within the cell around the data you type into it. For this example, do not change the cell padding, which you can adjust later on.

  ▶ When checked, the Table width setting controls how wide the table will be. You can pull down the menu to make the number you enter set the width as a percentage of the screen, or in pixels. If you make this a percentage, the table will scale automatically to fit different screen sizes. If you make this pixels, the table will not scale. For this example, do not change the table width padding, which you can adjust later on.

  ▶ When checked, the Table min. height setting guarantees that the table will occupy the specified minimum amount of height on the

Table 20-1 *(Continued)*

Netscape Composer

screen. You can pull down the menu to make the number you enter set the width as a percentage of the screen, or in pixels. If you make this a percentage, the table will scale automatically to fit different screen sizes. If you make this pixels, the table will not scale. For this example, do not check the Table min. height setting.

▶ When checked, the Use Color setting determines the color of the background of the table cells. Click the Color button if you want to set the background color. For this example, do not check the Use Color setting, which you can adjust later on.

▶ When checked, the Equal column widths option makes the columns have equal width. Otherwise, the width of the columns will adjust automatically to the relative width of the data. For this example, do not check Fast column layout.

▶ Click the Apply button whenever you want to preview the results of the settings you have made.

▶ Click the OK button to close the dialog.

Table 20-2 How to Create a Table on a Web Page with Microsoft FrontPage Express

Microsoft FrontPage Express

📝 Use Microsoft FrontPage Express to open the Web page on which you want to create a table. If this is your first time through these instructions, you'll be creating a table of the world's highest mountains, and you'll need a blank Web page to hold the table. Click the New Page button to create the blank Web page, then click the Save button and save the page in your *website* folder under the filename *highest.htm*. Then follow these steps:

▶ Position your cursor at the spot in the document where you want to insert a table.

▶ Pull down the Table menu and choose Insert Table; the Insert Table dialog appears as shown in Figure 20-6.

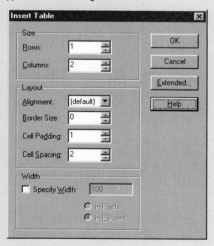

Figure 20-6 The Microsoft FrontPage Express Insert Table dialog.

▶ In the Rows field, enter the number of rows you want this table to have. For this example, enter 8.

▶ In the Columns field, enter the number of columns you want this table to have. For this example, enter 4.

▶ The rest of the controls enable you to modify certain table formatting parameters. You will be able to modify these parameters later on, if you decide you want to change the appearance of the table:

▶ The Alignment enables you to align the table with the left, center, or right of the screen. For this example, leave this set to the default setting, which is left.

▶ The Border Size field lets you define how wide you want the border around the table to be drawn, in pixels. If you do not want the table grid to be visible, set the border to 0. For this example, set the Border Width to 1.

▶ The Cell Padding field lets you specify how many pixels of blank space will appear within the cell around the data you type into it. For this example, do not change the cell padding, which you can adjust later on.

▶ The Cell Spacing field lets you specify how many pixels of blank space you want between the cells. If the grid is visible, this will increase the thickness of the grid. For this example, do not change the cell spacing, which you can adjust later on.

▶ When checked, the Specify Width setting controls how wide the table will be. By clicking the radio buttons below the width field, you can make the number you enter set the width either as a percentage of the screen or in pixels. If you make this a percentage, the table will scale automatically to fit different screen sizes. If you make this pixels, the table will not scale. For this example, do not change the width settings, which you can adjust later on.

▶ Click the OK button to close the dialog; the table appears on your Web page.

▶ 🖽 Another way to create a table is to click the Insert Table button; the table-size selector shown in Figure 20-7 will appear.

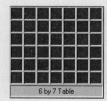

Figure 20-7 The Microsoft FrontPage Express table-size selector.

▶ Click and drag your mouse to form the size grid you want.

▶ Release the mouse button to create the table.

ENTERING THE CAPTION INTO A TABLE

You first time through these instructions, you will have created a table with 8 rows of 4 columns to hold data you will next enter concerning the world's highest mountains. To enter the caption into the table, follow the steps in Table 20-3.

Table 20-3 How to Caption a Table

Netscape Composer	Microsoft FrontPage Express
▶ In the Netscape Composer window, click once inside the caption field to position your cursor there.	▶ In the Microsoft FrontPage Express window, pull down the Table menu and choose Insert Caption.
▶ Type the caption; in this example, type **The World's Highest Mountains**	▶ Your cursor begins to flash where the caption will appear.
▶ The caption appears as shown in Figure 20-8.	▶ Type the caption; in this example, type **The World's Highest Mountains**
	▶ The caption appears as shown in Figure 20-9.

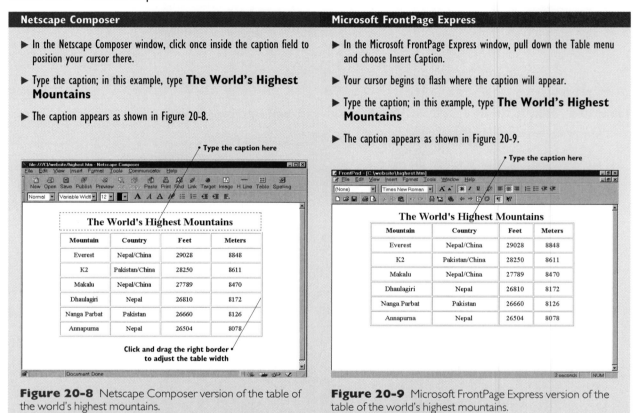

Figure 20-8 Netscape Composer version of the table of the world's highest mountains.

Figure 20-9 Microsoft FrontPage Express version of the table of the world's highest mountains.

ENTERING DATA INTO A TABLE

Once your table has been created, you can enter data into it. Simply click inside the cell into which you want to enter some data, and type what you want to enter. You can move from cell to cell by pressing the `Tab` key. Pressing `Shift`-`Tab` will move you back to the previous cell.

If this is your first time through these instructions, type the information displayed in Figure 20-8 or Figure 20-9 into the table.

To change the font, color, size, appearance, or justification of the text in a table, follow the steps in Table 20-4.

Table 20-4 How to Change Text Attributes in a Table

Netscape Composer	Microsoft FrontPage Express
▶ Drag your mouse over the text you want to modify, then click the appropriate button on the Format toolbar, as shown in Figure 20-10.	▶ Drag your mouse over the text you want to modify, then click the appropriate button on the Format toolbar, as shown in Figure 20-11.
▶ If the Format toolbar is not visible, pull down the View menu and choose Show Format Toolbar.	▶ If the Format toolbar is not visible, pull down the View menu and choose Format Toolbar.
▶ **A** For example, to bold the words *Mountain, Country, Feet,* and *Meters,* drag your mouse over them to select them, then click the Bold button.	▶ **B** For example, to bold the words *Mountain, Country, Feet,* and *Meters,* drag your mouse over them to select them, then click the Bold button.
▶ To center them, click the Alignment button, then choose Center.	▶ To center them, click the Center button.
▶ Click the Preview button to see how the table will appear on the Web. 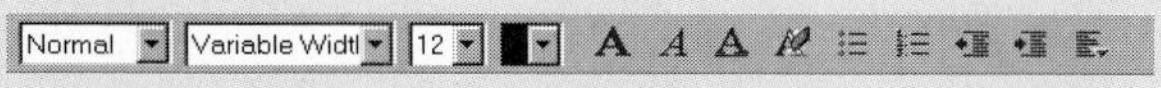	▶ Save the file, then use Microsoft Internet Explorer to open it so you can see how the table will appear on the Web. 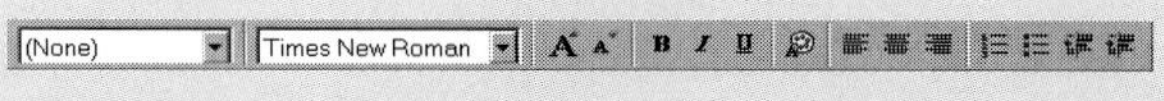

Figure 20-10 Use the Format toolbar to modify the appearance of text in a table.

Figure 20-11 Use the Format toolbar to modify the appearance of text in a table.

ADJUSTING THE PARAMETERS OF A TABLE

If you want to adjust the parameters of a table after you've created it, follow the steps in Table 20-5.

Table 20-5 How to Adjust the Parameters of a Table

Netscape Composer	Microsoft FrontPage Express
▶ Click once anywhere inside the table, then pull down the Format menu and choose Table Properties. The Table Properties dialog appears.	▶ Click once anywhere inside the table, then pull down the Table menu and choose Table Properties. The Table Properties dialog appears.
▶ Make the modification you want, then click the Apply button to preview the change.	▶ Make the modification you want, then click the Apply button to preview the change.
▶ Click the OK button to make the change, or click the Cancel button to cancel it.	▶ Click the OK button to make the change, or click the Cancel button to cancel it.
▶ To adjust the width of a table, you can click and drag the table's right border. The width of the columns will automatically scale proportionately.	▶ Another way to adjust a table is to click inside it with your right mouse button; when the menu appears, choose Table Properties.
	▶ To adjust an individual cell, choose Cell Properties instead of Table Properties.

INSPECTING YOUR HTML

If you inspect the HTML source code of the *highest.htm* file you created in this chapter, you will see how the table begins with the <TABLE> tag and ends with the </TABLE> tag. Each row of the table begins with <TR> and ends with </TR>, which stands for Table Row. Each cell begins with <TD> and ends with </TD >, which stands for Table Data. It's also possible for cells to have the tags <TH> and </TH>, which stand for Table Header. TH tags work the same as TD tags except that the data appear in a bolded heading style.

Note to Netscape Composer Users	Note to Microsoft FrontPage Express Users
To inspect your HTML, pull down the Composer's View menu and choose Page Source.	To inspect your HTML, pull down the FrontPage Express View menu and choose HTML.

The typical table uses these codes in the following structure:

```
<TABLE>
    <TR>
        <TD> row one, cell one </TD>
        <TD> row one, cell two </TD>
    </TR>
    <TR>
        <TD> row two, cell one </TD>
        <TD> row two, cell two </TD>
    </TR>
    <TR>
        <TD> row three, cell one </TD>
        <TD> row three, cell two </TD>
    </TR>
</TABLE>
```

Tables with more cells in a row than this example have more <TD></TD> tags. Tables with more rows add more <TR></TR> tags.

Attributes get added to the tags to specify the table formatting. The BORDER attribute gets added to the <TABLE> tag if the table has a border; for example, if a table has a border thickness of 2, the tag is <TABLE BORDER=2>. In Netscape Composer, if you check the Fast column layout option, the COLS attribute gets added to the <TABLE> tab, as in <TABLE BORDER COLS=4>.

The ALIGN attribute can modify the <TABLE>, <TR>, and <TD> tags to specify whether the element is to be aligned to the LEFT, CENTER, RIGHT, TOP, or BOTTOM. For example, a table cell in which the data is centered has the tag <TD ALIGN=CENTER>.

PUTTING IMAGES INSIDE TABLE CELLS

You can insert images inside any table cell. If the image is larger than the cell, the cell will expand to the size of the image, unless you've limited the size of the cell to a fixed pixel width or height. To insert an image into a table cell, follow the steps in Table 20-6.

Table 20-6   How to Insert an Image into a Table Cell

Netscape Composer	Microsoft FrontPage Express
▶ In the Netscape Composer window, click once inside the cell into which you want to insert an image.	▶ In the Microsoft FrontPage Express window, click once inside the cell into which you want to insert an image.
▶ 🖼 Click the Insert Image button; the Image Properties dialog appears.	▶ 🖼 Click the Insert Image button; the Image dialog appears.
▶ Click the Choose File button and choose the image file you want to insert.	▶ Activate the From File option and use the Browse button to choose the image file you want to insert.
▶ If the cell will include text as well as graphics, choose the text alignment option you want to control how the text flows around the picture.	▶ Click OK to close the Image Properties dialog; the picture will appear inside the cell.
▶ Click OK to close the Image Properties dialog; the picture will appear inside the cell.	▶ If the cell will include text as well as graphics, double-click the image and choose the text alignment option you want to control how the text flows around the picture.
▶ 🎇 Click the Preview button to see how the table will appear on the Web.	▶ 🖼 Save the file, then use Microsoft Internet Explorer to open it so you can see how the table will appear on the Web.

SUBDIVIDING TABLE CELLS

It is possible to subdivide any table cell by creating a table inside the cell. This puts a table grid inside the cell, providing another layer of structure on the Web page. There is no limit to the number of cells you can subdivide. Since this enables you to create any conceivable pattern of rectangular regions on the screen, it provides an unlimited array of possibilities for laying out Web pages. Figures 20-12 to 20-15 show layout analyses of Web pages that use subdivided table cells as design elements. As you can see, being able to create tables inside tables makes for some pretty interesting Web pages. To create a table inside a cell, follow the steps in Table 20-7.

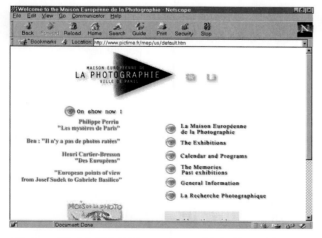

Figure 20-12 This Web page has a table inside a table.

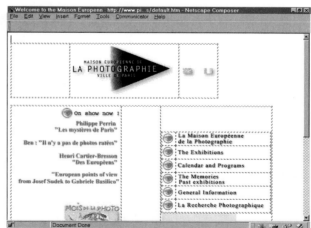

Figure 20-13 Layout analysis of Figure 20-12.

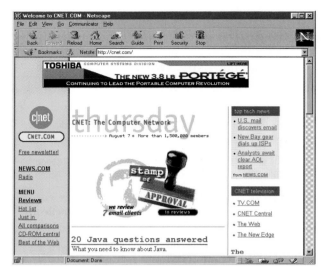

Figure 20-14 This Web page is built using one large outer table, a smaller table nested inside that one, and still smaller subtables inside that.

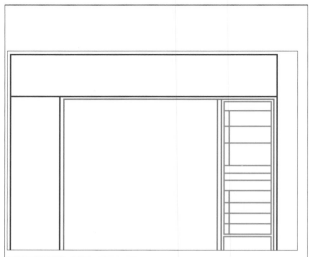

Figure 20-15 Layout analysis of Figure 20-14.

Table 20-7 How to Subdivide a Table Cell

Netscape Composer	Microsoft FrontPage Express
▶ Click inside the cell you want to subdivide to position your cursor in it. If your cursor doesn't want to go inside the cell, you probably have the centering attribute on; click in the center of the cell to position your cursor there.	▶ Click inside the cell you want to subdivide to position your cursor in it.
▶ Click the Insert Table button; the New Table Properties dialog appears.	▶ Pull down the Table menu and choose Insert Table; the Insert Table dialog appears.
▶ Enter the number of rows and columns you want in the subdivided cell.	▶ Enter the number of rows and columns you want in the subdivided cell.
▶ Adjust any other properties you want to modify. For example, if you do not want the grid visible, set the border thickness to 0. If you do not want any spacing between or around table cells, set the Cell Spacing and Cell Padding to 0.	▶ Adjust any other properties you want to modify. For example, if you do not want the grid visible, set the border size to 0. If you do not want any spacing between or around table cells, set the Cell Padding and Cell Spacing to 0.
▶ Click OK to close the dialog and create the table.	▶ Click OK to close the dialog and create the table.
▶ The newly created table subdivides the cell, providing another grid of rectangles to use as design elements on your Web page.	▶ The newly created table subdivides the cell, providing another grid of rectangles to use as design elements on your Web page.

In the next chapter, you will apply this method of inserting a table inside a table to create a really cool home page to mount on the Web.

MAKING CELLS THAT SPAN MORE THAN ONE ROW OR COLUMN

By default, each cell in a table is confined to just one row and column. To vary the layout of a table, you can expand a cell to make it span more than one row or column. To expand a cell to span more than one row or column, follow the steps in Table 20-8.

Table 20-8 How to Make a Table Cell Span More than One Row or Column

Netscape Composer	Microsoft FrontPage Express
▶ Click once inside the cell that you want to expand.	▶ Click once inside the cell that you want to expand.
▶ Pull down the Format menu and choose Table Properties; the Table Properties dialog appears.	▶ Pull down the Table menu and choose Cell Properties; the Cell Properties dialog appears, as shown in Figure 20-17.
▶ Click the Cell tab to make the Cell properties appear, as shown in Figure 20-16.	

Figure 20-16 The Cell tab of the Table Properties dialog.

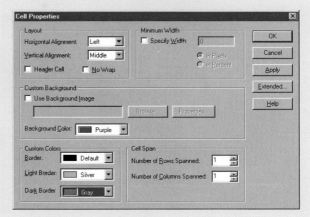

Figure 20-17 The Microsoft FrontPage Express Cell Properties dialog.

Netscape Composer (continued):

▶ In the Cell Spans field, enter the number of rows and columns you want the cell to span.

▶ Click the Apply button to preview how the cell will appear.

▶ Make any adjustments necessary, and click the Apply button to preview the cell again.

▶ Click the Close button when you are done formatting the cell.

▶ To delete any unwanted cells created by this process, position your mouse cursor inside an unwanted cell, click the right mouse button and choose Delete, then choose Cell.

Microsoft FrontPage Express (continued):

▶ In the Cell Span group, enter the number of rows and columns you want the cell to span.

▶ Click the Apply button to preview how the cell will appear.

▶ Make any adjustments necessary, and click the Apply button to preview the cell again.

▶ Click OK when you are done formatting the cell.

▶ To delete any unwanted cells created by this process, position your mouse cursor inside and toward the left of the unwanted cell, then press the [Delete] key.

NOTE If you inspect the HTML of a table that has a cell spanning more than one row or column, you will notice that the <TD> tag has ROWSPAN and COLSPAN attributes. For example, a cell that spans two rows and three columns has the tag <TD ROWSPAN=2 COLSPAN=3>.

E X E R C I S E S

1. The following exercises build upon one another and must be completed in the order presented.

2. Use Netscape Composer or Microsoft FrontPage Express to create a new blank Web page. On the blank page, create a table to hold the 1996 Summer Olympics scores printed below. Enter the caption, column labels, and data into the table. Save the page in your *website* folder under the name *olympics.htm*.

Summer Olympics Medal Count

Country	Gold	Silver	Bronze
USA	44	32	25
Germany	10	18	27
Russia	26	21	16
China	16	22	12

3. Experiment by turning the grid lines on and off. To do this, click anywhere inside the table. If you have Netscape Composer, pull down the Format menu and choose Table Properties. If you have Microsoft FrontPage Express, pull down the Table menu and choose Table Properties. The Table Properties dialog will appear. Type 0 into the border field to turn the grid lines off, or type 1 to turn them on. How do the grid lines affect the readability of the data? To answer this question, you must use your Web browser to view how the table will appear on the Web.

4. Repeat exercise 2. With the grid lines off, pull down the View menu and select View Source (Netscape Composer) or HTML (Microsoft FrontPage Express) to inspect the HTML source code. Find the <TABLE> tag. Does it have any attributes? Now turn the grid lines on, and inspect the source again. How does the <TABLE> tag appear now?

5. If you're using Netscape Composer, click and drag the grid lines of the table to the right or to the left to change the width of the table cells. If you have Microsoft FrontPage Express, right-click a table cell, then use Cell Properties to change the cell's minimum width. Use your Web browser to see how the reformatted table will appear on the Web. How does the width of the cells affect the readability of the data in the table?

6. This exercise is for Netscape Composer users only. Click anywhere inside the table. Pull down the Format menu and choose Table Properties, check the Fast column layout option, and click OK to close the Table Properties dialog. Now click and drag the right border of the table to adjust its size. Try making the table be lots of different widths. Observe what happens. Then pull down the Format menu, choose Table Properties, uncheck the Fast column layout option, and click OK. Click and drag the right border to make the table be lots of different widths. What is the difference you observe based on whether the Fast column layout option is checked?

7. At the Interlit Web site, you will find the flags of each country in the Olympics table. Download these four flags to the *website* folder on your computer. If you have trouble, refer to the instructions in Chapter 13 for downloading images from Web pages. In the Country column of the Olympics table, delete the country names, and use the Insert Image button to insert the appropriate flag instead. Notice how the height of the cells adjusts automatically to fit the image.

21 Making a Local Web and a Home Page

After completing this chapter, you will be able to:

- **Define the concept of a local web.**

- **Create a personal home page.**

- **Make a local web by linking your home page to your Web page résumé.**

- **Link your résumé to your home page.**

- **Test the links with a Web browser.**

- **Cope with case sensitivity in hypertext and hyperpicture links.**

WEBS are created by links that connect things together. If all of the objects of those links reside on your PC, you have what is known as a local web. In this chapter, you will create a home page and link it to the Web page résumé you created in Chapter 18. Since both of these pages will reside on your PC, this linkage will create a local web. After testing your local web with a Web browser to make sure it works properly, you will be ready to proceed to the next chapter, which shows how to mount your files on the World Wide Web.

HOME PAGE CREATION STRATEGIES

As you learned in Chapter 4, a home page is a person's focal point on the Web. When someone asks for your Web address, you give them the URL of your home page. By clicking on the links to your home page, people can access the resources you have provided. Thus, your home page establishes your identity on the Web.

Since it is the first page people will see when you invite someone to visit your Web site, it is important for your home page to make a good impression. The content, appearance, and layout of your home page will project an image on the Web and reflect on the kind of person you are. So you will want your home page to be your best page.

There are several ways to create a home page, including templating, wizardry, designing, and cloning. Templating uses the home page template that works with Netscape Composer. This is the quickest way for Netscape users to create a home page, and people who are pressed for time will find it convenient. Web pages constructed from templates, however, will share the design elements provided by the template, and as a result, your home page will appear similar to the thousands of other home pages created this way.

Wizardry involves the use of Web page creation software that prompts you for the information needed to make a Web page. The wizard asks you what kind of Web page you want to make (such as a home page or a menu), how you want to make it look (fancy, plain, or businesslike), and what kind of information you have to enter. Then the wizard generates the page for you, and you fine-tune the results.

The most original way to create a home page is to design your own custom layout. This takes the most time, but it's the best way to create a Web page that's uniquely suited to the image you want to project on the Web. You need to be aware, however, that if you come up with a design that's truly unique, it may not be long before other users clone it and create Web pages looking like yours.

Cloning involves the copying of someone else's Web page that you think is worthwhile. Both Netscape Communicator and Microsoft Internet Explorer make this easy to do. While cloning is a quick way to come up with a nice-looking Web page, it raises ethical questions with respect to copying other people's work. Unless the page is copyrighted, it is legally OK for you to borrow from it, and as a result, this practice is quite common on the Web. Since you're using someone else's design, however, your home page will not be original.

HOME PAGE NAMING CONVENTIONS

In the tutorials that follow, you'll learn how to create a home page using either Netscape's home page template or Microsoft's Home Page Wizard. You'll also learn how to clone Web pages and understand the copyright and ethical issues involved in borrowing other people's work. Then you'll learn how to design your own custom home page. At the end of each tutorial, when you save your new home page, you will need to give your page a filename. When someone asks for the address of your home page, you will respond with the URL (uniform resource locator) of this file. You see a lot of home page URLs that end with filenames like *home.html* or *welcome.html*, but the coolest home page addresses are the short ones that omit the filename. For example, Microsoft's home page is *http:// www.microsoft.com* with no filename specified.

Having a cool home page address with no filename in it indicates you understand that when someone visits a Web site folder without specifying a filename, the server looks to see if the folder contains that Web site's default filename, which is almost always *index.html*. If the default file exists, the server sends it. Since you will want the name of your home page to be cool, this tutorial names the file *index.html*. If your Web server uses some other default filename (such as *default.html*), use that name instead. If you are not sure what default filename your Web server uses, ask your ISP. If it's not possible for you to use a default filename, name your home page something intuitive, such as *home.html*. If you have Windows 3.1, which does not support long filenames, you won't be able to use the filename extension *.html*, so use *.htm* instead.

USING NETSCAPE'S HOME PAGE TEMPLATE

To create a home page from a template using Netscape Composer, your computer must be connected to the Internet, because the template uses software on the Web to ask you questions and to create a home page according to the options you select. Once you are connected to the Internet, get Netscape Composer running, and follow these steps:

 ▶ Click the New Page button in the Netscape Composer window; the Create New Page dialog appears.

▶ Click the From Template button; the Netscape Web Page Templates will appear in a browse window.

▶ Scroll down to the Personal/Family section and choose My Home Page. The home page template appears.

▶ Pull down the File menu and choose Edit Page. The home page template now appears in a Netscape Composer window.

▶ Modify the template by changing the text to say things about yourself. Delete things you don't want on your home page, such as the instructions at the top of the page.

 ▶ If you want a photo of yourself on your home page, double-click on the sample photo on the home page template to bring up the Image Properties dialog, then replace the filename with an image of yourself. Chapter 19 provides instructions on how to get your photo into an image file you can use here. Otherwise, if you do not want a picture on your Web page, delete the image.

 ▶ The links in the template are bogus, meaning they don't go anywhere. To make a link go somewhere, double-click on it to select it, then click the Link button. In the Link field, type the Web address (URL) of the resource you want to link to.

▶ Study your new home page carefully. Since it came from a template that provided sample information, it's possible that your home page may contain unwanted text. Read it very carefully, and make sure it says what you want.

▶ Pull down the Format menu and choose Page Title to make the Page Properties dialog appear. In the Title field, type the title you want the browser to display in the title bar when people visit your home page. Fill out any other information you care to provide in the Page Properties dialog, then click OK to close the dialog.

 ▶ Click the Save button, and save your new home page in your *website* folder. Make the name of your home page be either *index.htm* or *index.html* (if your computer supports long filenames).

 ▶ Click the Preview button to see how your home page will appear on the Web. If you see anything you don't like, use Netscape Composer to correct it.

MAKING A HOME PAGE WITH THE
MICROSOFT FRONTPAGE EXPRESS WEB PAGE WIZARD

To create a home page from a wizard using Microsoft FrontPage Express, get Microsoft FrontPage Express running, and follow these steps:

▶ Pull down the Microsoft FrontPage Express File menu and choose New; the New Page dialog appears, listing a variety of templates and wizards. Choose the Personal Home Page Wizard.

▶ The Wizard is totally self-prompting. Follow the instructions, and the Wizard will create your page.

▶ Once the page is created, you can use FrontPage Express to customize it as you wish. Make sure you scroll down and review all of the text and links carefully; several items are placeholders for information you need to provide.

 ▶ Click the Save button, and save your new home page in your *website* folder. Make the name of your home page be *index.html* (or *index.htm,* if you have Windows 3.1).

 ▶ Use the Microsoft Internet Explorer to view your new home page to see how it will appear on the Web. If you see anything you don't like, use Microsoft FrontPage Express to correct it.

THE ETHICS OF CLONING SOMEONE ELSE'S HOME PAGE

If you see a nicely designed page on the Web, and you want to make a page with a similar design, it is possible to clone the Web page, make modifications to customize it as you wish, then save the page under your own filename. When cloning Web pages, however, you must observe copyright law and the principles of Netiquette. Refer to the Copyright and Fair Use sections of Chapter 25, and follow the Interlit Web site links to Copyright, Fair Use, and Netiquette. If you get sued for copyright infringement, ignorance of these laws is no defense. A common myth about the Internet is that since the Internet is public, everything on the Internet is in the public domain. It just isn't so. You must assume that networked information is copyrighted, instead of believing it isn't. Always ask permission if you have any question regarding whether your use of the material is a fair use.

With the laws of copyright and the principles of ethics in mind, Table 21-1 shows how to create a home page by cloning someone else's page.

Table 21-1   How to Clone a Web Page

Netscape Communicator	Microsoft FrontPage Express
▶ Use Netscape Communicator to browse to the Web page you want to clone.	▶ Use Microsoft Internet Explorer to browse to the Web page you want to clone.
▶ Pull down the File menu and choose Edit Page. The Web page appears in a Netscape Composer window.	▶ Click the Edit button. The Web page appears in a Microsoft FrontPage Express window.
▶ Modify the page by changing the text to say things about yourself. Delete things you don't want on your home page.	▶ Modify the page by changing the text to say things about yourself. Delete things you don't want on your home page.

Table 21-1 *(Continued)*

Netscape Communicator	Microsoft FrontPage Express
▶ To replace an image on the cloned Web page with one of your own pictures, double-click on the image to bring up the Image Properties dialog, then replace the filename with one of your own pictures. Chapter 19 provides instructions on how to get a photo into an image file you can use here. Otherwise, if you do not want a picture on your Web page, delete the image.	▶ To replace an image on the cloned Web page with one of your own pictures, double-click on the image to bring up the Image Properties dialog, then replace the filename with one of your own pictures. Chapter 19 provides instructions on how to get a photo into an image file you can use here. Otherwise, if you do not want a picture on your Web page, delete the image.
▶ If you want to modify any of the links on the cloned Web page, double-click the link to select it, then click the Link button. In the Link field, type the Web address (URL) of the resource you want to link to.	▶ If you want to modify any of the links on the cloned Web page, right-click the link to pop out the Link menu, and choose Hyperlink Properties. In the URL field, type the Web address (URL) of the resource you want to link to.
▶ Study your new home page carefully. Since it was cloned from someone else's Web page, it's possible that your home page may contain unwanted text. Read it very carefully, and make sure it says what you want.	▶ Study your new home page carefully. Since it was cloned from someone else's Web page, it's possible that your home page may contain unwanted text. Read it very carefully, and make sure it says what you want.
▶ Pull down the Format menu and choose Page Title to make the Page Properties dialog appear. In the Title field, type the title you want the browser to display in the title bar when people visit your home page. Complete or modify information you want to provide in the rest of the Page Properties dialog, then click OK to close the dialog.	▶ Pull down the File menu and choose Page Properties to make the Page Properties dialog appear. In the Title field, type the title you want the browser to display in the title bar when people visit your home page. Then click OK to close the dialog.
▶ Click the Save button, and save your new home page in your *website* folder. Make the name of your home page be either *index.htm* or *index.html* (if your computer supports long filenames).	▶ Click the Save button, and save your new home page in your *website* folder. Make the name of your home page be either *index.htm* or *index.html* (if your computer supports long filenames).
▶ Click the Preview button to see how your home page will appear on the Web.	▶ Use the Microsoft Internet Explorer to view your new home page to preview how it will appear on the Web.

Since you cloned someone else's Web page, you should inspect the HTML code to make sure the page does not contain hidden comments that are derogatory, insulting, obscene, or otherwise inappropriate. Pull down the View menu and choose Page Source (Netscape Composer) or HTML (Microsoft FrontPage Express) to inspect the HTML codes. Look especially for <!> tags, which are comment tags that have the form <! your comment goes here>. If you find objectionable or unwanted comments in the HTML code, use a text editor such as the Windows Notepad to remove them, being careful not to create syntactical errors in the HTML by deleting a start tag without also deleting its stop tag, or vice versa. When you save the file, if there are file format options, make sure you choose plain text (also known as ASCII text or DOS text).

DESIGNING A CUSTOM HOME PAGE

The most original way to create a home page is to design your own. By using tables to divide the screen into the rectangles you practiced making in the previous chapter, you can lay out your Web page into different regions on the screen and enter your text and graphics into the different rectangles to create a unique screen layout with a custom look and feel.

To create a custom home page using a table-driven layout, you think of the page as consisting of primary and secondary rectangles. A primary rectangle is a table

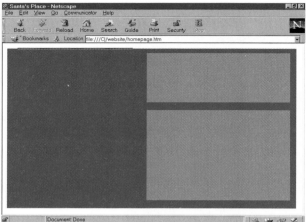

Figure 21-1 Rectangular layout consisting of primary (dark blue) and secondary (light blue) rectangles.

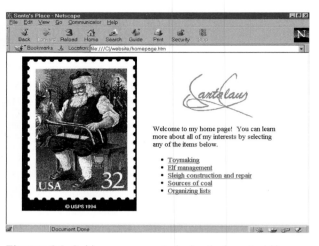

Figure 21-2 Home page created using the layout grid in Figure 21-1.

cell into which one or more secondary rectangles can be drawn. Secondary rectangles are created by subdividing a cell by inserting a new table into the cell. For example, Figure 21-1 shows a layout grid of primary and secondary rectangles, and Figure 21-2 shows the corresponding home page that was created using this layout.

To create a home page based on a rectangular table-driven layout, follow the steps in Table 21-2 for Netscape Composer or Table 21-3 for Microsoft FrontPage Express.

Table 21-2   How to Create a Custom Home Page with Netscape Composer

Netscape Composer

▶ Get Netscape Composer running.

▶ Click the Netscape Composer's New Page button. When the Create New Page dialog appears, choose Blank page.

▶ You're probably going to want your background color to be different from the default, which is gray. To set the background color, pull down the Format menu, choose Colors and Background, click the Background button, and choose a background color, such as white.

▶ Click the Table button to make the New Table Properties dialog appear.

▶ In the Number of rows field, enter the number of primary rectangles you want created vertically (i.e., up and down) on the page.

▶ In the Number of columns field, enter the number of primary rectangles you want created horizontally (i.e., left and right) across the page.

▶ You will probably want the table grid invisible; to make it invisible, set the Border line width to 0.

▶ If you turned the table grid off, you will probably want to set the Cell spacing and Cell padding to 0.

▶ Click OK to create the table. It will appear shorter than you want, but that's normal, because you haven't entered any data into it yet. The cells will expand automatically when you begin entering data into them.

▶ By default, the vertical spacing of the table cells is symmetrical. If you want to adjust the vertical position of the cell boundaries, follow these steps:

   ▶ Click once inside the column whose width you want to adjust, then pull down the Format menu and choose Table Properties to make the Table Properties dialog appear.

   ▶ Uncheck the Fast column layout option.

   ▶ Click the Cell tab.

   ▶ Check the Cell Width option, and adjust the percentage as you wish.

Table 21-2   *(Continued)*

Netscape Composer

▶ Click the Apply button to preview the width adjustment.

▶ Click OK to close the dialog.

▶ If your design calls for any of the cells to be subdivided into secondary rectangles, click inside the cell to be divided to position your cursor there, then click the Insert Table button to create the secondary table cells. You will probably want to set the options the same as for your primary table.

▶ At any time, you can begin entering your text and graphics into the table cells. Cell height will adjust automatically to the amount of information you enter.

▶ Use the Format toolbar to set the size, color, style, and appearance of your text.

▶ 🖫 Click the Save button, and save your new home page in your *website* folder. Make the name of your home page be either *index.htm* or *index.html* (if your computer supports long filenames).

▶ ❋ Click the Preview button to see how your home page will appear on the Web.

Table 21-3   How to Create a Custom Home Page with Microsoft FrontPage Express

Microsoft FrontPage Express

▶ 📝 Get Microsoft FrontPage Express running.

▶ 🗋 If Microsoft FrontPage Express has not automatically created a new page for you, click the New Page button.

▶ Pull down the Table menu and choose Insert Table to make the Insert Table dialog appear.

▶ In the Rows field, enter the number of primary rectangles you want created vertically (i.e., up and down) on the page.

▶ In the Columns field, enter the number of primary rectangles you want created horizontally (i.e., left and right) across the page.

▶ You will probably want the table grid invisible; to make it invisible, set the Border size to 0.

▶ If you turned the table grid off, you will probably want to set the Cell spacing and Cell padding to 0.

▶ Click OK to create the table. It will appear shorter than you want, but that's normal, because you haven't entered any data into it yet. The cells will expand automatically when you begin entering data into them.

▶ By default, the vertical spacing of the table cells is symmetrical. If you want to adjust the vertical position of the cell boundaries, follow these steps:

   ▶ Click once inside the column whose width you want to adjust, then pull down the Tables menu and choose Cell Properties to make the Cell Properties dialog appear.

   ▶ Click the Specify Width option, and adjust the width as you wish.

   ▶ Click the Apply button to preview the width adjustment.

   ▶ Click OK to close the dialog.

▶ If your design calls for any of the cells to be subdivided into secondary rectangles, click inside the cell to be divided to position your cursor there, then pull down the Table menu and choose Insert Table to create the secondary table cells. You will probably want to set the options the same as for your primary table.

▶ At any time, you can begin entering your text and graphics into the table cells. Cell height will adjust automatically to the amount of information you enter.

▶ Use the Format toolbar to set the size, color, style, and appearance of your text.

▶ 🖫 Click the Save button, and save your new home page in your *website* folder. Make the name of your home page be either *index.htm* or *index.html* (if your computer supports long filenames).

▶ 🔍 Use Microsoft Internet Explorer to open your new home page and preview what it will look like on the Web.

LINKING YOUR RÉSUMÉ TO YOUR HOME PAGE

Now that your home page has been created, you're ready to create a local web by linking your résumé to your home page. To link your résumé to your home page, follow the steps in Table 21-4.

Table 21-4 How to Link Your Résumé to Your Home Page

Netscape Composer	Microsoft FrontPage Express
▶ Use Netscape Composer to get your home page on screen.	▶ Use Microsoft FrontPage Express to get your home page on screen.
▶ If you have not already entered the text that will trigger your résumé, do so now. In an appropriate place on your home page, enter a phrase such as *Read my résumé to find out about my professional qualifications, career goals, and work experience.*	▶ If you have not already entered the text that will trigger your résumé, do so now. In an appropriate place on your home page, enter a phrase such as *Read my résumé to find out about my professional qualifications, career goals, and work experience.*
▶ Click and drag to highlight the word or phrase that will trigger the link. In this example, highlight *Read my résumé.*	▶ Click and drag to highlight the word or phrase that will trigger the link. In this example, highlight *Read my résumé.*
▶ Click the Link button to make the Link tab of the Character Properties dialog appear.	▶ Click the Link button to make the Create Hyperlink dialog appear; if the World Wide Web tab is not already selected, choose it now.
▶ Click the Choose File button and select the file you want to link. In this example, select *website\resume.html.* (If you have Windows 3.1, select *website\resume.htm.*)	▶ Set the HyperLink type to Other.
▶ The filename appears in the "Link to a page location or local file" field. Click OK to close the dialog.	▶ Edit the URL field to make it read as follows: **resume.html**
▶ Click the Save button to save the file.	▶ (If you have Windows 3.1, make the link say **resume.htm**)
▶ Click the Preview button to see how the link will appear on the Web.	▶ Click OK to close the Link dialog.
▶ Click the phrase that triggers your résumé to see if it brings up your résumé.	▶ Click the Save button to save the file.
	▶ Use the Microsoft Internet Explorer to view your home page to see how the link will appear on the Web.
	▶ Click the phrase that triggers your résumé to see if it brings up your résumé.

If your résumé appears when you click the phrase that triggers it on your home page, congratulate yourself, because you've just created a local web! If the link does not work, repeat these steps, reading the instructions more carefully. What you've done is to create a link to a **local file**. A local file is a link that resides in the same folder as the page that refers to it. In order for this link to work, both your home page and your résumé must reside in the same folder, which in this example is your *website* folder.

RETURNING TO YOUR HOME PAGE FROM YOUR RÉSUMÉ

Now that you have provided a way for the user to link to your résumé from your home page, it's time to create a link from your résumé back to your home page. While it is possible for users to return to your home page by clicking their Web browser's Back button, it is customary to provide a return link to your home page. Such a return link often appears at the bottom of a Web page, but sometimes it appears at the end of major sections, if the document is lengthy. The link to your home page will also come in handy for users who might enter your résumé some other way, such as through a search engine or via your résumé's URL.

Try to create such a return link on your own, but if you need help, follow the steps in Table 21-5.

Table 21-5 How to Create a Return Link to Your Résumé

Netscape Composer	Microsoft FrontPage Express
► Use Netscape Composer to get your Web page résumé on screen.	► Use Microsoft FrontPage Express to get your Web page résumé on screen.
► If you have not already entered the text that will trigger your home page, do so now. In an appropriate place on your home page, such as at the bottom of it, or at the end of major sections, enter a phrase such as *Go to my home page.*	► If you have not already entered the text that will trigger your home page, do so now. In an appropriate place on your home page, such as at the bottom of it, or at the end of major sections, enter a phrase such as *Go to my home page.*
► Click and drag to highlight the word or phrase that will trigger the link. In this example, highlight *Go to my home page.*	► Click and drag to highlight the word or phrase that will trigger the link. In this example, highlight *Go to my home page.*
► Click the Link button to make the Link tab of the Character Properties dialog appear.	► Click the Link button to make the Create Hyperlink dialog appear; if the World Wide Web tab is not already selected, choose it now.
► Click the Choose File button and select the file you want to link. In this example, select either *website\index.html* or *website\index.htm* (if your computer does not handle long filenames).	► Set the HyperLink type to Other.
► The filename appears in the "Link to a page location or local file" field. Click OK to close the dialog.	► Edit the URL field to make it read as follows: **index.html**
► Click the Save button to save the file.	► (If you have Windows 3.1, make the link say **index.htm**)
► Click the Preview button to see how the link will appear on the Web.	► Click OK to close the Link dialog.
► Click the phrase that triggers your home page to see if it goes to your home page.	► Click the Save button to save the file.
	► Use the Microsoft Internet Explorer to view your résumé to see how the link will appear on the Web.
	► Click the phrase that triggers your home page to see if it goes to your home page.

Now you should be able to click back and forth between your home page and your résumé with ease. Try this now. While viewing your home page in the Netscape Communicator window, click the trigger that goes to your résumé. When your résumé appears, click the trigger that goes to your home page. Practice going back and forth. You've successfully created a local web! In the next chapter, you will learn how to move this local web to the World Wide Web, and make your home page and your résumé available to everyone on the Internet.

CASE SENSITIVITY

When you create links to files on the World Wide Web, you need to be careful about when you use upper- and lowercase letters, because many file servers are case sensitive. The author recommends that you always keep your filenames in lowercase letters. That way, you will never get confused about whether to use upper- or lowercase when linking to your own files.

You need to be aware, however, that when you want to create a link to a Web address that contains a filename consisting of upper- and lowercase letters, you must type the filename exactly by observing the upper- and lowercase letters in the filename.

SPACES IN FILENAMES

You also need to be careful about putting spaces in filenames. Windows 95 and Windows NT allow this, but Unix does not. If you plan to mount your files on a Unix file server, do not put spaces in filenames.

INSPECTING YOUR HTML

Pull down the View menu and choose Page Source (Netscape Composer) or HTML (Microsoft FrontPage Express) to inspect the HTML code of your home page. Scroll down to the hypertext that triggers your résumé. Notice how the phrase that triggers your résumé appears inside the anchor tags <A> and </A>, as follows:

```
<A HREF="index.html">Read my résumé</A>
```

As you know, the tag <A> stands for anchor, and the attribute HREF stands for hypertext reference.

E X E R C I S E S

These exercises are designed to provide more practice creating Web pages via the methods of templating, wizardry, cloning, and designing. By trying all four methods, you will gain experience in being able to judge when it's best to clone, use a template or a wizard, or design your own custom Web page, depending on the purpose, whether you have a good model to follow, and how much time you have to spend creating the Web page. So you will know how long each method takes, time yourself as you complete each of these exercises.

1. For Netscape users only: Netscape Composer has a template for creating Web pages for clubs and other special-interest groups. You can use the Special Interest Group template to create a Web page for a club or organization to which you belong. To get started, click the New Page button in the Netscape Composer to make the Create New Page dialog appear. Click the From Template button, and, if you are connected to the Internet, the Netscape Web Page Templates will appear in a browse window. Scroll down to the Special Interest Group section and choose Windsurfing Club to make the template appear. Modify the template to create a Web page for a club or organization to which you belong. Remember to time yourself so you will know how long it takes to create a Web page this way. When you save this page, save it in your *website* folder under either the name *temp.htm* or the name *temp.html* (if your computer supports long filenames).

2. The Junior League of Bakersfield has a really beautiful Web page at http://www.goldenempire.com/jlb. The designers of this Web page, Brent and Melissa Palmer of World Leader Studios at http://www.worldleader.com, have graciously granted permission for you to create a similar design for your club or organization by cloning their Junior League page. To get started, use Netscape Communicator or Microsoft Internet Explorer to browse to http://www.goldenempire.com/jlb. To clone the page in Netscape, pull down the File menu and choose Edit Page; in Microsoft Internet Explorer, click the Edit button to clone the page. Modify the Web page to create a Web page for a club or organization to which you belong. Remember to keep track of how long this takes. When you save this page, save it in your *website* folder under either the name *cloned.htm* or *cloned.html* (if your computer supports long filenames). *Important:* The author obtained permission from the Palmers to use their Junior League of Bakersfield site in this cloning exercise. Whenever you clone a Web page, make sure you follow all copyright, fair use, and ethical guidelines. The Palmers, who are excellent Web page designers, invite you to visit their site at http://www.worldleader.com for a free consultation and to see the versatility of Web site designs in their design firm's portfolio.

3. The most creative way to make a Web page is to design your own. Use the table layout method taught in this chapter to create a Web page for your club or organization. When you save this page, save it in your *website* folder under either the name *designed.htm* or *designed.html* (if your computer supports long filenames). Remember to keep track of how long this takes.

4. Compare the results of the previous exercises. Which one took longest to complete? Which was most efficient? Which method—templating, wizardry, cloning, or designing—left you with the best feeling afterward regarding what you created? Why do you think it made you feel that way?

5. You probably like one of the Web pages you created in these exercises better than the others. Create a hypertext or hyperpicture link to it from your home page. If you have trouble, follow the steps provided earlier in this chapter under the section entitled "Linking Your Résumé to Your Home Page," except this time, you will link your club's page to your home page. Also put a link to your home page on your club's page, so the user will have an easy way to get back to your home page from your club's page. When you're finished, use your Web browser to go to your club's page and test the links to make sure you can go back and forth between your résumé and your club's page with ease.

6. If you're using this book in a class, work with your fellow classmates to create a Web page index of the home pages created in your class. E-mail the URL of this index to your professor, and in the message, tell your professor that you created the index to make grading your Web pages easier.

22 Publishing Files on the World Wide Web

After completing this chapter, you will be able to:

- **Define what it means to publish a file on the World Wide Web.**

- **Transfer files to your Web site.**

- **Inspect the folder of files at your Web site.**

- **Create folders and maintain a good directory structure at your Web site.**

- **Rename or delete files at your Web site.**

- **Cope with case-sensitive file servers.**

- **Set the file permission attributes at your Web site.**

- **Advertise the existence of your Web site.**

- **Understand what it means to be a WebMaster.**

O PUBLISH a file on the World Wide Web means to transfer the file into a folder on a Web server. Unless your computer happens to be a Web server, you need a way to transfer your files to the Web. This chapter provides you with the knowledge and the tools needed to transfer files from your PC to a World Wide Web file server.

As you work through this chapter, you will publish your home page and your résumé on the Web. Then you will be able to provide people with access to your Web pages by telling them what URL to go to. For example, suppose your Web server is www.northpole.com and your Web site is located on that server in a Web account named SantaClaus. Assume further that the default filename on your server is *index.html*. After you complete the exercises in this chapter, the URL of your home page will be http://www.northpole.com/~SantaClaus/index.html. Since *index.html* is the default filename, you will be able to shorten the URL and tell users to go to http://www.northpole.com/~SantaClaus to see your home page.

If *index.html* is not the default filename on your Web server, you will use your Web server's default filename instead. If you do not know what the default filename is on your Web server, you should contact your ISP to find out. If your Web server does not have a default filename, you can make your home page have an intuitive name such as *home.html*.

PUBLISHING FILES WITH NETSCAPE COMPOSER AND MICROSOFT FRONTPAGE EXPRESS

Both Netscape Composer and Microsoft FrontPage Express make it easy to transfer files to the Web. In order to make the transfer, however, you need to know the name of your Web server and the path to your filespace on that server. If you do not know this information, contact your ISP to find out. To publish a Web page, follow the steps in Table 22-1.

Table 22-1 How to Publish a Folder Full of Files on the World Wide Web

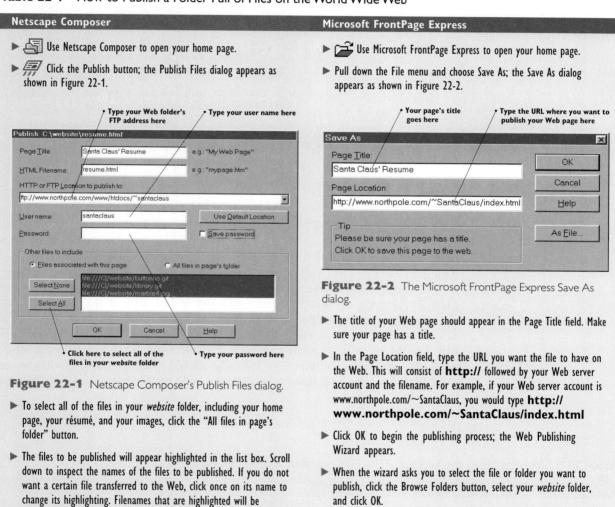

Netscape Composer	Microsoft FrontPage Express

Netscape Composer

▶ Use Netscape Composer to open your home page.

▶ Click the Publish button; the Publish Files dialog appears as shown in Figure 22-1.

Figure 22-1 Netscape Composer's Publish Files dialog.

▶ To select all of the files in your *website* folder, including your home page, your résumé, and your images, click the "All files in page's folder" button.

▶ The files to be published will appear highlighted in the list box. Scroll down to inspect the names of the files to be published. If you do not want a certain file transferred to the Web, click once on its name to change its highlighting. Filenames that are highlighted will be transferred; filenames that are not highlighted will not be transferred.

▶ In the "Upload files to this location" field, enter the upload address of your Web site. This will be something like **http:// www.northpole.com/~SantaClaus** or **ftp:// www.northpole.com/~SantaClaus** which would show what Santa Claus's Web site might look like. Contact your ISP if you do not know the upload address of your Web site.

▶ In the User name field, enter your user name, such as **SantaClaus**

Microsoft FrontPage Express

▶ Use Microsoft FrontPage Express to open your home page.

▶ Pull down the File menu and choose Save As; the Save As dialog appears as shown in Figure 22-2.

Figure 22-2 The Microsoft FrontPage Express Save As dialog.

▶ The title of your Web page should appear in the Page Title field. Make sure your page has a title.

▶ In the Page Location field, type the URL you want the file to have on the Web. This will consist of **http://** followed by your Web server account and the filename. For example, if your Web server account is www.northpole.com/~SantaClaus, you would type **http:// www.northpole.com/~SantaClaus/index.html**

▶ Click OK to begin the publishing process; the Web Publishing Wizard appears.

▶ When the wizard asks you to select the file or folder you want to publish, click the Browse Folders button, select your *website* folder, and click OK.

▶ When the wizard asks you to type a name describing your Web server, type something logical; the author typed **Fred's Web server**

▶ When the wizard asks you to type the URL provided by your ISP for publishing Web pages, do just that. If you were Santa Claus, this would be something like **http://www.northpole.com/ ~SantaClaus**

▶ The wizard may ask whether you want to use a LAN or dialup connection to publish your Web pages; answer according to the kind of connection you have.

Table 22-1   *(Continued)*

Netscape Composer	Microsoft FrontPage Express
▶ In the Password field, type your password. If you want Netscape to remember your password so you do not need to type it the next time you publish files, check the Save password box. For security reasons, the author recommends that you do not check this option. ▶ Click OK to publish the files.	▶ The wizard will go through a verification process to make sure the information you provided will work OK. If so, the wizard will publish your files, and you're done; skip the rest of these instructions. ▶ If the wizard says it cannot post your files, it's possible that your server does not permit you to post files to an http address. Instead, you need to use the FTP protocol. The wizard will help you solve this problem. Click the Next button. ▶ When the wizard asks you to select a protocol, choose FTP. ▶ When the wizard asks you to type your user name and password, do so. ▶ The wizard will ask you to verify the name of your FTP server; this is the name of the FTP server that your ISP gave you for your Web account. ▶ The wizard will ask you to confirm the directory and home root of your Web account; review the information and click Next. ▶ The wizard will go through another verification process; click Next. ▶ The wizard will keep repeating this process until it helps you come up with a scheme that works for publishing your files to the Web. If you have trouble, contact your ISP to verify that you are using the correct protocol, server address, account name, and password for your Web account.

If all goes well, you will see a status dialog informing you of progress as your files get transferred to the Web. If you get error messages, repeat these instructions carefully. If this procedure still does not work, it's possible that your Web server does not allow programs like Netscape Composer and Microsoft FrontPage Express to upload files. In this case, you should try transferring your files via the FTP software that is covered in the next part of this tutorial. If the FTP software won't work on your server, contact your ISP, who should either be able to help you get one of these methods working or provide you with another method for publishing files to your Web site.

To find out whether your files got published properly, follow the steps in Table 22-2.

Table 22-2   How to Verify the Success of the Publication of Your Home Page

Netscape Communicator	Microsoft Internet Explorer
▶ 🔳 Get your Web browser running. ▶ Pull down the File menu, choose Open Page, and type the URL of your home page. For example, if you are Santa Claus, you would type **http://www.northpole.com/~SantaClaus** ▶ Note that if you named your home page something else besides your Web server's default filename (*index.html*), you would need to include the filename when you type the URL of your home page, such as: **http://www.northpole.com/~SantaClaus/ home.html**	▶ 🔳 Get your Web browser running. ▶ If the Address field is not visible, pull down the View menu, and if the Toolbar is not checked, select the Toolbar to display it. If the Address field still is not visible, click your right mouse button on the Toolbar and select Address Bar. ▶ Delete anything that might already be in the Address field, then type the URL of your home page into the Address field. For example, if you are Santa Claus, you would type **http:// www.northpole.com/~SantaClaus**

Table 22-2 *(Continued)*

Netscape Communicator	Microsoft Internet Explorer
▶ Check the option to open the page in the browser. ▶ Click OK. If your home page appears, congratulate yourself! Then click the link that triggers your résumé. Try all of the different links on your Web pages, and make sure they work OK. Make note of any problems you find.	▶ Note that if you named your home page something else besides your Web server's default filename (*index.html*), you would need to include the filename when you type the URL of your home page, such as: **http://www.northpole.com/~SantaClaus/ home.html** ▶ Press ⎵Enter⎵. If your home page appears, congratulate yourself! Then click the link that triggers your résumé. Try all of the different links on your Web pages, and make sure they work OK. Make note of any problems you find.

CORRECTING PROBLEMS IN PUBLISHED WEB PAGES

It's rare to publish a Web page and not find any problems with it after you publish it on the Web. You're probably going to notice little problems like links that don't work, misspellings, or formatting problems. To fix the problems, use Netscape Composer or Microsoft FrontPage Express to open the file that contains the error and repair it. Then save the file, and follow the steps in Table 22-1 to publish it again. This time, since you're publishing a single file, you should choose the option to publish a single file, instead of publishing the entire folder full of files.

After you've republished the file, remember to test it again, following the steps in Table 22-2. Test, test, test. Make sure *everything* at your Web site works. It's embarrassing to publish files on the Web that don't work properly, because the whole world can see your mistakes.

USING FTP SOFTWARE TO MAINTAIN A WEB SITE

Another way to transfer files to a Web site is to use an FTP program such as WS_FTP for Windows, or Fetch for the Macintosh. These programs have a graphical user interface that makes it easy to upload and download files, inspect the contents of the folders at your Web site, delete and rename files, and create new folders.

IPSWITCH

Created by Ipswitch, Inc., WS_FTP stands for Windows Socket File Transfer Protocol. It's available in both a professional edition called WS_FTP PRO and a freeware version called WS_FTP LE, which may be used without fee by any United States government organization; by individuals for noncommercial home use; and by students, faculty, and staff of academic institutions.

Created by Dartmouth College, Fetch is licensed free to users affiliated with educational or charitable organizations. Other users can get an individual license for $25.

To download either WS_FTP for Windows or Fetch for the Macintosh, follow the steps in Table 22-3.

Installing the FTP Software

To download and install the FTP software, follow the steps in Table 22-3.

Table 22-3   How to Download and Install the FTP Software

WS_FTP LE for Windows	Fetch for Macintosh
▶ Click the link to download WS_FTP LE at the Interlit Web site.	▶ Fetch is distributed as a BinHex type self-extracting archive. In order to unpack this archive, you must first have StuffIt Expander installed on your Macintosh. If you do not have StuffIt Expander on your Mac, follow the Interlit Web site links to StuffIt Expander in Chapter 13 and install it.
▶ When your browser asks what folder you want to download the archive into, choose the folder you want to put it in. Normally you use your *temp* folder.	
▶ After the file gets downloaded, you will need to unzip it with PKZIP for Windows. If you don't have PKZIP for Windows, follow the steps in Table 13-4 to download and install it.	▶ Click the link to download Fetch at the Interlit Web site.
▶ Get PKZIP for Windows running.	▶ If StuffIt Expander has been installed on your computer, Fetch will automatically self-extract and put a Fetch Installer icon on your desktop.
▶ Pull down the File menu, choose Open, and open the WS_FTP LE zip file, which is named *wsftple.zip*.	▶ Double-click the Installer icon to install Fetch.
▶ Pull down the Unzip menu and choose Extract files; the Extract dialog appears.	▶ When the installer asks whether you want to install Fetch as a fat binary or application only, you can choose "application only" to install a copy of Fetch with native code for your kind of Macintosh, or a "fat binary" that will run natively on any Macintosh.
▶ Make sure the All Files option is selected; then click the Extract button to unzip the files.	
▶ Close the PKZIP for Windows program.	
▶ If you have Windows 95, click your Start button, choose Run, and run the *install.exe* program you will find in the folder where you unzipped the *wsftple.zip* file.	
▶ If you have Windows 3.1, pull down the Program Manager's File menu, choose Run, and run the *install.exe* program you will find in the folder where you unzipped the *wsftple.zip* file.	
▶ The WS_FTP LE install program will guide you through the installation; follow the on-screen instructions.	
▶ When you get to the screen that asks you what version of WS_FTP LE you want to install, the correct version for your system will be preselected. Do not change that unless you know for sure that you should choose something different.	

How to Configure a New FTP Connection

The first time you use your FTP software, you will need to configure a new connection for your Web site. The new connection configuration identifies the domain name of your Web server and your user ID on that server. To configure a new connection, follow the steps in Table 22-4.

Table 22-4 How to Configure a New FTP Connection

WS_FTP LE for Windows	Fetch for Macintosh
▶ Double-click the WS_FTP LE icon to get it running; if you have Windows 95, you can also click your Start button, choose Programs, and in the WS_FTP group, select WS_FTP95 LE.	▶ Double-click the Fetch icon to get it running. If you cannot find the Fetch icon, choose File from the menu, then Find, and do a search for the file containing the word Fetch.
▶ The Session Properties dialog shown in Figure 22-3 appears. The first time you run WS_FTP, you need to create a new profile for your World Wide Web server. Otherwise, you just select the profile you created in a previous session.	▶ With Fetch running, pull down the Customize menu and choose New Shortcut; the Bookmark Editor dialog appears as shown in Figure 22-4.

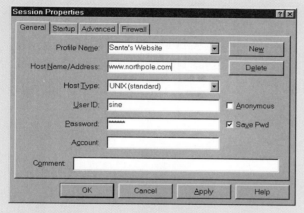

Figure 22-3 The WS_FTP Session Properties dialog.

To create a new profile, follow these steps:

▶ In the Session Properties dialog, click New; this clears the fields in the Session Profile dialog.

▶ In the Profile Name field, type the name you want the new session profile to be called; for example, if your name is Santa Claus, you might call it **Santa's Web site**

▶ In the Host Name field, type the domain name of your World Wide Web site, such as **www.northpole.com**

▶ Leave the Host Type set to Automatic detect, unless you have a reason to change it.

▶ In the User ID field, type the user ID by which you are known on your Web server; this will probably be the first part of your e-mail address, up to but not including the @ sign.

▶ If you are not concerned about the security of your password on your local PC, you can type your password into the Password field, but this is not recommended for security reasons; if you do not enter your Password here, your server will prompt you for it when you connect later on in this tutorial.

▶ Click Save to save the profile.

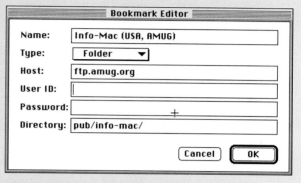

Figure 22-4 The Fetch Bookmark Editor dialog.

▶ In the Host field, type the domain name of your World Wide Web site, such as **www.northpole.com**

▶ In the User ID field, type the user ID by which you are known on your Web server; this will probably be the first part of your e-mail address, up to but not including the @ sign.

▶ Type your password into the Password field. If you are not using your own computer, you should erase the password field when you are done using Fetch, to prevent the user after you from accessing your Web site.

▶ Click OK to save the shortcut.

▶ When the Save dialog appears, give your shortcut a name you will remember, such as **Santa's Web site**

How to FTP Files to the Web

Figure 22-5 shows how the WS_FTP program has graphical controls that make it very easy for Windows users to FTP a file to your Web site. Figure 22-6 shows the Fetch controls that enable Macintosh users to do likewise.

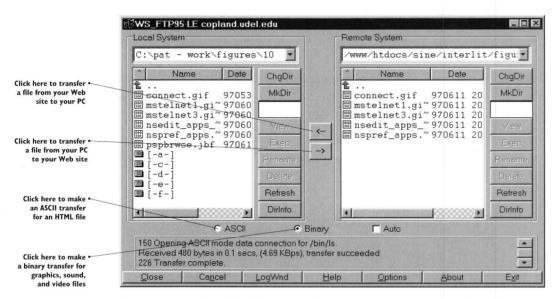

Figure 22-5 The WS_FTP program displays folder listings for your local system and the remote system.

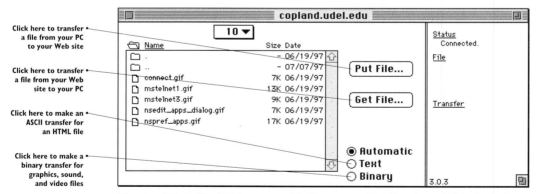

Figure 22-6 The Fetch program lists the names of the files at your Web site and enables you to upload and download files from the Internet.

For example, suppose you want to FTP your home page and your résumé from your computer to your World Wide Web account. Follow the steps in Table 22-5.

Table 22-5   How to FTP Files to the Web

WS_FTP LE for Windows	Fetch for Macintosh
▶ If you are not connected to the network, establish your network connection now	▶ If you are not connected to the network, establish your network connection now.
▶ If WS_FTP is not already running, double-click the WS_FTP icon; the Session Properties dialog appears.	▶ If Fetch is not already running, double-click the Fetch icon; the New Connection window appears.
▶ In the WS_FTP Session Properties dialog, pull down the Profile Name selection box and choose your Web site's profile; if your Web site is not listed in the selection box, follow the steps in Table 22-4 for creating an FTP session profile.	▶ Click Cancel and then pull down File and choose Open Shortcut.
▶ To transfer HTML files to the Web, you must make sure the ASCII button is checked. ASCII stands for American Standard Code for Information Interchange; ASCII is the format for plain text files, which is what HTML files are. Click the ASCII button now.	▶ Click the Shortcuts menu, and choose the shortcut you saved when you configured your FTP connection in Table 22-4.
▶ On the Local System side of the WS_FTP window, browse to the folder in which the file you want to transfer resides; in this example, browse to the Web site folder on your hard drive.	▶ When you're connected to your Web site, the Fetch window will display a listing of the names of the files residing at your Web site.
▶ On the Remote System side of the WS_FTP window, browse to the folder in which you want to transfer the files; in this example, that will be the main folder of your World Wide Web account.	▶ To transfer a file to the Web, drag and drop the file from your desktop into the Fetch window.
▶ To transfer your résumé, click once on *resume.htm* on the Local System side of the WS_FTP window; then click the ⮕ button to transfer the file to the Web. After the transfer completes, you will see your *resume.htm* file listed on the Remote System side of the WS_FTP window in your World Wide Web folder.	▶ Another way to transfer a file is to pull down the File menu and click the Put File button to make the Open File dialog appear; select the name of the file you want to transfer to the Web, and click the Open button.
▶ To transfer your home page, click once on *index.htm* on the Local System side of the WS_FTP window; then click the ⮕ button to transfer the file to the Web. After the transfer completes, you will see your *index.htm* file listed on the Remote System side of the WS_FTP window in your World Wide Web folder.	
▶ To transfer the image files on your Web pages, you must click the binary button, because images are binary files. Click the binary button now.	
▶ To transfer your images, click once on the name of an image on the Local System side of the WS_FTP window, then click the ⮕ button to transfer the file to the Web. After the transfer completes, you will see your image file listed on the Remote System side of the WS_FTP window in your World Wide Web folder. Repeat this step for each image you want to publish on the Web. If you click and drag your mouse over the list of filenames, you can select multiple files to transfer all at once. To add a single file to a group of selected files, hold down the Ctrl key and click the filename once.	

How to Delete and Rename Files at a Web Site

Your FTP software provides a way to delete files you no longer want on the Web. It also lets you rename files. To delete and rename files at a Web site, follow the steps in Table 22-6.

Table 22-6   How to Delete and Rename Files at a Web Site

WS_FTP LE for Windows	Fetch for Macintosh
▶ If WS_FTP is not already running, double-click the WS_FTP icon; the Session Properties dialog appears.	▶ If Fetch is not already running, double-click the Fetch icon; the New Connection window appears.
▶ In the WS_FTP Session Properties dialog, pull down the Profile Name selection box and choose your Web site's profile.	▶ Click Cancel and then pull down File and choose Open Shortcut.
▶ Click once on the name of the file you want to delete or rename on the Remote System side of the WS_FTP window in your World Wide Web folder.	▶ Click the Shortcuts menu, and choose the shortcut you saved when you configured your FTP connection in Table 22-4.
▶ To delete the file, click the Delete button. WS_FTP will ask if you really want to delete it. Click the Yes button if you really want to.	▶ Click once on the name of the file you want to delete or rename to select it.
▶ To rename the file, click the Rename button. WS_FTP will prompt you to type the new name for the file. Type the new filename, and click OK.	▶ To delete the file, pull down the Remote menu and choose "Delete Directory or File."
	▶ Fetch will ask if you are sure you want to delete the file. If you're sure, click Delete.
	▶ To rename the file, pull down the Remote menu and choose Rename Directory or File. Fetch will prompt you to type the new name for the file. Type the new filename, and click OK.

Coping with Case-Sensitive File Servers

Remember that many World Wide Web servers are case sensitive. If your Web server is case sensitive, you need to make sure that the filenames you FTP to the server match the case that you gave them in your HTML source code. For example, the Unix operating system is case sensitive. On a Unix-based server, if an image is named *PORTRAIT.GIF* and your HTML file attempts to access it as *portrait.gif,* you will get a "File Not Found" error. Folder names are also case sensitive; make sure the case of your folders on the Web matches the case you gave them in your HTML source code.

To cope with case-sensitive file servers, always keep the names of your files and folders in all uppercase or all lowercase. Most people use all lowercase, which is what the author recommends you do. You should also avoid typing spaces or special symbols in your filenames and folder names.

RELATIVE VERSUS ABSOLUTE LINKS

Links on the Web can be relative or absolute. A relative link means that a file has been specified without its complete URL. The browser will look for it in folders related to the current Web page's folder; hence the term *relative.* An absolute link means that the complete URL has been specified.

Suppose that Santa Claus has a folder at his Web site called *wishlist.* In the *wishlist* folder, there's a file called *danny.html* that contains the list of presents Danny wants for Christmas. On Santa's home page, Santa can link to Danny's wish list either as a relative link or as an absolute link. The relative link would be wishlist/danny.html. The absolute link would be:

```
http://www.northpole.com/~SantaClaus/wishlist/danny.html
```

A lot of Web page creation software uses relative links instead of absolute links. For example, both Netscape Composer and Microsoft FrontPage Express use relative links when you create links to files relative to the page you're creating. In order for the relative links to work when you transfer the files to the Web, you must maintain a good directory structure on your PC and at your Web site.

MAINTAINING A GOOD DIRECTORY STRUCTURE

You need to be careful how you create folders and subfolders when you make a local web that you plan to mount on the World Wide Web. Because the links you make to local files are made relative to those files, the directory structure of the local web must be exactly the same as you intend to have out on the World Wide Web. Otherwise, the links will fail when you transfer your local web to the World Wide Web.

Suppose you have lots of HTML files, pictures, sounds, and movies that you plan to mount on the World Wide Web. You should keep them organized in a neat directory structure like this:

```
📁 website
   📄 index.htm
   📁 sounds
      📄 ambient.wav
      📄 welcome.wav
   📁 pictures
      📄 logo.gif
      📄 portrait.gif
   📁 movies
      📄 dance.mpg
      📄 effects.mpg
   📁 html
      📄 resume.htm
      📄 essay.html
      📄 research_paper.html
```

If your files are scattered across multiple folders and multiple drives on your PC, it will be time-consuming and tedious to recreate that same directory structure on your World Wide Web server. It is also more difficult to troubleshoot problems that occur on Web sites that are not well organized.

How to Create New Folders on the Web

As the number of files at your Web site increases, you may choose to create folders to help keep your site organized. For example, if you create a series of Web pages related to your work, you might create a folder called *work* to keep them in. The directory structure you create on the Web must mirror the structure of the *website* folder on your PC. If you create a *work* folder at your Web site, then you must also create a *work* subfolder in the *website* folder on your PC. To create a folder at your Web site, follow the steps in Table 22-7.

Table 22-7   How to Create a New Folder at Your Web Site

WS_FTP LE for Windows	Fetch for Macintosh
▶ 📠 If WS_FTP is not already running, double-click the WS_FTP icon; the Session Properties dialog appears.	▶ 📠 If Fetch is not already running, double-click the Fetch icon; the New Connection dialog appears.
▶ In the WS_FTP Session Properties dialog, pull down the Profile Name selection box and choose your Web site's profile.	▶ In the Fetch New Connection dialog, pull down the Shortcuts menu and choose your Web site's server. Then click OK to open the connection.
▶ On the Remote System side of the WS_FTP window, make sure your current directory is the one in which you want to create a new folder. If it's not, double-click on a directory name to select it, or double-click on the two dots at the top of the directory listing to move back a level of directory structure.	▶ In the Fetch directory window, make sure your current directory is the one in which you want to create a new folder. If it's not, double-click on a directory name to select it, or double-click on the two dots at the top of the directory listing to move back a level of directory structure.
▶ Click the MkDir button to make the Input dialog appear.	▶ From the menu bar, choose Directories, then Create New Directory to make the dialog appear.
▶ Enter the name of the folder you want to create, and click OK.	▶ Enter the name of the folder you want to create, and click OK.
▶ Wait for a second or two, while the new folder gets created. Then WS_FTP will refresh the directory listing, and the new folder will appear in it.	▶ Wait for a second or two, while the new folder gets created. Then Fetch will refresh the directory listing, and the new folder will appear in it.
▶ If you want to enter the new folder, double-click its icon.	▶ If you want to enter the new folder, double-click its icon.

SETTING THE FILE PERMISSION ATTRIBUTES

After you FTP your files to the Web, you will probably want to set the file permission attributes to let anyone in the world read your files but allow only you to modify or delete them. If your Web server is Unix-based, the command to type is **chmod 644**. For example, if the folder in which your Web files are kept is called *public_html*, you would type the following command at your Unix prompt:

```
chmod 644 public_html
```

Chmod is pronounced *shmode* in Unix land. For more information about chmoding files, type **man chmod** at your Unix prompt.

If you're using Fetch on the Macintosh, you can avoid the need to use Unix, because Fetch can change the permission attributes. To change the permission attributes of a file with Fetch, follow the steps in Table 22-8.

Table 22-8   How to Change the Permission Attributes with Fetch (Macintosh Only)

Fetch for Macintosh

▶ 📠 Get Fetch running, if it isn't already.

▶ Select the file whose permission attributes you want to change.

▶ Pull down the Remote menu and choose Set Permissions to make the Permissions dialog appear as shown in Figure 22-7.

▶ Check the boxes to let Owner, Group, and Everyone read your files, but allow only the Owner to write them. (The owner is you!)

▶ Click OK to close the dialog and make the changes take effect.

Figure 22-7
The Fetch Permissions dialog.

PROMOTING YOUR NEW WEB SITE

After you publish your Web site, you will want to let other people know about it. Adding your home page's URL to the signature file of your e-mail software is a quick way of letting everyone to whom you send e-mail know what your Web address is. You can also submit your Web site to the search engines, so your site gets indexed by the Web crawlers. Follow these steps:

- **Yahoo.** At www.yahoo.com, go to the appropriate subject category and click the Add URL button. You'll get an online form to fill out and submit. The Add URL page at http://add.yahoo.com/fast/add provides detailed instructions for doing this.

- **AltaVista.** At www.altavista.digital.com, click the Add URL button at the bottom of the page. AltaVista will prompt you for the URL you want added to the AltaVista database.

- **Lycos.** At www.lycos.com/addasite.html, check to see if your URL is already indexed by typing it into the form. If not, the form gets returned, and you're asked for your e-mail address. Your URL will be added to the Lycos database in about two to four weeks.

- **Submit-it.** There's a free service at www.submit-it.com, where you can submit Web pages to about 20 different search engines and indexes.

- **Broadcaster.** www.broadcaster.co.uk has you fill out a single form and then submits your Web page to 200 search engines and Web indexes.

BECOMING A WEBMASTER

An exciting new profession that has emerged along with the World Wide Web is that of WebMaster. A WebMaster is a person in charge of a Web site. The WebMaster keeps track of all the files in the Web site, maintains a good directory structure, and makes sure the links in the Web site work properly.

WEBMASTER MAGAZINE
http://www.web-master.com/

If you found this tutorial easy to complete, you may well have the knack for becoming a WebMaster. To learn more about this new profession, you may be interested in subscribing to *WebMaster* magazine. To apply for a free subscription, click the *WebMaster* icon at the Interlit Web site.

Also linked to the Interlit Web site is CNET's builder.com site, which provides access to a wide variety of tools for Web site builders.

1. Find a few friends who have Web browsers, and send e-mail to your friends asking them to try out your new home page and résumé. Be sure to include the URL of your home page so your friends know its address on the Web. Ask your friends to write you back, letting you know how they liked your page and if they had any trouble using it. Ask for comments and suggestions for improving your page.

2. Use your Web browser to get on the Web, go to your home page, and test the mailto link that you put at the end of your Web page when you identified yourself as the Web page owner and provided a mailto link so people can get in touch with you. Click on the link and see if you can send an e-mail message to yourself. If you get a message telling you that your browser has not been configured for e-mail, pull down your browser's Options or Preferences menu, find the e-mail settings dialog, and fill in your name and e-mail address. Then click OK and try your e-mail link again.

3. After you complete the steps in the "Promoting Your New Web Site" section of this chapter, see if the search engines find your Web pages. Go to AltaVista, for example, and enter your last name as a key word. See if AltaVista finds your page. If you have a common name like Smith or Jones, you'll need to be more specific; type your complete name, exactly as it appears on your résumé. Typing your own name into the Web's search engines is known as egosurfing, by the way. Try typing other phrases on your Web page as key words. Make sure you used the advanced search syntax, putting the phrase in quotes, such as **"Peter G. Smith's Resume"** to make the search engine look for the entire phrase. Now go to Yahoo and Lycos to see if they find your Web pages when you type your name as the key word for a search. Remember that it can take a couple of days for the search engines to begin indexing your material. If the search engines don't find your Web pages right away, wait a couple of days, and try again. Finally, reflect on the communication power this process provides. Anyone in the world can publish Web pages and index them into the Internet's search engines. Thus, everyone becomes a provider as well as a consumer of information.

Part Six

Using Multimedia on the Internet

Multimedia brings Web pages to life with stereo sound, active movies, and colorful animations. This part of the book introduces you to multimedia on the Internet. After exploring how Web browsers do multimedia with helper apps, plug-ins, and add-ins, you'll learn how to record waveform audio and add sound to your Web pages.

23

How Web Browsers
Do Multimedia

After completing this chapter, you will be able to:

■ **Understand how Web browsers use helper apps, plug-ins, and add-ins to do multimedia.**

■ **Explain the difference between a helper app, plug-in, and add-in.**

■ **Configure your Web browser to use helper apps.**

■ **Download and install multimedia plug-ins and add-ins.**

■ **Use multimedia Web pages containing sound and video.**

■ **Find hot multimedia Web sites.**

ULTIMEDIA brings Web pages to life with sound, video, and animations. In order to hear the sound or see the video on a Web page, your Web browser must be configured to handle the multimedia resource contained on the Web page. Multimedia is an emerging technology that is undergoing a lot of research and development. As a result of this research, there are a lot of different ways to do multimedia. In the review of commonly found Internet file types in Chapter 12, for example, you learned about several different kinds of audio and video formats.

Web browsers use a clever approach to handling the diversity of multimedia file types. First, the browser has built-in support for the most-common kinds of multimedia. You don't need to do anything special to get these to work, as long as you have a multimedia PC capable of making sound and showing movies. Second, multimedia companies make plug-ins and add-ins which install inside the browser to play their company's brand of multimedia files. Third, some browsers enable you to define so-called helper apps that the browser launches to handle other kinds of multimedia files.

This chapter shows you how to do all three kinds of multimedia browsing. You'll learn how to use built-in support and define helpers for file types that are not built in. The Interlit Web site will enable you to download the most-popular plug-ins and add-ins for handling proprietary multimedia file types. Then you'll be ready to visit some of the hottest multimedia Web sites in the world.

BUILT-IN BROWSER SUPPORT FOR MULTIMEDIA

The first browsers didn't have any support for multimedia built in. Everything had to be handled through helper apps. Today, the trend is for browsers to contain built-in support for the most-common multimedia file types. Both Netscape Composer and Microsoft Internet Explorer contain built-in support for the most-common kinds of audio and video files.

Embedded Audio

Audio that's built into a Web page is known as embedded audio. There's an example of embedded audio at the Interlit Web site. It's a waveform audio file of the author greeting you. To hear this greeting, go to the embedded audio section of Chapter 22 at the Interlit Web site. Depending on whether you have Netscape Composer or Microsoft Internet Explorer, you'll get different controls to play the audio. Figures 23-1 and 23-2 show how to use the controls.

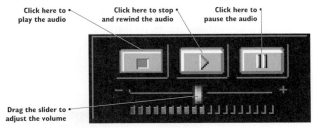

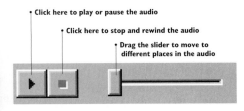

Figure 23-1 Netscape Composer's audio controls.

Figure 23-2 Microsoft Internet Explorer's audio controls.

Video Controls

Both Netscape Communicator and Microsoft Internet Explorer have built-in support for the video file types of *.mpg* (MPEG), *.avi* (Microsoft Video for Windows), and *.mov* (Apple QuickTime). Under Windows 3.1, movies get played by a program called the Media Player (*mplayer.exe*). In later versions of Windows, Microsoft's ActiveMovie controller gets called upon to play the movie, as shown in Figure 23-3. On the Macintosh, movies get played by the QuickTime plug-in, as shown in Figure 23-4. You can download the latest version by following the Interlit Web site links to Microsoft's ActiveMovie or Apple's QuickTime plug-in.

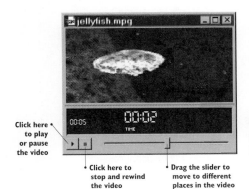

Figure 23-3 Microsoft's Active-Movie controller.

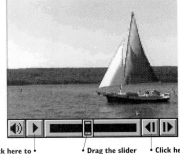

Figure 23-4 Apple's QuickTime movie controller.

HELPER APPS FOR NETSCAPE COMMUNICATOR

In the beginning, the only way browsers handled multimedia was via helper apps. When the user triggered a link to a multimedia file type, the browser would launch a so-called helper application to play the file. Netscape Communicator still uses helper apps. There's a table of file types inside the Netscape browser that associates a helper app with each kind of multimedia file the browser knows about. When you want to make Netscape Communicator handle a certain file type a different way, you can go in and edit this table, and change the helper app associate with that filetype. You can also add new file types and tell your browser how to handle them; this comes in handy when a new multimedia file type gets invented that the browsers do not yet know how to handle.

To inspect the helper apps associated with different file types in Netscape Communicator, follow the steps in Table 23-1. If you're going to modify the helper app for a certain file type, it's a good idea first to jot down the current settings for that file type's helper app. That way, if the change you make doesn't work properly, you can revert to the former setup. These days, most helper apps come with a setup program that installs the helper into your browser automatically, thereby saving you the need to modify the settings by hand.

Table 23-1   How to Inspect and Modify
the Helper App Settings in Netscape Communicator

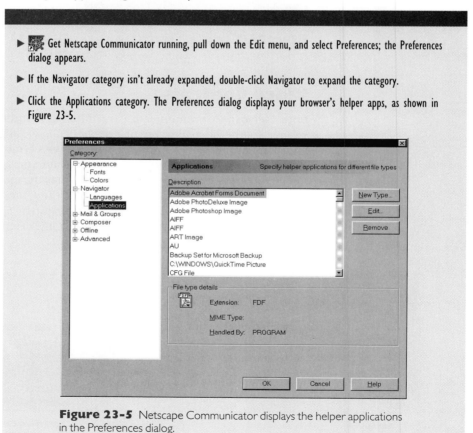

▶ Get Netscape Communicator running, pull down the Edit menu, and select Preferences; the Preferences dialog appears.

▶ If the Navigator category isn't already expanded, double-click Navigator to expand the category.

▶ Click the Applications category. The Preferences dialog displays your browser's helper apps, as shown in Figure 23-5.

Figure 23-5 Netscape Communicator displays the helper applications in the Preferences dialog.

Table 23-1   *(Continued)*

▶ Use the scrollbar to scroll down and inspect the list of file types for which helper apps have been defined.

▶ To inspect the current settings for a helper app, click once on the description of the file type to select it; that file type's helper app settings appear beneath the listbox in the File Type Details group.

▶ To modify a helper app setting, click once on the description of the helper app you want to modify, then click the Edit button. An Edit dialog will appear with a Browse button to let you browse for a different application to handle this type of file. Before you make a change, take note of the current setting, just in case things don't work out and you need to revert to the current settings.

▶ To add a new helper category, click the New Type button; the New Type dialog will appear to help you define the new type. It's rare that you will need to add a new type, however. Only do this if you're sure that the type of file you need to handle isn't already listed in the scrolling list of defined file types.

PLUG-INS AND ADD-INS

Plug-ins and add-ins are software modules that add functionality to computer applications. There's a subtle and almost trivial difference between the terms plug-in and add-in—Netscape calls them plug-ins, and Microsoft calls them add-ins. Most people use the terms interchangeably. From now on, this book will call them plug-ins.

The advantage of plug-ins over helper apps is that the plug-in gives you better integration of the media than the helper app, which uses a separate window to play the file. Plug-ins make multimedia play in the browser's window.

Shockwave

The most-popular plug-in on the Internet is Shockwave. As you learned in Chapter 12, Shockwave is the Macromedia product that enables multimedia created with Director, Authorware, and Flash to plug in to Web pages. If you haven't already downloaded and installed the Shockwave plug-in, you can do so now by following the links to Shockwave at the Interlit Web site. The latest version includes a technology known as Streaming Shockwave, which allows video files to be played over the Internet before they are completely downloaded. In the previous version, a typical Shockwave movie of 200 KB took about 60 seconds to start playing. With Streaming Shockwave, the movie begins playing in about 1 second.

Crescendo MIDI Plug-In

Crescendo is a MIDI plug-in for Netscape Communicator and Microsoft Internet Explorer that outperforms the standard helper apps by a wide margin. Not only does Crescendo give you a better set of controls for playing MIDI songs, but it also enables you to add streaming MIDI music to your Web site. You can download the Crescendo MIDI plug-in by following the links to Crescendo at the Interlit Web site.

Browser Support for Plug-Ins

 Both Netscape and Microsoft have special support for plug-ins. If you have Netscape Communicator, you can pull down the Help menu and choose About Plug-ins to find out what plug-ins are installed in your browser. Then you follow the links to Netscape's Index of Plug-ins to download plug-ins you don't have.

 If you have Microsoft Internet Explorer, you can follow the Interlit links to Microsoft's ActiveX plug-in site. This Web site uses ActiveX to detect what Microsoft plug-ins are already installed in your browser; then you can download and install any plug-ins you don't already have. You can also find out how to use Netscape plug-ins in the Microsoft Internet Explorer by following the Interlit links to Netscape plug-ins for Microsoft Internet Explorer.

Security Risks

Every user needs to be aware that whenever you download code that executes on your computer, you run the risk of getting a virus that could cause serious problems on your PC. If you're downloading code from reputable vendor sites, such as Netscape, Microsoft, and Macromedia, the chance of your getting a virus is highly unlikely. Downloading code from unknown sources, however, could open the door to trouble.

Even if the code you download is virus-free, it could contain back doors and loopholes through which malicious programmers called crackers could send you viruses or cause other problems on your computer. For example, a security hole in one of the major vendor's plug-ins allowed malicious Web page developers to create a movie that could read a user's e-mail messages and upload them to a server, without the user knowing anything about it. Instructions on how to do this were published on the Internet, where any malicious programmer could learn how to do it.

The vendors respond quickly to plug such loopholes, and the chance of your being affected by one is not great, but you need to be aware of the risks involved. Supercautious users don't download plug-ins, to guard against the possibility of security breaks. If you're running a supersecure facility, such as the CIA or the NSA, you'll probably want to guard further against the possibility of these attacks by disabling Java as well. Most users can use plug-ins and Java confidently, as long as you avoid going to sites you suspect of being malicious.

E X E R C I S E S

1. Go to the Embedded Audio section of the Interlit Web site, and play the waveform audio recording of the author greeting you. Do you like the audio controls your browser provides to play the greeting? How could the controls be improved? What features do you want in an audio player that your browser's audio controls lack?

2. Go to the Embedded Video section of the Interlit Web site, and play the video recording of the author greeting you. Do you like the video controller your browser provides to play the greeting? How could the controller be improved? What features do you want in a video player that your browser's video controller lacks?

3. A MIDI file has been linked to the plug-in section of the Interlit Web site. Go there and listen to the MIDI file. If you are using Netscape Communicator, follow the steps in Table 23-1 to inspect your browser's MIDI handler, and jot down the current settings for the helper app that's being used to play MIDI files. You may need this information at the end of this exercise. Then follow the Interlit Web site links to the Crescendo MIDI plug-in. Download and install the Crescendo MIDI plug-in. Now trigger the MIDI file that's linked to the plug-in section of the Interlit Web site. What difference does having the Crescendo MIDI plug-in make? Do you like the Crescendo MIDI plug-in better than the handler your Web browser was using before? If not, follow the steps in Table 23-1 if you are using Netscape Communicator and make your Web browser revert to the MIDI handler you made note of at the beginning of this exercise.

4. Shockwave can make your Web browser do some really neat stuff. Follow the links to Shockwave at the Interlit Web site. Download and install the Shockwave player. Then use your browser to visit some of the Shockwave-enabled Web sites you'll find at http://www.macromedia.com/shockzone. Make a list of the features you find Shockwave supporting that you haven't seen on Web pages that don't use it. What is your favorite Shockwave feature?

24 Waveform Audio Recording

After completing this chapter, you'll be able to:

- [ ] **Make a waveform audio recording.**

- [ ] **Adjust the quality of a waveform audio recording.**

- [ ] **Explain the difference between sampling rate and bits per sample.**

- [ ] **Link a waveform audio recording to your Web page.**

- [ ] **Embed audio on a Web page.**

- [ ] **Make audio start automatically on a Web page.**

WAVEFORM audio is a great way to begin adding multimedia content to your Web pages. Because every multimedia computer comes with the hardware needed to create waveform audio recordings, you're already equipped to do it.

This chapter steps you through the process of recording waveform audio and linking it to your Web pages. You'll learn how to create hypertext and hyperpicture links which, when clicked, cause your audio to play. You'll also learn how to put sound into the background of a Web page, thereby making the sound start automatically when the Web page appears.

PREPARING TO MAKE YOUR FIRST WAVEFORM AUDIO RECORDING

Windows comes with a program called the Sound Recorder that enables you to create waveform audio recordings. On the Macintosh, you use a shareware program called Sound Effects, which you can download by following the links at the Interlit Web site.

You can record either from a microphone, or from a so-called line output from a tape recorder, audio CD player, or VCR. Your computer has jacks into which you can plug a microphone or a line output. Most computers have two separate jacks—one labeled Mic, the other Line; make sure you plug into the correct jack. If the connectors on your microphone or other audio source don't fit the jacks on your computer, you can purchase the necessary adapters from your local Radio Shack store.

Once your audio source is connected, you need to make sure it's selected as the source in the recording section of your computer's sound-mixing software. Follow the steps in Table 24-1 to do that.

Table 24-1 How to Select the Record Sound Source

Windows Sound Recorder	Macintosh Sound Effects

▶ 🔊 If there's a sound icon on your Windows 95 taskbar, double-click it to bring up your sound mixer controls. Otherwise, look on your Windows 95 Start menu or your Windows 3.1 Windows menu for a group related to sound, in which you should be able to find your sound mixer software.

▶ Pull down the Options menu and choose Properties; the Properties dialog appears as shown in Figure 24-1.

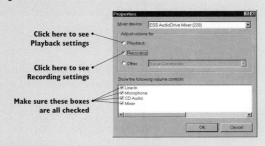

Click here to see Playback settings

Click here to see Recording settings

Make sure these boxes are all checked

Figure 24-1
The Sound Properties dialog.

▶ Click the Recording button, if it is not already selected.

▶ The listbox identifies the different recording controls on your computer. Make sure they're all selected, so they'll show up in the Recording Control window in the next step.

▶ Click OK; the Recording Control window appears as shown in Figure 24-2.

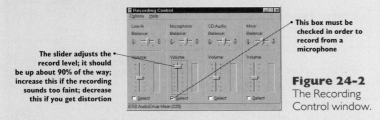

This box must be checked in order to record from a microphone

The slider adjusts the record level; it should be up about 90% of the way; increase this if the recording sounds too faint; decrease this if you get distortion

Figure 24-2
The Recording Control window.

▶ Make sure the checkbox for the source you're recording is selected. If you're recording from a microphone, for example, check the microphone source.

▶ Pull down the Options menu and choose Properties to make the Properties dialog shown in Figure 24-1 reappear.

▶ Click the Playback button.

▶ The listbox identifies the different playback controls on your computer. Make sure they're all selected, so they'll show up in the Volume Control window in the next step.

▶ Click OK; the Volume Control window appears as shown in Figure 24-3.

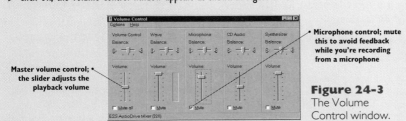

Microphone control; mute this to avoid feedback while you're recording from a microphone

Master volume control; the slider adjusts the playback volume

Figure 24-3
The Volume Control window.

▶ If you're recording from a microphone, you'll probably want to mute the microphone; otherwise, sound from the microphone will feed back through your speakers. Feedback can cause distortion, but it can also create an interesting depth effect if your microphone is not positioned too close to the speakers. The author recommends you mute the Mic setting your first time through; later on, you can try making depth effects.

▶ Make sure the master volume control is turned up.

▶ 🐾 Get the Sound Effects program running.

▶ Pull down the File menu and choose Preferences, then Recording—Sound Input Device. The Sound Effects Preferences dialog appears as shown in Figure 24-4.

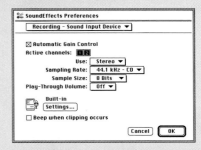

Figure 24-4 The Sound Effects Preferences dialog.

▶ Click Settings to make the Input Source dialog appear, as shown in Figure 24-5.

Figure 24-5
The Sound Effects Input Source dialog.

▶ Don't click the Playthrough box unless you want to experiment with feedback effects; it's best not to try this your first time through.

▶ Click OK to close the Input Source dialog.

▶ Click OK to close the Sound Effects Preferences dialog.

MAKING A WAVEFORM AUDIO RECORDING

Now that you've got your sound source connected and selected, you can make the recording by following the steps in Table 24-2.

Table 24-2   How to Make a Waveform Audio Recording

Windows Sound Recorder	Macintosh Sound Effects

Windows Sound Recorder

▶ ⌨ If you have Windows 95, get the Windows Sound Recorder running by following these steps:

▶ Click the Windows 95 Start button.

▶ Choose Programs, then Accessories, then Multimedia, then Sound Recorder.

▶ ⌨ If you have Windows 3.1, get the Windows Sound Recorder running by following these steps:

▶ If your Accessories group is not visible, pull down the Program Manager's Windows menu and choose Accessories.

▶ In the Accessories group, double-click the Sound Recorder icon.

▶ The Sound Recorder appears as shown in Figure 24-6. The green line in the black window is an oscilloscope that shows you the incoming sound wave. When you click the Record button to begin recording, the green line should oscillate as the sound comes in. If the line does not move, your sound source is not active—review the instructions in Table 24-1 to fix the problem.

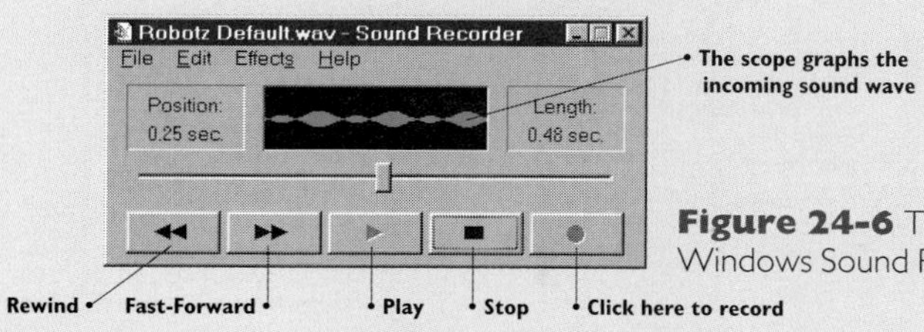

Figure 24-6 The Windows Sound Recorder.

The scope graphs the incoming sound wave

Rewind • Fast-Forward • • Play • Stop • Click here to record

▶ ⬤ To begin recording, click the Record button. If you're using a microphone, hold it close to your mouth so your recording will have good presence of sound. Speak in a loud, clear voice.

▶ ⬛ To stop recording, click the Stop button.

▶ ▶ To hear the recording, click the Play button. If you don't hear anything, your sound source is probably not connected properly. Make sure your microphone or line input is plugged in to the proper jack, and follow the steps in Table 24-1 to select it as the recording source.

▶ ◀◀ To rewind the recording, click the Rewind button.

▶ To save the recording, pull down the File menu and click Save As; the Save As dialog appears. If you plan to put this recording on the Web, save it in your *website* folder. Make sure you give the recording a *.wav* filename extension; *wav* stands for waveform.

▶ If the recording sounds too faint, you need to adjust the record level; pull down the Edit menu, choose Audio Properties, and turn up the recording level.

▶ If you hear distortion, you need to turn the record level down; pull down the Edit menu, choose Audio Properties, and turn down the recording level.

▶ It may take you several tries to get a good recording. Keep adjusting the settings and rerecord until you get the result you want.

▶ To rerecord, pull down the File menu and choose New to empty the waveform buffer. If you do not choose New, what you record next will get inserted into what's already been recorded.

Macintosh Sound Effects

▶ 🔊 Get the Sound Recorder program running.

▶ ⬤ Click the Record button; the Sound Recording window appears as shown in Figure 24-7.

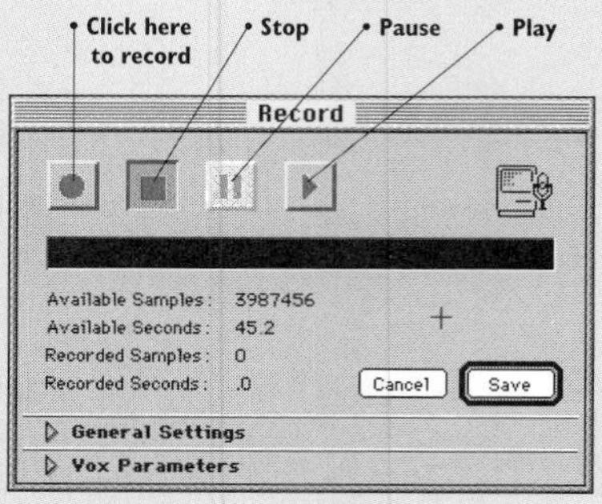

Click here to record • Stop • Pause • Play

Figure 24-7 The Macintosh Sound Effects recording window.

▶ ⬤ To begin recording, click the Record button. If you're using a microphone, hold it close to your mouth so your recording will have good presence of sound. Speak in a loud, clear voice.

▶ ⬛ To stop recording, click the Stop button.

▶ ▶ To hear the recording, click the Play button. If you don't hear anything, your sound source is probably not connected properly. Make sure your microphone or line input is plugged into the proper jack, and follow the steps in Table 24-1 to select it as the recording source.

▶ To save the recording, click the Save button, then pull down the File menu and choose Save As to make the Save dialog appear.

▶ Make sure you save the file in the AIFF file format, which is the format in which Macintosh sound files play on the Web. Both Windows and Macintosh users will be able to play back your AIFF files from the Web.

EDITING WAVEFORM AUDIO RECORDINGS

In addition to letting you record waveform audio, the Sound Recorder enables you to edit the audio. For example, if you pressed the Record button too soon, there's extra sound at the beginning of the recording that you need to delete. Similarly, if you pressed the Stop button too late, there's extra sound at the end that you'll want to remove. To edit a waveform audio recording, follow the steps in Table 24-3.

Table 24-3   How to Edit a Waveform Audio Recording

Windows Sound Recorder	Macintosh Sound Effects
▶ 🎙 Get the Sound Recorder running, if it isn't already.	▶ 🐾 Get the Sound Effects program running, if it isn't already.
▶ Pull down the File menu, choose Open, and open the *.wav* file you'd like to edit. If the file is already open, you can skip this step.	▶ Pull down the File menu, choose Open, and open the sound file you'd like to edit. If the file is already open, you can skip this step.
▶ ▶ Play the file, and make note of the spots at which you want to delete things. You can drag the slider to move quickly to different positions in the recording. The Position counter shows where you are in hundredths of seconds.	▶ ▶ To delete the first part of the recording, click and drag your mouse to select the first part of the waveform, and click Play to audition the selection. Make sure you select only what you want to delete.
▶ To delete the first part of a recording, position the slider at the spot where the good stuff starts, then pull down the Edit menu and choose Delete Before Current Position.	▶ If your recording is in stereo, make sure you click and drag over both the left and right channels.
▶ To delete the last part of a recording, position the slider at the end of the good stuff, then pull down the Edit menu and choose Delete After Current Position.	▶ To delete the selection, pull down the Edit menu and choose Clear, or press the [Delete] key.
▶ Play the file to make sure you got what you wanted.	▶ Play the file to make sure you got what you wanted.
▶ Save the file.	▶ To delete the last part of a recording, repeat these steps, drag your mouse over the last part of the waveform, click Play to audition the selection, and when you have selected just what you want to delete, press the [Delete] key.
	▶ Play the file to make sure you got what you wanted.
	▶ Save the file.

ADJUSTING THE QUALITY OF WAVEFORM AUDIO RECORDINGS

Most waveform audio recording software lets you adjust two parameters that govern the quality of a waveform audio recording: **sampling rate** and **bits per sample.** Be aware that the higher you set these parameters, the larger your waveform audio file will be.

Sampling Rate

The sampling rate determines the frequency response of the recorded sound. To record frequencies faithfully, your sampling rate must be at least two times greater than the highest frequency you want to record. However, the higher you set the sampling rate, the larger your waveform audio file will be. Since the size of the file increases, you shouldn't choose a higher sampling rate than you need because of

Table 24-4   The Relationship Between
Sound Quality and Sampling Rate

Samples per Second	Sonic Equivalent
6,000	Telephone
15,000	AM Radio
37,500	FM Radio
40,000	Phonograph Records
44,100	Compact Disc

the increased bandwidth required to transfer the file over the Internet. To help you grasp the relationship between sampling rate and sound quality, Table 24-4 compares different sampling rates to real-world audio devices of differing fidelities.

Bits per Sample

Table 24-5 illustrates how the number of bits per sample determines the dynamic range, which determines how much of a volume change you will hear between the loudest and softest sounds in a recording. Waveform audio devices typically give you a choice of 8 or 16 bits per sample. The original MPC standard required that multimedia computers be capable of recording at 8 bits per sample, while the MPC2 and MPC3 standards require 16.

Since file size is determined by multiplying the bits per sample by the sampling rate, you don't want to choose a higher bits-per-sample setting than required. Try recording first at 8 bits per sample. Only if that does not provide adequate sound quality should you increase the setting to 16 bits. To help you grasp the relationship between bits per sample and sound quality, Table 24-6 shows the dynamic range equivalents of some real-world sound sources.

Table 24-5   The Relationship Between Bits Per Sample and Dynamic Range

Bits per Sample	Dynamic Range	Bits per Sample	Dynamic Range
1	8dB	10	62dB
2	14dB	11	68dB
3	20dB	12	74dB
4	26dB	13	80dB
5	32dB	14	86dB
6	38dB	15	92dB
7	44dB	16	98dB
8	50dB	17	104dB
9	56dB	18	110dB

Table 24-6 Bits-per-Sample Equivalents of Traditional Sound Sources

Sound Source	Bits-per-Sample Equivalent
AM Radio	6 bits
Telephone	8 bits
FM Radio	9 bits
Phonograph Record	10 bits
Reel-to-Reel Tape	11 bits
Compact Disc	16 bits

Bandwidth Considerations

If you're using the Windows Sound Recorder, you can modify the sound quality settings by pulling down the Edit menu and choosing Audio Properties to make the Audio Properties dialog appear as shown in Figure 24-8. To adjust the quality, pull down the Preferred quality menu, and choose the setting you want. If you understand how bits per sample and dynamic range affect sound, you can click the Customize button to create your own custom settings. Be careful to keep bandwidth in mind, however, because the higher you set the quality adjustments, the larger the file will become, and the longer it will take to download the sound from the Web.

Figure 24-8 The Audio Properties dialog.

If you're using the Macintosh Sound Effects program, you change the bandwidth settings by pulling down the File menu, choosing Preferences, then Recording—Sound Input Device. In the Preferences dialog, you can change the sampling rate, word size, and choose stereo or mono recording.

LINKING AUDIO TO YOUR WEB PAGE

Now that you've learned how to record audio, it's time to put it on your Web page. There are two ways to do that. You can either link it, or you can embed it. If you link it, the user will click a hypertext or hyperpicture trigger, which will cause your browser to download and play the audio. If you embed the audio, it will be more tightly coupled to your Web page. To link audio to a Web page, follow the steps in Table 24-7.

Table 24-7   How to Link Sound to a Trigger on a Web Page

Netscape Composer	Microsoft FrontPage Express
▶ Use Netscape Composer to open the page in your *website* folder on which you want to link the audio.	▶ Use Microsoft Internet Explorer to browse to the page on which you want to add some audio.
▶ Select the picture or text to which you want to link the audio. Click once on a picture to select it, or click and drag to select some text.	▶ Click the Edit button; the page appears in a Microsoft FrontPage Express window.
▶ Click the Link button; the Link dialog appears.	▶ Select the picture or text to which you want to link the audio. Click once on a picture to select it, or click and drag to select some text.
▶ Click the Choose File button, and select the *.wav* file you want to link.	▶ Click the Link button; the Link dialog appears.
▶ Click OK to close the Link dialog.	▶ Set the HyperLink type to Other. In the URL field, type the filename of your waveform audio file. Do not type a drive letter; just type the filename, such as **greeting.wav**
▶ Click the Save button and save the modified Web page.	▶ Click the Save button; the Microsoft Publishing Wizard will help you transfer the modified Web page to the Web.
▶ Click the Preview button to make the page appear in a browser window; test the link to make sure it works the way you want.	▶ Click the Save button once again; this time, use the Microsoft Publishing Wizard to transfer your waveform audio file to the Web.
▶ Close the browser window; the composer window reappears.	▶ Use Microsoft Internet Explorer to test the files on the Web to make sure they got published correctly. If there are any problems, repeat these steps until the audio link works properly on the Web.
▶ Make any changes that are needed and, if necessary, click the Preview button to test the file again.	
▶ Click the Publish button to publish the Web page to your Web site. Make sure you publish the audio file along with the revised Web page. To do this, you'll need to select the option to show all pages in the file's folder, press the Select None button, then select the files you want to publish.	
▶ Use Netscape Communicator to test the files on the Web to make sure they got published correctly.	

Make sure you test your sound files on the Web with your browser to make sure they got published correctly. Click every link on your Web page to make sure it works. If any link fails to work, follow the steps in Table 24-7 carefully to troubleshoot the problem.

EMBEDDING AUDIO ON A WEB PAGE

To embed audio on a Web page, you use the <EMBED> tag. The <EMBED> tag has parameters that let you preset the volume and the size of the audio controller. You can make the audio autostart, and you can also hide the audio controller. If you hide the controller, however, the user will not be able to turn the audio off. Many people do not like it when Web pages play audio that the user cannot control. Tables 24-8 and 24-9 show how to embed audio on a Web page using Netscape Composer and Microsoft FrontPage Express, respectively.

Table 24-8 How to Embed Audio on a Web Page with Netscape Communicator

Netscape Communicator

▶  Use Netscape Composer to open the page in your Web site folder on which you want to embed the audio.

▶ Position your cursor at the spot where you want to embed the audio.

▶ Pull down the Insert menu and choose HTML Tag; the HTML Tag dialog appears as shown in Figure 24-9.

Figure 24-9 The Netscape Composer HTML Tag dialog.

▶ Type the following HTML code, replacing *filename.wav* with the filename or URL of the audio file you want to play:

> **<embed src="*filename.wav*" volume="100" height=60 width=144>**

▶ If you want to make the audio start automatically, include the following parameter prior to the > that ends the <embed> tag:

> **autostart="true"**

▶ If you're making the audio start automatically, and you want the audio control to be invisible, include the following parameter prior to the >

that ends the <embed> tag:

> **hidden="true"**

▶ Click the Verify button; Netscape will tell you if there's anything wrong with your HTML. Fix it, if there is.

▶ Click OK to close the HTML Tag dialog.

▶ Click the Preview button to make the page appear in a browser window; make sure the embedded audio works the way you want.

▶ Close the Browser window; the Composer window reappears.

▶ Make any changes that are needed, and if necessary, click the Preview button to test the file again.

▶ 🖳 Click the Publish button to publish the Web page to your Web site. Make sure you publish the audio file along with the revised Web page. To do this, you'll need to select the option to show all pages in the file's folder, press the Select None button, then select the files you want to publish.

▶ Use Netscape Communicator to test the files on the Web to make sure they got published correctly.

▶ Later on, if you want to edit the <EMBED> tag, use Netscape Composer to open the Web page, then double-click on the embedded audio. Your <EMBED> tag will appear in a dialog box that lets you edit it.

Table 24-9 How to Embed Audio on a Web Page with Microsoft FrontPage Express

Microsoft FrontPage Express

▶ Use Microsoft Internet Explorer to browse to the page on which you want to add some audio.

▶ 📝 Click the Edit button; the page appears in a Microsoft FrontPage Express window.

▶ Position your cursor at the spot where you want to embed the audio.

▶ Pull down the Insert menu and choose HTML Markup; the HTML Markup dialog appears as shown in Figure 24-10.

Figure 24-10 The Microsoft FrontPage Express HTML Markup dialog.

▶ Type the following HTML code, replacing *filename.wav* with the filename or URL of the audio file you want to play:

> **<embed src="*filename.wav*" volume="100" height=60 width=144>**

▶ If you want to make the audio start automatically, include the following parameter prior to the > that ends the <embed> tag:

> **autostart="true"**

▶ If you're making the audio start automatically, and you want the audio control to be invisible, include the following parameter prior to the > that ends the <embed> tag::

> **hidden="true"**

▶ Click OK to close the HTML Markup dialog.

▶ 💾 Click the Save button; the Microsoft Publishing Wizard will help you transfer the modified Web page to the Web.

▶ Click the Save button once again; this time, use the Microsoft Publishing Wizard to transfer your waveform audio file to the Web.

▶ 🔍 Use Microsoft Internet Explorer to test the files on the Web to make sure they got published correctly. If there are any problems, repeat these steps until the audio link works properly on the Web.

▶ Later on, if you want to edit the <EMBED> tag, use Microsoft FrontPage Express to open the Web page, then pull down the View menu and choose HTML. Find your <EMBED> tag, and edit it as you wish.

1. Record a waveform audio file to welcome people to your home page. Save the file in your *website* folder. Call it *greeting.wav*. You'll need this file in the next exercise.

2. Link the greeting you recorded in exercise 1 to a hyperpicture or hypertext on your home page. Publish the revised page and the greeting to your Web site. Test the link on the Web to make sure it works properly.

3. Embed the greeting you recorded in exercise 1 to your Web page. If you have any trouble doing this, review the steps in Table 24-8 (Netscape) or Table 24-9 (Microsoft). At first, do not include the autostart parameter, so the audio will not start until the user clicks the Play button. Then use the autostart parameter to make the greeting start playing automatically when your Web page appears. Which way do you prefer? Do you think it is impolite for a Web page to begin playing audio automatically?

4. This exercise has you rerecord the greeting you made in exercise 1 at a higher quality of audio. Get your sound recorder software running. If you're using the Windows Sound Recorder, pull down the Edit menu and choose Audio Properties, then pull down the Preferred Quality menu and set the quality a notch or two higher. If you've got the Macintosh Sound Effects, pull down the File menu, choose Preferences, then Recording—Sound Input Device, and in the Preferences dialog, increase the sampling rate. Rerecord the greeting you made in exercise 1, except this time, when you save the file in your *website* folder, call it *greet2.wav*. Now use the Windows Explorer or File Manager, or the Macintosh Finder, to inspect the size of the greeting files. How much larger is the *greet2.wav* file than the *greeting.wav* file? Can you hear any difference in quality between the two files? Which file sounds better?

5. Go to your home page on the Web, and time how long it takes for the greeting you have there now to start playing after you click on it. Click your browser's Refresh button to make sure it rereads the file. Make a note of how long it takes for the greeting to begin playing. Then edit your home page, and replace the *greeting.wav* link with the *greet2.wav* file. Publish the modified file, then open it with your browser on the Web. Time how long it takes for the greeting to start playing. How much longer does it take for the higher-quality recording to begin playing? What implications does this have for bandwidth considerations on the Internet?

6. Unless you heard a big difference and you're willing for people to wait longer to hear your greeting, change your home page greeting link back to *greeting.wav*. Publish the revised page to the Web, and test it to make sure it works properly. To save space at your Web site, delete the waveform file you're no longer using there. Table 22-6 shows how to use WS_FTP to delete a file from a Web site.

7. You can add depth, technically known as reverberation, to a waveform audio recording if you let the sound feed back a little through the speakers while you record. You vary the amount of depth by turning the playback volume up or down, and by moving the microphone closer or further away from the speakers. Be careful, however, because you can cause a bad-sounding feedback if you move the microphone too close to the speakers. If your amp is turned up real loud, the feedback could damage your speakers. If you'd like to experiment adding depth to your recordings, repeat the steps in Tables 24-1 and 24-2. This time, instead of muting the microphone, turn the microphone on, and manipulate its playback volume to create more or less depth. What depth setting makes you sound best?

Part Seven

Planning for the Future of the Internet

Because the Internet is the communications infrastructure for the twenty-first century, its future is vitally important. This part of the book introduces you to the many ways in which the Internet will affect your future. You'll probably learn about some issues you haven't thought about. Many of these issues are controversial, and some could shock or even offend you.

The Internet is a public resource used by tens of millions of people. Like any public resource, what's found on the Internet reflects the people who use it. Unfortunately, not everyone using the Internet is well-meaning. Chapter 25 will make you aware of what's bad about the Internet, prepare you to guard against evil, and provide you with a way to voice your opinions about how the Internet should be regulated.

In spite of the bad things done by some hateful users, the Internet is a strategic resource to which everyone needs access. Citizens who cannot access the Information Superhighway will be disenfranchised in the twenty-first century. This part of the book will make you aware of the equity issues and suggest things you can do to help everyone gain access.

The Internet is growing and changing rapidly. New technologies are emerging that promise to help solve not only the technical issues regarding the Internet, but many of the societal issues as well. For example, declining costs caused by advances in microelectronics will make it possible for more people to become connected, thereby helping to solve the equity problem. Chapter 26 defines and discusses the emerging technologies that are creating new directions for the Internet.

Finally, since the Internet is constantly evolving, Chapter 27 will conclude the book by suggesting ways you can keep up with the new technology. People often ask how the author keeps up with all the changes in technology. In Chapter 27, you'll find out how to use the technology to help you keep up with the changes in technology.

25 Societal Issues

After completing this chapter, you'll be able to:

☐ **Summarize what's being done to help the technological underclass gain access to the Internet.**

☐ **Understand how the Internet threatens your right to privacy, and know what you can do about that.**

☐ **Take steps to avoid being stalked on the Internet.**

☐ **Exercise the appropriate security measures to protect the privacy of your information on the Internet.**

☐ **Understand why protectionists seek to censor certain kinds of material on the Internet.**

☐ **Realize how much Internet traffic is pornographic or obscene, and consider who should have access to such material.**

☐ **Reflect on the impact of the evil side of technology that is being used to spread electronic hate on the Internet.**

☐ **Understand the concept of copyright and fair use in cyberspace, and realize how important it is to exercise your right of fair use of electronic resources.**

 **S THE** communications infrastructure for the twenty-first century, the Internet is the most strategic resource in modern society. But will its true potential be reached? Who will control access? Almost any good thing can be misused; how will the Internet harm society?

EQUITY, COST, AND UNIVERSAL ACCESS

As this book goes to press, only about 20 million Americans are using the Internet. We have a long way to go before achieving universal access.

In his 1997 State of the Union Address, President Clinton called for every 12-year-old to be able to log on to the Internet by the year 2000. This is a noble goal that involves connecting every school to the Internet. The Clinton administration has done a good job of leveraging the telecommunications industry to make it possible for every school to afford to connect.

As a result of these efforts, the Telecommunications Act of 1996 provides a Universal Service Fund whereby schools and libraries can receive subsidized access to the Internet. Discounts range from 20 to 90% on telecommunications services, Internet access, and cabling in school buildings. The amount of the discount is based on two factors: need, and whether the organization is in an urban or a rural area. For more information, follow the Interlit Web site links to the Universal Service Fund. You'll also find links to the full text of the Telecommunications Act, and President Clinton's 1997 State of the Union Address.

How Long Will It Take?

A grassroots volunteer effort called NetDay is working to connect schools sooner rather than later. Volunteer labor and materials come from companies, unions, parents, teachers, students, and school employees. Figure 25-1 shows the connection status in 1997 of the 140,000 K–12 schools in the United States. To query the connection status for your local schools, follow the Interlit Web site links to NetDay.

Making it possible for every student to log on from school, however, does not provide equal access to the Internet. Citizens who do not have convenient access outside of school constitute a technological underclass that is seriously disadvantaged in the information society. In California, for example, the regional Bell company Pacific Telesis will spend about $15 billion over five years to develop a network that can deliver television and high-speed data services throughout California. Phase one called for wiring 1.5 million homes by the end of 1996; phase two will hook up 3.5 million more by the end of the decade. California's remaining 4 million customers would be wired by 2010 (*New York Times* 11 Nov 93: C4).

Imagine having to wait until 2010. Given the fast pace of the computer industry, 2010 is so far in the future that several new generations of technology will have passed in the meantime. Won't citizens getting wired for today's technology in 2010 be just as disadvantaged then as they are now?

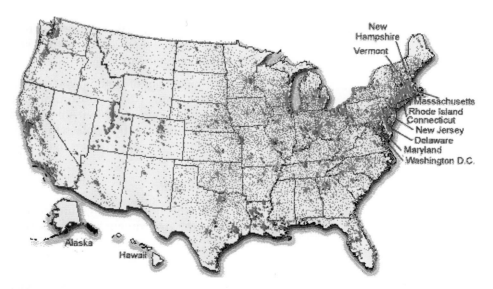

Figure 25-1 The NetDay map of U.S. schools. Internet connection key: red = none
blue = single user
green = multi user

By following the Interlit Web site links to *Universal Access to the Information Superhighway,* you'll come to the Yuri Rubinsky Insight Foundation report on universal access. The report warns that the Internet "must be used to bring Americans together, as opposed to allowing further polarization between the information haves and have nots."

How Much Will It Cost?

The Clinton administration has estimated the cost of building the Information Superhighway at between $50 billion and $100 billion over the next 10 to 15 years. But industry analysts say that figure could double, up to $200 billion by the time the network is built (*BNA Special Report: Outlook '94* 28 Jan 94: S21).

Taxation could further increase the cost of using the Internet. While the federal government has rejected the notion of a national Internet sales tax, the states of Connecticut, Massachusetts, Tennessee, Pennsylvania, Texas, Ohio, and Wisconsin are already taxing some Internet services. Meanwhile, Governor George Pataki has made New York the first state to exempt Internet service providers from state taxes (AP 26 Feb 97).

PRIVACY

The constitution guarantees every American the right to privacy. The Internet threatens this right. Most users are unaware of how real the threat is.

Sniffing Messages on the Internet

When you use the Internet, the information you send and receive gets routed through the gateways and bridges that connect the networks on the Information Superhighway. Each gateway is a computer that can (and often does) make a copy of your messages for backup purposes. If your message doesn't make it to the next node on the Internet, the gateway can route your information a different way. Crackers who hack their way into the gateway can read your message. Intercepting information this way on the Internet is known as **sniffing**, which is the Internet's equivalent of a telephone wiretap.

To protect against the danger of sniffing, you can encrypt your messages. As you learned in Chapter 6, both Netscape Communicator and Microsoft Internet Explorer have encryption options. When someone sniffs an encrypted message, the message will be unintelligible, unless the person who sniffs the message knows the encryption key or can somehow figure it out.

The Clipper Chip

Criminals are using the Internet to communicate because they can encrypt messages to prevent the government from eavesdropping on conversations. Thus, the Internet is safer for criminals than the telephone, which is easily tapped. The government believes that it should have the ability to decipher encrypted communications between criminals, just as it can obtain a court order to tap a criminal's telephone line. The government wants all electronic devices to contain a so-called Clipper Chip, which is an encryption device with a "back door" that allows detectives with the proper access to decipher the messages. The Clipper Chip has been denounced by industry groups as well as civil liberties groups concerned about privacy (*New York Times* 5 Feb 94: A1). The CPSR (Computer

Professionals for Social Responsibility) has organized a protest; for more information, follow the Interlit Web site links to the Clipper Chip.

InfoWorld publisher Bob Metcalfe opposes Clipper Chip technology for technological reasons: "I am against Clipper simply because it will not work, and it will cost an unnecessary amount of tax money to outfit government computers with the chips.... Smart criminals can easily get around Clipper by using additional encryption. Stupid criminals will continue to do stupid things and get caught" (*Wall Street Journal* 22 Mar 94: A14).

Cookies

Do you remember the PacMan game that was popular in video arcades in the 1980s? The game contained magic cookies which, when devoured, made you more powerful. On the Internet, cookies work a little differently, but they're much more powerful. They're also one of the greatest threats to your privacy.

On the Internet, a cookie is a record that stores information about you and can track your mouse clicks through a Web site. Intended originally for use by advertisers to track buyer preferences, cookies have created an outcry from privacy advocates, who believe that the creation and collection of personal information resulting from transactions between users and Web servers is an invasion of privacy.

In response, the Internet Engineering Task Force (IETF) has proposed a change in the specifications for third-party cookies in order to direct the browser not to accept the cookie. The Association of Online Professionals has objected to the proposal, citing the loss of a major method used to assess the success of Web advertising, and the potential loss of services from online providers who rely on cookies for passwords, preferences, and other tasks. The loss of cookies would also require hundreds of hours to reprogram retail Web sites (*BNA Daily Report for Executives* 23 May 97). For the latest information, follow the cookie links at the Interlit Web site. The Cookie Central link tells how to inspect the cookies on your computer.

Certification

To verify that a Web site has committed to following privacy principles and will not make unethical use of information obtained from users, two organizations are offering certificates. When you visit a certified Web site, you can be reasonably sure that it adheres to these principles.

TRUSTe licenses service marks called trustmarks that are awarded to sites considered to be safe and secure places to conduct business, education, communication, and entertainment activities. The trustmarks are served remotely from the TRUSTe servers and are linked to a site's privacy statement, which describes the kind of information a site gathers, what the site does with that information, and with whom the information is shared. In addition to the baseline guidelines, TRUSTe members may adopt one of several model policies which address specific privacy issues, such as children-oriented sites. For more on trustmarks, follow the Interlit Web site links to TRUSTe.

The National Computer Security Association (NCSA) is an independent organization that certifies Web sites as being secure. NCSA-certified sites undergo on-site evaluation, remote testing, and random spot-checking to ensure that the Web site follows the NCSA guidelines, which are based on a portfolio of industry-endorsed best practices. To learn more about NCSA certification, follow the Interlit Web site links to the National Computer Security Association.

Privacy Legislation

Senators Dianne Feinstein (D, California) and Charles Grassley (R, Iowa) have introduced legislation that would bar commercial use of social security numbers and make it illegal for credit bureaus to disseminate your social security number, unlisted phone number, birthdate, or your mother's maiden name. In the House of Representatives, Congressman Paul E. Kanjorski (D, Pennsylvania) submitted legislation that would create a Commission on Privacy of Government Records and ban your social security and Internal Revenue Service records from being posted on the Internet without your written permission being obtained first (*Washington Post* 17 Apr 97).

 ## Platform for Privacy Preferences

With a Microsoft executive saying "this is unprecedented, but we realized that we need to work together for the common good," Microsoft has decided to abandon plans to create its own Internet software privacy standards, and endorse instead the standard proposed by its rival Netscape and Firefly Network Inc. Part of the World Wide Web Consortium's Platform for Privacy Preferences, the standard is supported by a hundred hardware and software companies, both large and small. It will enable Web surfers to control what personal information can be obtained about them during their travels on the Internet (*New York Times* 12 Jun 97). For more information, follow the Interlit Web site links to the Platform for Privacy Preferences.

 ## Center for Democracy and Technology

The Center for Democracy and Technology (CDT) is developing an Online Privacy Clearinghouse to raise the public's awareness of privacy issues on the Internet. By following the Interlit Web site links to the CDT, you can examine the privacy policies of the four major commercial online service providers.

In the future, the CDT will be providing information on the privacy policies of a broad range of Internet players. You will be able to look for a particular company or Web site by name in the CDT's Policy Warehouse, for example, or you can get an overview of policies within specific industries such as commercial online service providers, Internet service providers, Internet Web browsers, commercial Web sites, political Web sites, nonprofit Web sites, telecommunication services, and financial services.

 ## Electronic Frontier Foundation

The Electronic Frontier Foundation (EFF) is a nonprofit civil liberties organization working in the public interest to protect privacy, free expression, and access to public resources and information online, as well as to promote responsibility in new media. Anyone interested in protecting their right to privacy on the Internet should visit the EFF. Follow the Interlit Web site links to the Electronic Frontier Foundation.

 ## Internet Privacy Coalition

The Internet Privacy Coalition is urging members of the Internet community to display a Golden Key & Envelope symbol on their Web pages to show support for the right of privacy and the freedom to use good tools of privacy without government restraints. Follow the Interlit Web site links to the Internet Privacy Coalition.

 Electronic Privacy Information Center

The Electronic Privacy Information Center (EPIC) is a public-interest research center that was established in 1994 to focus public attention on emerging civil liberties issues and to protect privacy, the First Amendment, and constitutional values. EPIC is a project of the Fund for Constitutional Government. EPIC works in association with Privacy International, an international human rights group based in London, and is also a member of the Global Internet Liberty Campaign and the Internet Privacy Coalition. For more information, follow the Interlit Web site links to EPIC.

STALKING

Believe it or not, there's a home page for stalkers on the Internet. In researching this part of the book, the author was visitor number 278,379 to the Stalker's Home Page, which you'll find linked to the Interlit Web site. The purpose of the Stalker's Home Page is not so much to enable you to stalk, but rather to make you aware of the tools that stalkers could use against you on the Internet.

The Stalker's Home Page

Let's face it, when you use the Internet, you leave tracks. Little snippets of information about you litter the Information Superhighway. A social security number here, a phone number there. Here a résumé, there a newsgroup message. A stalker who is network savvy can use the techniques described at the Stalker's Home Page to put this information together and find out an amazing amount of information about you.

The Stalker's Home Page quotes Congressman Frank Horton, who predicted the threat of electronic stalking in a statement made more than 25 years ago:

> One of the most practical of our present safeguards of privacy is the fragmented nature of personal information. It is scattered in little bits across the geography and years of our life. Retrieval is impractical and often impossible. A central data bank removes completely this safeguard.

Discreet Data Research

There's even a service on the Internet called Discreet Data Research that will do stalking for you (or sleuthing as they like to refer to it). While the fees are steep, the range of services offered is incredible. You can surf the Discreet Data Research Web site for free to see the kinds of services offered, which fall into the categories of telephone, pager, and voice mail research; asset locator, for finding someone's checking or savings accounts or other assets; missing persons, for finding people who are unintentionally lost; skip tracing, to find people who have intentionally become missing; and "unusual requests" for asking anything else you want to know. For more information, follow the Interlit Web site links to Discreet Data Research.

SECURITY

To protect networks against unauthorized access by users seeking information to which they are not entitled, several steps can be taken. Security measures include passwords, encryption, firewalls, and proxy servers.

Passwords

The simplest form of protection is the **password**, which is an alphanumeric string of characters the user must type in order to gain access. Unless the user knows the password, access to the data is denied. Passwords are not failsafe, however, because it's possible for someone to guess your password. To protect against people guessing your password, choose an unlikely string of characters containing a combination of upper- and lowercase letters and numbers. Never use your name (or your mother's maiden name, to which passwords are often set initially), and avoid using the names of hobbies or other things you're interested in. As you learned in the section on stalking, it's possible for people to find out things about you, and crackers can use information learned by stalking you to try and guess your password.

Encryption

As you learned in the section on privacy, messages on the Internet can be sniffed. When you type your password to gain access to a resource on the Internet, your password is sent as a message to the server you're trying to access. Anywhere along the way from your PC to the server, it's possible that your password could be sniffed. To protect against this, you can encrypt your messages. Both Netscape Communicator and Microsoft Internet Explorer contain built-in encryption capability. Unless the sniffer knows the encryption key, your password remains private.

There is considerable debate regarding national encryption policy. Should individuals have the right to encrypt their messages? Should the government have the right to decipher these communications? To learn more about this debate, follow the Interlit Web site links to the Encryption Policy Resource Page, which is dedicated to educating Internet users, policymakers, and the public about the issues surrounding encryption policy. Here you will find background information on the encryption policy debate, including legislation, government documents, and statements by members of Congress and administration officials.

Firewalls

In the housing industry, firewalls are constructed between dwellings in an apartment building to prevent a fire that might break out in one unit from spreading to another. The fire is thereby contained to the domain of the apartment in which it started. On the Internet, firewalls work like that, keeping data from moving outside its domain, and preventing access to users from other domains. Even if someone from another domain guesses your password, access will be denied by the firewall.

To learn more about firewalls, follow the Interlit Web site link to the Firewall site. The mission of the Firewall site is to provide a focal point on the Web where users can find links to all sorts of firewall and Internet security information.

Proxy Servers

A proxy server is an intermediary computer through which user requests are routed. The proxy can filter or translate outgoing requests and incoming data, thereby protecting the network from receiving unwanted transmissions. Thus, proxy servers provide a safe way to allow users inside firewalls to access information resources outside the firewall.

To block access to sites inappropriate for schoolchildren, for example, Lee County School District connected its schools to the Internet with Microsoft Proxy Server. The proxy server monitors the Internet access provided to 4,100 students at 13 schools. To learn more about this, follow the Interlit Web site links to Lee County School District's proxy server.

PROTECTIONISM

Some countries view technology as a cultural threat and are taking steps to counteract it. To protect the French language, for example, France passed a law in 1996 requiring that all software sold in France must be provided in a French-language version. People who live in France should protest such a Machiavellian law.

China has a history of human rights abuses and denial of individual freedom. Continuing that tradition, China is building a centrally administered Internet backbone that will allow government monitoring of e-mail and other online activities (*Wall Street Journal* 31 Jan 96: A1).

Viewing the Internet as the end of civilization, Iraq has denied access to all of its citizens. An editorial in the Iraqi government newspaper *Al-Jumhuriya* says that the Internet is "the end of civilizations, cultures, interests, and ethics," and "one of the American means to enter every house in the world. They want to become the only source for controlling human beings in the new electronic village" (AP 17 Feb 97). This viewpoint fails to realize that many of the key Internet inventions came from outside the United States. Packet switching originated in Great Britain, for example, and the Web was invented in Switzerland.

The Internet is a worldwide resource in which every country should participate and become a co-inventor. Restricting or denying access to the Internet will severely retard a nation's status in the twenty-first century. Every citizen in the world should have the right to unrestricted Internet access.

CENSORSHIP

Many people are concerned that in addition to being able to monitor electronic communications that stream across the Internet, network administrators also have the ability to censor them. To what extent and under what circumstances should the government act as a censor on the Information Superhighway?

In a well-publicized criminal trial in Toronto, the Canadian government exercised its right to ban any publicity about the case, lest prospective jurors become biased and the hearings end in mistrial. So the University of Toronto stopped carrying an Internet bulletin board that disclosed banned information about the case. But that did not stop people from distributing the information through e-mail (*Toronto Globe & Mail* 2 Dec 93: A4).

There has been a lot of controversy surrounding the Communications Decency Act of 1996, which makes it illegal to distribute indecent or offensive materials on the Internet. Ruling that the act violates free speech, a three-judge federal court has blocked enforcement of the CDA, describing it as "a government-imposed content-based restriction on speech," in violation of the Constitution. The full text of the decision is available on the Web at http://www.cdt.org. The Justice Department has appealed to the Supreme Court. President Clinton defended the Communications Decency Act by saying: "I remain convinced, as I was when I signed the bill, that our Constitution allows us to help parents by enforcing this act to prevent objectionable material transmitted through computer networks" (*New York Times* 13 Jun 96: A1). For the latest information, follow the Interlit Web site links to the Communications Decency Act.

PORNOGRAPHY AND OBSCENITY

Too much bandwidth on the Internet is devoted to the transmission of pornographic and obscene sexual content. The JPEG file format, which makes it possible to include beautiful full-color images on Web pages, can also transmit full-color photos of explicit "hardcore" pornography and child pornography. The federal government has been searching and seizing servers that contain such material. These sites are so popular that Delft University in the Netherlands has had to limit each user to eight downloads per day from its erotic image file server.

The Supreme Court's 1973 *Miller* ruling gave communities the right to legislate obscenity. To help interpret the laws, Godwin (1994: 58) developed the following four-part test for obscenity:

1. Is the work designed to be sexually arousing?

2. Is it arousing in a way that one's local community would consider unhealthy or immoral?

3. Does it picture acts whose depictions are specifically prohibited by state law?

4. Does the work, when taken as a whole, lack sufficient literary, artistic, scientific, or social value?

Distributing such materials over the Internet raises some difficult issues. For example, while an erotic picture might not be immoral in the community where it was uploaded, it may very well be considered obscene in the place it gets downloaded. Screen-capture utilities make it easy to take things out of context; who can prevent users from circulating an image devoid of the supplementary material that made it legitimate? Moreover, children can easily access materials over the Internet that were intended for adults.

 The U.S. child protection laws forbid any pornographic images that use children, whether or not they meet Godwin's obscenity test. Individuals convicted can be fined up to $100,000 and imprisoned up to 10 years. For example, as the result of a nationwide FBI investigation of online porn, a distributor of child pornography was sentenced to five years in prison for sending sexually explicit photos of children via his America Online account (*Tampa Tribune* 24 Feb 96: A6).

 Canada's best-known computer science school, the University of Waterloo, banned from its campus five Internet bulletin boards dealing with violent sex out of concern that their contents break laws on pornography and obscenity (*Toronto Globe & Mail* 5 Feb 94: A1).

Recreational Software Advisory Council The Recreational Software Advisory Council (RSAC) has begun to issue Web ratings that allow parents to block Web sites rated as having a high degree of violence, nudity, sex, or objectionable language (*USA Today* 29 May 96: 1D). Web page sponsors fill out an electronic questionnaire to get their sites rated on a scale of 0 (innocuous) to 4 ("X-rated"). Parents can set the level at which content will be blocked and can also block all unrated sites. A password gives parents access to areas blocked from children (*Investor's Business Daily* 10 May 96: A18).

PREJUDICE AND HATRED

Unfortunately, the world contains many insecure individuals who, for some sick reason, are made to feel superior by defaming people based on race or ethnic origin. Not only does the Internet reflect the hatred in society, but it provides bigots with a wider audience.

According to the Anti-Defamation League's annual report, "electronic hate is the dark side of technology, and anti-Semites have particularly taken to the medium." The report states that in 1996, anti-Semitic incidents in traditional forms of communication declined by 7% from 1,843 to 1,722 incidents, but anti-Semites and Holocaust deniers shifted to the Internet. According to the report, because the Internet is unregulated, "bigots can spew their hatred without ever running the risk of being identified" (*USA Today* 26 Feb 97).

A study of e-mail use at a large mid-Atlantic university found that sexual harassment of women by e-mail is four to five times more likely than racial or ethnic harassment. The Prejudice Institute, a nonprofit group in Baltimore that released the study, found that 10% of the women who responded to its survey said that they received threatening e-mail, while 3% of the survey respondents said they had received racial or ethnic hate mail (*New York Times* 16 Feb 97).

For more information on issues related to prejudice and hatred on the Net, follow the Interlit links to the University of Iowa's Internet Resources on Hate Speech Web site.

CHAT ROOM DECENCY IN MOOs, MUDs, IRCs, AND MUSHes

In her fascinating book *Life On the Screen*, Sherry Turkle (1995) describes what it is like to participate in Multi User Domains (MUDs). In Chapter 9, you learned how MUDs are virtual spaces in which you can navigate, strategize, and converse with other users. Turkle views MUDs as a new kind of parlor game and a new form of community that lets people generate experiences, relationships, identities, and living spaces that arise only through interaction with technology. One of the dangerous aspects is how men can stalk women in MUDs. For example, Turkle tells of a virtual rape:

> One MUD player had used his skill with the system to seize control of another player's character. In this way the aggressor was able to direct the seized character to submit to a violent sexual encounter. He did all this against the will and over the distraught objections of the player usually "behind" this character, the player to whom this character "belonged." Although some made light of the offender's actions by saying that the episode was just words, in text-based virtual realities such as MUDs, words *are* deeds. (Turkle, 1995, p. 15)

Parents need to be aware of the dangers of MUDs because young people are especially susceptible. Discussing childhood encounters with Net sex, Turkle warns:

Parents need to be able to talk to their children about where they are going and what they are doing. This same commonsense rule applies to their children's lives on the screen. Parents don't have to become technical experts, but they do need to learn enough about computer networks to discuss with their children what and who is out there and lay down some basic safety rules. The children who do best after a bad experience on the Internet (who are harassed, perhaps even propositioned) are those who can talk to their parents, just as children who best handle bad experiences in real life are those who can talk to an elder without shame or fear of blame. (Turkle, 1995, p. 227)

COPYRIGHT

Article I, section 8 of the United States Constitution grants Congress the power "to promote the progress of science and useful arts, by securing for limited times to authors and inventors the exclusive right to their respective writings and discoveries." Congress used this power to pass the Copyright Act of 1976, which defines and allocates rights associated with "original works of authorship fixed in any tangible medium of expression, now known or later developed, or otherwise communicated, either directly or with the aid of a machine or device" (U.S. Constitution, 17 § 102). This means that all of the elements presented in Chapter 12 ("Commonly Found Internet File Types") of this book—including illustrations, text, movies, video clips, documentaries, animations, music, and software—are protected by copyright. There are stiff penalties for copyright offendors. For example, the Software Publishers Association took action in 1993 against 577 organizations for pirating commercial software, resulting in $3.6 million in fines (*Atlanta Journal-Constitution* 3 Feb 94: C2). Whenever you plan to publish a Web page on the Internet, you must make sure you have the right to use every object in it.

Similarly, you should register a copyright for your Web pages. To copyright a Web page, include the following copyright notice on the page, replacing *xx* by the current year:

Copyright © 19*xx* by your_name_goes_here. All rights reserved.

UNITED STATES
COPYRIGHT OFFICE
The Library of Congress

Although this notice legally suffices to protect your copyright, it is also a good idea to register the copyright with the U.S. Copyright Office. If someone infringes your copyright and you take legal action to defend it, copyright registration can help your case. To register a copyright, follow these steps:

▶ Go to the U.S. Copyright Office Web page at http://www.loc.gov/copyright and choose "copyright registration."

▶ Choose "multimedia works" to display the policies and procedures for multimedia copyright registration. (Web pages are multimedia documents.) Read the policy to determine what form to use to register your copyright.

▶ Go back to http://www.loc.gov/copyright and choose "copyright application forms." Download the form you need.

▶ Complete the application form and make a copy to retain in your files.

▶ Mail the application along with a printout of the work and the $20 registration fee to the Register of Copyrights, Copyright Office, Library of Congress, Washington, D.C. 20559.

If you want a receipt, have the Post Office mail your application "return receipt requested." It will take several weeks for the Library of Congress to process your application and send you the registration number. For more information, follow the links to Copyright at the Interlit Web site.

FAIR USE

Fair Use is a section of the U.S. Copyright Law that allows the use of copyrighted works in reporting news, conducting research, and teaching. The law states:

> Notwithstanding the provisions of section 106 [which grants authors exclusive rights], the fair use of a copyrighted work, including such use by reproduction in copies or phonorecords or by any other means specified by that section, for purposes such as criticism, comment, news reporting, teaching (including multiple copies for classroom use), scholarship, or research, is not an infringement of copyright. In determining whether the use made of a work in any particular case is a fair use the factors to be considered shall include:
>
> 1. the purpose and character of the use, including whether such use is of a commercial nature or is for nonprofit educational purposes;
> 2. the nature of the copyrighted work;
> 3. the amount and substantiality of the portion used in relation to the copyrighted work as a whole; and
> 4. the effect of the use upon the potential market for or value of the copyrighted work.

Interpreting Fair Use for Education

To summarize the Fair Use law for education, one may shorten its first paragraph as follows: "... the fair use of a copyrighted work for... teaching (including multiple copies for classroom use)... is not an infringement of copyright." The difficulty arises from interpreting the four tests, which are intentionally left vague, as the law goes on to state, "Although the courts have considered and ruled upon the fair use doctrine over and over again, no real definition of the concept has ever emerged. Indeed, since the doctrine is an equitable rule of reason, no generally applicable definition is possible, and each case raising the question must be decided on its own facts."

The Fair Use Guidelines for Educational Multimedia

To help educational institutions interpret the Fair Use law with regard to multimedia and the Internet, the CCUMC (Consortium of College and University Media Centers) spearheaded the creation of the new *Fair Use Guidelines for Educational Multimedia*. The committee that created these guidelines consisted of representatives from print, film, music, and multimedia publishing companies who spent many months discussing and debating fair use issues with representatives from educational institutions. Professor Lisa Livingston, Director of the Instructional Media Division of the City University of New York, chaired the committee, and well-known copyright attorney Ivan Bender (who died too young in 1996) was retained to advise on legal issues. As a member of this committee, the author can attest to the rigor of the process.

The *Fair Use Guidelines for Educational Multimedia* are linked to the Interlit Web site. They specify what's fair for students as well as for teachers. The author encourages you to study these guidelines carefully and use them to exercise your right of Fair Use.

1. Follow the Interlit Web site links to the national NetDay Web site. Do you find your local schools in the NetDay database? If not, do you know whether your local schools are participating in NetDay? Check with your local K–12 school administrators, and encourage them to join the NetDay movement.

2. As you learned in this chapter, the Telecommunications Act of 1996 provides a Universal Service Fund whereby schools and libraries can receive subsidized access to the Internet. Check with your local school administrators to find out whether they are aware of the USF. What level of support are your K–12 schools getting?

3. Where do you stand on the issue of privacy and encryption technology? Do you believe that every citizen should have the right to use any encryption scheme they please? Should the government have the right to decipher encrypted messages under court order to eavesdrop on electronic communications among criminals? Is the Clipper Chip the answer, or would you recommend some other approach? To help answer these questions, follow the Interlit Web site links to Privacy.

4. Find the cookies file on your computer. It's called *cookies.txt,* and you'll find it somewhere in your Web browser's folder. If you have Windows 95, you can find the file easily by clicking the Start button, choosing Find, and doing a file search. If you have a Macintosh, you can do a file search by clicking the Apple icon in the upper left corner of the screen to pull down the menu, then choose Find File. Inspect your *cookies.txt* file with any text editor. What information does it contain about the history of your activity at commercial Web sites? Did you realize this kind of information is being kept? Do you think companies should be permitted to collect this kind of information about you? Why or why not?

5. Follow the Interlit Web site links to the Stalker's Home Page. Peruse the different stalking resources provided there. Do any of the resources surprise you? In what ways could you be stalked, of which you were unaware before visiting this Web site? Do you think any of these methods should be illegal? Why? Now go to the Discreet Data Research site. What stalking services do you find here that are not supported at the Stalker's Home Page? Do you think any of the Discreet Data Research services should be illegal? If so, which ones? Why do you feel they are improper?

6. Where do you stand on the issue of protectionism? Do you think France was justified in creating the law requiring that software cannot be sold in France unless it's a French-language version? State why you agree or disagree with the French government on this issue.

7. As explained earlier in this chapter, a lot of traffic on the Information Superhighway deals with sex. Do you believe this large amount of sexual traffic detracts from the goals and objectives of the Internet? Do you object to the use of public funds to transmit such material? Why or why not?

8. Do you agree that the University of Waterloo was justified in banning obscene bulletin boards from its network? Should obscene bulletin boards be banned from the Information Superhighway altogether? Are obscene bulletin boards accessible from your connection to the network?

9. Has a government regulation ever prevented you from accessing services you felt you had a right to? For example, when the FCC ruled that cable companies cannot rebroadcast FM signals, the author's community lost its cable access to National Public Radio and several other FM stations. Since we live in an area too remote for good FM reception, we became disconnected from these important stations. And without any warning! Have you had a similar experience? If our government cannot regulate access to a simple FM radio station, how will it ever manage an Information Superhighway?

10. Follow the Interlit Web site links to the *Fair Use Guidelines for Educational Multimedia.* Read the guidelines, and as you do so, reflect on whether the resources on your Web pages adhere to the guidelines. Have you done anything at your Web site that's not a fair use? If so, have you obtained the necessary copyright permission to use the material?

11. The Clinton administration has promised the public that everyone will have equal access to the Information Superhighway. Do you believe this, or do you feel that its construction will create a technological underclass in our society? What do you see as the major obstacles that must be overcome to provide equal access for everyone?

26 Emerging Technology

After completing this chapter, you'll be able to:

- **Explain the methods being used to speed up the Internet, and know how to avoid consuming unnecessary bandwidth when you use the Net.**

- **Prepare yourself to take advantage of the real-time communications technologies that are emerging.**

- **Understand how artificial intelligence makes it possible for people to make more efficient use of the Internet.**

- **Define HDTV and consider the role digital television will play in the future of the Internet.**

- **Understand the push-pull metaphor and experience some exciting push technologies on the Internet.**

- **Reflect on the human interface and the role that personal digital assistants (PDAs) will play in the future of the Internet.**

N E W technologies follow a cycle that includes invention, prototyping, proof of concept, productizing, and manufacture. Throughout this process, the inventions are called emerging technologies. It often takes many years for an emerging technology to achieve widespread use in the marketplace. One reason why this takes so long is because consumers have a hard time seeing the benefit. As Bane and McMahon (1994:89) describe the problem:

> Customers are typically incapable of understanding the value of a new technology until they actually experience it. Microwave ovens, for example, were a kitchen curiosity and a perceived health hazard in the 1970s, but they are now found in 87 percent of U.S. homes.

A problem particularly related to information technologies is the rapid rate of change. Any PC you buy this year, for example, will be considered outdated in just a year or two. The computer will still do the job for which you purchased it, but newer models will be faster and more fully featured. Ira Fuchs, vice president for computing and information technology at Princeton University, articulates this problem with a principle that has become known as Fuchs's law:

> "The time to acquisition is longer than the time to obsolescence."
> (*Chronicle of Higher Education* 28 Mar 97)

This chapter will introduce you to emerging technologies that promise to improve the Internet substantially in coming years. Then the next chapter, which deals with how to keep up with changes in technology, will provide you with ways of tracking the progress of these inventions as they emerge. In the end, you'll be prepared to take advantage of these innovations sooner rather than later.

IMPROVING THE INFRASTRUCTURE

You've undoubtedly experienced some problems with the Internet's physical transport layer. Network delay is the most obvious problem. You click a hypertext trigger to go to a Web site, and you wait, and you wait, and you wait. Sometimes it seems like WWW stands for World Wide Wait.

W3C Speeding Up the Web with HTTP 1.1

The World Wide Web Consortium is working on a redesign of the HTTP 1.0 protocol that has been the basis of the Web since 1990. By the time you read this, browsers should be supporting the new protocol, which is known as HTTP 1.1. The new protocol uses an invention known as pipelined HTTP.

Pipelined HTTP speeds up the Web by reducing the number of connects needed to display a Web page. Under the original HTTP 1.0 protocol, Web servers hang up on you several times during the downloading of a Web page. First, the server downloads the text and hangs up. Then, your browser makes a new connection and asks for the first image that goes on the page; the server obligingly downloads the image and hangs up. Then your browser makes another connection to download the second image. This process continues until all of the objects on the Web page have come down.

Having to establish a new connection several times per Web page really slows down the Web. Pipelined HTTP speeds up the Web by maintaining a single connection throughout the downloading of the Web page. Depending on the number of objects per page, Web speed increases by a factor of 2 to 8 times faster than the original HTTP 1.0 protocol. For more information, follow the Interlit Web site links to Pipelined HTTP.

THE MBONE INFORMATION WEB Multimedia MBONE

MBONE stands for Multicast Backbone. It's a network of computers on the Internet specially designed for the transmission of simultaneous live video and audio broadcasts. In a traditional packet-switched network, if you send a video to four different people, four identical copies of the information are sent over the network. Multicasting the video over the MBONE sends only one copy of the message and replicates the information only at branch points in the network.

As the television, telephone, and computer industries continue to converge, real-time audio and video will grow in importance on the Internet. Look for the MBONE, or a technology like it, to have a significant impact on the Web in the years ahead.

Connecting to the MBONE requires that your ISP have special routing and switching equipment. Follow the Interlit Web site link to Multicasting and the MBONE for a technical description of how the MBONE works.

Internet II

An EDUCOM-based consortium of research universities is conducting a project called Internet II. The goal is to create a higher-speed version of the Internet that will revolve around a high-speed connection point called the Gigapop. Strategically placed throughout the network, Gigapops will guarantee high-speed bandwidth between universities implementing the Internet II standards.

Internet II uses three protocols to provide high-speed transmission and guaranteed bandwidth:

- RSVP permits a user to reserve bandwidth from the workstation to the network host computer.

- IPv6 is a packet-delivery protocol that lets the user assign priority to certain kinds of information. You may want your Web search traffic to have a higher priority than your e-mail traffic, for example, so your searches get completed faster.

- Multicast, as described above in the section on the MBONE, will use IP tunneling and multithreading to increase multimedia throughput.

To find out the current status, follow the Interlit Web site links to Internet II.

Wireless Communications

At present, most Internet use occurs at the end of a wire or cable that connects your computer to the Internet. Emerging wireless technologies promise to untether you. If you follow the Interlit Web site links to Wireless Design and Development, for example, you can read about new products that enable you to access the Internet without needing a conventional telephone line or network cable.

AT&T is taking wireless technology a step further by developing what it calls the "communications medium for the twenty-first century," which is a wireless system that bypasses the local phone network to link residential and business phones directly to AT&T's long-distance network. A small transceiver attached to the side of your house will provide telephone service and data transmission at twice the speed currently available over Bell company lines. AT&T President John Walter says: "When we call this a breakthrough, we're placing it in the same category as satellite and fiber-optic transmission and electronic switching." Walter predicts that this emerging technology, which is code-named Project Angel during the development phase, will surpass regular wired service in call quality and error-free data transmission (*Wall Street Journal* 26 Feb 97). For more information, follow the Interlit Web site links to AT&T and Project Angel.

REAL-TIME COMMUNICATIONS

In the past, the Internet has been used primarily for communications that do not occur in real time. The most-popular services on the Internet, for example, are not real-time technologies. E-mail is based on a store-and-forward protocol that delivers mail to your in-box, where the message waits until you open your in-box to read it. Traditional Web pages reside on a server, where they wait for you to access them with a browser.

Real-time communications, on the other hand, don't wait for someone to open them. Instead, they stream across the Internet and play on your PC in real time.

These emerging technologies are converging radio, telephone, and television into a networked supermedium.

Internet Telephone Services

Rapid progress is being made in Internet telephone services. Microsoft Phone, for example, combines the Windows 95 telephony features with new voice-enabled modems. This converges into your PC the capabilities of a speakerphone and a telephone answering machine. Microsoft Phone has text-to-speech technology that lets you listen to your e-mail messages aloud over the phone, and speech-recognition technology that enables users to dial a telephone number merely by saying the name of the person they want to call. You can even tell the computer to beep you on your pager when new messages arrive. To learn more, follow the Interlit Web site links to Microsoft Phone.

As Internet telephony services emerge, traditional long-distance telephone companies will see revenues begin to fall. The London consulting firm Philips Tarifica predicts that Europe's largest telecom company, Deutsche Telekom, will see revenues from international phone calls decline by at least $171 million in 2001 as the result of Internet telephony (*Financial Times* 26 Apr 97). To increase further the rate at which Internet telephony emerges, Motorola has licensed VocalTec's Internet telephony software, which hooks up to corporate switchboards and routes long-distance calls to the Internet. Because this has the potential to eliminate long-distance telephone charges, many companies will consider adopting it (*Wall Street Journal* 3 Mar 97). For more information, follow the Interlit Web site links to VocalTec.

The America's Carriers Telecommunications Association (ACTA) believes it is unfair for the Internet to compete for long-distance telephony, because computer companies are not subject to the same FCC regulations that govern long-distance carriers. On the other hand, a coalition of high-tech groups known as Voice on the Net (VON) argues that it's in the public interest for voice telephony on the Internet to remain unregulated. An attorney for the FCC says that "one thing is for sure. The commission is not interested in refereeing between technologies" (*US News & World Report* 15 Apr 96: 53).

In Germany, meanwhile, Deutsche Telekom is the first major telephone company to offer Internet-based voice telephony in a trial involving 1,000 customers in Germany, Japan, and the United States. These customers will be able to use ordinary handsets, rather than computers, to make their calls, which will cost about 13 cents a minute, which is less than a fifth of the cost of a regular voice call from Germany to the United States. "The targets of this project are to test the technology, to analyze the usage, and to evaluate whether Internet telephony can be offered at lower rates than conventional telephone service," says the company (*TechWire* 18 Jul 97).

Internet Radio

Figure 26-1
PlayerPlus is a streaming audio and video player.

Progressive Networks is producing software that takes the Internet radio metaphor literally. Lee (1996:30) tells how "there are six preset station buttons and a scan mode that goes through all of the live RealAudio stations. It works with RealAudio's Web site, TimeCast (www.timecast.com), to save individual user preferences to the site." For more information, follow the Interlit Web site links to PlayerPlus. As illustrated in Figure 26-1, PlayerPlus now plays RealVideo as well as RealAudio streams.

Real Time Streaming Protocol (RTSP)

A coalition of 40 companies led by Netscape and Progressive Networks has proposed to the Internet Engineering Task Force that the Real Time Streaming Protocol (RTSP) become the Internet standard for streaming media. The RTSP underlies Progressive's RealAudio and RealVideo products and Netscape's LiveMedia. The coalition includes IBM, Apple, Sun, Macromedia, Xing, Digital Equipment, Hewlett-Packard, and Silicon Graphics. A notable exception is Microsoft, which elected not to participate (*New York Times* 14 Oct 96: C3). To learn more about the Real Time Streaming Protocol, and to find out the status of the proposal to make it an Internet standard, follow the Interlit Web site links to RTSP.

ARTIFICIAL INTELLIGENCE

Artificial intelligence (AI) is for real. It's not just a theoretical science for researchers. Featured here are several AI technologies that promise to improve your use of the Internet in years to come.

Voice Recognition

Many people do not type very fast, and even those who do wish there were an easier way to enter information into a computer. Voice recognition is rapidly emerging as a solution to this problem. Apple's Speech Recognition Manager is a software development kit (SDK) that lets developers incorporate speech recognition into any Macintosh application. Among the first to take advantage of this new technology is the *Star Trek Omnipedia* CD-ROM from Imergy, a voice-activated guide to a galaxy of Star Trek facts, characters, and movies. Imergy was amazed at how accurate the recognition is, even for phrases like "Denibian Slime Devil." Known as PlainTalk, Apple's Speech Recognition Manager enables the application developer to define how many words are active and to build custom vocabularies or language models. The PlainTalk SDK is available free of charge; Macintosh developers can get it by following the links to Apple's Speech Web site.

For Windows users, Creative Labs produces a SoundBlaster add-on called Creative VoiceAssist, which you can train to recognize up to 1,024 voice commands. For more information, follow the Interlit Web site links to the Creative zone and do a search for voice recognition.

Of course, there is a world of difference between a system that can recognize only 1,024 words, and a continuous-speech system such as Dragon Systems' DragonDictate for Windows, which can recognize up to 60,000 words. DragonDictate applications include legal dictation, environmental control systems, and word processing by persons with physical disabilities, such as repetitive stress injuries. DragonDictate consumes a lot of RAM—16 megabytes for the 60,000-word edition. For more information, follow the Interlit Web site links to DragonDictate.

Text-to-Speech Conversion

In Chapter 9, you learned about Time Warner's virtual chat environment, which is called the Palace on the Internet. If you have a Macintosh, Apple's text-to-speech extension enables you to hear the conversations as well as see them on screen in the cartoon talk balloons.

For more information about Apple's text-to-speech technology, follow the Interlit Web site links to PlainTalk.

Image Recognition

If you've ever tried to find an image that you're looking for in a database, you know how difficult it is to locate an image via key words. Virage is working on software that can compare images with a visual template, which is how the human brain recognizes images. The Virage software reduces the image into a 1-kilobyte file called a feature vector, which is based on the placement, color, and texture of shapes in the image. You search for images by describing the visual properties of what you're seeking (*Forbes* 2 Dec 96: 240).

The commercial graphics provider PhotoDisc uses the Virage software to help users search for images. For a demonstration, follow the Interlit Web site links to the Virage image recognition demo.

Knowbots

Knowbots are software applications programmed to act as intelligent agents that go out on the network and find things for you. You tell a knowbot what you want, and it worms its way through the Internet finding all the relevant information, digesting it, and reporting it to you succinctly.

Likening them to robotic librarians, Krol (1992: 259) refers to knowbots as "… software worms that crawl from source to source looking for answers to your questions. As a knowbot looks, it may discover more sources. If it does, it checks the new sources, too. When it has exhausted all sources, it comes crawling home with whatever it found."

Quarterdeck won Best of Show at Comdex '95 for a knowbot called WebCompass. You can set WebCompass to go out on the Net automatically at regular intervals and bring back the information you need. For more information, follow the Interlit Web site links to Quarterdeck, where you can download the personal edition of WebCompass for free.

House Hunter is intelligent agent software that uses General Magic's Telescript technology to watch for new house listings that fit your profile. You simply specify the type of house and the locale and price range you're looking for. House Hunter monitors the Coldwell Banker real estate listings for houses that fit your profile and sends you an e-mail alert when such a listing appears. For more information, go to http://www.genmagic.com. There's also a General Magic listserv for discussing the Magic Cap operating system. The listserv is MAGICCAP on LISTSERV@BrownVM.Brown.Edu. If you need help subscribing to the listserv, refer to the instructions in Chapter 7.

For more information about knowbots and intelligent agents, follow the Interlit Web site links to intelligent agents.

DIGITAL TELEVISION AND VIDEO

Computer technology is creating fundamental changes in the way televisions are made and videos are distributed. Almost everyone reading this book will be purchasing one of the new TVs during the next few years.

High-Definition Television (HDTV)

HDTV stands for high-definition television. It will replace NTSC as the television standard for the United States. HDTV is based on four technologies:

- MPEG digital video compression

- Transmission in packets that will permit any combination of video, audio, and data

- Progressive scanning for computer interoperability up to 60 frames per second at 1920 × 1080 pixels

- Compact-disc quality digital surround sound using Dolby AC-3 audio technology

It's taken longer than expected for HDTV to emerge. The planned rollout at the 1996 Summer Olympic Games never happened. Instead, the first HDTV sets will come onto the market sometime in 1998. Chances are that by the time you read this, you'll be able to visit your local television store to get an HDTV demonstration.

How soon will your analog TV become obsolete? The current plan is for HDTV and NTSC to be broadcast concurrently until the year 2006, when broadcasts will be transmitted in digital form only. At that time, the 240 million TV sets now in use in the United States will become useless (*New York Times* 4 Apr 97). For more information, follow the Interlit Web site links to HDTV.

Figure 26-2 DirecTV uses MPEG to deliver more than 175 channels of digital TV programming over the nation's first high-powered direct broadcast satellite (DBS) service using 18-inch satellite dishes. For more information, go to http://www.directv.com.

MPEG Digital Video

MPEG stands for Motion Picture Experts Group, the name of the ISO standards committee that created it. MPEG compresses video by using a discrete cosine transform algorithm to eliminate redundant data in blocks of pixels on the screen. MPEG compresses the video further by recording only changes from frame to frame; this is known as **delta-frame encoding**. MPEG is expected to become the digital video standard for compact discs, cable TV, direct satellite broadcast, and high-definition television. Bell Atlantic is already using MPEG in its Stargazer service, and MPEG is the standard for the DirecTV system, as advertised in Figure 26-2. For the DirecTV dealer nearest you, follow the Interlit Web site links to DirecTV.

See the discussion of the MPEG file type in Chapter 12 for an explanation of the four versions of MPEG that have been worked on so far. For more information on MPEG, follow the MPEG links at the Interlit Web site.

WebTV

WebTV came on the market during the holiday shopping period at the end of 1996. As illustrated in Figure 26-3, WebTV is a device that essentially connects your telephone line to the video input on your TV or VCR. When you start up the WebTV, it connects via your telephone line to your local WebTV Internet service provider, and you see the Web pages

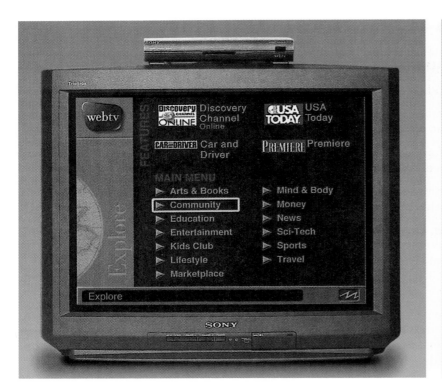

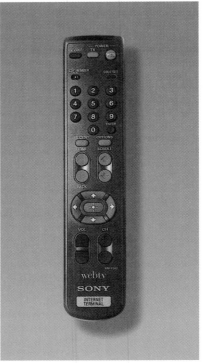

Figure 26-3 WebTV connects your telephone to your TV for access to the World Wide Web and e-mail.

Figure 26-4 The WebTV hand control, called the Universal Remote, with one-thumb surfing.

 on your TV screen. As depicted in Figure 26-4, there's a cleverly designed hand control that let's you do one-thumb surfing on the Internet, but to really take advantage of all the features of WebTV, you need to purchase the optional computer keyboard. In addition to providing access to the Web, the WebTV has electronic mail services. Your mail messages can even include pictures and audio clips.

In April of 1997, Microsoft bought WebTV for $425 million. The computer giant hopes to achieve its goal of integrating the television, the telephone, and the computer into a networked supermedium. Withrow (1993) credits technology prophet George Gilder with coining the phrase **telecomputer** to describe such a device. To learn more about WebTV and what Microsoft plans to do with it, follow the Interlit Web site links to WebTV.

There is some doubt as to whether products like WebTV and other diskless devices such as network computers (NCs) will be successful. A study by Aragon Consulting Group predicts that consumer demand will fall short of vendor expectations. "If you look at the 45% of U.S. households that have computers (which is the market targeted by NC makers), 85% of those have children, and those kids want the same level of computing at home that they have in school—the ability to run different applications and store data, for example. The cost factor is diminished when you consider you can buy a used Pentium running at 75 MHz for about the same price as an NC. So why would you want to buy a low-grade home appliance?" says Aragon's president, who sees the outlook for WebTVs as equally dismal: "With this type of adjunct appliance, the industry hopes to address the 55 or 60% of American homes without computers, but, again, they haven't thought it through. Half of those households don't care at all about computers or the Internet and never will. And the other half, 25% or so of households, aren't very eager to enhance the capabilities of their TVs" (*Investor's Business Daily* 20 Feb 97).

Intercasting in TV's Vertical Blanking Interval

The vertical blanking interval is the gap between the frames of a television picture. You see the vertical blanking interval if your television is out of horizontal adjustment, causing the frames to scroll down the screen. Ever since the invention of television, the vertical blanking interval has had the capability of carrying additional information, but no one has used it effectively. Until now. Intel has trademarked the term **intercast**, which means to transmit Web pages and other digital information in the vertical blanking interval. Partnering with Intel in the Intercast venture are NBC, CNN, Viacom, WGBH, QVC, Comcast, America Online, Asymetrix, En Technology, Netscape, Gateway, and Packard Bell. NBC did its first intercast during the 1996 Summer Olympic Games, and CNN is already intercasting news stories. For more information, follow the Interlit Web site links to the Intercast Industry Group.

PUSH TECHNOLOGIES

When you use a browser to get a page from the Web, you're effectively pulling the page from the Web into your computer. Until you pull, the page stays put. The push-pull metaphor is changing this paradigm.

The Push-Pull Metaphor

Push is obviously the opposite of *pull*. Push means that someone can make information appear on your computer screen, without your having to pull each page down from the Web individually.

You're already familiar with one of the world's most popular push technologies: television. Once you tune to a channel, you can just sit back and watch, like a couch potato, while the TV station pushes the program onto your screen.

On the Web, push works a lot like TV. You use your browser to select a channel on a Web server, and the server pushes a stream of multimedia information that plays automatically on your screen. In effect, your Web browser becomes a switchboard capable of connecting you to thousands of different push channels.

Webcasting

Webcasting is a generic term that means to use push technologies to deliver channels of information on the Web. The term Webcasting is akin to television broadcasting, with one huge difference. In TV broadcasting, anyone with a TV can tune to any channel being broadcast. In Webcasting, on the other hand, the server can decide what PCs it's willing to push the information onto by filtering requests according to Internet domain names. A company-private Webcasting server at the Sony corporation, for example, could refuse to push programming onto any user who doesn't belong to the sony.com domain.

The Webcasting SIG (special-interest group) has a Web site where you can find out the latest information about push technologies. Clicking the WCGuide button takes you to a list of the Webcasting and push guides available on the Internet. To peruse a wide variety of Webcasting resources, follow the Interlit Web site link to the Webcasting SIG.

PointCasting

PointCasting was invented by PCN, which stands for PointCast Network. Think of your PC as being at a certain "point" on the Internet. PointCasting means to push to that point a personalized stream of information, which plays on your screen.

Figure 26-5 shows PCN's personalization settings. The user can click tabs that display sets of options for news, weather, sports, stocks, and lifestyle. When the user tunes into PCN, the PointCast server pushes onto the user's PC a multimedia show containing the kind of information the user wants. Plus, as an added bonus, you get commercial advertising! That's why PCN, which is one of the hottest services on the Web, is free. Like broadcast television, the programming is paid for by commercial advertisers, whose ads appear on screen in the midst of the show, as shown in Figure 26-6. Unlike TV, however, the PCN ads are clickable. If you're interested in one of the products appearing in the ad, you can click on it, and PCN will take you to the product's Web site.

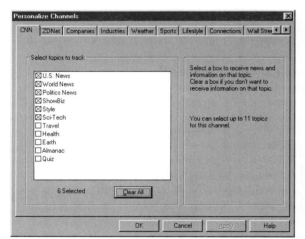

Figure 26-5 The PointCast personalization settings.

Figure 26-6 Commercial advertising appears in a PointCast.

DOWNLOADING THE POINTCAST CLIENT

You can download and install the PointCast client software for free. Follow these steps:

▶ Use your Web browser to go to http://www.pointcast.com.

▶ Click the option to download the PointCast Network.

▶ Choose the version you want to download (Windows or Macintosh).

▶ When you download the file, make sure you remember the folder you save it in.

▶ PCN is a self-extracting, self-installing archive; to install it, simply run the file you downloaded in the previous step. If you have trouble running the archive, review the section at the end of Chapter 13 on downloading and installing self-extracting archives.

POINTCAST AS SCREEN SAVER

When you install the PointCast Network, PCN gives you the option of installing it as a screen saver. Whenever your computer sits idle, the PointCast Network appears, providing you with a multimedia show. This so-called **idle-time interface** is one of the smartest ideas PCN had. Imagine how the commercial advertisers must love this. Whenever your computer sits idle, it becomes a multimedia kiosk hyping retail products. It also shows the information you selected when you personalized PointCast, enabling you to find out the value of the stock you bought this morning, or see the scores of your favorite sports teams.

WEBCASTING ON POINTCAST

PointCast Connections is a Webcasting product from PCN that enables you to become a Webcaster. Anyone can use Connections to create a channel and run it alongside other channels in the PointCast Network like CNN, Companies, and Weather. There's a comprehensive directory of PointCast Connections at Excite. To peruse the channels that are available, follow the Interlit Web site links to the Excite directory of PointCast Connections. There you will find a button to click if you want to add your own Connection to the directory.

NOTE When this book went to press, Connections was in the beta test phase and was available for Windows users only. By the time you read this, Connections should be released as a standard feature of the PointCast Network.

PERSONAL DIGITAL ASSISTANTS

Personal digital assistants (PDAs) are portable, handheld computers that you can take with you to work, school, or anyplace where a PC might come in handy. It's not uncommon to see people in supermarkets, for example, using PDAs instead of handwritten shopping lists. There are two main families of PDAs: Windows CE and Newton. Both have taken on exciting new capabilities as PDA technology continues to emerge.

Windows CE is a handheld PC version of the Windows 95 operating system. If you know how to use Windows 95, you know how to use Windows CE. Casio makes a very popular Windows CE device called the *Cassiopeia*. As illustrated in Figure 26-7, you use the Windows 95 Start button to choose programs, which include special handheld versions of Microsoft Office programs—MS Word, MS Excel, and MS

Figure 26-7 Casio's *Cassiopeia* uses the Windows CE operating system.

Figure 26-8 The MessagePad 2000 uses Apple's Newton operating system.

Schedule—as well as e-mail and the Pocket Explorer Web browser. Instead of using a mouse, you choose things on screen with a stylus via Microsoft's pen computing interface. To learn more about these emerging technologies, follow the Interlit Web site links to Windows CE and Cassiopeia.

Also based on a pen computing interface is Apple's Newton operating system, which is Newton found on Apple's MessagePad 2000 and eMate products. As depicted in Figure 26-8, the MessagePad eliminates the need for a computer keyboard by using handwriting software that recognizes characters you write on the screen with a stylus. Most users find that instead of recognizing your style of handwriting, however, the MessagePad ends up training you to write in a style of handwriting that it understands. The eMate, which is a portable Newton product intended for use by schoolchildren, has a standard computer keyboard that is shockproof and spillproof. To learn more about Apple's emerging line of PDA products, follow the Interlit Web site links to Newton.

E X E R C I S E S

1. Where do you stand on the issue of Internet telephony? Do you believe that it is unfair for the Internet to compete with long-distance telephone companies? Should the Internet be regulated or taxed in order to provide phone companies with a level playing field? Or should the phone companies be encouraged to get more actively involved with the Internet?

2. Go to the RealAudio and RealVideo Web site at www.timecast.com, and tune in to some of the radio and TV broadcasts you find there. What do you think about the quality of what you see and hear? Do you think the Internet will ever be capable of carrying high-quality audiovisual data streams throughout the network?

3. Follow the Interlit Web site links to Voice Recognition, and explore the material you find there. Then reflect on how voice recognition might help make computers easier to use. What ways can you think of? How would you use voice recognition in your daily life? How long do you think it will take before the common mass-market retail computer can do voice recognition without needing to have special hardware and software installed?

4. Follow the Interlit Web site links to the Virage image recognition demo, which will help you learn how to search for images at the PhotoDisc site. After trying the example search in the demo, construct a custom search in which you look for images having visual characteristics you describe. How well do you think the Virage software works? Is this an effective way to search for images? How does image recognition software need to be improved?

5. If you could program a knowbot to go out on the Internet periodically and collect information or do things for you automatically, what would you make it do? After you answer this question, follow the Interlit Web site links to Quarterdeck's WebCompass site, download the WebCompass software, and try to make WebCompass do your bidding. Of the things you wanted to do, what does WebCompass enable you to do, and what can it not yet do? Do you think programs like WebCompass will ever be able to do the things you want?

6. By the time you read this, HDTV should be available commercially. Go to your local television store and check it out. Can you see the difference in quality between an HDTV picture and a standard NTSC television signal? How much do HDTV sets cost? Are you willing to pay that much to get one, or will you wait for the price to come down? How many of your friends have HDTV sets?

7. Go to your local television store and ask if they have WebTV. If not, check your local Sears store— Sears carries WebTV. Use the WebTV remote control to browse to some of your favorite Web pages. How do the Web pages look on the WebTV? What has the WebTV done to reformat the Web page to make it look good on TV? How do you like the one-thumb surfing capability of the WebTV hand control? Now try creating an e-mail message with the hand control. If you have trouble, ask the sales representative for help. Can you see why the author believes that every WebTV should ship with a computer keyboard, instead of making you buy it separately at an added cost?

8. Follow the Interlit Web site links to PCN, and download and install the latest version of the PointCast Network. If you have trouble, review the section on downloading and installing self-extracting archives at the end of Chapter 13. When you run PointCast, choose the customize option, and set your personal preferences for the kind of information you want. Also choose the option to make PointCast be your screen saver. After having PointCast be your screen saver for a few days, reflect on whether this is a good idea or not. Do you like having your computer screen pop up PointCast during your idle time? Does this help or hinder your work? If you decide you don't like it, go back to the user preference settings and turn the screen-saver option off.

9. Follow the Interlit Web site links to the directory of PointCast Connections at Excite. Peruse the directory of PCN channels that people have created. Try those that interest you. Do you feel like creating your own push channel? PCN claims it's easy to do with the latest version of the PointCast Network. Give it a try, and see if PCN Connections lives up to this claim.

10. Go to your local computer store and ask to see a demonstration of Windows CE running on a personal digital assistant such as the Cassiopeia. Are you impressed? How could you use such a device in your line of work? What features would you like to see added to Windows CE? Or can it already do everything you want?

11. Go to your local computer store and ask for a demonstration of the MessagePad 2000. Use the stylus to write a message on screen. How well does the Newton software recognize your handwriting? Do you have to alter your style of writing, or can Newton recognize your natural handwriting style? Do you think it will ever be possible for a computer to recognize a person's native handwriting?

27

How to Keep Up

After completing this chapter, you'll be able to:

- **Keep up with the changes that are occurring on the Internet.**

- **Subscribe to listservs that send updates in your e-mail.**

- **Bookmark Web sites that announce and explain changes in technology.**

- **Peruse catalogs for new products that may interest you.**

- **Subscribe to free magazines that review and compare the new products.**

- **Read books that will extend your knowledge of computers, multimedia, and the Internet.**

COMPUTER technology is advancing so rapidly that even the so-called experts feel overwhelmed sometimes by the fast pace of change. Never has a field had so many new inventions happening so rapidly. There's so much hype surrounding the new-product announcements. How can you see through the hype when you consider purchasing new technology? How will you know what model of computer to buy, what software to use, and how best to connect to the Internet?

Happily, you can use the technology to keep up with what's new. This chapter provides you with a list of recommended listservs, Web sites, catalogs, periodicals, and books. These recommendations are succinct and strategic; instead of providing you with a list so long that you wouldn't know where to start, this chapter provides you with a short list of the most strategic ways to keep up with changes and advances in technology.

LISTSERVS

Table 27-1 recommends listservs that will send you periodic e-mail messages to keep you up to date with what's happening in technology. If you have time to join only one of these recommended listservs, EDUPAGE is the one.

Table 27-1   Recommended Listservs

Name of Listserv	What the Listserv Does	How to Subscribe
EDUPAGE	Sends you news about new technology three times each week	Send e-mail to listproc@educom.unc.edu; leave the subject line blank, and as your message, type: **Subscribe EDUPAGE *Firstname Lastname***
Netsurfer Digest	Reviews the latest hot spots on the Internet	Send e-mail to nsdigest-request@netsurf.com; leave the subject line blank, and as your message, type: **Subscribe nsdigest-text**
Seidman's Online Insider	Puts you on the inside track of what's happening on the Internet	Send e-mail to: listserv@peach.ease.lsoft.com; leave the subject line blank, and as your message, type: **Subscribe ONLINE-L *Firstname Lastname***
TOURBUS	Provides a virtual tour of the best Internet sites and tools	Send e-mail to: listserv@listserv.aol.com; leave the subject line blank, and as your message, type: **Subscribe TOURBUS *Firstname Lastname***

CATALOGS

One of the best catalogs for people considering computer purchases is the *Computer Shopper*. It's filled with new-product announcements, evaluations, advertisements, technology reviews, and shopper's guides to multimedia peripherals, input/output devices, and modems. You'll find the *Computer Shopper* on the magazine rack of most newsstands. It's very popular, and new editions come out monthly. Although the *Computer Shopper* is called a magazine, it looks and feels more like a catalog, which is why it's listed here as a catalog. To subscribe, call (303) 665-8930, fax (303) 604-7455, or write P.O. Box 52568, Boulder, CO 80322-2568.

There are also Web sites where you'll find annotated lists of computer products for sale, including multimedia PCs, peripherals, and networking. Table 27-2 lists the recommended technology catalogs on the Web.

Table 27-2   Technology Catalogs on the World Wide Web

World Wide Web Address	What You'll Find There
http://i-shop.iworld.com	Wide range of information technology products, including network connections, Internet providers, World Wide Web products, digital cameras, video products, and more
http://www.isn.com	Internet Shopping Network (ISN) for computer products, software, and multimedia accessories

PERIODICALS AND WEB SITES

Listed here are periodicals that will help keep you up to date on the new technology. Several of these periodicals are free. Each month, you'll receive a printed magazine in the mail. These periodicals also have Web sites where you can search for information by key word and read extra material that expands on the printed edition.

Internet World

A good source for the latest news about the Information Superhighway, *Internet World* features articles about new trends on the network, advertises Internet addresses of new online resources, reviews books about the Internet, and presents profiles of the key companies, people, and products that impact the Internet's growth and development. Penetrating analyses probe legal, social, and ethical issues. Labs educate users and buyers about important new Internet products and technologies for home and business.

Internet World is published monthly by Mecklermedia Corporation, 20 Ketchum Street, Westport, CT 06880. Phone (203) 226-6967. Fax (203) 454-5840. E-mail info@mecklermedia.com. A subscription costs $29 per year. There is an online version at http://www.internetworld.com.

NetGuide

Published monthly, *NetGuide* magazine is the official publication of the Internet Developers Association. Filled with Internet news, product reviews, and insider stories, the subscription cost is $29 per year.

To subscribe to *NetGuide,* write to 600 Community Drive, Manhasset, NY 11030. Phone (800) 829-0421. E-mail amarotta@cmp.com.

NetGuide also has a Web site at http://www.netguidemag.com, where you'll find information and features not printed in the magazine, such as NetGuide Live.

NewMedia

NewMedia magazine is probably the best single source for keeping up with what's new in multimedia. It appears monthly and publishes an annual buyer's guide. *NewMedia* contains dozens of full-color pictures that illustrate the products it describes, and the layout is visually appealing.

To subscribe to *NewMedia,* write to P.O. Box 1771, Riverton, NJ 08077-7331. Phone (415) 573-5170. Fax (415) 573-5131. Be sure to ask about a free subscription, which is available to qualified readers.

NewMedia is also available on the Web at http://www.newmedia.com, where you'll find even more information than what is contained in the printed version.

T.H.E. Journal

T.H.E. stands for Technological Horizons in Education. *Now in its 25th year, T.H.E. Journal* appears monthly except for July; each issue contains academic papers plus application highlights and hundreds of new-product announcements. Each year, *T.H.E. Journal* publishes special supplements from vendors like IBM, Apple, and Zenith.

T.H.E. Journal is free to qualified individuals in educational institutions and training departments in the United States. To subscribe, phone (714) 730-4011 or fax (714) 730-3739. The mailing address is 150 El Camino Real, Suite 112, Tustin, CA 92780. There is also a companion Web site online at http://www.thejournal.com. It features back issues from 1994 on, additional articles not found in the printed journal, a search engine, and road maps of educational Web links.

Technology & Learning

Technology & Learning is published monthly, except in December and the summer months. Targeted primarily at precollege educators, it reviews software, advertises grants and contests, contains vendor supplements, articulates classroom needs, reviews authoring tools, and has a Q&A section to answer questions about technology and learning. Plus it has great cartoons.

To subscribe, phone (513) 847-5900. The mailing address is Peter Li, Inc., 330 Progress Road, Dayton, OH 45449. The online version at http://www.techlearning.com has searchable software reviews.

Wired

Wired is an award-winning monthly magazine that captures the excitement and the substance of the digital revolution. The best writers and designers in the world help you identify the people, companies, and ideas shaping our future.

To subscribe, contact Wired, 520 Third Street, San Francisco, CA 94107. Phone (800) SO WIRED. Fax (415) 222-6399. E-mail subscription@wired.com. Web address http://www.wired.com.

Syllabus

Syllabus magazine informs educators on how technology can be used to support teaching, learning, and administrative activities. Each issue includes feature articles, case studies, product reviews, and profiles of technology use at the individual, departmental, and institutional levels. Regular features cover multimedia, distance learning, the Internet, quantitative tools, publishing, and administrative technology. A variety of multiplatform technologies are covered, including computers, video, multimedia, and telecommunications. Special supplements to *Syllabus* are published on a regular basis, including the *Arts and the Humanities, Business Education, Computer Science, Engineering,* the *Social Sciences,* and *Science and Medicine. Syllabus* is published ten times per year, following the academic calendar.

Syllabus is published by Syllabus Press, 1307 S. Mary Ave., Suite #211, Sunnyvale, CA 94087. Phone (408) 746-2000. Fax: (408) 746-2711. Highlights from recent issues are found at http://www.syllabus.com.

INTERNET BOOK LIST

There are more than 700 books about the Internet. Happily, there's a Web site that catalogs and organizes these books according to category, level, and platform. To peruse the list, follow the Interlit Web site links to the Unofficial Internet Booklist. Even though the list is called unofficial, it's really pretty good. And it's published in association with amazon.com, where you can purchase the books at a discount online.

1. Subscribe to all of the listservs recommended in Table 27-1. As you begin receiving information from the listservs, you'll develop a feel for which ones you like best. After a few weeks of comparing the messages you'll receive, you can unsubscribe from the listservs you no longer want. To unsubscribe from a listserv, use the Unsubscribe command as documented in Table 7-3 toward the end of Chapter 7.

2. Subscribe to the free printed journals *NewMedia* and *T.H.E. Journal*. For the first few months, when you receive the printed magazines, also visit their Web sites. *NewMedia* is at www.newmedia.com, and *T.H.E. Journal* is at http://www.thejournal.com. How do you prefer reading these journals—on the Web, or in print? What are the advantages and disadvantages of print versus electronic media? Did you find anything helpful at the Web sites that wasn't printed in the magazines? Which medium makes it easier for you to find things in back issues: the printed journal or the Web site? If you were forced to read the journal only in one form, which would you choose, the printed edition or the Web site?

3. Go to your local newsstand and have a look at the latest issue of the *Computer Shopper*. What new products do you find listed there that you did not already know about? Do you think it would be practical to subscribe to a magazine so large? Would you enjoy receiving such a magazine each month? Now visit the online catalogs linked to the Interlit Web site. Compare how they're organized to the way the information is presented in the *Computer Shopper*. Which medium—printed or online—would you prefer for your computer shopping,? Why do you feel that way?

4. Go to Yahoo and do a search for emerging technology. What new technologies do you find listed at Yahoo that were not discussed in this book? Which ones merit inclusion in the next edition?

Appendix A
Basic Windows and Macintosh Tutorials

Throughout this book, instructions have been provided on how to perform basic Windows tasks. Experienced users will not need these tutorials, but beginners will find them helpful. To make it easy for both students and instructors to find these basic Windows tutorials, this appendix lists the names of the tutorials and tells where to find them.

Title of Tutorial	Windows	Macintosh
How to Use a Vertical Scroll Bar	Table 4-2	Table 4-2
How to Resize and Position a Window	Table 4-5	Table 4-5
How to Hide and Reveal a Window	Table 4-6	Table 4-6
How to Create a File Folder	Table 6-9	Table 6-9
How to Create a Plain Text File	Table 6-10	Table 6-10
How to Start a Program When Its Icon Isn't Visible	Table 13-5	Table 13-5

Appendix B
Internet Toolkit for Windows and Macintosh

Listed here is a collection of the tools used in this book. All of these tools can be downloaded from the Interlit Web site. Follow the links to Appendix B, Internet Toolkit on the Interlit Web site.

Web Browsers

Name of Package	Windows	Macintosh
Netscape Communicator	Yes	Yes
Microsoft Internet Explorer	Yes	Yes

HTML Translators

Name of Package	Windows	Macintosh
Microsoft Word	Yes	Yes
WordPerfect	Yes	Yes

HTML Editors

Name of Package	Windows	Macintosh
HoTMetaL	Yes	Yes
WebEdit	Yes	No

Graphics Editors and Converters

Name of Package	Windows	Macintosh
Paint Shop Pro	Yes	No
Graphic Converter	No	Yes

Animated GIF Tools

Name of Package	Windows	Macintosh
GIF Construction Set	Yes	No
GifBuilder	No	Yes

FTP Software

Name of Package	Windows	Macintosh
WS_FTP LE	Yes	No
Fetch	No	Yes

Waveform Audio Recording Software

Name of Package	Windows	Macintosh
Sound Recorder	Yes	No
SoundEffects	No	Yes

Glossary

account A subscription with an Internet service provider that provides the basic Internet services of e-mail, listserv, newsgroup, FTP, telnet, and the Web.

ActiveX A technology invented by Microsoft that enables a wide variety of applications and content to be embedded in Web pages and other computer applications.

APA style The bibliographic style guidelines developed by the American Psychological Association (APA).

applet A little computer application typically created with the Java language that can be downloaded along with a Web page to bring the page to life. *See* Java.

Archie A search tool for finding files available on the Internet via FTP servers. *See* FTP.

ARPA The U.S. Department of Defense Advanced Research Projects Agency (ARPA), for which the Internet Protocol was invented.

ASCII American Standard Code for Information Interchange; the file format of a plain text *(.txt)* file.

avatar An icon or representation of a user in a shared virtual reality.

bandwidth The volume of information per unit of time that a computer, person, or transmission medium can handle.

bits per sample In waveform audio recording, the dynamic range setting, which determines how much of a volume change you will hear between the loudest and softest sounds in the recording.

bookmark The record of a Web site location that makes it easy for the user to return to that site later on.

broadband The kind of cabling used on a high-speed local area network.

browser *See* Web browser.

cable modem The network interface cards used to connect PCs to television cable systems that carry broadband Internet services.

cache The place on your hard disk and RAM where your browser keeps copies of the most recently visited Web sites.

CGI Common gateway interface; the protocol that enables the Web page author to link buttons, fields, and controls on a Web page to programs on a server that can process them.

client-server The manner in which computers exchange information over the Internet by sending it (as servers) and receiving it (as clients).

Clipper Chip An encryption device with a "back door" that allows government agents with the proper access to decipher the messages.

CMS style The bibliographic style guidelines developed by the University of Chicago Press and published in a book called *The Chicago Manual of Style*.

convergence The process of digitalization through which all of the traditional ways of communicating are merging into a networked supermedium on the Internet.

cookie Record that stores information about you and can track your mouse clicks through a Web site.

DirecTV The satellite service that uses MPEG to deliver more than 175 channels of digital TV programming throughout North America; *see* MPEG.

DNS Domain name system. *See* domain name.

domain name The alphabetical name that substitutes for a numeric IP address on the Internet; for example, the Library of Congress, which has the IP address 140.147.248.7, can also be addressed by its domain name, which is www.loc.gov.

EDUPAGE A highly rated listserv that sends you news about new technology three times each week. *See* listserv.

EFF The electronic Frontier Foundation, a nonprofit civil liberties organization working in the public interest to protect privacy, free expression, and access to public resources and information online, as well as to promote responsibility in new media.

e-mail client The software used to receive, read, and respond to electronic mail messages.

embedded audio Audio that's built in to a Web page, as opposed to being linked to it.

embedded video Video that's built in to a Web page, as opposed to being linked to it.

emoticon A character combination used in e-mail or news to indicate an emotional state; the most famous is the smiley :)

encryption The process of encoding a message with special symbols and algorithms so the message cannot be deciphered by anyone who does not have the encryption key.

Ethernet The high-speed network invented in Bob Metcalfe's Harvard Ph.D. thesis in 1973 that fueled the explosion of local area networks (LANs) throughout academia and industry.

Fair Use A section of the U.S. Copyright Law that allows the use of copyrighted works in reporting news, conducting research, and teaching.

FAQ Frequently asked question; also, a list of frequently asked questions and their answers.

firefighter A peacemaker on the Internet who intervenes to stop a flame war; *see* flame.

firewall A computer that provides security by preventing unauthorized data from moving across a network.

flame To send an e-mail message intended to insult or provoke; also used as a noun to refer to the insulting e-mail message.

folder On a hard disk, a place where computer files get stored; file folders provide a way to organize the files on a computer.

frame On a Web page, a window in a document that often has its own scrollbar; provides a way for a Web page to display more than one document simultaneously.

FTP File Transfer Protocol; the method used to transfer files from one computer to another over the Internet.

GIF The Graphics Interchange Format; one of the most popular graphics formats for transferring images over the Web.

giga A billion; abbreviated G, as in GB, meaning a billion bytes, which is also called a *gigabyte.*

Gopher Named after the mascot at the University of Minnesota where it was invented, a protocol for hierarchically organizing and providing access to texts, pictures, audio clips, and videos on the Internet.

HDTV High-definition television, the digital television format that will replace NTSC as the television standard in the United States and Japan.

host The computer that provides a service, such as a bulletin board, chat room, or MUD, to which other computers connect. *See* MUD.

HTML Hypertext markup language; the file format for a Web page. *See* markup; Web page.

hypertext A word coined by Ted Nelson in 1965 referring to text that has been linked; the linkage gives the text an added dimension, thereby making it hyper.

IETF Internet Engineering Task Force, the official working group that develops standards and specifications for Internet protocols and services.

information warfare An electronic invasion of a nation's computer networks intended to disable the networks and give the aggressor a strategic advantage during wartime.

interlaced In the Graphics Interchange Format (GIF), a special subformat that creates a venetian-blind effect when the file opens, due to the interlacing of the horizontal lines full of pixels that create the image. *See* GIF.

Internet A worldwide connection of more than 10 million computers and 45,000 networks that follow the Internet Protocol (IP).

Internet Protocol (IP) A specification for how information gets routed across a network in packets that are addressed to a specific destination; if a node on the network goes down, the information will seek an alternate path to its destination because of the addressing in the packets.

IRC Internet Relay Chat, a worldwide "party line" network that allows one to converse with others in real time in chat rooms on the Internet.

ISDN Integrated Services Digital Network, the digital telephone system that is being installed by regional Bell companies in most of the United States, as well as in other countries.

ISP Internet service provider, a type of company that sells Internet access.

Java An object-oriented programming language that can be used to develop applications and applets that will run on any computer on which the Java virtual machine (VM) has been installed. *See* applet.

JavaScript A scripting language intended to decrease the complexity of creating active Web pages so that people who do not know how to program in Java can still create some of the special effects. *See* Java.

JPEG Joint Photographic Experts Group, one of the most popular file formats for transmitting full-color images on the Web.

kilo A thousand; abbreviated K, as in KB, meaning a thousand bytes, which is also called a *kilobyte.*

Knowbot A software application programmed to act as an intelligent agent that goes out on the network and finds things for you.

link A trigger on a Web page which, when clicked, brings up the object of the link.

listserv Short for list server and built on top of the Internet's e-mail protocol; works like an electronic mailing list, sending e-mail messages to groups of people whose names are on the list.

lurker One of the silent majority in an electronic forum who posts occasionally or not at all but reads the group's postings regularly.

markup The special codes, called tags, that mark up a text in the Web's HTML file format, controlling how the text will flow onto the screen and automatically arrange itself with respect to pictures and other screen design elements.

MBONE Multicast backbone, the network of computers on the Internet specially designed for the transmission of simultaneous live video and audio broadcasts.

mega A million; abbreviated M, as in MB, meaning a million bytes, which is also called a *megabyte.*

MIDI Musical Instrument Digital Interface; also, the file format for transmitting synthesized music over the Internet.

MLA style The bibliographic style guidelines developed by the Modern Language Association (MLA).

modem A combination of the terms *mo*dulate and *dem*odulate; a device that makes it possible for a computer to send and receive digital information over analog phone lines.

MPEG Motion Picture Experts Group, the name of the ISO standards committee that created the digital video file format known by the same name (MPEG).

MUD Multi User Dimension, also Multi User Dungeon; a synchronous multiuser communication environment that enables participants to take on a persona and create virtual worlds out of their own imaginations.

Netiquette Network etiquette, the observance of certain rules and conventions that have evolved in order to help users get along with one another and make proper use of the Internet.

newsgroup One of Usenet's many discussion groups; *see* Usenet.

NSFNET A backbone that connects the nation's five super-computer centers at high speed.

PDA Personal digital assistant; a generic term for a portable, handheld computer that you can take with you to work, school, or anyplace where a PC might come in handy.

Perl A scripting language used especially for creating CGI programs on CGI servers. *See* CGI.

plug-in A software module that adds functionality to an existing computer application such as a Web browser.

PointCasting Invented by the PointCast Network (PCN); a method of pushing a personalized stream of information across the Internet to play on your computer screen.

POTS Plain old telephone service.

PPP Point-to-point protocol; the communications software that permits computers to connect to the Internet via ordinary telephone lines and a modem.

RADSL Rate adaptive digital subscriber line, a special kind of modem that can send data at speeds up to 2 million bits per second, making it possible to send video over ordinary telephone lines.

RTSP   Real Time Streaming Protocol; a method and a standard for streaming audio and video over the Internet.

sampling rate   In waveform audio recording, the setting that determines the frequency response of the recorded sound.

self-extracting archive   A compressed computer file into which the files that comprise an application or set of data have been packed, and which extract themselves automatically when the archive is run.

shareware   Software that you can try out before you buy; typically you download it from the Web, try it out for 30 days, and if you decide to keep it, you pay a reasonable fee to the producer.

Shockwave   The plug-in that makes it possible for a Web browser to play multimedia sequences created with Macromedia Director, Authorware, and Flash. *See* plug-in.

shouting   On the internet, typing a message ALL IN CAPITAL LETTERS to add emphasis; almost always, this is considered in bad taste and should be AVOIDED.

signature file   A block of text that automatically gets appended to the e-mail messages a person originates, intended to identify the sender by providing information such as your name, address, telephone number, and home page Web address.

sniffing   Intercepting information as it moves across the network; the Internet's equivalent of a telephone wiretap.

spam   To send unwanted messages to newsgroups, listservs, or individuals; also used as a noun to refer to the unwanted messages.

surf   To browse the Internet in search of interesting stuff, especially on the World Wide Web.

target   A named location on a Web page intended to provide the user with a quick way to jump around among the various topics on a Web page.

TCP/IP   Transmission Control Protocol/Internet Protocol; the wide area networking protocol that makes the Internet work; *see* Internet Protocol.

telecommuting   Working from home, using your Internet connection instead of your automobile (or other form of physical transportation) to get to work.

telephone modem   *See* modem.

telnet   The Internet resource that enables you to login remotely to other networks on the Internet, once you've connected to your local network.

terminal program   A computer software utility that allows you to dial up to a remote computer using a telephone modem; you are not really "on" the Internet when you use a terminal program. *See* PPP.

TLA   Three-letter acronym; codes and abbreviations consisting of three letters, such as FYI (for your information), used especially in chat rooms to shorten the amount of keyboarding required to write a message on the Internet.

Token Ring   A type of high-speed network that passes data in tokens that move around the network in a ring.

TOURBUS   One of the most popular listservs on the Internet, providing you with a biweekly tour of the most interesting and informative sites on the Internet.

URL   Uniform resource locator, an address that identifies a document or resource on the World Wide Web.

Usenet   A distributed bulletin board system hosting more than 10,000 newsgroups.

virus   A cracker program that searches out other programs and infects them by embedding a copy of itself in them; when these programs are executed, the embedded virus is executed too, thus propagating the infection.

VRML   Virtual Reality Modeling Language; a standard and a file format that enables Web page designers to add dimensions, texture, and lighting to Web sites.

W3C   World Wide Web Consortium, the standards body that officially registers new features into HTML. *See* HTML.

Web   *See* World Wide Web.

Web browser   Software that enables you to use your computer to surf the Web and download texts, pictures, sounds, databases, software applications, and movies to your computer. *See* surf.

Web page   The display created when a Web browser accesses an HTML file. *See* HTML.

Web site   The place on the Web where persons or companies stores their collections of Web pages, images, audio files, videos, and any other files used in conjunction with their Web pages.

Webcasting   A generic term that means to use push technologies to deliver channels of information on the Web; *see* PointCasting.

WebTV   A settop box that accesses the Internet via your telephone and displays its output through the video input on your TV or VCR; on startup, the WebTV automatically dials up to your local WebTV Internet service provider, and you see the Web pages on your TV screen.

whiteboard   A computer program that enables remote users to share a common screen across the network; Microsoft's NetMeeting, which comes as part of the Microsoft Internet Explorer, combines a whiteboard with audio and video-conferencing.

World Wide Web   A networked hypertext system that allows multimedia documents to be shared over the Internet without requiring people to travel anywhere physically in order to obtain the information.

WYSIWYG   What you see is what you get; a type of software that lets you edit a document such as a Web page via graphical controls instead of requiring you to learn the HTML codes. *See* HTML.

WWW   World Wide Web; *see* World Wide Web.

zip file   An archive into which one or more files has been compressed to save space and packed into a single file that can be transmitted easily over a network. *See* self-extracting archive.

Bibliography

Most of the resources used in this book are online references linked to the Interlit Web site. Listed here are the references you won't find at the Web site. For the hundreds of online references, go to the Interlit Web site at http://www.udel.edu/interlit.

Bane, P. William, Stephen P. Bradley, and David J. Collis. "Colliding Worlds," Harvard Business School Colloquium, October 5–7, 1994. Revised March 1995.

Bane, P. William, and Debra B. McMahon. "Learning to Grow: The New Marketing Challenge in Telecommunications," *Mercer Management Journal*, vol. 2 (1994): 83–92.

Godwin, Mike. "Sex and the Single Sysadmin: The Risks of Carrying Graphic Sexual Materials," *Internet World*, vol. 5, no. 2 (March/April 1994): 11–13.

Lee, Lydia. "RealAudio Goes Mainstream: SDK in Beta," *NewMedia* (October 7, 1996): 30.

Nelson, Theodore H. "The Hypertext," *Proceedings of the World Documentation Federation*, 1965.

Index